HEGEL: NEW DIRECTIONS

HEGEL: NEW DIRECTIONS

Edited by Katerina Deligiorgi

McGill-Queen's University Press
Montreal & Kingston • Ithaca

ISBN-13:978-0-7735-3173-4   ISBN-10:0-7735-3173-4 (hardcover)
ISBN-13:978-0-7735-3174-1   ISBN-10:0-7735-3174-2 (paperback)

Legal deposit third quarter 2006
Bibliothèque nationale du Québec

Published simultaneously outside North America
by Acumen Publishing Limited

McGill-Queen's University Press acknowledges the financial support of the
Government of Canada through the Book Publishing Development Program
(BPIDP) for its activities.

Library and Archives Canada Cataloguing in Publication

    Hegel : new directions / edited by Katerina Deligiorgi.

    Includes bibliographical references and index.
    ISBN-13: 978-0-7735-3173-4   ISBN-10: 0-7735-3173-4 (bound)
    ISBN-13: 978-0-7735-3174-1   ISBN-10: 0-7735-3174-2 (pbk.)

    1. Hegel, Georg Wilhelm Friedrich, 1770-1831.
    I. Deligiorgi, Katerina, 1965-

    B2948.H38 2006   193   C2006-902312-3

Designed and typeset by Kate Williams, Swansea.
Printed and bound by Cromwell Press, Trowbridge.

CONTENTS

CONTRIBUTORS

John Burbidge is Professor of Philosophy Emeritus at Trent University. He is the author of *On Hegel's Logic* and *Hegel on Logic and Religion*. From 1988 to 1990 he was President of the Hegel Society of America.

Allegra de Laurentiis is Assistant Professor of Philosophy at the State University of New York, Stony Brook. She is the author of *Subjects in the Ancient and Modern World: On Hegel's Theory of Subjectivity*.

Katerina Deligiorgi is Senior Lecturer in Philosophy at Anglia Ruskin University, Cambridge. She is the author of *Kant and the Culture of Enlightenment* and articles on Kant, Hegel and German Idealism.

Jason Gaiger is Lecturer at the Open University. His publications include *Art in Theory 1815–1900* and *Art in Theory: 1648–1815* and *Frameworks for Modern Art*. He is the editor and translator of Johann Gottfried Herder's *Sculpture: Some Observations on Shape and Form from Pygmalion's Dream*.

Rolf-Peter Horstmann is Professor of Philosophy at the Humboldt University. He is the author of several books, including *Die Grenzen der Vernunft. Eine Untersuchung zu Zielen und Motiven des Deutschen Idealismus, Bausteine kritischer Philosophie: Arbeiten zu Kant* and *G. W. F. Hegel: Eine Einführung* (with D. Emundts).

Kimberly Hutchings is Reader in International Relations at the London School of Economics. Her books include *Kant, Critique and Politics* and *Hegel and Feminist Philosophy*.

Iain Macdonald is Associate Professor of Philosophy at the Université de Montréal. He has written on Hegel, Adorno and Heidegger and is currently working on Hegel and Adorno, focusing on metaphysics, history and the future of transcendental philosophy.

John McDowell is University Professor at the University of Pittsburgh. He is the author of *Mind and World* and two volumes of collected papers: *Mind, Value and Reality* and *Meaning, Knowledge and Reality*.

Angelica Nuzzo is Associate Professor of Philosophy at Brooklyn College, City University of New York. Her books include *System* and *Kant and the Unity of Reason*.

Robert B. Pippin is the Raymond W. and Martha Hilpert Gruner Distinguished Service Professor in the Committee on Social Thought, the Department of Philosophy, and the College at the University of Chicago. He is the author of several books, including *Hegel's Idealism: The Satisfactions of Self-Consciousness* and *Henry James and Modern Moral Life*.

Sally Sedgwick is Professor of Philosophy at the University of Illinois. Her publications include numerous essays on Kant and Hegel. She edited the volume *The Reception of Kant's Critical Philosophy: Fichte, Schelling, and Hegel*, and is working on a book on Hegel's critique of Kant.

Ludwig Siep is Professor of Philosophy at the University of Muenster. He is the author of several books, including *Der Weg der Phänomenologie des Geistes: Ein einführender Kommentar zu Hegels "Differenzschrift" und "Phänomenologie des Geistes"* and *Konkrete Ethik: Grundlagen der Natur- und Kulturethik*.

Allen Speight is Assistant Professor in Philosophy at Boston University. He is the author of *Hegel, Literature and the Problem of Agency*, numerous articles on Hegel's philosophy and *The Philosophy of Hegel* (Acumen, 2007).

Nicholas Walker is Associate Lecturer in Philosophy at the University of Essex. He has written extensively on Hegel and German philosophy.

ACKNOWLEDGEMENTS

The editor wishes to thank Alison Ainley, Jason Gaiger, Ulrich Haase, Stephen Houlgate, Iain Macdonald, Ludwig Siep for his help in the English version of his article, Robert Stern, Sabine Vogt, Nicholas Walker, Tristan Palmer and the anonymous readers for Acumen.

With the following exceptions, the essays appear in print for the first time. John McDowell's "The Apperceptive I and the Empirical Self: Towards a Heterodox Reading of 'Lordship and Bondage' in Hegel's Phenomenology" was previously published in the *Bulletin of the Hegel Society of Great Britain* 47/48 (2003). Sally Sedgwick's "Hegel, McDowell, and Recent Defenses of Kant" appeared in the *Journal of the British Society for Phenomenology* 31(3) (2000 © The British Society for Phenomenology). Robert B. Pippin's "Recognition and Reconciliation: Actualized Agency in Hegel's Jena *Phenomenology*" was previously published in the *Internationales Jahrbuch des Deutschen Idealismus*, K. Ameriks and J. Stolzenberg (eds), volume 2 (2004 © Walter de Gruyter, Berlin and New York). Rolf-Peter Horstmann's "The Finite and the Infinite in Hegel's Thought" appears here for the first time in English in a translation by Nicholas Walker. It appeared in German with the title "Das Endliche und das Unendliche in Hegels Denken" in the *Internationales Jahrbuch des Deutschen Idealismus*, volume 1 (2003 © Walter de Gruyter, Berlin and New York). Ludwig Siep's "The Contemporary Relevance of Hegel's Practical Philosophy" appears here for the first time in English in a translation by Katerina Deligiorgi. It appeared in German with the title "Die Aktualität der praktischen Philosophie Hegels" in *Das Interesse des Denkens: Hegel aus heutiger Sicht*, W. Welsch and K. Vieweg (eds) (2003 © Wilhelm Fink Verlag, München). The editor is grateful to the copyright holders for granting permission to publish this material.

ABBREVIATIONS

A   *Hegel's Aesthetics: Lectures on Fine Art* (1975)

Ascheberg   *Vorlesung über Ästhetik* (1995)

Bernhardy   *Naturphilosophie: Band I: Die Vorlesungen von 1819/20* (1982)

Bonsiepen   W. Bonsiepen, "Hegels Raum-Zeit-Lehre" (1985)

Br   *Briefe von und an Hegel* (1952)

D   *Dokumente zu Hegels Entwicklung* ([1936] 1974)

EL   *Encyclopaedia of the Philosophical Sciences I: Logic* (1991)

EM   *Encyclopaedia of the Philosophical Sciences III: Hegel's Philosophy of Mind* (1971)

EN   *Encyclopaedia of the Philosophical Sciences II: Hegel's Philosophy of Nature* (1970)

ET   *Early Theological Writings* (1948)

FK   *Faith and Knowledge* (1977)

Griesheim   *Vorlesungen über Naturphilosophie Berlin 1823/24* (Griesheim Nachschrift) (2000)

GW   *Gesammelte Werke* (1968)

Hotho   *Vorlesung über die Philosophie der Kunst* (1998; student edition, 2003)

HW   *Hauptwerke in sechs Bänden* (1999)

L   *Science of Logic* (1976)

LHP   *Lectures on the History of Philosophy* ([1892–96] 1995)

LPW   *Lectures on the Philosophy of World History: Introduction* (1975)

N *Hegels theologische Jugendschriften* ([1907] 1971)

Pfordten *Philosophie der Kunst: Vorlesung von 1826* (2005)

PH *The Philosophy of History* (1956)

PhG *Phenomenology of Spirit* (1977)

PR *Elements of the Philosophy of Right* (1991)

Ringier *Vorlesungen über die Philosophie der Natur: Berlin 1819/1920* (Ringier Nachschrift) (2002)

SW *Sämtliche Werke: Jubiläumsausgabe in zwanzig Bänden* (1941)

Uexküll *Vorlesungen über Naturphilosophie Berlin 1821/22* (von Uexküll Nachschrift) (2002)

Vorlesungen *Vorlesungen. Ausgewählte Nachschriften und Manuskripte* (1983–)

VPW *Vorlesungen über die Philosophie der Weltgeschichte* (1955)

W *Werke in zwanzig Bänden* (1986)

INTRODUCTION

ON READING HEGEL TODAY

Katerina Deligiorgi

> Whatever happens, every individual is a child of his time; so
> philosophy too is its own time apprehended in thoughts.
>
> Hegel, Philosophy of Right, 11

What is a timely reading of Hegel? In what ways does Hegel's philosophy
speak to current concerns? These are the guiding questions for the essays
gathered in this volume, which explore different aspects of Hegel's thought
in the context of contemporary philosophical debates. The thematic range
and variety of perspectives represented here are signs of the fertility of the
continuing engagement with his ideas. It is the purpose of this Introduction
to examine the reasons for this sustained interest and to look at some of the
different ways in which Hegel is read today.

Agreement about Hegel's lasting significance is more easily secured than
agreement about the nature of his achievement. There is little dispute over
the plurality of projects – including monism, pluralism, metaphysical aprior-
ism and pragmatism that have claimed Hegelian inspiration. Such variety
of interpretation is intimately related to the critical animus that continues to
pervade evaluations of his legacy today. A clear lesson to be drawn from the
reception history of Hegel's thought is that opposition to his ideas has been
a vital force in instigating renewed engagement with his philosophy. This, in
turn, goes some way towards explaining the diversity of approaches to his
work. The question "why his constituency of friends and foes is so heterogeneous?" (Stern 2002: xii) must be addressed alongside the question why
Hegel is the thinker "with the best and the worst reputation" (Pinkard 2002:
217).[1] It is instructive to remind ourselves of the way his immediate legacy
was divided between disciples who sought to pursue a broadly conservative,
theistic and philosophically systematic programme, and the so-called "Young"
or "Left" Hegelians who sought Hegel's true meaning through a critical and

humanistic interpretation.[2] This original split is reproduced at several important stages in the history of appropriation of Hegel's thought, a history that is shaped not only by those who saw themselves as preserving his teachings, but also by those who criticized them, thereby inspiring fresh interpretative attempts. By providing both new critical perspectives from which to attack what was thought to be pernicious about Hegel's influence and new conceptual frameworks for the study of his work, movements such as Marxism, existentialism, phenomenology and pragmatism contributed centrally to the history of Hegelianism. It seems that the stronger the criticism, the more vigorous the effort to think afresh about Hegel. To give just a few examples: Benedetto Croce's search for "what is living and what is dead"[3] in Hegel's philosophy in Italy at the start of the twentieth century was prompted at least in part by historicist commitments that were articulated within Neo-Kantian thought by figures such as Wilhelm Windelband and Heinrich Rickert (see Köhnke 1991); the interpretations of Hegel presented by Jean Wahl and Alexandre Kojève in France were influenced by existentialist and Marxist themes;[4] and in England in the 1950s it was in response to Karl Popper's censure that J. N. Findlay undertook the task of "rehabilitating the philosophical reputation of Hegel" (Findlay 1955–56: 1) from the cold ashes of the defunct school of British Idealism led by F. H. Bradley and J. E. McTaggart.[5] It is no exaggeration to say that the reception history of Hegel's thought is a history of reappraisal, rethinking, reinterpretation and, indeed, of rehabilitation.

Confronted with the sheer diversity of historical Hegelianism, it is worth considering whether Hegel's philosophy is especially amenable to changing concerns and intellectual priorities. What is it about his philosophy that has prompted time and again the question: "do we know what to make of Hegel?" (Hartmann 1972: 101). One response is to suggest that the very complexity of Hegel's thought – which is, by universal acknowledgement, difficult, indeed "so very difficult that it requires far more effort than a thinker has a right to exact of others" (Findlay 1955–56: 23)[6] – makes it a particularly apt object for interpretative ingenuity. But difficulty alone is not sufficient to account for the variety of interpretations that his writings continue to generate, and even less for the repeated efforts of serious engagement that characterize the reception of his thought. Instead, we need to consider how elements internal to Hegel's philosophy speak to live philosophical questions. This opens on to broader issues concerning the relation of philosophy to its history and the historicality of our current philosophical concerns.

I

Writing in 1883, Edward Caird sought to encapsulate Hegel's legacy by explaining the "modernity" of his thought:

2

> It is this also which lends interest to the great movement of thought which began with Kant, and the ultimate meaning of which was expressed by Hegel. For that movement was, above all, an attempt to find a way *through* the modern principles of subjective freedom – the very principle which produced the Reformation of the sixteenth and the Revolution of the eighteenth century – to a reconstruction of the intellectual and moral order on which man's life had been based in the past.
> (Caird 1886: 3)

Caird already flags the key issues of subjectivity and of freedom that have shaped subsequent attempts to "recognize the existence of a living development" in his philosophy (*ibid.*: 224). From our present standpoint, Caird's claim that we need to "find a way through the modern principles of subjective freedom" is rendered yet more urgent in the light of twentieth-century criticisms of the normative content of the "modern project" in works such as Edmund Husserl's *The Crisis of European Sciences* and Theodor W. Adorno and Max Horkheimer's *Dialectic of Enlightenment*. Out of this debate about the nature and value – and the achievements and pathologies – of modernity has emerged a distinctive way of formulating philosophical problems that has proved especially productive in opening up new perspectives on Hegel's philosophy.[7]

Charles Taylor, for example, has justified his claim that Hegel's thought "remains of perennial interest" by offering a diagnosis of modernity that focuses on the political dilemma confronting modern liberal democracies that are forced to respond to competing demands for differentiation and cohesion (Taylor 1992: 1). Taylor seeks to establish the "unbroken continuity into our time" of central themes in Hegel by drawing attention to his "attempt to realize the synthesis between rational autonomy and expressive unity" (*ibid.*: 14). Jürgen Habermas goes a step further by identifying Hegel as the first philosopher to develop a systematic understanding of modernity. His interpretation of Hegel's significance forms part of a broad narrative that is shaped by pressing contemporary concerns about truth, justice, rationality and power. Habermas's reconstruction of Hegel's thought depends on the identification of a normative problem of modernity, the "new age", which "can and will no longer borrow the criteria by which it takes its orientation from models supplied by another epoch; *it has to create its normativity out of itself*" (Habermas 1987: 7). Robert Pippin attempts to construct a similarly ambitious interpretive framework. In a series of influential studies, he has identified the possibility of genuine freedom both as the central question in Hegel's philosophy and as the characteristic feature of his claim to modernity. The challenge from our contemporary perspective remains that of giving a satisfactory account of the modern ideal of freedom understood as "a law, a compelling norm, wholly unto oneself, in a wholly self-legislated, self-authorized way" (Pippin 1997: 7). While such ambitious narratives of modernity may not always form the basis for sympathetic reconstructions of Hegel's thought, they do display a distinctly Hegelian discipline of thinking, which demands that we should turn to the past in order better to reflect on the present. Such large-scale reconstructive projects invite us to retrace our steps in order to see where we stand and to make a more informed assessment of our gains and our losses in relation to the past.

Two further developments contribute to and refine current interest in this broad-based historical–philosophical approach. The first is the growing avail-ability of scholarly studies of the intellectual and cultural context in which Hegel's ideas were formed. The title of a conference held in Stuttgart in the early 1980s, "Kant or Hegel?", describes an intellectual crossroads (Henrich 1983). For the contemporary reader the situation is rather different: there is much philosophical instruction to be had from traversing the path *between* Kant and Hegel. A number of recent works have contributed to this state of affairs, including translations of key texts, Frederick Beiser's (1987, 1992) analyses of historical developments in the Kantian aftermath and Terry Pink-ard's (2000) biography of Hegel, as well as several important studies on par-ticular aspects of German idealism (Pinkard 2002; Pippin 1989, 1997).[8] As a consequence of this detailed examination of a formative period in modern European culture, Hegel is now read alongside thinkers such as J. G. Fichte and F. W. J. Schelling, as well as F. H. Jacobi, K. L. Reinhold, F. D. Schleiermacher, Novalis and the brothers August and Friedrich Schlegel, who engaged critically with their post-Enlightenment inheritance. Far from diluting their potency, this contextualization of Hegel's ideas has encouraged different interpretations by thinkers from a range of philosophical backgrounds.

Equally important, however, is a new willingness to bridge the traditional division between the history of philosophy and philosophical argument. In a direct challenge to the prevailing philosophical orthodoxy that saw the history of philosophy as at best a marginal pursuit, Taylor claimed in the mid-1980s that "philosophy and the history of philosophy are one" (Taylor 1984: 17). Since then there has been a swelling stream of historically informed discussions about philosophical methods and positions that were once held to stand above the coming to be and passing away of intellectual fashion. Genetic–philosophical works such as Alberto Coffa's (1991) account of the semantic tradition, or recent histories of the analytic movement, such as those by Michael Beaney (1990) and Michael Dummett (1993), permit a reflective exploration not only of particular problems and topics, but also of how these problems and topics came to matter in the way they did. Such historical investigations need no longer be seen as external to philosophy: analysis of the hidden assumptions and pre-suppositions in the very way in which a philosophical problem presents itself to us is central to philosophy's critical and self-critical tasks. That a *historical* exploration can have a role in such self-reflection is a recognizably Hegelian idea. It is therefore fitting that this idea has had a beneficial effect in awaken-ing and sustaining contemporary interest in Hegel.

Wilfrid Sellars's observation that when Kant appears Hegel cannot be far behind is borne out by much current work on Hegel. A number of commentators see in Hegel an intellectual ally in their effort to rethink the Kantian categories of *a priori* and *a posteriori*, and the relation between form and content, schema and substance, principle and its application. This allows Hegel to be read as offering either a corrective or an alternative to projects in epistemology as well as in moral and political theory that take their bearings from Kant. The initial reception of Kant's philosophy was dominated by his problematic claim that we have no direct knowledge of things in themselves. Kant's answer to the question "What can I know?" limited knowledge to content that is made accessible for cognition through the subjective forms of sensibility and the concepts of the understanding. What remain unknowable are things in abstraction of these forms, or things as they are in themselves. While sympathetic to Kant's reversal of the relation of subordination of concepts to objects, many post-Kantian thinkers saw his account of "things in themselves" as rekindling scepticism. Kant's argument threatened to render meaningless existential claims about perception-independent objects and to open an insuperable gap between ourselves and the world.[9]

The identification of a distinctly Hegelian solution to this problem requires that we recognize Hegel's dissatisfaction with the Kantian division of labour between theoretical and practical philosophy. Not only for Hegel, but also for those within his immediate intellectual environment, Kant's four questions – What can I know? What ought I to do? What may I hope? What is man? – were intimately related and treated synthetically. The early correspondence between Hegel, Friedrich Hölderlin and Schelling brims with enthusiasm for the tasks of philosophy, which are seen as both urgently relevant and practical. Inspired by his reading of Kant, Hegel proclaimed a coming revolution in Germany:

> Humanity is represented as worthy of respect in itself; this is proof that the nimbus surrounding the heads of the oppressors and the earthly gods is disappearing. The philosophers have expounded human dignity, the people will learn to experience it; they shall not content themselves merely with claiming their rights, which are trampled in the dust, they will appropriate them for themselves. (*Br* 24, letter to Schelling, 16 April 1795)

That there is a public and ethical side to philosophical calling – indeed that philosophy is a calling – is a thought that Hegel shares with many of his contemporaries. It remains central to his work even when he is at his most abstruse. As a number of contributors to this volume argue, for Hegel the claims of science and logic are intimately connected to ethical and political claims. Once again, we can clarify this argument through reference to Kant. Hegel's motivation for drawing closer together theoretical and practical concerns – his determination to give a worldly expression to the rational order

5

identified by Kant – is best understood as a response to the Kantian claim that human beings are "rational beings who spontaneously impose lawfulness on the world and thereby create its basic order" (Schneewind 1998: 484). Hegel's discussion of "objective spirit", the realm of relations and institutions, of existing rights and obligations, is nothing less than an account of the procedures and structures that give shape to our freedom and allow our capacity for judgement to flourish. Hegel's conception of freedom in terms of the conditions of its realization, that is, in terms of the constraints that make freedom possible, cannot be understood if it is severed from its Rousseauean and Kantian heritage. This is vividly revealed in Hegel's criticism of the early German Romantics, especially Novalis and the Schlegels, whom he saw as elaborating a conception of freedom as sheer self-determination that eroded the link between freedom and morality (see Menke 2005).[10]

Lest we become complacent in our response to the call for historical receptivity, we should remember that as a historical philosopher and philosophical historian Hegel is not always a congenial past master. Having taught us to think of philosophy as its own time apprehended in thought, Hegel also compares the realm of thought with "God as he is in his eternal essence" (L: 50) and in the preface to the *Philosophy of Right* he promises to provide his readers with "something that is neither new nor old but perennial" (PR: 3). Richard Rorty's qualified Hegelianism arises from, and at the same time exemplifies, the difficulty of philosophy's dialogue with its own history. Rorty's insistence that he is an ironist is meant to guard against the identification of history and reason. Mindful of the young Marx's lesson that "man is not an abstract being, squatting outside the world ... he is the human world" (Marx 1978: 53), Rorty sets out to show that reason is both worldly and historical. However, he is equally concerned to show that the historicization of reason need not – and most emphatically ought not – commit us to the rationalization of history. In a strongly deflationary philosophical environment, a great deal of sympathetic current commentary on Hegel seems to be undertaken under the maxim: "Avoid the perennial". Making the "turn to history"[11] without a historical teleology is one way of solving the problem of establishing a living connection with the philosophical past. But this problem has another side to it: that of giving a philosophical account of the present. Arthur Danto draws an arresting picture of the history of philosophy, which he likens to:

> a long nightmare from which philosophy longs to waken, and from which it seems at any given moment to the working philosopher that he has awakened – even if, from the vantage point of his successors, it will instead seem as if he had been but part of the nightmare.　　　　　　　　　　　　　　(Danto 1997b: 5)

There is a temptation to view the present as philosophically irrelevant, as providing a mere occasion for philosophical reflection. Yet, at least since

Descartes's willingness to trace the origin of his enquiries back to his own philosophical culture, philosophers have sought to claim a link between historical origin and philosophical beginning. Exemplary in this respect are Husserl's opening remarks in his *Cartesian Meditations*: "The splintering of present-day philosophy, with its perplexed activity, sets us thinking ... In this unhappy present, is not our situation similar to the one encountered by Descartes in his youth? If so, then is not this a fitting time to renew his radicalness?" (Husserl 1988: 4–5). Cartesian radicalness is not mandatory for striking out in new directions. As the essays gathered here testify, although our present philosophical culture presents us with a similarly perplexing multiplicity, Hegel's writings can form a point of contact for interlocutors from across its different regions. Furthermore, the perspective on the present opened up through this engagement with Hegel's thought owes its interest and animation not only to the capacity to recognize shared trends of thought: it also requires us to acknowledge ideas that strike us as strange or remote from our concerns.

In recent years, there has been an unprecedented scholarly effort to establish reliable texts for the Hegel's lecture series.[12] Already benefiting from this work are those aspects of Hegel's philosophy, such as his writings on art, religion, science and history, that are often held to be esoteric or simply dated. For a long time, the fate of these writings has been either to languish in the obscurity of relative neglect, or to be approached in terms of slogans, such as "the end of art" or "the end of history", which eclipse Hegel's argument even as they proclaim its significance. As the contributors to this volume show, however, taking up Hegel's challenge to think historically is also a matter of learning to read these texts anew.

II

"Sparingness in giving", Hegel wrote in the preface to the *Phenomenology of Spirit*, "does not ... befit Science" (*PhG*: 5). Hegel's intellectual generosity has not always found an appreciative readership. One of his contemporaries, Jacob Friedrich Fries, declared his disappointment that Hegel's metaphysical ambition drowns the movement of thought in the "Dead Sea of the absolute" (Fries to Jacobi, December 1807, in Zoeppritz 1869: 20).[13] While many commentators subsequently found themselves in agreement with Fries's observation, others have seen Hegel as elucidating our "learning-as-we-go" navigational skills in uncharted waters. The role of the dialectic within Hegel's work plays a key role in these radically divergent evaluations. Dialectic can be seen either as a progressive, self-perfecting and ampliative process that leads ultimately to secure and unrevisable insights about ourselves and our world, or as a regressive process that uncovers the hidden presuppositions and implications of any position that presents itself as final truth. Defenders of the former perspective argue that if we are to form a cohesive account of Hegel's thought, we must place the *Logic* at its centre and take seriously Hegel's ambition to provide us with a truly presuppositionless philosophy (Houlgate 1985; Winfield 1986, 1989). But there is an equally long tradition of thinkers who emphasize the aporetic – even ironic – character of Hegel's intimations of reconciliation and who point instead to the mobility or plasticity of his thought (Flay 1990).[14] These contrasting interpretations of Hegel's systematic ambition do not merely recreate earlier splits from his reception history: they help to illustrate how his ideas can be used to question our own acquired certainties about metaphysics and ontology.[15] It is instructive in this context to consider Beiser's view that Hegelian metaphysics, which he defines as "knowledge of the absolute", is perfectly compatible with a naturalistic outlook from which "all occult forces" are banished (Beiser 1993: 5).

The concept of "recognition" is central to a number of interpretative projects that proclaim the ethical significance of Hegel's thought. There are several ways of spelling out the importance of this concept, which places inter-subjective and social commitments at the centre of ideas of moral agency and action. Readings of Hegel developed in direct response to twentieth-century attacks on metaphysical idealism have focused on recognition as the key to understanding both Hegel's positive claims and his exploration of the failures of intersubjectivity.[16] Sensitive to Lévinas's "protest on behalf of the other", such studies identify reciprocal recognition as an indispensable requirement in the social and historical life of a community. Similar themes are explored in interpretations that follow the "communicative model" developed in Germany under the influence of Habermas (1984/1987, 1990) and Karl-Otto Apel (1994). In the work of Axel Honneth (1991, 1996), the communicative model plays a central role in the historical reconstruction of successive theoretical attempts to define the social domain and, at the same time, forms the basis for a normative conception of "the social".[17] This double perspective, at once both historical and normative, is also evident in interpretations that come out of political and social theoretical projects developed in response to John Rawls's groundbreaking treatise, *A Theory of Justice*.[18] Here, Hegel's critique of Kant's moral philosophy is seen as anticipating the liberal-communitarian debate of the latter half of the twentieth century, with Hegel giving voice to concerns about the substantive ethical commitments embodied in particular social relations, roles and institutions. Hegel's emphatic conception of ethics as the set of normative practices – the *ethos* or *habitus* – of the community in which agents find themselves is encapsulated in the idea that "others matter fundamentally to the development and exercise of our capacities for self-understanding and for flourishing" (Eldridge 1989: 4). This idea is perhaps convenient shorthand for a Hegelian position in current debates. However, it can also function as a hermeneutic premise for serious engagement with the detail of Hegel's ethical and political thought, notably in the work of Allen Wood (1990) and more recently Alan Patten.[19]

The recent rediscovery of Hegel for an Anglo-American audience can be attributed in part to the resurgence of interest in Hegelian positions in ethics and politics, in part to internal developments within certain strands of the analytic tradition. Two important points of reference and philosophical signposts on the way to this rediscovery are Wilfrid Sellars's criticism of the "Myth of the Given" in his paper on "Empiricism and the Philosophy of Mind" (1956) and, nearly twenty years later, Donald Davidson's paper, "On the Very Idea of a Conceptual Scheme" (1984). The target of Sellars's attempted mythicide was the positivist account of sense data. He argues that the sense-datum theorist:

> construes as data the particulars and arrays of particulars which he has come to be able to observe, and believes them to be antecedent objects of knowledge which have somehow been in the framework from the beginning. It is in the very act of *taking*, that he speaks of the *given*. (1956: 328)

Drawing on a tradition that reaches from Kant to Quine, Davidson also uncovers a dualism of schema and content, arguing that the very notion of "uninterpreted content", the raw material that is supposedly ordered by the scheme, is fundamentally obscure. These criticisms are reflected in a number of philosophical projects that place Hegel at their centre, including recent work by John McDowell (1994) and Robert Brandom (2002). McDowell's turn to Hegel forms part of a larger project that takes as its starting-point the idea that it must be possible to think that we are answerable to the world without committing ourselves to the dualism of active intellect and passive intuition. Brandom sees in Hegel an ally in identifying as a pseudo-problem the problem of how knowledge hooks on to the world. He urges us to concentrate instead on our discursive tasks and commitments, the game of giving and asking for reasons. Despite important differences, both approaches focus on the epistemic and ethical practices that underpin our cognitive commitments and give interpretative privilege to the inter-subjective context in which we negotiate competing normative claims. Indeed, one can see these broad themes as forming the communicative bridges that join together the different philosophical projects that make up the contemporary landscape of Hegel studies.

III

The following chapters are self-contained and therefore can be read in any order. There is, however, a rationale for their present sequence. Given the centrality of the question of history and philosophy already broached in this

Introduction, the book begins and ends with Hegel's own explorations of the history of philosophy, including his discussion of the anticipations of the modern self in the Socratic *daimonion*, Lutheran conscience and Aristotelian *psyche*. This concern with modern subjectivity is followed through in the other chapters, starting with Kant's apperceptive "I" and moving on to the broader issue of the subjective contribution to our knowledge of objects and to a discussion of the forms of thought analysed in the *Logic*. The essays on the *Logic* form in turn a bridge to the essays that treat Hegel's analysis of the inter-subjective domain in his political writings as well as in his writings on art, religion and history.

Allen Speight focuses on Hegel's discussion of conscience in his *Lectures on the History of Philosophy*, the *Phenomenology* and the *Philosophy of Right*. Challenging recent accounts of the historical significance of the idea of "conscience", Speight vindicates a Hegelian view and argues that conscience is not a recalcitrant element in tension with the universalistic and legalistic claims of enlightened reason. Rather than constituting an irrational break that is in opposition to the rational ethical order, conscience has an incipiently inter-subjective and ethical dimension and is internally connected to the rational forms of ethical life.

John McDowell draws attention to Hegel's acknowledged debt to Kant's concept of the original synthetic unity of apperception and sets out to show how it shapes the Hegelian doctrine of the free self-development of the Notion. McDowell's defence of Hegel's "whole-hearted counterpart" to the apperceptive I is guided by the need to show that Hegel's position does not commit us to abandoning the idea of objective reality. He presents a reading of the "master–slave" section of the *Phenomenology* as a post-Kantian philo-sophical parable, arguing that the stages of the struggle between master and slave are stages in the formative process of a self. The struggle between self and other is a struggle to acknowledge that the self's worldly life, against which the apperceptive I stakes its spontaneity and independence, is neces-sary for self-consciousness.

McDowell's critique of Kant and his Hegelian alternative are the topics of Sally Sedgwick's chapter. She sets out to refute the charge that, having mis-understood Kant's critical idealism, Hegel and McDowell impute sceptical implications to the Kantian doctrine of the unknowability of things in them-selves. Against the charge that the Hegelian alternative leads to an enhanced subjectivism that deprives nature of its independent reality, Sedgwick argues that it is Kant's contemporary defenders who are guilty of misunderstanding. She points out that Hegel fully endorses Kant's refutation of transcendental realism, but that he argues for a "two-way dependence" between subjective form and mind-independent content. She shows that rather than seeking to close the gap between mind and world, both Hegel and McDowell try to persuade us that the problem resides in our conviction that such a gap exists in the first place.

Rolf-Peter Horstmann argues that current neo-pragmatic, non-metaphysical interpretations of Hegel's philosophy, which emphasize the importance of the *Phenomenology* and the *Philosophy of Right*, fail to take fully into account Hegel's "monistic and organological model of reality" developed chiefly in the *Logic*. This failure risks burdening Hegel with the view that knowledge claims can only be justified contextually and that states of affairs can be "dissolved entirely into epochally or culturally dependent conceptual constellations". To avoid this conclusion, Horstmann shows that close attention to the triad of subject, substance and infinity reveals just how distant Hegel's systematic and scientific intentions are from those of his neo-pragmatic interpreters.

Angelica Nuzzo engages with the notorious problem of the status of the *Logic*. Central to her argument is the claim that dialectic is a "logic of transformative processes" that enables us to conceptualize change. Placing Hegel's thought firmly in its historical context, she argues that the political fragment on "the ever-growing contradiction", provides a crucial insight into Hegel's attempt to develop the logic of change that is fully elaborated in the *Logic*. In Nuzzo's non-ontological interpretation, dialectic is seen as the logic of modernity that provides us with the means to think philosophically about the transitions and contradictions of our own time.

Kimberly Hutchings also focuses on the *Logic*, using Hegel's analysis of universal, particular and singular judgement to show how it maps onto current debates in moral and political philosophy. Taking as central Hegel's argument that forms of thought are not indifferent to their content, she reconstructs his "logic of relation", emphasizing the absence of finality that such a logic forces us to confront. In applying these Hegelian insights to contemporary ethics, Hutchings is able to reveal some of the limitations of current universalist, utilitarian, communitarian and particularistic positions. While acknowledging the motivation behind these different perspectives, she argues for the superiority of a fallibilistic approach modelled on the logic of relation.

Hegel's account of human dependence is central to Robert Pippin's discussion of concerns that arise in the context of contemporary discussions of neo-Hegelian positions in ethics and politics, especially with regard to the potentially illiberal implications of Hegel's theory of the state. Pippin focuses on Hegel's account of intentionality to formulate a criticism of "the ultimacy of individuality". He argues that by granting primacy to the deed, rather than to inner states, Hegel opens up intention to the social world and transforms individuality into a public matter. The shattering of a private fantasy of self-sufficiency opens a path to a different conception of independence, even though, on Pippin's admission, we have no safe conduct to this promised land.

The broader issue of the political and social significance of Hegel's arguments in the *Philosophy of Right* is discussed by Ludwig Siep. He argues that the best way to approach the question of the contemporary relevance of

Hegel's practical philosophy is to focus on three key features: Hegel's normative social model, which allows for the integration of a fully differentiated social world; his multi-layered concept of right, which accommodates a range of claims; and his conception of political life as essential to individual self-realization. These ideas resonate with much contemporary writing in social and political theory. For this reason, Siep argues, they can contribute to revitalizing current debates about the role of the state and of individual citizens.

Jason Gaiger addresses the contemporary relevance of Hegel's aesthetics by analysing two contrasting interpretations of abstract art from a Hegelian perspective. Whereas Stephen Houlgate maintains that Hegel provides a normative account of painting that enables us to criticize subsequent developments in art, Robert Pippin contends that the emergence of abstraction is fully compatible with the underlying tendency of Hegel's lectures. Drawing on newly available textual sources, Gaiger identifies a number of problems with both of these positions. He argues that the contemporary relevance of Hegel's aesthetics resides not in any prior set of normative commitments, but in his demand that we acknowledge art's constantly changing function and character.

John Burbidge invites us to rethink our preconceptions about Hegel's philosophy of nature, which, as he acknowledges, is one of the least studied elements of his philosophy. Taking issue directly both with critics and defenders who see Hegel as presuming to tell us *a priori* what nature should be like, he develops an interpretation that takes as its starting-point the sheer wealth of empirical material found in Hegel's texts. Making sense of this, Burbidge argues, requires that we acknowledge the logic of "double transition" that Hegel employs in his thinking about the empirical world. This logic, Burbidge concludes, allows not only a more positive evaluation of Hegel's project, but also a more sanguine perspective about its relevance to current scientific thinking.

Nicholas Walker discusses the Kantian and Enlightenment themes that permeate Hegel's early writings on religion. On the basis of this analysis, Walker argues that there is continuity between the ideas contained in these early works and Hegel's mature thinking on the ethical and social role of religion and on the relation between philosophy and religion. The early writings on religion are revealing about Hegel's absorption of Kant's ideas and their role in shaping the distinctively Hegelian concern with an "autonomous and self-authenticating spirit within an inter-subjective context".

The question of philosophical history is taken up by Iain Macdonald. Taking as his starting-point the term "conceptual history", found in the closing lines of the *Phenomenology*, Macdonald investigates some of the broader issues that arise at the intersection of philosophy and history, and in particular the question of how Hegel reconciles "the concrete, contingent events of history with the universal demands of reason". Using Hegel's criticism of pragmatic historians of the eighteenth century, and Adorno's criticism of Hegel's account of history, Macdonald argues that conceptual history offers a demonstration of the "concrete self-corrective power of reason".

Allegra de Laurentiis uses Hegel's discussion of Aristotle in his *Lectures on the History of Philosophy* to explore the broader question of how thought relates to its history and how Hegel's praise for Aristotle's "speculative insight" can be seen as consistent with the progressive account of reason's coming to self-consciousness in modernity. She argues that in attributing "speculative insights" to Aristotle, Hegel is referring to the double metaphysical status of *psyche* implicit in the Aristotelian doctrines of wakefulness and sleep, of the activity and passivity of *nous*. For de Laurentiis, Hegel's discussion of Aristotle's dialectic of active and passive provides an important clue for understanding his resolution of the problem of self-knowledge.

NOTES

1. It is customary for defenders of Hegel, or at least defenders of certain aspects of his thought, to preface their efforts with the dismissive comments of his critics. Karl Popper and Bertrand Russell are often pressed to this task, but it is Arthur Schopenhauer who upbraids Hegel with most relish: "the greatest effrontery in serving up sheer nonsense, in scrabbling together senseless and maddening webs of words, such as had previously been heard only in madhouses, finally appeared in Hegel. It became the instrument of the most ponderous and general mystification that has ever existed, with a result that will seem incredible to posterity and be a lasting monument of German stupidity" (cited in S. Houlgate, *An Introduction to Hegel: Freedom, Truth and History* (Oxford: Blackwell, 2005), 1).

2. For a survey of the Hegelian school, see J. Toews, *Hegelianism: The Path Toward Dialectical Humanism 1805–1841* (Cambridge: Cambridge University Press, 1980). For a general survey of Hegelianism, see R. Stern & N. Walker, "Hegelianism", in *Routledge Encyclopaedia of Philosophy*, E. Craig (ed.), 280–302 (London: Routledge, 2000). A useful anthology of the writings of the Young Hegelians is L. S. Stepelevich, *The Young Hegelians* (Cambridge: Cambridge University Press, 1987). The split between so-called "left" and "right" Hegelianism was reinforced by the division into the "young" and the "mature" Hegel that occurred early on in the reception history of his thought. See, for instance, G. Lukács, *The Young Hegel* (London: Merlin Press, [1938] 1975).

3. The phrase "what is living and what is dead" comes from Benedetto Croce's 1907 work, *Cio che é vivo e cio che é morto nella filisofia di Hegel* (Bari: Laterza, 1907).

4. For an account of the reception history of Hegel in France see J. D'Hondt, *Hegel et hégélianisme* (Paris: Presses Universitaires de France, 1982) and J. Butler, *Subjects of Desire: Hegelian Reflections in Twentieth Century France* (Ithaca, NY: Cornell University Press, 1988). Very helpful is B. Bauch, "Limiting Reason's Empire: The Early Reception of Hegel in France", *Journal of the History of Philosophy* 31(2) (1993), 259–75.

5. A timely reappraisal of British Idealism itself can be found in S. Houlgate (ed.), *Hegel and British Idealism*, *Bulletin of the Hegel Society of Great Britain* 31 (1995) and R. Stern, "James and Bradley on Understanding", *Philosophy* 68 (1993), 193–209.

6. Theodor W. Adorno's essay on the difficulty of reading Hegel is rather unpromisingly titled "*Skoteinos*, or How to Read Hegel", in T. W. Adorno, *Hegel: Three Studies*, S. Weber Nicholsen (trans.) (Cambridge, MA: MIT Press, 1993).

7. A good account of the German context of the debate can be found in Robert M. Wallace's "Introduction", in H. Blumenberg, *The Legitimacy of the Modern Age*, R. M. Wallace (trans.), xi–xxxi (Cambridge MA: MIT Press, 1983); see also K. Löwith, *Weltgeschichte und heilgeschehen: Die theologischen Voraussetzungen der Geschichtsphilosophie* (Stuttgart: Lohlammer, 1953).

8. Other important studies include K. Ameriks (ed.), *The Cambridge Companion to German Idealism* (Cambridge: Cambridge University Press, 2000), which contains a number of helpful pieces, not least Ameriks's "Introduction", 1–17, and *Kant and the Fate of Autonomy: Problems in the Appropriation of the Critical Philosophy*. (Cambridge: Cambridge University Press, 2000); S. Sedgwick (ed.), *The Reception of Kant's Critical Philosophy: Fichte, Schelling and Hegel* (Cambridge: Cambridge University Press, 2000); A. Bowie, *Aesthetics and Subjectivity from Kant to Nietzsche*, 2nd edn (Manchester: Manchester University Press, 2003). See also J. van der Zande & R. H. Popkin (eds), *The Skeptical Tradition Around 1800: Skepticism in Philosophy, Science, and Society* (Dordrecht: Kluwer, 1998).

9. See especially this volume, Ch. 3. The problem of things-in-themselves played a central role in the so-called Spinozism dispute; see G. di Giovanni, "Hegel, Jacobi and 'Crypto-Catholicism' or Hegel in Dialogue with the Enlightenment", in *Hegel on the Modern World*, A. Collins (ed.), 53–72 (Albany, NY: SUNY Press, 1995).

10. An interesting early treatment of the freedom and constraint theme in Hegel can be found in R. Brandom, "Freedom and Constraint by Norms", *American Philosophical Quarterly* 16(3) (1979), 187–96.

11. The expression "historical turn" is used in R. Campbell, "The Covert Metaphysics of the Clash between 'Analytic' and 'Continental' Philosophy", *British Journal for the History of Philosophy* 9(2) (2001), 341–59.

12. Hegel's writings and lectures are now being made available in new editions and translations. Meiner Verlag are in the process of publishing a series of new editions of Hegel's major works and lectures; in the English-speaking world, Cambridge University Press is embarking on an ambitious publishing project to bring out an edition of the *Collected Works* under the editorship of Robert Pippin. Another major project is the four volume reception history by R. Stern (ed.), *G. W. F. Hegel: Critical Assessments*, 4 vols (London: Routledge, 1993).

13. Twentieth-century versions of this criticism can be found in C. Taylor, *Hegel* (Cambridge: Cambridge University Press, 1975) and M. Rosen, *Hegel's Dialectic and its Criticism* (Cambridge: Cambridge University Press, 1982). For a discussion of Rosen see K. Deligiorgi, "Kant, Hegel, and the Bounds of Thought", *Bulletin of the Hegel Society of Great Britain* 45/46 (2002): 56–71.

14. G. di Giovanni (ed.), *Essays on Hegel's Logic* (Albany, NY: SUNY Press, 1990) offers a good illustration of the divergent perspectives discussed here. See also this volume, Chs 4, 5, 6 and 10. The mobility of Hegel's thought is a central theme of non-immanentist interpretations issuing from a variety of philosophical traditions; see, for instance, H. Marcuse, *Hegel's Ontology and the Theory of Historicity*, S. Benhabib

(trans.) (Cambridge MA: MIT Press, 1987) and C. Malabou, *L'Avenir de Hegel: Plasticité, Temporalité, Dialectique* (Paris: Vrin, 1996).

15. Houlgate argues that Hegel employs the term "metaphysics" to refer both to traditional philosophical enquiries and to the basic categories that inform our experience; see Houlgate, *An Introduction to Hegel,* 4ff., 26ff.. For different approaches to this see A. W. Wood, *Hegel's Ethical Thought* (Cambridge: Cambridge University Press, 1990); R. B. Pippin, "Hegel on the Rationality and Priority of Ethical Life", *Neue Hefte für Philosophie* 35 (1995), 95–126; and S. Sedgwick, "Metaphysics and Morality in Kant and Hegel", *Bulletin of the Hegel Society of Great Britain* 37/38 (1998), 1–16. See also G. Jarczyk, *Système et Liberté dans la Logique de Hegel* (Paris: Aubier, 1980); B. Longuenesse, *Hegel et la Critique de la Métaphysique* (Paris: Vrin, 1981); and A. Doz, *Parcours Philosophique, Tome 1: Avec Hegel* (Paris: L'Harmattan, 2001). For an aporetic but also absolutist and speculative reading see G. Rose, *Hegel contra Sociology* (London: Athlone, 1981).

16. An early exponent of the recognitive interpretation is M. Theunissen, *Sein und Schein* (Frankfurt: Suhrkamp, 1978). See also J. Flay, *Hegel's Quest for Certainty* (Albany, NY: SUNY Press, 1984) and V. Hösle, *Hegels System: Der Idealismus der Subjektivität und das Problem der Intersubjektivität* (Hamburg: Felix Meiner, 1987). Drawing on this tradition, but developing an interpretation that seeks directly to address postmodern and deconstructionist concerns, is R. R. Williams, *Recognition: Fichte and Hegel on the Other* (Albany, NY: SUNY Press, 1992).

17. For a Hegelian perspective on the "communicative model", see G. Finlayson, "Does Hegel's Critique of Kant's Moral Theory Apply to Discourse Ethics?", *Bulletin of the Hegel Society of Great Britain* 37/38 (1988), 17–34.

18. See especially this volume, Chs 6, 7 and 8. Interestingly Rawls's project can also be seen as containing a Hegelian dimension, see C. Kukathas & P. Pettit, *Rawls: A Theory of Justice and Its Critics* (Cambridge: Polity, 1995), 144.

19. A. Patten, *Hegel's Idea of Freedom* (Oxford: Oxford University Press, 1999) is a useful study of the "Sittlichkeit thesis". For a more sombre assessment of Hegel's conciliatory hopes, see A. Negri, "La Tragedia nell'Etico", *Giornale Critico della Filosofia Italiana* 41 (1962), 65–86.

CHAPTER ONE

HEGEL ON CONSCIENCE AND THE HISTORY OF MORAL PHILOSOPHY

Allen Speight

Conscience, Hegel claims, "represents an exalted point of view, a point of view of the modern world" (*PR*: §136A). The notion that conscience is indeed closely linked to the experience of modernity has played an important role in a number of approaches to the history of moral philosophy, but these approaches often differ in terms of their accounts of what precisely it is that makes conscience a modern phenomenon. In what follows I want to show what is distinctive about Hegel's view of the modernity of conscience, in the process re-examining some conventional assumptions about Hegel's relation to the history of moral philosophy. I hope thereby to make some contribution to the still not entirely developed philosophical subdiscipline of the history of moral philosophy, as well as to the broader connection it shares with political and religious concerns that were always central to Hegel's treatment of the concept of conscience.

The issue of conscience and the history of moral philosophy might in general be framed at the start in terms of recent discussion of it in Edward G. Andrew's *Conscience and its Critics: Protestant Conscience, Enlightenment Reason and Modern Subjectivity* (2001), more specifically in Andrew's response to the history of moral philosophy he finds implicit in J. B. Schneewind's *The Invention of Autonomy* (1998). Andrew's concern is the development of particularly the Protestant notion of conscience between the sixteenth and nineteenth centuries. On the one hand, Andrew sees something of an overall trend in these centuries. First, there is a development in the sort of activity that conscience could be allowed as describing; he follows here C. S. Lewis's famous characterization of conscience as moving from the activity of the witness box to that of the judge and ultimately even the legislator (Lewis 1960). Secondly, there is a division between the two terms "conscience" and "consciousness"; in the post-Lockean Enlightenment, he argues, the "elevation of consciousness as the basis of personal identity accompanied the rejection of conscience as innate practical principle" (Andrew 2001: 7).

On the other hand, and despite this general trend, Andrew sees in the relevant time period an underlying *tension* between conscience and reason that he appears to take to be in some sense unresolvable: there are views and philosophical moments that seem more dominated by Enlightenment reason and others that seem more dominated by Protestant conscience. Here Andrew sets out his account in terms of a set of determinate oppositions: the Enlightenment view of reason enshrines itself often in *law*, while conscience has an *antinomian* streak; *rational* judgement is opposed to the conscientious judgement that is simply *one's own*; reason is *sceptical* and conscience is *certain*; reason strives for a *sociality* while conscience is the province of the *individual*; reason is *communicative* while conscience is often portrayed as deeply *silent* (*ibid*.: 8–9).

This view of conscience as representing a recalcitrant element in tension with reason is articulated in part as a contrast to what Andrew calls Schneewind's "harmonious conjunction of Protestantism and Enlightenment" (*ibid*.: 179). Some of the differences between Andrew's and Schneewind's projects can be attributed to a difference of focus. Andrew is concerned to examine primarily the development of views of conscience in the English-speaking tradition; Schneewind has a broader perspective that is not focused on simply the concept of conscience but on the broader issue of autonomy and that includes the rather different development within German cultural and intellectual history.

Andrew explains away his avoidance of figures such as Kant as connected with the desire to focus on philosophical approaches that do not suggest so strongly possible grounds of synthesis between the notions of Protestant conscience and Enlightenment reason (*ibid*.: 8). He further suggests that Schneewind gives insufficient consideration to *social* counter-movements to the notion of conscience, especially, he holds, "the rise of society and the regulation of conduct by social expectations" in the eighteenth century (*ibid*.: 180). This latter point is somewhat of a strained claim, since Schneewind makes clear that he thinks the history of moral philosophy is frequently more driven by social developments than the history of philosophy more generally often recognizes (Schneewind 1998: 5–8). Nonetheless, a brief consideration of Andrew and Schneewind has yielded a question concerning the relation between conscience and reason that bears underlining: is there a way of understanding the relation between *individual self-certainty* in judgements of conscience and normative judgements of *reason* that does not simply view them as opposed tensions? I shall claim that Hegel's approach to the issue of conscience does in fact offer such a synthetic possibility for construing both the rational and self-certain sides of the experience of conscience.

CONSCIENCE IN HEGEL'S HISTORY OF PHILOSOPHY

At first glance, we might think that Hegel tells a story similar to Andrew's about the place of conscience within the history of moral philosophy. It appears, to begin with, to be a developmental story of conscience as a distinctively modern phenomenon. Hegel often makes the point, for example, that conscience is a notion that was not available to the ancient Greeks: "of the Greeks in the first and true shape of their freedom, we can insist that they had no conscience; among them ruled the habit of living for the fatherland, without further reflection" (*PH*: 253; *SW* 12: 308). Even more decisively, and closer to the specific developmental account that Andrew gives, the experience of conscience appears for Hegel to be a crucial marker not just of the Christian as opposed to the classical era but of the distinctively Protestant moment within Christianity itself. Among Hegel's more famous remarks is this from the preface to the *Philosophy of Right*:

> It is a great obstinacy [*Eigensinn*], the kind of obstinacy which does honor to human beings, that they are unwilling to acknowledge in their attitudes anything which has not been justified by thought – and this obstinacy is the characteristic property of the modern age, as well as being the distinctive principle of Protestantism. What Luther inaugurated as faith in feeling and in the testimony of the spirit [*Zeugnis des Geistes*] is the same thing that the spirit, at a more mature stage of its development endeavors to grasp in the *concept* so as to free itself in the present and thus find itself therein.   (*PR*: 12, emphasis added)

Hegel's remark here may suggest the two sides of Andrew's tension: although Hegel speaks about an appropriation of this experience into a conceptual or rational form, the description of a characteristic Protestant "obstinacy" certainly suggests a recalcitrant, not-necessarily-rational side of the claim to trust one's own judgement. (The German word for "obstinacy", *Eigensinn*, is one that Hegel uses otherwise in the *Philosophy of Right* when talking about topics such as the unwavering and occasionally impolite insistence he thinks uncultured persons can place on the satisfaction of their own rights in various situations.)

But Hegel's view of the relation between these two sides is actually quite different from Andrew's. A first window on to the differences in their views can be seen etymologically: while the notion of *conscience*, as Andrew argues, increasingly comes to be defined in the English language in distinction from its emergent cognate *consciousness*, the German *Gewissen* – as Hegel's account of it famously exploits at a number of levels – instead is linked at once both to the related terms *gewiss* ("certain") and *Wissen* ("knowledge"). The difference in Hegel's view can be glimpsed

19

from a section of the account of conscience in the "Morality" section of the *Philosophy of Right*:

> This subjectivity, as abstract self-determination and pure certainty of itself alone, evaporates into itself all *determinate* aspects of right, duty, and existence [*Dasein*], inasmuch as it is the power of *judgment* which determines solely from within itself what is good in relation to a given content, and at the same time the power to which the good, which is at first only an Idea and an *obligation*, owes its *actuality*.
>
> The self-consciousness which has managed to attain this absolute reflection into itself knows itself in this reflection as a consciousness which cannot and should not be compromised by any present and given determination. In the shapes which it more commonly assumes in history (as in the case of Socrates, the Stoics, etc.) the tendency to look *inwards* into the self and to know and determine from within the self what is right and good appears in epochs when what is recognized as right and good in actuality and custom is unable to satisfy the better will.
>
> (PR: §138 and Remark, emphasis added)

The first thing to notice is that Hegel is talking here about a coordinate power that seems to work in two directions: on the one hand, to evaporate or condense ethical actuality, and, on the other hand, to give it fullness and actuality (perhaps we could call this a kind of "solidifying"). The examples Hegel gives to illustrate his conception of conscience as a sort of evaporated form of rational ethical life are striking: Socrates and the Stoics, he says, are instances of "the tendency to look *inwards* into the self and to know and determine from within the self what is right and good" which appear "in epochs when what is recognized as right and good in actuality and custom is unable to satisfy the better will": "When the existing world of freedom has become unfaithful to the better will, this will no longer finds itself in the duties recognized in this world and must seek to recover in ideal inwardness alone that harmony which it has lost in actuality" (PR: §138 Remark).

The double image of evaporation and solidification, as well as the appeal to exceptional figures who, like Socrates and the Stoics, can in some relevant sense withdraw from the ethical whole, suggests that Hegel views conscience and reason not as two separate elements that are in tension with one another, as though, on Andrew's view, there are simply moments in history when either conscience or reason just happens to dominate; rather, the extreme inward experience of conscience must be thought of in terms of being a concentrated power of judgement that is, in fact, the source of the actuality of the rational ethical whole that is *Sittlichkeit*. Or we might say it in this way: it appears that Hegel appeals to the notion of a conscience that must act in a world in which it can find its own purposes present. Presumably, then, conscience must not be regarded as a sudden eruption of what opposes rational ethical order but rather as having a more intimate conceptual connection to that order.

In addition to this conceptual point – what we might call Hegel's "holistic" stance toward conscience – there is a further issue raised by Hegel's use of examples in this passage: paradoxically, given the stress Hegel places on the modernity of conscience, it is two *ancient* ethical examples, Socrates and the Stoics, that play a central role in this passage. What sort of historical account is Hegel actually giving, then, of the notion of conscience?

To begin with, we must notice that it is not the history of moral philosophy that we might perhaps expect of someone who makes Hegel's claim about the essential modernity of conscience: that is to say, a history that might track the development of the notion of *conscientia* from late antiquity in the writings of figures such as St Paul through its medieval appropriation in figures such as Peter Lombard, Thomas Aquinas and Bonaventure.[1] Hegel does not, in fact, give an explicit developmental account of the notion of conscience, and his own brief references, for example, to conscience in its medieval context are limited to a framework defined by his familiar criticism of the "external" orientation of Catholic religious views more generally. (Characteristic are these comments about conscience and the medieval Church: "In the same way that the administration of the means of grace belongs as an outward possession to the Church in relation of worship, so is the Church also in possession of a moral estimate for judging of the actions of individuals; it is in the possession of the conscience, as of knowledge as a whole, so that man's inmost essence, his accountability, passes into other hands and to another person, and the subject is devoid of individuality even in his inmost self" (*LHP* 3: 56; *SW* 19: 538).

Instead, as we have begun to see, Hegel's account of the history of the concept of conscience is surprisingly punctate, emphasizing the historical moments defined by individual figures such as Socrates and Luther (and to a lesser extent the Stoics) in whom subjective self-awareness is in especially stark relief to the conventional order. And, perhaps more problematically, while Hegel does mark a difference between the inauguration of the modern age in Luther and the ancient figures of Socrates and the Stoics, it is not initially clear why he seems to want to stretch the "modern" notion of conscience to include these ancient "exceptions". A brief comparative look at Hegel's description of these moments seems warranted.

Socrates and the Stoics

Hegel describes the Socratic moment of conscience in terms that we have seen already employed for that of Luther's devotion to the "witness" or "testimony" of the Spirit (*Zeugnis des Geistes*), and that stress that this "witness" must involve, on Hegel's view, both the side of self-certainty and that of rationality and universality:

> According to the Socratic principle, nothing has any value to men to which the spirit does not testify. Man in it is free, is at home with himself, and that is the subjectivity of spirit ... But what spirit derives from itself must come from it as from the spirit which acts in a universal manner, and not from its passions, likings, and arbitrary desires ... Socrates opposed to the contingent and particular inward, that universal, true inward of thought. And Socrates awakened this real conscience, for he not only said that man is the measure of all things, but that man as thinking is the measure of all things. (*LHP* 1: 410–11; *SW* 18: 470–71)

Hegel's description of Socrates here is reminiscent of the *Phenomenology*'s account of conscience as a *concrete* knowledge of all that is involved in a specific case of action. As opposed to the conflicting duties that may be discerned by the non-concretely knowing universal moral consciousness, conscience "knows and does what is concretely right" and in its "simple moral action" puts aside the analysis that breaks apart into various claims to pure duty (*PhG*: §635). Hegel describes Socrates as confronting in his conscientious judgement a similar case of concrete action:

> When we have the perfect consciousness that in actual life fixed duties and actions do not exist, for each concrete case is really a conflict of many duties which separate themselves in the moral understanding, but which mind treats as not absolute, comprehending them in the unity of its judgment, we call this pure, deciding individuality, the knowledge of what is right, or conscience, just as we call the pure universal of consciousness not a particular but an all-comprehensive one, duty. Now both sides here present, the universal law and the deciding spirit which is in its abstraction the active individual, are also necessary to the consciousness of Socrates as the content and the power over the content. (*LHP* 1: 420; *SW* 18: 487–8)

Hegel contrasts Socrates' inward awareness of subjective certainty and the individual decisiveness it implies with the external character of the Greek experience of decision-making, the latter determined by oracles and other outside influences. Hegel is careful to insist that Socrates' famous interior experience of the divine "voice" – his "genius" or *daimonion* – *cannot* be regarded as an experience of something that could be called *conscience*:

22

> For conscience is the idea of universal individuality, of the mind certain of itself, which is at the same time universal truth. But the Genius of Socrates is rather all the other and necessary sides of his universality, that is, the individuality of mind which came to consciousness in him equally with the former ... The deficiency in the universal, which lies in its indeterminateness, is unsatisfactorily supplied in an individual way, because Socrates' judgment, as coming from himself, was characterized by the form of an unconscious impulse. The Genius of Socrates is not Socrates himself, not his opinions and conviction, but an oracle which, however, is not external but is subjective, his oracle. (*LHP* 1: 422; *SW* 18: 490)

The Socratic *daimonion* thus "stands midway between the externality of the oracle and the pure inwardness of the mind" (*LHP* 1: 425; *SW* 18: 494).

Because of its inwardness, the "turning-point in the whole world-famed change of views constituting the principle of Socrates" (*LHP* 1: 425; *SW* 18: 494–5) is one that puts him at odds with the contemporary norms of Greek ethical life. Hegel's description of Socrates' relation to the Athenian court that tries and sentences him sets up an important set of questions for the ultimate Hegelian account of conscience and its relation to the state, a relation that Hegel frames, quite interestingly, in terms of what he here calls the "privileged" conscience implicit in the law court itself:

> Socrates thus set his conscience in opposition to the judges' sentence, and acquitted himself before its tribunal. But no people, and least of all a free people like the Athenians, has by this freedom to recognize a tribunal of conscience which knows no consciousness of having fulfilled its duty excepting its own consciousness. To this government and law, the universal spirit of the people, may reply: "If you have the consciousness of having done your duty, we must also have the consciousness that you have so done." For the first principle of a State is that there is no reason or conscience or righteousness or anything else, higher than what the State recognizes as such ... [L]aw also has a conscience and has to speak through it; the law-court is the privileged conscience.
> (*LHP* 1: 442–3; *SW* 18: 509–10)

Hegel's difficult claims here set up the concern of his own ethical and political philosophy with marking off a difference between the subjectivist demands of merely "formal" conscience and what can be termed "true" conscience, that is, one whose content is defined by the dispositions attached to the various institutions and norms of actual ethical life. I shall briefly look at Hegel's distinction between these two kinds of conscience in the section "Conscience in Hegel's account of modern agency" below, but before taking up the remainder

23

of Hegel's historical references to conscience, it is important to say a brief word about Hegel's reference to conscience and the ancient Stoics. Although the *Philosophy of Right* paragraph quite clearly cites both Socrates and the Stoics as examples of conscientious "withdrawal" from conventional moral life, Hegel is somewhat more careful in the *Lectures on the History of Philosophy* to insist that the Stoics do not yet employ a notion that could be called conscience: "[t]he Stoic principle has not yet reached to this more concrete attitude, as being on the one hand abstract morality, and, on the other, the subject that has a conscience" (*LHP* 3: 275; *SW* 19: 294). Why, then, does he mention the Stoics as examples in the *Philosophy of Right* passage? The point of connection would seem to be the Stoic principle that "everything is true or good in the simplicity of thought" – or, as Hegel puts it in the *Phenomenology*: the "principle" of Stoicism "is that consciousness is a being that *thinks*, and that consciousness holds something to be essentially important, or true and good only insofar as it *thinks* it to be such" (*PhG*: §198)[2] – a formulation that may be compared, as we have seen already in the case of Socrates, with the *Phenomenology*'s later claim in the discussion of "Conscience" at the end of the "Spirit" chapter that a case of moral action is known there "only as conscience knows it" (*PhG*: §635).[3]

Luther and the Reformation

Central to Hegel's historical account of conscience is the role of the Protestant Reformation, and particularly that of Luther, in making conscience a religious phenomenon. As we have noted, Hegel does not offer any sustained account in his history of conscience linking Luther's notion of conscience to medieval or earlier Christian claims about conscience.[4] Hegel's account instead focuses directly on Luther's famous appeal to conscience in his speech before the Diet of Worms and on the consequences of that appeal for the character of reformed thought more generally.[5]

As with the Socratic turn to conscience's inwardness in opposition to the external oracular character of Greek religious and ethical life, there is with Luther also the overcoming of an external element, which is for Hegel perhaps most clearly symbolized in the division between laity and clergy that is altered by Luther:

> [O]n the side of knowledge man turned back into himself from the Beyond of authority; and reason was recognized as the absolutely universal, and hence as divine. Now it was perceived that it is in the mind of man that religion must have its place, and the whole process of salvation be gone through – that man's salvation is his own affair, and that by it he enters into relationship with his conscience and into immediate connection with God, requiring no

mediation of priests having the so-called means of grace within their hands. There is indeed a mediation [*Vermittlung*] present still by means of doctrine, perception [*Einsicht* – Hegel's word also for Socrates' conscientious "insight"], the observation of self and of one's actions; but that is a mediation without a separating wall [*Scheidewand*], while formerly a brazen wall of division was present separating the laity from the church.

(LHP 3: 147; *SW* 20: 48–9)

On the face of it, Hegel's account of Lutheran conscience seems to be framed in terms that make it sound quite similar to the Socratic conscience: in both cases, Hegel stresses the importance of the *Zeugnis des Geistes* (an *internal*, as opposed to an external criterion for the rightness of action) and the role of a distinctive individual self-certainty (Luther's *Eigensinn*, Socrates' "pure deciding individuality") in becoming aware of that criterion. Luther's notion of conscience clearly must involve an advance over Socrates', however: to be sure, as Frederick Neuhouser has emphasized in his discussion of the Hegelian concept of conscience, Luther appeals both to a new notion of unconditionality associated with a different conception of God and to a more thoroughgoing universality (Neuhouser 2000: 232–5). But we might notice two other distinct developments between Luther and Socrates precisely in terms of the issues we have emphasized, the *Zeugnis des Geistes* and the importance of the *Eigensinn* associated with the Protestant conscience:

(i) Hegel seems to notice in Luther an advance over Socrates in terms of his appeal to the criterion of non-externality: while it was the peculiarity of Socrates' experience of individual self-certainty and conscientious "insight" that it was "characterized by the form of an *unconscious impulse*" – and hence represented in Hegel's view a sort of "internal oracle" – Luther's notion of conscience goes further in allowing the experience of that insight, along with the "observation of self and of one's actions", to be understood by the self as its own, requiring not even the "internal" oracularity associated with the Socratic *daimonion*. This "non-oracular" character of conscience may be the most decisive break toward the *modern* in Hegel's view,[6] since the further development that occurs over the ensuing 300 years may be regarded as a concern with finding an internal source of – rational, non-given, non-revealed – *content* that is appropriate to the essential internality of the *mode* of "testimony of the Spirit" involved in Luther's appeal to conscience.[7]

(ii) The *Eigensinn* associated with Protestant conscience frames in many ways for Hegel a deep connection between the two quintessentially modern concerns of his *Philosophy of Right*: the moral subjectivity represented in conscience and the demands of inalienability associated with claims of *right*. Conscience is, in fact, in Hegel's political philosophy, a claim of right – not of *abstract* right in Hegel's sense, but of the right of a subject in conditions of modernity, something guaranteed within the wider scope of the rights and duties associated with *Sittlichkeit* – and it may be that a Hegelian notion of holistic conscience could offer a construal of these two practices (those of conscientious speech and claims of right) that can be understood to have a connection to one another as moves within a set of emerging ways in which modern subjects regard themselves as free.

In any case, Hegel's curiously "modern" reading of both Socrates and Luther has raised a number of questions. First, we might ask more specifically what the Socratic and Lutheran concerns with individuality and witness of the spirit yield in terms of the role that conscience plays in Hegel's philosophy of agency more generally. And secondly, we might still ask about what sort of historical distinctiveness contemporary – non-Greek, non-Protestant – claims of conscience might have, given the rather unconventional history of moral philosophy Hegel has presented. I shall take up these two issues respectively in the following sections.

CONSCIENCE IN HEGEL'S ACCOUNT OF MODERN AGENCY

Our discussion of the character of conscience as revealed in Luther and Socrates raises some interesting questions about the role of conscience in Hegel's philosophy of agency. Hegel is, for example, often taken to be simply a *critic* of the notion of conscience. Especially in the later phase of his ethical writing, in the *Philosophy of Right*, Hegel severely attacks the subjectivity and relativism he finds implicit in the Romantic versions of conscience espoused by contemporary figures such as J. F. Fries and W. M. L. deWette. Moreover, the place of conscience in Hegel's writing appears to shift: while the moment of conscience is the concern of the final section of the "Spirit" chapter of the *Phenomenology* – representing thereby a development beyond the Greek moment of *Sittlichkeit* with which that chapter begins – the *Philosophy of Right* places conscience as a moment of transition on the way to a more comprehensive doctrine of ethical institutions in the section devoted to *Sittlichkeit*.

While Hegel is undoubtedly a critic of the notion of conscience as presented by certain of his contemporaries, and while there are significant differences between the relevant accounts of conscience in the *Phenomenology* and the *Philosophy of Right*, these considerations can nonetheless obscure the underlying importance of conscience and its relation to right in Hegel's thought. As we have framed it, our question about the peculiar "holistic"' claim concerning conscience that Hegel makes must be something like this: how can we view the sort of inward self-certainty represented by the first-personal experience of conscience as at all having a necessary tie to reason, especially to the norms of ethical life as a whole? Several important relations are implicit in Hegel's claims about conscience and rationality: (i) the relation between conscience and action; (ii) the relation between what Hegel calls "true" and "formal" conscience; and (iii) the relation of conscience to the inter-subjective experience of forgiveness. I shall explore each of these briefly.

(i) The relation between conscience and action

First, the importance of the relation between conscience and *action*. I have suggested that the Hegelian account of conscience is one that is tightly linked to the account he gives of ethical practices. The philosophical root of this connection may best be seen by considering how Hegel's philosophy of action – visible first in the *Phenomenology* and articulated systematically in the *Philosophy of Right* – directly requires the notion of conscience (and vice versa). The final section of the "Spirit" chapter of the *Phenomenology*, which is devoted to conscience, offers a central window into Hegel's philosophy of action. What is distinctive about the shape of conscience, after all, is that – unlike the moral consciousness, which is riven by an empty opposition – it actually *acts*; and – unlike other prior moments within "Spirit", where agents (such as the tragic Antigone) find themselves opening up unknown oppositions in their action – it acts with complete *assurance of its knowledge* of the concrete ethical situation in front of it. Conscience is thus a self (unique among the "selves" sketched within the "Spirit" chapter) which has a determinate content, a content that it derives from its agent's knowledge of its own purposes.

Conscience is not, on Hegel's presentation in either the *Phenomenology* or the *Philosophy of Right*, a special *faculty* but rather a mode of (rational) intentionality. As "action *qua* actualization" it is thus "the pure form of will – the simple conversion of a reality that merely *is* into a reality that results from *action*" (*PhG*: §635). The *Philosophy of Right* can be understood as giving a similar importance to the notion of conscience in its official discussion of action (*PR*: §§115–20), a section that is significantly placed as the transition between the claims of (impersonal) "abstract right" and the (distinctly first-personal) claims of "morality" including, ultimately, conscience. Hegel's account here, as Michael Quante has suggested (Quante 1993: 104–8), owes much to Anscombean notions of (non-observational) knowledge of one's own purpose, a feature that is essential to the first-personal claims of conscience being knowledge at all.

As a knowledge of its own purposes – which is thus (as implicit in Anscombe's view of agent's knowledge) a knowledge of the *world* as well as itself – conscience thus opens up the whole realm of determinate claims within that world. But these claims are just what Hegel calls right, in the larger sense of Hegel's

Philosophy of Right: not just the "abstract right" that Hegel associates with the Kantian and Fichtean philosophies of right, but right in the determinate sense that characterizes all of the moments of *Sittlichkeit*.[8]

Thus a consideration of the relation between conscience and action suggests already part of Hegel's solution to one of the great problems of German Idealism: how to ground a comprehensive ethics that could include both claims of both right and morality.[9] If it is true for conscience that where I have a reason, I also have a purpose that I can construe as *mine*, this casts some light on the *Philosophy of Right*'s famous (but not so readily understood) claim that "duty and right coincide in ... [the] identity of the universal and the particular will" (PR: § 155).

(ii) The relation between what Hegel calls "true" and "formal" conscience

As Hegel's problematic remarks concerning the "privileged conscience" of Socrates' jury suggests, a good deal of the difficulty in comprehending Hegel's view of the relation between conscience and right lies, of course, in another distinction that Hegel draws – that between true and formal conscience (*PR:* §137); it is formal conscience that involves the subjectivist claims against which Hegel rails so much, whereas true conscience is linked in the *Philosophy of Right* to the "ethical disposition" at the root of an agent's connection to the various institutions of ethical life. The knowledge of its own purposes in the world that is so central to Hegel's account of true conscience has much to do with Hegel's ability to concern himself with an ethical agent's right *to* conscience – unlike Fichte, who claimed that it was "invalid to talk of a right to freedom ... of conscience" (SW 3: 55).

(iii) The relation of conscience to the inter-subjective experience of forgiveness

A full account of Hegel's position here would need to address more fully both the ways in which true conscience structures the ethical institutions of the *Philosophy of Right* and the degree to which conscientious criticism of those institutions is essential to Hegel's political theory.[10] Yet it must be noted that neither in the *Phenomenology* nor in the *Philosophy of Right* does Hegel seem to make conscience by itself an ultimate term. The *Phenomenology* famously moves from a description of the conscientious "beautiful soul" to a scene of reconciling forgiveness between beautiful soul and acting subject: while the conscientious subject is in some sense rightly to be regarded as the final and unifying "self" of the "Spirit" chapter, the judgements of this conscientious self have authority only because of the inter-subjective moment of recognition of the conditions of agency that forgiveness provides. The point could perhaps be put this way: only *consciences* may forgive, but it is the act of forgiveness that enables their judgements, a point inscribed as well in the *Philosophy of Right*'s view of the monarch who pardons.[11]

CONSCIENCE IN ITS CONTOURS: MODERNITY IN POLITICAL LIFE AND RELIGIOUS EXPERIENCE

We have left, however, something of a problem regarding the relation between conscience and the history of moral philosophy: if the conscientious agent for Hegel is one that ultimately owes a great deal to its Socratic and Lutheran embodiments, how "modern" is conscience, in the end, and what is the connection the concept of conscience has to Hegel's approach to the history of moral philosophy? One way of considering a potential Hegelian answer to this question is to examine two transitions that conscience effects in Hegel's writings: the first in the *Phenomenology* (from "Spirit" to "Religion") and the second in the *Philosophy of Right* (from "Morality" to "*Sittlichkeit*" and the world of ethical, economic and political institutions that make up the latter).

In both transitions, as noted in the final point of the previous section, there is a concrete mediation involved: in the ethical case, a mediating range of specific ethical institutions that are capable of integrating, as the moment of forgiveness does, both impersonal and personal sides of the action; in the religious case, as Hegel's lectures on the philosophy of religion make polemically clear, there is no conscientious stance apart from the content of an articulated theological doctrine. As a way of concluding the foregoing discussion, I shall briefly look at the essential Hegelian claim about the modernity of each of these mediations.

- Conscience and the transition to ethical life: Hegel's stress on conscience, from his treatment of Socrates forwards, as involving both "universal law and deciding Spirit" implies a concern with how inner decision can be bound up with the range of specific duties and ethical concerns involved in any actual case of ethical action. Whether in its "evaporated" or "solidified" form, conscience must, in other words, involve precisely a reflective consideration of ethical norms in their historicity, and thus of their revisability. A complete account of modern conscience must, then, involve an account of the ethical institutions of modern life and the norms associated with those institutions.
- Conscience and the transition to religion: One way of considering the transition that the final section of the *Phenomenology*'s treatment of "conscience" effects to the standpoint of "Religion" is to view it in terms

of the further development of an essentially internal, "non-oracular" voice of authority in moral experience. As Socrates and Luther were both associated with moves to a more internal view of moral authority, free of external interventions such as oracular command or a priestly class, so Hegel may be seen in the "Conscience" section of the *Phenomenology* to be offering an account of how the distinct moments of post-Kantian appropriations of conscience develop in their turn into a view of agency that is free of even the seemingly more internal notion of an ideal judge. In a longer account of the role of conscience in this section of the *Phenomenology*, we might, for example, view the Hegelian interpretation of the development of the post-Kantian notion of conscience as a series of idealist and romantic attempts to break free from Kant's claim that conscience is "the subjective principle of being accountable to God for all one's deeds", or an "accountability to a holy being (morally lawgiving reason) distinct from us yet present in our inmost being" (Kant 1996: 190).[12] From this perspective, Hegel can be seen to be offering an examination of the recognitive potential of moments associated with – but not fully integrated into – Fichtean, Jacobian and Schlegelian accounts of conscience.[13]

Taking both of these transitions into account, conscience's "modernity" can be seen to be related on the one hand to the self-conscious awareness of the historical task of revision of norms central to modernity's ongoing realization and on the other hand to perhaps the most singular shift that makes for modernity itself: the awareness that religious experience is no longer merely of an other that is "beyond".

NOTES

1. Such an account can be found, for example, in E. D'Arcy, *Conscience and Its Right to Freedom* (New York: Sheed & Ward, 1961) and T. C. Potts, *Conscience in Medieval Philosophy* (Cambridge: Cambridge University Press, 1980).
2. Hegel's emphasis here may interestingly be considered in light of the Stoic stress on rationality as inherent in a particular agent's *assent*, rather than on the rationality of *deliberation* (as is characteristic, for example, of Aristotelian ethics), a point central to the account of Stoic ethics in B. Inwood, *Ethics and Human Action in Early Stoicism* (Oxford: Clarendon Press, 1985).
3. "[S]ince the separation of the in-itself and the self has been done away with, a case of moral action is, in the sense-*certainty* of knowing, directly as it is *in itself*, and it is *in itself* only in the way that it is in this [kind of] knowing" (*PhG*: §635).
4. Luther's early appropriation of the notions of conscience and *synteresis* is discussed in M. G. Baylor, *Action and Person: Conscience in Late Scholasticism and the Young Luther* (Leiden: E. J. Brill, 1977).

5. "Luther repudiated that authority [of the Church], and set up in its stead the *Bible* and the testimony of the Human Spirit. And it is a fact of the weightiest import that the Bible has become the basis of the Christian Church: henceforth each individual enjoys the right of deriving instruction for himself from it, and of directing his conscience in accordance with it" (*PH*: 417–18).

6. Compare Baylor's summary comments about the importance of conscience to Luther's essential modernity; Baylor, *Action and Person*, 271–2.

7. Neuhouser, for example, traces the development of this concern with the content of ethical standards, but still maintains that "[t]he conception of conscience Hegel ascribes to the Enlightenment is to a large extent merely a synthesis of the Socratic and Lutheran views of moral subjectivity" (F. Neuhouser, *Foundations of Hegel's Social Theory* (Cambridge, MA: Harvard University Press, 2000), 234).

8. Such a move is implicit already in the *Phenomenology*'s account of conscience, which is there said to be "simple in action in accordance with duty, which fulfills not this or that duty, but knows and does what is concretely right [*das konkrete Rechte*]" (*PhG*: §635).

9. Reconciling right and morality was a "Kantian" problem (for Fichte, among others) even before the appearance of Kant's own *Rechtslehre* in 1797; see W. Kersting, "Sittengesetz und Rechtsgesetz – Die Begründung des Rechts bei Kant und den frühen Kantianern", in *Rechtsphilosophie der Aufklärung*, R. Brandt (ed.), 148–77 (Berlin: Walter de Gruyter, 1982) and A. Speight, "The *Metaphysics of Morals* and Hegel's Critique of Kantian Ethics", *History of Philosophy Quarterly* 14(4) (1997), 379–402.

10. There is an important literature on this topic, but I shall cite here especially F. Neuhouser, *Foundations of Hegel's Social Theory* (Cambridge, MA: Harvard University Press, 2000), as well as L. Siep, "The *Aufhebung* of Morality in Ethical Life", in *Hegel's Philosophy of Action*, L. Stepelevich & D. Lamb (eds), 137–55 (Atlantic Highlands, NJ: Humanities Press, 1983) and D. Dahlstrom, "The Dialectic of Conscience and the Necessity of Morality in Hegel's *Philosophy of Right*", *The Owl of Minerva* 24(2) (1993), 181–9.

11. On the importance of forgiveness and pardon in Hegel's ethics, see K. Brinkmann, "Hegel on Forgiveness", in *Hegel's Phenomenology of Spirit: New Critical Essays*, A. Denker & M. Vater (eds), 243–64 (Amherst, NY: Humanity Books, 2003); R. Bernasconi, "Hegel and Lévinas: The Possibility of Forgiveness and Reconciliation", *Archivio di Filosofia* 54 (1986), 325–46; and A. Speight, "Butler and Hegel on Forgiveness and Agency", *Southern Journal of Philosophy* 43(2) (2005), 299–316.

12. For an account of issues involved in Kant's various treatments of conscience, see, among others, H. J. Paton, "Conscience and Kant", *Kant-Studien* 70(3) (1979), 239–51.

13. I offer a fuller account of this section in A. Speight, *Hegel, Literature and the Problem of Agency* (Cambridge: Cambridge University Press, 2001), 94–121.

CHAPTER TWO

THE APPERCEPTIVE I AND THE EMPIRICAL SELF
TOWARDS A HETERODOX READING OF "LORDSHIP AND
BONDAGE" IN HEGEL'S *PHENOMENOLOGY*

John McDowell

1. Hegel's *Phenomenology* traces an education of consciousness, as a result of which it is to attain the standpoint of absolute knowing. For consciousness (as such) its object is other than itself. The goal is for this otherness to be *aufgehoben* – cancelled as the simple otherness it at first appears to be, although preserved at a higher level, as a "moment" in a more comprehensive conception. Enquiry will then in principle be able to avoid a certain sort of philosophical anxiety. We shall no longer need to be troubled by the spectre of a gulf between subject and object, which is the pretext for a transcendental scepticism.

2. At the standpoint of absolute knowing, the progress of knowledge is to become intelligible as the free self-development of "the Notion".[1] Hegel sees this conception as indebted to Kant, in a way he makes explicit when he writes, in the *Science of Logic*: "It is one of the profoundest and truest insights to be found in the *Critique of Pure Reason* that the *unity* which constitutes the nature of the Notion is recognized as the *original synthetic* unity of *apperception*, as the unity of the *I think*, or of self-consciousness" (L: 584).[2] This is obviously an allusion to the transcendental deduction. There – especially in the second-edition recasting – Kant comes close to Hegel's conception of absolute knowing.

I shall begin by spending some time on this Kantian background. That will place the apperceptive I, whose unity is the unity of the *I think*, in the picture.

Intuitions are immediately of objects. In the so-called "Metaphysical Deduction" Kant says: "The same function which gives unity to the various representations *in a judgment* also gives unity to the mere synthesis of various representations *in an intuition*; and this unity, in its most general expression, we entitle the pure concept of the understanding" (A79/B104–5). The

33

objective purport of intuitions is to be understood, then, in terms of their exemplifying logical unities that are characteristic of judging. And in the Transcendental Deduction Kant says judging is bringing given cognitions (*Erkenntnisse*) to the objective unity of apperception (B141). Given that conception of judging, the identification of the unity of judgement with the unity of intuition explains why he says: "The transcendental unity of apperception is that unity through which all the manifold given in an intuition is united [into] a concept of the object. It is therefore entitled objective ..." (B139).[3] By "concept of the object" here, Kant must mean something like "conceptually informed awareness of the object". That intuitions are of objects, he is urging, is to be understood in terms of their possessing the kind of unity that results when, in judging, one brings cognitions to the unity of apperception.

So Kant places spontaneous apperceptive activity at the centre of his picture of the objective purport of sensory consciousness. The free activity of bringing cognitions to the unity of apperception is a precursor, in Kant, to what figures in Hegel as the free self-development of "the Notion" – a setting within which the idea of thought's directedness at objects no longer includes anything that could appear as a gulf between subject and object.[4]

3. Kant's idea is that categorial unity – conformity to the requirements of the understanding – accounts for the possibility of subjective states that are cases of consciousness of objects. The Deduction is intended to vindicate the objective validity of the categories. But the structure of Kant's conception poses a threat to this aim, a threat to which he is especially sensitive in the second-edition version (which I shall call the "B Deduction"). A condition for objects to be thinkable (one might suppose) is not thereby a condition for them to be able to be given to our senses. Surely (one might go on) conditions for objects to be able to be given to our senses are for Kant a separate topic, dealt with independently in the Transcendental Aesthetic. So for all any deduction can show, objects could be present to our senses, conforming to the requirements considered in the Aesthetic, without meeting the requirements of the understanding.[5] And now the requirements of the understanding look like mere subjective imposition on our part, needed for us to get objects into our thoughts, but perhaps nothing to do with objects themselves.

In the B Deduction Kant aims to avert this threat, by arguing that the conditions for objects to be able to be given to our senses are not, after all, separate from the conditions he connects with apperceptive spontaneity. In the second half of the B Deduction, he works out consequences of the fact that space and time, as "formal intuitions" (B160n.), are themselves cases of the combination of a manifold into a single intuition. By the basic principle that governs the Deduction, it follows that the spatiotemporal form required by our sensibility is not, after all, intelligible independently of appealing to apperceptive spontaneity.[6] As Hegel appreciatively puts the point in "Glauben und Wissen":

> Here [in the Transcendental Deduction], the original synthetic unity of apperception is recognized also as the principle of the figurative synthesis, i.e., of the forms of intuition; space and time are themselves conceived as synthetic unities, and spontaneity, the absolute synthetic activity of the productive imagination, is conceived as the principle of the very sensibility that was previously characterized only as receptivity. *(FK*: 69–70)

The Aesthetic does not, after all, lay down independent conditions for objects to be available to our senses, in a way that leaves it still open whether they are conformable to the activity of apperceptive spontaneity. So Kant takes himself to be entitled to claim that the categories apply to "whatever objects may present themselves to our senses" (B159). There is, after all, no threat that objects might be present to our senses but not meet the requirements of the understanding.

If we describe them as requirements of the understanding, we attribute categorial requirements to a faculty of the cognitive subject, and thus depict them as subjective conditions. But by extending the scope of apperception's unifying activity into what had seemed the independent terrain of the Aesthetic, Kant aims to undermine a picture in which objects satisfy independent requirements for them to be able to be sensibly present to us, and we then impose on them conditions demanded by the understanding. Thereby he aims to show that the requirements of the understanding, although as so described they have to be counted as subjective conditions, are simultaneously and equally conditions on objects themselves.[7] In this conception, with its equipoise between subjective and objective, between thought and its subject matter, we have something it is plausible to see as an inspiration for Hegel's conception of absolute knowing.

4. However, Kant's way of making out that the requirements of the understanding are equally conditions on objects themselves depends essentially on its being acceptable to gloss "objects themselves" with "objects as they are given to our senses". And in Kant's thinking this gloss embodies its own subjective imposition, at a different point from the one where the threat arose.

In the second half of the B Deduction Kant contrives to represent the combination of manifolds into the "formal intuitions", space and time, as the work of apperceptive spontaneity. But he leaves it a separate fact about us, a reflection of the specific character of our sensibility, that what are so unified, in our case, are manifolds that are specifically spatial and temporal. The Aesthetic encourages us to entertain the thought that there could be differently formed sensibilities, which would be associated with different "formal intuitions". That makes it irresistible to contemplate a different gloss on "objects themselves": things in themselves, as that idea figures in the Aesthetic – things such that it is beyond our ken whether they themselves are spatially or temporally ordered.[8]

35

Kant tries to demonstrate objective validity for the categories by arguing that they are applicable to things as they are given to *our* sensibility. He is clear that according to his argument it is "only *our* sensible and empirical intuition" that can confer *Sinn* and *Bedeutung* on the pure concepts of the understanding (B149). But in view of his doctrine that our sensibility is the way it is independently of the character of things in themselves, and independently of our capacity for apperceptive unification, to which it furnishes materials, that means there is an unassimilated subjectivity, a subjectivity with no balancing objectivity, within what purported to be the objective side of a proto-Hegelian equipoise. The most Kant can claim to establish in the Deduction is that there is no extra subjective imposition in demanding that objects of our experience conform to the requirements of the understanding, over and above the subjective imposition involved in requiring that our world be spatially and temporally ordered. But this latter is, as Kant conceives it, a subjective imposition. There is a mere reflection of a fact about us at the foundation of Kant's construction. And corresponding to this unassimilated subjectivity at the putatively objective pole of the attempted equipoise, there is an unassimilated objectivity, the perhaps non-spatial and non-temporal thing in itself, left outside the equipoise altogether, and looking as if it would have to be the genuine article.[9]

A genuine equipoise between subjective and objective would require discarding Kant's distinction of things as they are available to our senses from things as they may be in themselves.[10] It would require not leaving the spatial and temporal character of our sensibility outside the scope of intellectual freedom. Here we can begin to see a point in insisting that there is nothing outside the free unfolding of "the Notion". Absolute knowing is a wholehearted counterpart to the activity of apperceptive spontaneity as Kant conceives it in the Transcendental Deduction, where, just because the specific character of our sensibility is left outside its scope, the intended equipoise between subjective and objective is not genuinely achieved.

Hegelian wholeheartedness brings everything within the scope of free subjective activity. If one takes such a description out of context, it can seem that the move abandons the realism of common sense – that it obliterates anything genuinely recognizable as objective reality, in favour of projections from unconstrained movements of the mind.[11] But the context gives the lie to this. It is Kant's half-heartedness that spoils his attempt at an equipoise between subjective and objective.[12] Expanding the scope of intellectual freedom does not tip the scale to the side of the subjective, as if the objective (so-called, we would have to say) can only be a projection of subjective activity, taken to be independently intelligible. That is just what happens in Kant's unsuccessful attempt at the equipoise. Because there is unassimilated subjectivity at the base of Kant's construction, it amounts to no more than a subjective idealism. That is a Hegelian accusation often thought to be outrageous, but we are now in a position to find justice in it. The point of expanding the scope of intellectual freedom is to achieve a genuine balance between subjective and objective, in which neither is prior to the other. Achieving a genuine balance would allow subjectivity to be conceived as engaging with what is genuinely objective. To hold that the very idea of objectivity can be understood only as part of such a structure is exactly not to abandon the independently real in favour of projections from subjectivity.[13]

5. Clearly there is more to be said.[14] But perhaps that is enough to let us begin to understand why, in the remark I began with, Hegel praises Kant for equating the unity of "the Notion" with the unity of apperception. When Hegel says "With self-consciousness we have entered the homeland of truth" (PhG: §167), we can put his point in Kantian terms, like this: we have begun to see how to understand knowledge in terms of the unifying powers of apperceptive spontaneity.[15]

But this can make what Hegel does in the "Self-Consciousness" chapter of the Phenomenology mysterious. How is someone's balking at a struggle to the death and submitting to enslavement by someone else related to the Aufhebung of otherness between consciousness and its object, the balance between subjective and objective that Kant aimed at but failed to achieve?[16] Much commentary seems unconcerned with such questions. For instance, commentators often take Hegel to be arguing in "Lordship and Bondage" that there can be self-conscious individuals only in mutually recognitive communities. To me the text there does not seem to say what these commentators would like it to: that recognition by an unrespected inferior cannot validate a superior's self-certainty – so that self-consciousness can find a truth corresponding to its certainty only in a community of equals. At any rate I find it hard to read that thought into Hegel's play with the mismatch between the master's self-certainty and the servile consciousness as the truth of that certainty (PhG: §192). But anyway, even if that is the point, how does it advance us towards Reason's certainty of being all reality, the Aufhebung of otherness between subjective and objective that is the culmination of this chapter (PhG: §230)?

In what follows, I shall go through the first two sections of the chapter, working towards a reading that would not be vulnerable to this puzzlement. At least to begin with, I shall stay so close to the text as to risk merely duplicating its obscurities; I hope things will become clearer as I go along.

I do not mean to suggest that this, or any other, section of the Phenomenology traces the route into Hegelian thinking from a Kantian starting-point that I began with. I am not trying to find in "Lordship and Bondage" a Hegelian improvement on Kant's treatment of the forms of our sensibility. The point of starting with the Kantian material was only to provide a frame for the significance that Hegel credits to self-consciousness at the beginning of the "Self-Consciousness" chapter.

6. We begin with self-consciousness on the scene as the result of the final movement in the experience of (mere, as it were) consciousness, whose object

is conceived as simply other than it. That object – empirically knowable reality – does not just disappear with the advent of self-consciousness. If it did, we would have only "the motionless tautology of: I am I". Without otherness in the picture, self-consciousness could not be in the picture either. The otherness of the object of consciousness must be *aufgehoben*, not simply obliterated. So self-consciousness "has a doubled object", or an object with two moments. The first moment is "the whole expanse of the sensible world", what previously figured as the independent object of consciousness. The second moment is self-consciousness itself. These two moments show up as mutually opposed, the first as "*for* self-consciousness marked with the *character of the negative*",[17] and the second "only, at first, in opposition to the first". Hegel says: "Self-consciousness presents itself here as the movement wherein this opposition is *aufgehoben* and the identity of itself with itself gets to be [explicit] for it" (all citations in this paragraph are from *PhG*: §167).

So far so good, we might say, given that we are trying to find in this text a progression towards absolute knowing. Supposing we can make sense of the so far only schematic idea of overcoming an opposition between those two moments in the object of self-consciousness, the result should be a picture in which the otherness of the empirically accessible world is prevented from threatening to constitute a gulf, by being embraced within the object of self-consciousness, which is seen as having an internal complexity, while as the object of self-consciousness it is not other than the conscious self. In one sense apperception has only itself for object. But we are to work towards seeing how it can have "the whole expanse of the sensible world" as its object, in another sense that is unthreatening just because of how it is integrated with the first.

We might be tempted to derive a less schematic understanding of the movement here attributed to self-consciousness from Hegel's invocation of desire. But I think the text should discourage this hope. Hegel offers "Self-consciousness is desire *Überhaupt*" (*PhG*: §167) as a paraphrase, not here further elaborated, of one of his schematic descriptions of the required movement. The explanatory relation seems to be the wrong way around for that hope of concreteness. We understand what Hegel means by introducing desire only to the extent that we understand those schematic descriptions of the movement of self-consciousness. "Desire *Überhaupt*" functions as a figure for the general idea of negating otherness by appropriating or consuming, incorporating into oneself, what at first figures as merely other. That is, schematically, what self-consciousness has to do to the first moment in its doubled object. There is no suggestion here of anything as specific as a mode of consciousness that has objects in view only in so far as they can be seen as conducive or obstructive to its purposes.[18]

7. Hegel says that the first of those two moments in the object of self-consciousness has, for us or in itself, returned into itself and become life (*PhG*: §168). Here he is harking back to the closing phase in the experience

of consciousness (see *PhG*: §162), where what had appeared as the independent object of consciousness turned out to be the self-developing movement of "the absolute Notion".[19] That was what brought self-consciousness on to the scene. As it often does in Hegel, life there served as a figure or model for his conception of "the Notion", which generates differentiation within itself rather than being externally related to a subject matter that is simply other than it. But here, in the opening section of the "Self-Consciousness" chapter, life becomes more than a figure. It becomes, so to speak, itself.

Hegel now gives an exposition of life as the genus dissolving all differences, having its actuality in the living individual separating itself out from that negative universality (*PhG*: §§169–72). This is the second pole in "the antithesis of self-consciousness and life", into which "this Notion [life] sunders itself" (*PhG*: §168). At this stage life is not *for itself* (*PhG*: §§168, 172); it is *for* the consciousness, now self-consciousness, that is the first pole in the antithesis of self-consciousness and life.

All I want from this obscure material at this stage is the structure. Life as the difference-dissolving genus, actual in the shape of a living individual, is the guise in which the first moment in the doubled object of self-consciousness now appears – the moment in respect of which self-consciousness continues to be consciousness, and "the whole expanse of the sensible world is preserved for it" (*PhG*: §167). At this stage, this object, or moment in a doubled object, is not for itself, not a subject, but in view only as an object for a subject, for self-consciousness as consciousness.

This belongs with the fact that the unfolding of life Hegel has given so far has been "for us" rather than for the consciousness whose experience we are about to witness. The exposition, as is usual after a mutation of consciousness, recapitulates how this new consciousness appeared on the scene, although from its own point of view it is simply present, having forgotten what constrained it to take its present shape. The previous movement ("Force and the Understanding") reached a position in which the otherness of the object of consciousness was in principle *aufgehoben*. The object of consciousness turned out to be the freely self-developing "Notion", in which consciousness was in principle enabled to see nothing other than itself. But this new object, the Notion – which is life – "sunders itself", and, at the beginning of the "Self-Consciousness" chapter, consciousness finds itself immediately present as self-consciousness but, because of the lack of mediation, still confronted with unassimilated otherness. That much is typical of the transitions in the *Phenomenology*. The point for now is that the unassimilated otherness is here in the form of life.

8. Now we start to observe the experience of this consciousness as self-consciousness, the subject for which life has so far appeared as object. Hegel describes the experiencing subject as "this other life, for which the genus as such is" (*PhG*: §173). It is another life, because it was life that sundered itself

into the antithesis between self-consciousness – now referred to as "this other life" – and life as Hegel has just expounded it, life as object for the consciousness that self-consciousness is (*PhG*: §168).

The subject life, he says, is "for itself genus". That fits with its being life, and picks up the conception of the genus as dissolving differences. This life is self-consciousness, which "has itself as pure I for object" (*PhG*: §173), and "is certain of itself only by the *Aufheben* of this other that presents itself to it as independent life" (*PhG*: §174). It is aware of itself as needing to dissolve the difference between itself and "this other", the first of the two moments in its doubled object. This is what we had already (in *PhG*: §167) as the movement of self-consciousness – overcoming the antithesis between the two moments of its object. Here we have the added specificity that the moment that first appears as opposed to self-consciousness, the moment whose antithesis with self-consciousness is to be overcome, has been elaborated as life.

The simplest way to effect this required overcoming of otherness would be by reducing to nothingness (*vernichten*) the independent other. Self-consciousness is, as we already know, desire *Überhaupt* (*PhG*: §167). But desire in particular (so to speak) cannot reduce otherness to nothingness by its activity of appropriation and consumption. It needs independent objects to be what it appropriates and consumes. In the experience of desire specifically (as opposed to desire *Überhaupt*), self-consciousness learns that reducing to nothingness is not what it needs to do to its other. As was promised in §168, it thereby "makes the experience of the self-standingness [*Selbständigkeit*: independence]" of its object – that is, of the first of the two moments of its doubled object.

But to find a truth corresponding to its self-certainty, it still needs the otherness of that object to be *aufgehoben*. What it has learned is that it is no good attempting a unilateral annihilation of the other; the other must preserve its independence. The object must present itself as negative of its own accord, rather than being marked with the character of the negative by something other than itself, namely the self-consciousness that is trying to overcome the otherness of (one moment in) its object. This requirement of independent negativity reveals the object – the other moment in the doubled object – as itself consciousness after all, not, as it hitherto appeared, something that is only an object for consciousness. It is in the nature of consciousness to maintain its independence even while, in distinguishing itself from its object, it presents itself as negative.

And in fact this object is not just consciousness but self-consciousness. We know anyway, from the end of the "Consciousness" section, that if it is consciousness it is self-consciousness. ("Consciousness of an other, of an object as such, is indeed itself necessarily *self-consciousness*"; *PhG*: §164.) But here Hegel reveals this object as self-consciousness by noting that in the sphere of life independent negativity takes the form of "the universal independent nature in which negation is present as absolute negation", and that "is

40

the genus as such, or self-consciousness" (*PhG*: §175). This is just how self-consciousness conceived itself at the beginning of the experience he has just described (*PhG*: §§173–4). It has now turned out that its object, or the first moment in its doubled object, needs to be conceived in just the same way. After the initial exposition of it, life, as one of the two moments in the object of self-consciousness, was not for itself but only for consciousness (*PhG*: §172). But now it has emerged that that moment in the doubled object "is itself for itself genus, universal fluidity in the peculiarity of its separateness; it is a living self-consciousness" (*PhG*: §176).

9. It is in summing up this result that Hegel says: "*Self-consciousness achieves its satisfaction only in another self-consciousness*" (*PhG*: §175).[20] I think this is usually taken to claim that there can be a self-conscious individual, say a self-conscious human being, only if there are at least two, each recognizing the other as another of what it is one of. And I do not dispute that much in what follows can be made out to fit this conception of multiple individuals mutually recognizing one another. But this raises in an urgent form the puzzlement I started from, about the role of Hegel's moves here in the progress towards absolute knowing. Or, another way of making the same point, there is a problem about how to fit this remark, so taken, into the flow of the text I have been working through.

The otherness that needs to be *aufgehoben* by the movement of self-consciousness appeared in the first instance as the otherness of "the whole expanse of the sensible world" (*PhG*: §167), one moment in the doubled object of self-consciousness, whose movement is to overcome the antithesis between that moment and the other, namely itself. It was that moment in the doubled object, "the whole expanse of the sensible world", that returned into itself and became life (*PhG*: §168), and then revealed itself as consciousness and finally as self-consciousness. This is the "another self-consciousness" of our passage. It should surely be in some sense the same object, or moment in a doubled object, that we began with, only now more hygienically – less immediately – understood. But if "another self-consciousness" here is a literally other mind, say a different human being, what has happened to "the whole expanse of the sensible world"? How does replacing that first moment in the doubled object of self-consciousness with someone else's self-consciousness belong with the unfolding of that moment that Hegel seemed to be offering in the text up to this point? And how does it help towards disarming a threat that might be posed by the otherness of the object of consciousness?

These questions are forestalled, and the progression I have been working through begins to fall into place, if we take it that when Hegel talks of "another self-consciousness" here, he is saying how things are, not for us or in themselves, but for a consciousness still in the midst of the movement of self-consciousness, the overcoming of the antithesis between those two moments. This consciousness is one for which *Aufhebung* of otherness is still an unfinished task (as indeed it is at all stages short of absolute knowing). So "another", in "another self-consciousness", reflects how things seem to consciousness at this stage of its education, not how things actually are.[21]

The otherness that confronts my self-consciousness, at the beginning of the chapter, is the otherness of the world as the scene of conscious life – in fact my life, although it will take a while before that specification is straightforwardly available. When "the whole expanse of the sensible world" returns into itself and becomes life, that makes available another way of pointing to that otherness, by speaking of an antithesis between my self-consciousness and the individual conscious life whose scene is my world. It is that life, or the individual living it, that is progressively revealed as itself consciousness and then self-consciousness. What it actually is is my self-consciousness, not someone else's.[22] When that becomes clear, empirical consciousness will be integrated with apperceptive consciousness, and the otherness of the world that confronts my empirical consciousness will be purged of its threat to open a gulf between subjective and objective. But by the stage we have reached – the end of the first section of the "Self-Consciousness" chapter – that is not yet clear. As Hegel will say early in the next section, self-consciousness must "*aufheben* this its other-being" (*PhG*: §180).

This suggestion – that Hegel is not here talking about multiple human beings – may seem to ignore the very end of the first section, where Hegel says that with its final development, "the Notion of spirit is already present for us" (*PhG*: §177). But that remark does not, as is often supposed, salute the appearance before us of a concept of communal being. Hegel makes it clear that by "spirit" here he means an object that "is just as much I as object".[23] That is exactly what becomes present for us when the problematic moment of the doubled object of self-consciousness is revealed as itself self-consciousness, itself I. And that is so whoever the I thus revealed as an object is: it does not need to be someone other than the subject of the experience we are observing.

I am not denying that the spiritual will not be fully in view for us until communal being is in the picture. But Hegel here locates "I that is we and we that is I" in "what still lies ahead for consciousness", "the experience of what spirit is". That seems to amount to saying that the interplay of singular and plural will come into view only later. It is not supposed to be the result of the experience we have so far witnessed.

10. What I am proposing may become clearer if I say a little, at last, about what may by now be obvious, how this reading of the chapter's opening section carries over into "Lordship and Bondage". I shall be sketchier here, partly because there is no space for more, but partly because I hope the ground has been sufficiently laid for it to be plausible that the details can in principle be made to fall into place.

Hegel introduces the struggle to the death like this:

> The *presentation* of itself, however, as the pure abstraction of self-consciousness consists in showing itself as pure negation of its objective mode, or in showing it to be connected to no determinate *existence*, not to be connected to the universal singularity of existence as such, not to be connected to life.   (*PhG*: §187)

This fits the suggestion I am making, that only one biological individual is really in play. The description of the struggle to the death works as an allegorical depiction of an attempt, on the part of a single self-consciousness, to affirm its independence, by disavowing any dependence on "its objective mode", which is the life that has come to stand in for the otherness of the world whose scene that life is. So far, the life that is the "objective mode" has revealed itself as the life of a consciousness, indeed a self-consciousness. In fact it is the very same self-consciousness that here tries to disavow it. It is that self-consciousness not *qua* attempting to affirm its independence but *qua* living through "the whole expanse of the sensible world". But the subject that is undergoing this experience is not yet aware that those are two different specifications of what is in fact itself. Unassimilated otherness now takes the form of an alienation from what is in fact its own consciousness as living through its world, its own empirical consciousness. Hegel makes this alienation vivid with the image of one living individual confronted by another.[24] And he makes the attempt to disavow dependence on what is in fact one's own life vivid with the image of trying to end the life of the other that confronts one.

There is a textual curiosity in this vicinity. Immediately after the passage I just quoted as introducing the struggle to the death, Hegel says: "This presentation is the *doubled* doing [cf. §182]: doing of the other and doing of oneself. In so far as it is doing of the *other*, each goes after the death of the other" (*PhG*: §187). This is quite mysterious at the level of the image of two individuals trying to kill each other.[25] How can pursuing the death of the other be the doing of the *other*? But if the other is really the subject itself, *qua* "sunk in the being of life" (*PhG*: §186), the idea makes a certain sense. If one is to affirm one's independence as a self consciousness by showing that one is indifferent to mere life, it is actually oneself *qua* alive – what figures here as the other – that must subject itself to the risk of death. "However", as Hegel goes on to say, "therein the second [aspect of the doubled doing], *the doing through oneself*, is also present; for the former doing implies the staking of one's own life". This works both within the image – one cannot seek the death of another without staking one's own life – and as anticipating what self-consciousness trying to affirm its independence learns in this phase of its experience: that the life it is attempting to disown is something whose continuation is necessary to its continuing independence, so that its own life is at risk when it goes after the death of the supposed other. This is actually because the supposedly other life just is its own life, but that is not how the lesson immediately strikes the consciousness whose experience we are observing.

43

On this account, the struggle to the death gives allegorical expression to the need to acknowledge that self-consciousness cannot be independent of what, in the frame of mind its experience is here dislodging it from, it would like to think of as mere life, only inessentially related to it. "In this experience, it becomes [clear] to self-consciousness that life is as essential to it as pure self-consciousness" (*PhG*: §189).

This takes us smoothly to lordship and bondage. Hegel's presentation here makes good sense if understood as a continuation of the allegory. Enslaving another individual who backs down in a struggle to the death stands in for an attempt on the part of self-consciousness – the apperceptive I – to acknowledge the indispensability to it of, but refuse to identify itself with, the subject of a life lived through and conditioned by "the whole expanse of the sensible world" – which is in fact itself, *qua* empirical subject, although self-consciousness at this stage cannot see how to combine acknowledging that with continuing to affirm its independence. This self-consciousness conceives its "objective mode" as a distinct consciousness, bound up with and dependent on external objects. It tries to preserve its own independence of external objects by delegating dealings with them to a consciousness that it attempts to appropriate or see as its own in some sense, while holding back from identifying itself with it.

We might be reminded here of how Kant sees apperceptive self-awareness as contentless. For him, content for self-knowledge can be supplied only by (inner) intuition, which is distinct from apperception (cf. B157–9). This certainly makes it hard to identify the I of apperception with the self that figures in substantive knowledge of the course of one's experiential life.

This attempt to affirm that one's real self is independent of one's empirical self, although the empirical self is in a way one's own, is vividly captured in the way the master interposes the slave between himself and the objects of consciousness, thereby putatively achieving independence with respect to them (see *PhG*: §190). The project fails because in thus consigning its "objective mode" to mere dependence, this masterly self-consciousness, attempting to affirm its own independence, ensures that it can find no objective truth answering to its self-certainty (see *PhG*: §192).

At the beginning of the last section of the "Self-Consciousness" chapter, a new shape of consciousness has appeared on the scene: "consciousness that *thinks*, or is free self-consciousness" (*PhG*: §197). This new shape of consciousness emerges not out of the master consciousness's failure to affirm its independence, but out of an achievement on the part of the servile consciousness. The servile consciousness manages to emerge from the dependence to which the master consciousness relegates it – to "posit *itself* as a negative in the element of abiding" (*PhG*: §196), in activity whose significance is informed by the prospect of death. The details of this development are too complex and difficult to go into now. But even without trying to be specific, it seems clear that at least it makes for no extra difficulty of interpretation if

44

we suppose, as I have suggested, that it is only within an allegorical presentation that the master consciousness and the servile consciousness are embodied in two separate individuals. The real topic is two aspects of the consciousness of a single individual, although at a stage at which that is not clear to the individual in question. The immediate appearance of thinking consciousness marks a temporary integration of the two aspects, in which a consciousness bound up with the world it lives through, a consciousness that was previously seen as merely dependent on that world, achieves a kind of independence in its formative activity, which becomes the freedom of thought ("movement in Notions"; *PhG*: §197). We might put this by saying an empirical consciousness *becomes* an apperceptive consciousness.

The achievement of integration by thinking consciousness, as it immediately makes its appearance, is short-lived. Self-consciousness can have individuality only as the individuality of a living being, bound up with its specific immersion in the world. Thinking consciousness is a descendant of the servile consciousness, not the master consciousness, of "Lordship and Bondage". But the shift to thinking itself makes it harder to keep hold of the importance of immersion in life, because with the introduction of "movement in Notions", a new temptation arises to separate the ideal, conceptual aspect of one's relation to reality from a material residue that is then naturally conceived as the merely animal aspect of one's engagement with one's life-world. Stoicism attempts to locate itself exclusively in the separated ideal, withdrawing from immersion in life, and thus loses determinate content for its thinking. Scepticism oscillates between the separated ideal and what is left for immersion in life to be once the ideal is skimmed off (the "animal life" of *PhG*: §205). The unhappy consciousness sees that it must have both aspects, but cannot see how to bring them together. Seeing that it must have both aspects is an advance over the consciousness that undergoes the experience narrated in "Lordship and Bondage". Hegel registers the advance when he says, in introducing the unhappy consciousness, that "the duplication that formerly divided itself into two individuals, the master and the slave, is here lodged in one" (*PhG*: §206). This remark might seem difficult for me. But as before, I can say that the point about division into two individuals is that that is how things looked to the consciousness in question, not that that is how things really were.

11. I have urged that "Lordship and Bondage" describes a failure and then a temporary success at integrating, within a single individual, a consciousness aiming to affirm itself as spontaneously apperceptive and a consciousness that is conceived as immersed in life in the world. This immersion in life is at first conceived mainly as a matter of theoretical cognition, in line with the experience of mere consciousness. But with the temporary success, which turns on finding oneself in one's formative activity, immersion in life becomes centrally a practical matter.

A complete case for such a reading would of course require not only much more about how the passage itself works, but also an assessment of how it fits into the movement of the whole book. But I hope I have said enough to suggest that a proposal on these lines might be worthy of consideration. [26]

NOTES

1. This section and the next two use material from J. McDowell, "L'idealismo di Hegel come radicalizazzione di Kant", *Iride* **34** (2001): 527–48 and "Hegel's Idealism as Radicalisation of Kant", in *Hegel contemporaneo: La ricezione americana di Hegel a confronto con la tradizione europea*, L. Ruggiu & I. Testa (eds), 451–77 (Milan: Guerini e Associati, 2003). The inspiration for arriving at Hegel from the Kantian material I shall exploit comes from R. B. Pippin, *Hegel's Idealism: The Satisfactions of Self-Consciousness* (Cambridge: Cambridge University Press, 1989). The reading of Kant comes from working through him with James Conant and John Haugeland.

2. Pippin cites this passage as central to his reading of Hegel's idealism; Pippin, *Hegel's Idealism*, 18.

3. I substitute "into" for Kemp-Smith's "in" (Kant wrote "in einen Begriff", not "in einem Begriff"). See R. E. Aquila, *Matter in Mind: A Study of Kant's Transcendental Deduction* (Bloomington, IN: Indiana University Press, 1989), 136.

4. Kant describes the understanding – which is "the faculty of apperception" (B134n.) – in terms of spontaneity (e.g. at A50/B74). And spontaneity is the theme of the opening section of the B Deduction.

5. See A89–91/B122–3 (in the preamble to the Transcendental Deduction, common to both editions). Kant is here explaining why the task of a Transcendental Deduction (showing "how *subjective conditions of thought* can have *objective validity*") is so difficult.

6. Kant puts the basic principle like this (in the opening section of the B Deduction, which is devoted to elaborating the thought): "But the combination (*conjunctio*) of a manifold in general can never come to us through the senses, and cannot, therefore, be already contained in the pure form of sensible intuition. For it is an act of spontaneity of the faculty of representation ..." (B129–30).

7. See B138: "The synthetic unity of consciousness is ... an objective condition of all knowledge. It is not merely a condition that I myself require in knowing an object, but is a condition under which every intuition must stand in order to become *an object for me*." ("For me" spoils this formulation, in a way that should begin to become intelligible when I discuss how Kant's conception is still, by Hegel's lights, a merely subjective idealism: §4 below.) For the general idea of conditions that are subjective and objective together (not primarily subjective and thereby allegedly objective), see A158/B197: "the conditions of the *possibility of experience* in general are likewise conditions of the *possibility of the objects of experience*".

8. For the localization to the Aesthetic, see J. Hyppolite, *Genesis and Structure of Hegel's Phenomenology of Spirit*, S. Cherniak & J. Heckman (trans.) (Evanston, IL: Northwestern University Press, 1974), 144. The noumenon of the Analytic is different, and the related notion in the Dialectic is different again.

9. See *PhG*: §238. In what follows, I shall modify Miller's translation, or substitute my own, in which I shall allow myself to count words like the untranslatable "*aufheben*" as English.

10. It does not help with the problem I am posing for Kant to inveigh against "two-world" readings of Kant. Let it be acknowledged, by all means, that he identifies "things as objects of experience" with "those same things as things in themselves" (Bxxvii). But this does not alter the fact that according to him the spatial and temporal organization of things as objects of our experience reflects a fact about us rather than characterizing the things themselves. And he himself stresses that his attempted vindication of the objective validity of the categories essentially turns on that feature of things as objects of experience.

11. For an understanding of "post-Kantian absolute idealism" on these lines, see Michael Friedman, "Exorcising the Philosophical Tradition: Comments on John McDowell's *Mind and World*", *Philosophical Review* 105 (1996), 427–67, esp. 439–44.

12. Hence the unhappy addition of "for me" at B138, cited above; and hence also his willingness to accept the Copernican image (Bxvi–xviii), which certainly suggests a priority of subjective over objective.

13. These remarks bear on Henry Allison's characterization of transcendental idealism as insisting on a distinction between "conditions of the possibility of knowledge of things" and "conditions of the possibility of the things themselves" (*Kant's Transcendental Idealism: An Interpretation and Defense* (New Haven, CT: Yale University Press, 1983), 13). Transcendental realism rejects the distinction by seeing conditions of the possibility of knowledge as merely derivative from autonomous conditions of the possibility of things. Allison maintains that the only other way to reject the distinction is to embrace a subjectivistic phenomenalism, which one might describe, as in my text, as an abandonment of the independently real in favour of projections from subjectivity. That would be a symmetrical counterpart to transcendental realism, taking subjective conditions to be autonomous as such where transcendental realism takes objective conditions to be autonomous as such. What goes missing here is the Hegelian alternative, which is inspired by how Kant wants to think of the requirements of the understanding. Hegel rejects Allison's distinction on the grounds that the relevant conditions are inseparably both conditions on thought and conditions on objects, not primarily either the one or the other.

14. For one thing, a proper treatment of Hegel's relation to Kant would need to take account of Fichte's intervening contribution. For another, something would need to be said about how what in Kant is the activity of the understanding becomes, in Hegel, the self-fulfillment of reason, in the face of Kant's sharp distinction between understanding and reason. For yet another, something would need to be said about how Hegel sees his idealism as related to Kant's practical philosophy, which I have not mentioned at all. (These are all no doubt connected.)

15. We need to arrive at the significance of apperception through the experience of mere consciousness, rather than just starting with it (like Kant and Fichte), because just starting with it leads only to the subjective idealism of *Phenomenology* (§238). See H.-G. Gadamer, "Hegel's Dialectic of Self-Consciousness", in *Hegel's Dialectic: Five Hermeneutical Studies*, P. Christopher Smith (trans.), 54–74 (New Haven, CT: Yale University Press, 1976), 54–5.

16. See Pippin: "Suddenly we are talking about desire, life, struggles to the death, masters and slaves" (*Hegel's Idealism*, 143). Pippin tries to read the chapter's first two sections

47

(the third is, as he remarks, easier to accommodate) so as to fit his overall conception of the *Phenomenology*'s point, but his details (for instance, desire as emerging out of the idea of a lack that drives the pursuit of knowledge) strike me as far removed from what actually happens in the text.

17. Self-consciousness is the shape in which consciousness is now present, and for consciousness the essential thing about its object is that it is not – is other than – itself.

18. See Pippin, *Hegel's Idealism*, 149. Pippin says that "this chapter ... does not begin a case for the primacy of practical reason" (*ibid.*, 288 n. 11). I am not sure about this claim, when we come to the slave's emancipation through work. But Pippin is talking about the role of desire in the chapter, and I think he is right that that feature of it does not point us to practical reason. However, Pippin's denial is muted by his taking "desire *Überhaupt*" too literally.

19. Fortunately, in this chapter I do not have to try to explain how this happens.

20. "Achieves its satisfaction" rather than, more plainly, "finds its truth" because we are still working with the conception of self-consciousness as desire *Überhaupt*, although in the experience of *Phenomenology* (§175) it learned not to conceive itself as appropriating its object in anything like a literal sense. See n.6 above.

21. No doubt the remark also works if taken straightforwardly, without that understood frame. I think this is quite common in the *Phenomenology*. What I am disputing is only that the straightforward reading captures what Hegel has argued for in his approach to the remark.

22. Self-consciousness starts this movement in its experience with "itself as *pure I* for object" (*PhG*: §173). Hegel announces there that in its subsequent experience "this abstract object will enrich itself and undergo the unfolding we have seen in life". It is going to turn out to *be* what was there unfolded.

23. Compare what he says in the preface about "grasping and expressing the true not [just] as *substance*, but no less as *subject*" (*PhG*: §17). Compare also *Phenomenology* (§790), where he says (ironically), of Observing Reason's culminating identification of the soul with a thing, that "according to its concept it is the most richly spiritual". The concept of spirit as it figures here is the concept of something that is equally object and subject.

24. It is part of the image that, for the consciousness whose experience we are considering, the other views it in the same way. But this symmetry need not carry over into what the image is an image for.

25. I have not seen this obvious point noted by commentators.

26. I have seen a few precedents for this proposal. J. Flay says that "master" and "slave" refer not to separate individuals but to different aspects of consciousness; *Hegel's Quest for Certainty* (Albany, NY: SUNY Press, 1984), 86. Kelly offers an intra-personal reading as a supplement to the more typical interpersonal readings; "Notes on Hegel's 'Lordship and Bondage'", in *The Phenomenology of Spirit Reader*, J. Stewart (ed.), 172–91 (Albany, NY: SUNY Press, 1998). And Robert M. Wallace, in an unpublished book manuscript, says that "a self-consciousness ... can, in principle, be its own 'other'". But none of these authors has what seems to me to be the essential connection between the master–slave dialectic and the project of overcoming otherness.

CHAPTER THREE

HEGEL, McDOWELL AND RECENT DEFENCES OF KANT
Sally Sedgwick

According to Graham Bird, the interpretation and critique of Kant recently defended by John McDowell in his book *Mind and World* is "fundamentally mistaken" (Bird 1996: 219). Bird is not alone in holding this view; it is also shared by other prominent Kantians such as Henry Allison and Michael Friedman.[1] All agree that the account McDowell provides of what he calls the "transcendental" side of Kant perpetuates unfortunate myths about the nature and implications of Kant's idealism, myths forcefully articulated by P. F. Strawson, and by Hegel more than a century earlier.

In the name of setting the record straight, Allison, Bird and Friedman undertake to defend Kant's idealism anew. The myths, they tell us, are products of misinterpretation. What is more, the myths can set us off on an unfortunate philosophical track, as is evident, they argue, in the case of McDowell. The myths can in other words encourage in us the misguided view not merely that there is something valid about the Hegelian critique of Kant, but also that there is something compelling or attractive about the Hegelian alternative. This explains why in the course of their efforts to correct misinterpretation, the Kantians in addition seek to convince us of the virtues of transcendental over absolute idealism. While Kant, they suggest, has the good sense to draw attention to the limits of our knowledge, Hegel seems intent upon persuading us to ignore them.

We learn more about what the Kantians understand the Hegelian alternative to be from the following passage quoted by Bird:

> Kant opened the door to nineteenth century idealism and it rushed ... past him, agreeing with him that mind was not a part of nature, but pressing on boldly to the even more liberating doctrine that nature itself was an externalization, or self-objectification, of Mind.
>
> (John Skorupski, quoted in Bird 1995: 399)

Although hardly self-explanatory, the terms "externalization" and "self-objectification" suggest at least this: that what is "bold" and therefore troubling about post-Kantian idealism is that it deprives nature of its independent reality, of its irreducibility to mind. The flip side of this objection is the worry that this form of idealism awards mind too much creative power and therefore too much free rein. If nature is no more than an "externalization" of mind, mind has nothing outside itself to be answerable to. Its freedom is without limits (or "frictionless", as McDowell would put it). In Michael Friedman's words, "post-Kantian idealism views the objects of rational knowledge as manifestations of an absolute rational freedom *entirely unconstrained by anything outside itself*" (1996: 442, emphasis added).

Kant "opened the door" to this form of idealism, presumably, because of the degree of creative power he awarded our form of cognition. In opposition to empiricism, he argued that mind is more than just a repository of ideas originating from elsewhere; it is more, too, than the mere capacity to perform logical operations on those ideas. Rather, mind according to Kant is productive of its own ideas or forms. These ideas or forms, far from deriving from our perception of objects, in fact determine or make objects possible, in his view.

But while it is true that Kant awards human cognition this degree of creative power, his form of idealism does not imply that nature is a mere externalization or objectification of mind. Kantians remind us that this cannot be his view because he argues that the forms we bring to our cognitions of nature determine a content we do not make: the given content or matter of sensation.[2] Human cognition is thus to this degree limited in its productive powers: it is incapable of simply producing nature out of its own cognitive activity. At most, it is productive of the form through which it is possible for us to know or experience nature. This is why Kant insists that we know nature only as "appearance", not as a "thing in itself".

So in the name of ensuring that we not mistake Kant's idealism for the Hegelian alternative, Kantians remind us that transcendental idealism is committed to the thesis of the irreducibility of nature to mind as well as to the thesis that there are limits to what we can know. They sing the praises of his modesty. But in responding in this way to the worry that Kant is somehow responsible for later and less plausible forms of idealism, Kantians invite an objection of a different kind. Kant's thesis of the irreducibility of nature to mind and his resulting restriction of our knowledge to appearances is precisely what gives rise to the representation of his idealism as having ultimately sceptical implications for the possibility of human knowledge. For if we know nature not as it is "in itself" but only as "appearance" (only as conditioned by our subjective forms), it would seem that what we know of nature is at best something "subjective": a mere representation or projection. And, on Kant's account, we have no means of determining whether our projections are also valid of things in themselves.

It is just this portrayal of the implications of Kant's modesty that commentators such as Allison, Bird and Friedman dismiss as a "myth". Transcendental idealism does not commit us to the platonistic tendencies of post-Kantian idealism, they argue, but is not it an ultimately sceptical thesis about the scope of our knowledge either. Any suggestion to the contrary, they claim, is evidence of misunderstanding.

In this chapter I challenge the Kantians' account of both the Hegelian critique of and the Hegelian alternative to Kant. However successful they may be in responding to persistent misrepresentations of transcendental idealism, the recent defences of Kant by Allison, Bird and Friedman do not in my view begin to address the Hegelian critique. What I hope will emerge from this discussion is that Hegel's critique is significantly more interesting than the Kantians make it out to be. And although I shall not argue for this directly, I believe it will follow from my discussion that McDowell's critique of Kant is more interesting as well, at least if we are warranted in taking him at his word when he characterizes his position in *Mind and World* as Hegelian.[3]

I

As just noted, Kantians respond to the charge that transcendental idealism "opens the door" to excessive claims about the creative capacities of human cognition by emphasizing Kant's modesty, by drawing attention to the fact that in his view we must depend in our knowledge of nature on a sense-content we do not make. It follows from the fact that our form of cognition is "discursive" rather than "intuitive", Kant explains, that it is incapable of producing the content of experience out of its own activity; the most it can do is produce the form through which the given *a posteriori* content must be thought and known. Because we are dependent on an independently given sense-content, objects of nature are not for us mere products or externalizations of our cognitive powers; we know of them, he writes in the B preface of the first *Critique*, only "what we put into them" (Bxviii). We know them as conditioned by our subjective forms, not as they are in themselves.

So in response to those who suggest that Kant is responsible for later developments in German Idealism, Kantians urge us to take his dualism seriously. It follows from his insistence that our form of understanding is discursive, that nature on his account cannot be a mere product of or reducible to mind. In response to those who suspect that his dualism has sceptical consequences for our knowledge, the Kantians remind us of his dualism's precise nature and implications. Although it is true for Kant that we know nature only as appearance, only as given via our subjective forms of intuition and as thought through the categories, this does not imply, the Kantians argue, that objects of our knowledge are no more than mere representations and therefore necessarily less than real. It is a mistake to understand transcendental idealism as entailing that what is "really real" are things in themselves or noumena, and that our knowledge, because limited to appearances, must be an imperfect version of the real thing. If we understand Kant's distinction between appearances and things in themselves in this way, we fall prey to what Allison has called the "myth of the noumenal". This myth, he writes:

> consists in the assumption that Kant is committed to the doctrine that the "real" is equated with a supersensible (and hence noumenal) realm, of which we can know nothing save that it somehow affects us, and that the cognition of appearances of which we are capable is merely a pale substitute for genuine knowledge.
>
> (1997: 45)[4]

Along with Bird and Friedman, Allison is convinced that the worries Hegelians such as McDowell raise depend on the fact that they attribute to Kant this "myth". This is an assumption I shall challenge. But before doing so and suggesting an alternative way of understanding the Hegelian critique, it will be useful to review strategies the Kantians adopt in exposing and correcting their opponent's mistakes. This will provide a clearer picture of just who the Kantians take their opponent to be.

II

Again, those persuaded by the "myth of the noumenal" assume that Kant's doctrine of the unknowability of things in themselves implies the unknowability for us of what is "really real". They then attribute to appearances and our knowledge of them a "second class status", as Bird has put it (1996: 234; see also 226, 228).[5] They take transcendental idealism to be a form of scepticism in just this sense.

But as the Kantians point out, numerous passages in the *Critique of Pure Reason* warn us against interpreting the distinction between appearances and things in themselves in this way. It follows from the fact that we cannot know things in themselves, Kant argues, that we also cannot know that they, rather than appearances, are the "really real". If we have understood the distinction correctly, in what he calls its "transcendental" versus "empirical" sense, we will recognize that the predicates "real" and "illusory" or "merely apparent" legitimately apply only to appearances. Again, this has to do with the fact that what "objects may be in themselves" or apart from our forms of sensibility, remains in Kant's words, *completely* unknown to us" (B59/A42, emphasis added).[6] As unknown, we can have no warrant for claims about their reality.

This is indeed what Kant says. But of course it could be the case that he is inconsistent. It could be the case, for example, that in spite of his many warnings against our supposing to know things in themselves, he nonetheless measures the adequacy of our knowledge of appearances against them. In response to this kind of worry the Kantians remind us not merely of passages in which Kant is explicit in drawing the limits to our knowledge, but of the arguments that lead him to do so. Those tempted to impute to him the "myth of the noumenal", they claim, fail to grasp the basic aims (or, as Allison puts it, the "critical nature") of his form of idealism. We understand the "critical" nature of Kant's idealism, the Kantians argue, only when we appreciate the following two points: first, that it is not the transcendental idealist but rather the transcendental realist, according to Kant, who assumes the knowability of things in themselves; and secondly, that a central aim of the *Critique of Pure Reason* is to provide an *alternative* to transcendental realism.[7]

Let us take a closer look at this strategy for defending Kant. If we ask why Kant was convinced that he needed to find an alternative to transcendental realism, the Kantians recall for us a principal motivation of his critical project: to "save metaphysics". In Kant's view, transcendental realism threatens the very possibility of metaphysics because it can secure for us no necessary knowledge of objects of nature. Kant argued this point with reference to both the Lockean and Leibnizian versions of transcendental realism that he reviewed in the first *Critique*. In assuming that all our concepts derive from sense experience, Lockean empiricism delivered metaphysics into the hands of the Humean sceptic. This is because, as Hume rightly pointed out, we cannot via an appeal to experience demonstrate any *necessary* connection between our concepts and their objects. The "course of nature", he famously reminds us, "may change" (Hume [1777] 1989: 378). Leibniz's effort to guarantee necessity, while not vulnerable to Hume's sceptical arguments, was nonetheless no more successful than Locke's, in Kant's estimation. This is because Leibniz relied on the mistaken assumption that we can ground our claims about the nature and existence of objects on the basis of an analysis of their concepts alone. The strategy Kant seized on in the name of "saving metaphysics", then, involved rejecting assumptions he believed Locke and Leibniz held in common, not the least of which was the assumption he came to identify as transcendental realism.

Given how very different the Lockean and Leibnizian theories of knowledge are, it is not obvious that these theories share *anything* in common. But, as the Kantians rightly point out, we need to understand what Kant thought they shared in common if we are to appreciate what he rejected in both approaches and offered in their place. Kant noticed, first of all, that both Leibniz and Locke took for granted that our knowledge of nature depends on one faculty rather than two, on either thought or sensation.[8] One key to Kant's alternative, therefore, was his introduction of the thesis that our knowledge is dependent on the cooperation of two independent or irreducible faculties: the faculty of understanding (of concepts) and the faculty of recep-tivity (of intuition).[9] In contrast to the empiricist approaches of Locke and Hume, Kant argued that we possess at least some concepts that are not simply derived from sensation but are "original" or "*a priori*". In contrast to Leib-niz, on the other hand, he claimed that our knowledge of nature depends on more than just conceptual analysis. Although we can think via concepts what-ever we please (provided that we conform to the law of non-contradiction), knowledge of nature requires in addition that our concepts apply to a con-tent given in empirical intuition (Bxxvi(a) and Transcendental Aesthetic, §1). Our knowledge of nature requires intuition as well as concepts, Kant argued in the "Ideal of Pure Reason", because existence is not analytically contained in any concept.[10]

So one key to Kant's effort to save metaphysics was his commitment to the thesis that neither concepts nor sensations by themselves can provide for the possibility of necessary knowledge of nature; our knowledge of objects of experience, in his view, requires both. A second key has to do with the constraint he placed on how it is that objects of nature must be given to us in sensation: they are given, he tells us in the Transcendental Aesthetic, via our *a priori* forms of sensible intuition, space and time. Any possible object of empirical knowledge not only must be thought through *a priori* concepts or categories but must in addition appear to us via these forms of intuition.

Strictly speaking, it is this second constraint that is responsible for Kant's insistence that our knowledge is limited to appearances. For the claim that we know nature only as conditioned by our forms of sensible intuition is on his account equivalent to the claim that we know nature only as appearance. The "thing in itself", then, is what remains when we abstract this constraint on how objects of possible experience must be given to us.

But why does Kant assert that the positions of Locke and Leibniz are instances of "transcendental realism", and how is "transcendental realism" distinct from his own alternative, "transcendental idealism"? In the Transcen-dental Aesthetic, Kant argues that space and time are "transcendentally ideal" forms of experience. They are "ideal", he says there, because they inhere "in the subject" as necessary *a priori* conditions of human knowledge. We have no grounds for supposing in addition that they are valid or have reality for objects "absolutely", for objects "in themselves". Their validity, in other words, is restricted to their role as subjective conditions of human knowledge. They are "ideal" because "in us" or *a priori*; they nonetheless have "empirical reality", Kant claims, just because they condition what is empirically real or a possible object of perception for us.[11]

Locke and Leibniz are transcendental realists, according to Kant, because neither identifies the role of space and time as *a priori* or subjective condi-tions determining how objects of experience must appear to us. Neither is therefore in the position to acknowledge a distinction between appearances and things in themselves in the Kantian sense. For Locke, we can by means

54

of sensation know the nature of things in themselves; for Leibniz, we know things in themselves via thought alone.

This explains Kant's insistence that it is the transcendental realist and not the transcendental idealist who claims that we can know nature as a thing in itself. As Allison puts it, the transcendental realist assumes, "that what can alone satisfy the truth conditions of human knowledge must be something to which the mind has access *independently of its own conditions of cognition*" (Allison 1997: 46, emphasis added).[12] Allison and others then argue that if we have understood the "critical nature" of Kant's idealism – its opposition, namely, to transcendental realism – we shall recognize the absurdity of imputing to Kant the claim that we can know things in themselves. Again, it is the transcendental realist who is committed to this position, but transcendental realism in Kant's view provides us with no way to save metaphysics. Precisely because Kant rejects transcendental realism, he must rule out as illegitimate or as instances of "transcendental illusion" any claims about the possible reality or existence of things in themselves, including the claim that they are more real than appearances. In his words, the thing in itself or noumenon is no more than a "limiting concept", the function of which is "to curb the pretensions of sensibility" or remind us of the limits to what we can know (A255/B311).[13]

III

The above line of defence takes itself to establish that there can be no justification for either of the following two charges against Kant: (i) that he is inconsistent because although he claims that we have no knowledge of things in themselves on the one hand, he nonetheless assumes their reality on the other; and (ii) that his idealism is ultimately a form of *scepticism* because it implies an *unbridgeable gap* between what is "merely real for us" and what is "really real". In his recent review of McDowell's *Mind and World*, Friedman defends Kant against these charges as well and tells us that, on a proper reading of Kant's critical philosophy, we discover that rather than imply scepticism, transcendental idealism in fact "closes" the gap between mind and world. Like Allison and Bird, Friedman employs the strategy of interpreting Kant's philosophy in light of the transcendental realist alternatives to which he was responding. It is not Kant who leaves us with a gap between mind and world, Friedman claims, but his transcendental realist opponents. Transcendental realism implies for Kant a gap between mind and world, Friedman argues, in precisely the ways we have just reviewed: neither empiricist nor rationalist versions can guarantee necessary knowledge of nature and therefore "save metaphysics". Thanks to his two-faculty doctrine and introduction of "revolutionary new doctrines of a priori sensibility", however, Kant succeeds in "closing" the gap, Friedman suggests (1996: 437), that transcendental realism leaves open.

Friedman focuses his attention on the way in which Kant closes the gap left open by the rationalist or Leibnizian version of transcendental realism. We have already considered why Kant was unpersuaded by Leibniz's effort to demonstrate that we can have necessary knowledge of nature. Because Leibniz did not regard intuition as an independent source of knowledge, irreducible to conception, he presumed that the necessary application of our concepts to nature could be demonstrated by way of an appeal to conceptual analysis alone. In Kant's terminology, Leibniz failed in this effort because he in effect conflated the "logical" with the "real" possibility of concepts.[14] Kant set out to close the transcendental realist gap between mind and world, Friedman reminds us, by adopting the following strategy. First, he argued that sensation is not reducible to or a mere species of conception, but rather an independent source of knowledge. Secondly, he introduced his doctrine of *a priori* sensibility in arguing that objects of sensation are necessarily given to us via our *a priori* forms of intuition, space and time, and are therefore known to us as appearances rather than as things in themselves. Finally, he set out in the Analytic section of his Transcendental Logic to demonstrate the necessary application of our *a priori* concepts or categories to nature as appearance. Friedman reminds us, then, of the three principal steps of Kant's effort to "save metaphysics", the three principal steps of his "Copernican Revolution".

If we bear in mind that the "gap" Kant "closes", according to Friedman, is the gap between our *a priori* concepts and nature as appearance (between what Friedman refers to as "mathematical reason" and "sensible nature"), then there is no reason to doubt that Friedman gets Kant's Copernican story perfectly right. Again, Kant's task in the Transcendental Analytic is to close this gap by demonstrating the necessary application of our categories to appearances. How does he do this? By arguing that the categories are forms without which what is given in empirical intuition could not be thought or known by us at all. In the absence of concepts, Kant famously insists, intuitions are blind. By "synthesizing" or "unifying" the content of appearance, the categories first make nature possible for us as an object of thought and scientific enquiry. In Friedman's words:

> For Kant, our sensible experience is necessarily governed by and framed within a "space of reasons" consisting, essentially, of logical and mathematical relations; … there can be no question, therefore, of an epistemological gap between such rational relations on the one side and our sensible experience on the other.
>
> (1996: 438ff.)[15]

As I said, I find nothing to criticize in this retelling of Kant's Copernican story. What is puzzling, however, is the fact that Friedman along with

Allison and Bird believe that this retelling of the Copernican story counts as a response to the Hegelian critique. Kant closes the gap between mind and world, they tell us, by demonstrating that appearances could not be for us possible objects of thought or knowledge in the absence of the subjective conditions of our thinking and knowing them.[16] If the Hegelian persists in charging that Kant's restriction of human knowledge to appearances in effect leaves another gap open, namely the gap between what is "really real" and what is "merely real for us", then clearly the Hegelian has failed to grasp the fact that for Kant the categories, including the category of "reality", have valid application only for appearances.[17] If the Hegelian assumes that for Kant our knowledge of appearances must be something merely "subjective" or "second rate", it is because he persists in misinterpreting the term "appearance" in an unKantian or "colloquial" sense.[18]

What can be wrong with this as a response to Hegel? Very simply, it ascribes to him interpretative errors he did not commit. Hegel was aware of the essential features of Kant's idealism and its specifically "critical" nature.[19] The same, I believe, may be said of McDowell. If I am right, then it should be possible to provide an alternative account of the Hegelian worry about the Kantian gap between mind and world, an account that does not depend on the assumption that Hegel and McDowell fail to appreciate the "critical" nature of Kant's idealism.

IV

To get this alternative reading underway, we first need to bear in mind that the success of Kant's effort to close the gap between "mathematical reason" and appearances or "sensible nature" requires, as even the Kantians admit, keeping another gap open. The key to Kant's Copernican alternative to transcendental realism depends, as we have seen, on the fact that, as Allison puts it, Kant "factors in" our subjective conditions. In providing his alternative account of how necessary knowledge of nature is possible for us, Kant in other words factors in the role of the categories and forms of space and time. Having done so, he then derives the central tenet of his idealism: that we know objects only as conditioned or determined by these forms, only as appearances. In this way, the success of Kant's Copernican alternative depends on keeping open the gap between our subjective conditions and things considered in abstraction from them. Because the Kantians consider this alternative to transcendental realism an instance of philosophical progress, they applaud Kant's restriction of our knowledge to appearances. They sing the praises of his modesty.

Should the Hegelian raise doubts about *this* gap between mind and world (the gap, namely, between our subjective forms and things considered in abstraction from them), the Kantians respond by pointing out that this gap does not imply for Kant that we must give up hope of knowing what is "really real". But here it is important that we not overlook the fact that in responding to the Hegelian's doubts in this way, the Kantians merely rehearse for us what Kant's critical form of idealism requires. They assume, in other words, that the Hegelian critique calls merely for a *reminder*, as opposed to a *defence*, of Kant's Copernican strategy.

Surely, however, one can be sceptical about that strategy. One can be sceptical, for example, about the conception of mind and world that leads Kant to conclude that "we can know a priori of things only what we ourselves put into them" and that we therefore have no warrant for knowledge claims about objects independent of our subjective forms. And one can raise doubts about this without failing to acknowledge the implication of transcendental idealism that from the standpoint of theoretical knowledge objects considered in abstraction from our subjective forms can have for us, strictly speaking, no reality. Furthermore, one can raise doubts about Kant's Copernican strategy, as Hegel does, without reviving either a Lockean or a Leibnizian form of realism.

V

Assuming that what I have just suggested is true – namely, that Hegel neither fails to recognize the critical nature of Kant's idealism nor adheres to a Lockean or Leibnizian form of realism – how should we begin to piece together the fundamentals of his critique of and alternative to Kant? The first point to bear in mind is that, contrary to what is commonly supposed, Hegel is in sympathy with Kant's claim that our knowledge requires not one faculty but two, neither reducible to the other. As just noted, he embraces Kant's rejection of the reductionist transcendental realisms of Locke and Leibniz. The problem with Kant has to do, then, not with his assumption that our knowledge requires the cooperation of two faculties, but with his particular conception of the nature and contribution of those faculties. The problem, in Hegel's terminology, is that Kant assumes that the contributions of sensation on the one hand and of the mind's forms on the other are "originally heterogeneous" or "absolutely opposed".[20] As McDowell has put it, the problem is that Kant assumes that form and content are not merely separate but also "separable".[21]

On the face of it, the charge that Kant assumes the "separability" or "absolute opposition" of form and content seems anything but plausible. The key implication of his Copernican turn, after all, is that the objects of our thought and knowledge are not bare contents, but unities of form and content: contents which must be thought through the categories and, if knowable, given via our forms of space and time. But this Kantian thesis that subjective form plays an indispensable role in making possible human thought and experience is not what Hegel rejects. What *does* he then have in mind in charging that Kant assumes the opposition or separability of form and content? Recall what I identified above as the Kantian inference Hegel finds unpersuasive: that from the fact that experience for us requires the contribution of our subjective forms it is supposed to follow, according to Kant, that we have no warrant for knowledge claims about objects considered in abstraction from those forms. Hegel points out that this inference is only conditionally valid – valid, that is, only if we assume a particular conception of form: namely, as already given or *a priori*.[22] Kant's conclusion that we cannot know mind-independent content depends on his commitment to the separability or opposition of form and content in *this* sense. When Hegel insists in his provocative way, then, that things in themselves are indeed knowable for human cognition, he means to challenge Kant's conception of the already given or *a priori* nature of form.[23]

So in opposing the thesis of separability or absolute opposition, Hegel calls into question not Kant's insight that our cognitive access to content is dependent on the role of subjective form, but rather Kant's failure to acknowledge that a relation of dependence obtains in the other direction as well. Subjective form, Hegel seems to suggest, is in some way dependent on content. And this point about two-way dependence is presumably what motivates his mysterious assertion that form and content, rather than absolutely opposed, are in fact "originally identical" elements of a synthetic unity or totality.[24]

Needless to say, the idea that form according to Hegel is inseparable from content is not easy to grasp. It is no easier to grasp than his alternative expression of what is essentially the same point, his claim that reason is "in the world" or "in history".[25] These claims are particularly baffling because, as we saw above, Hegel's idealism is not a return to reductive realism, including the empiricist version of realism that takes form to be reducible to or a mere species of content. Although we might be tempted to say that, in claiming that the nature of form depends on content, Hegel in effect naturalizes the subjective forms that according to Kant are *a priori*, it is essential that we add the qualification that he aims to do so without reviving the reductive empiricism according to which form is nothing but a product of passive sensible affection.

We can derive some idea of the way in which form is dependent on and so inseparable from content, in Hegel's view, from a principal strategy he adopts in his critique of Kant. It is a strategy about which our Kantians have nothing to say because they in fact overlook Hegel's objections to Kant's conception of form. What I have in mind are Hegel's repeated efforts to persuade us that the formal features of experience that Kant identifies as *a priori*, and therefore as universal and necessary, are in some way contingent or only conditionally valid. Hegel employs this argumentative strategy again and again, whether his topic be Kant's Table of Categories, his treatment of substance in the Analogies, or his attempt in the *Metaphysical Foundations of Natural*

Science to construct the forces of matter. Underlying Kant's account of the *a priori* or pre-given conditions of experience, Hegel argues, are assumptions that escape Kant's critical notice, assumptions that in no obvious way are necessarily and universally valid.

Surely one lesson Hegel wishes us to derive from these discussions is that Kant is insufficiently appreciative of some of the conditions of his own philosophizing (his Newtonianism, for example). But although part of Hegel's aim is to convince us is that Kant is to be faulted for in this way failing to live up to his own rigorous standards of philosophical reflection, Hegel's deeper philosophical objective is to urge us to call into question the standards themselves. That is, Hegel believes we should call into question the conception of philosophical reflection that assumes that when we undertake to identify features of our experience, it is possible for us to leave the influences of our own intellectual culture thoroughly behind. This is why in the opening paragraphs of the introduction to the *Phenomenology* he challenges Kant's conception of a "critique" of reason.[26] The claim of "critique" is that reflection can unburden us of the merely relative or contingent assumptions that tie us to a particular philosophical tradition. The benefit of being unburdened, of course, is that only by this means do we gain access to non-contingent or timeless truths. Hegel finds this conception of philosophical reflection deeply suspect. It presumes, he writes in the preface to his *Philosophy of Right*, that "philosophy can transcend its contemporary world" or that "an individual can overleap his time" (*PR*: 11). Granted, the truths Kant claims to derive from critique are intended to reveal the nature and limits not of things in themselves but of merely human experience. Nonetheless, Kant believes that he has, via critique, revealed to us unconditionally necessary and universal conditions of human experience. He is confident that he has done so, because he believes that his discovery of the *a priori* features of subjective form does not depend on assumptions he has inherited from his "contemporary world". In this way, he presupposes that the forms he discovers are already given or separable from content. Relying on the method of critique, he assumes he is warranted in his claims about the nature of form "in itself".

For Hegel, this understanding of the nature and accomplishments of critique is an instance, not of philosophical modesty, but of vanity.[27] Because Hegel denies that critique in this sense is possible for us, he also denies the validity of the kinds of claims critique is supposed to be uniquely fit to defend. He rejects the supposed pre-givenness of form in favour of a conception of form as having a history and as revisable in response to the forces of history.[28] If we conclude from this that he is a reductive naturalist or positivist about form, then we miss what we saw above is implied by his denial of the thesis of separability: that the relation of logical dependence between form and content obtains in both directions, and that there can be for us as thinkers and knowers no bare or mind-independent content that form is somehow reducible to.

VI

Summing up the points covered so far: we have seen that, according to Hegel (and to McDowell as well, I believe), Kant's account of form implies a gap between mind and world: a gap, namely, between the subjective conditions of our knowledge of nature and things considered in abstraction from those conditions. Our Kantians do not deny that this gap is implied by Kant's idealism, nor do they consider this gap cause for concern. Keeping this gap open, they correctly point out, is key to the success of Kant's effort to save metaphysics. It is what allows him to close another gap, namely the gap between subjective form and nature *qua* appearance. The fact that for Kant we can have no warrant for claims about objects independent of the subjective conditions of our knowing them, the Kantians tell us, does not imply that transcendental idealism is a sceptical thesis about the possibility of human knowledge. If we take it to imply this, then we have yet to free ourselves from the grip of transcendental realism.

In light of the fact that the Hegelians object to the gap left open by Kant's idealism, we might suppose that what they are after is some way to close it. This is true in one sense but not in another. Clearly, the Hegelians seek an alternative to Kant's conception of form. They find unsatisfactory the implication of Kant's conception of form that we can know of things only what we put into them. But it would be inaccurate to suggest that in their effort to close the gap between mind and world, Hegel and McDowell set out to re-establish for us justification for supposing that we can transcend the realm of subjective form. This cannot be what they are after for the simple reason that this strategy ignores the side of Kant's idealism they accept. They accept what we might refer to as Kant's half-hearted commitment to the thesis of inseparability: his insight that we can know and think content only as already formed.

In what way, then, *do* Hegel and McDowell seek to close the gap between mind and world? Perhaps what we should say is that they undertake to persuade us that we are mistaken in believing that there is a gap that needs to be closed. This response – the response that we have been fretting over a pseudo-problem – may seem too easy. But it is nonetheless implied by Hegel and McDowell's commitment to the thesis of inseparability. The thesis of inseparability, remember, denies the validity of the terms that define the supposed gap between subjective form, on the one side, and mind-independent content, on the other. It asserts that, for our cognition, form and content considered "in themselves" or in isolation from each other are empty abstractions: expressions of what McDowell (following Sellars) refers to as the myths of the "exogenous" and the "endogenous" Given.[29] If we assume that securing the possibility of our knowledge of nature requires that we find some way of bridging the gap between subjective form and mind-independent content, then it is clear that we still cling to these myths.

So closing the gap between mind and world, according to the Hegelian, cannot be a matter of appealing outside the realm of subjective form or presuming to know the exogenous Given. Nonetheless, Hegel and McDowell seek to bridge the gap between mind and world in some sense. As mentioned above, they seek an alternative to the conclusion that we can know of things only what we can put into them. Otherwise put, they set out to persuade us that subjective form is more than, in McDowell's words, a "frictionless spinning" valid merely "for us" (see McDowell 1994: 11). How do they argue this? The answer is that they draw our attention to an implication of the thesis of inseparability. As we saw above, giving up the idea of form as already given or inseparable from content is equivalent to granting that form has a history and is in principle revisable. If we grant this, we in effect admit that form does not determine experience simply of its own accord; it adjusts to forces that are not of its own design or creation. (Hence Hegel's emphasis on the *conditioned* or *contingent* character of form or law and McDowell's emphasis on the *partially passive* nature of experience.) According to the Hegelian idealist, we cannot justify the claim that form has friction or is objective by appealing outside the realm of subjective form, because no such appeal is possible for us. If a case is to be made for closing the gap between mind and world, then, it must depend on rejecting the assumption that the nature of form is already given. For the Hegelian idealist, in other words, form owes whatever friction or objectivity it has to its inseparablility from content. If we follow Hegel and McDowell in "exorcising" the myths of both the "exogenous" and the "endogenous" Given, this is all the realism we get. But for the Hegelian, it is all the realism we should ever want or need (see McDowell 1996: 285).

The Hegelian alternative to Kant thus ends up looking like this: the Hegelian accepts Kant's thesis that we can think and know content only by means of our subjective forms. The Hegelian in other words accepts the thesis of the inaccessibility for our cognition of the "exogenous Given". But the Hegelian does not follow Kant in concluding in light of the indispensable role of subjective form that we can know of things only what we put into them. Again, the Hegelian avoids this conclusion by rejecting Kant's conception of form as already given and as therefore in no way a reflection of or responsive to content. The key to Hegel and McDowell's effort to bridge the gap between mind and world, then, is their insistence that the idea of an already given form "absolutely opposed" to or "separable" from content, is for our cognition as much of an empty abstraction as the idea of a bare or unformed content.

VII

We might ask, in conclusion, why the Kantians we have been considering suppose that the Hegelian's worry about a gap between mind and world is based on the mistake of ascribing to Kant the "myth of the noumenal", that is, of assuming that Kant "demotes" our knowledge of appearances and inconsistently awards noumena the status of the "really real". Why do they miss the point stressed above that the Hegelian is critical of Kant's insistence that our subjective forms are *a priori* or already given versus to some extent dependent for their nature on and inseparable from content? Regarding their reading of McDowell, why do they overlook what is clearly a central proposal of *Mind and World:* that we give up the idea not merely of the exogenous but also of the endogenous Given and therefore think of subjective form on the model of a partially naturalized versus "rampant" form of Platonism (McDowell 1994: 92)?

In responding to these questions we need to expose some of the Kantians' own myths. We saw evidence of the principal myth in the opening pages of this chapter. This is the myth that to be a Hegelian is to be a platonist of the most rampant sort. This type of platonist, we saw, is committed to the thesis that nature is nothing other than an "externalization" or "self-objectification" of mind. Our Kantians apparently interpret the Hegelian in this way because they assume that the Hegelian's only suggestion for how we can successfully close the gap between mind and world is that we reduce the latter to the former, and in so doing deny world or nature independent reality. They assume that, for the Hegelian, the creative capacities of the human mind are unlimited and without external constraint. This is supposed to explain why the Hegelian is frustrated with Kant's restriction of our knowledge to appearances, and why the Hegelian insists, against Kant, that we can indeed know the absolute.

Friedman among others subscribes to this myth, which is why he writes that the tendency of "post-Kantian absolute idealism" is to "distance rational thought from sensible experience and to minimize the empiricist elements in Kant's own conception" (1996: 440). Because the post-Kantian idealist minimizes the role of the empirical and downplays the necessary role in our experience of an external or intuitive constraint, it is "not surprising", Friedman continues, that this form of idealism "eventually leads to explicitly Coherentist conceptions of the objects of rational knowledge" (*ibid.*).[30] This is a relatively common representation of Hegel; it is as common, perhaps, as the equally inaccurate portrayal of him as a reductive naturalist or positivist. But if what I have been suggesting here is correct, we are more on the right track if we say not that the Hegelian encourages us to minimize the role of the empirical in cognition, but rather that the Hegelian encourages us to pay more attention to it. On the interpretation I have proposed, the possibility of knowing things themselves and therefore of closing the gap between mind and world, depends for the Hegelian on our recognizing what is empirical or historically conditioned in the purportedly universal and necessary.[31]

NOTES

1. Friedman describes as "seriously misleading" the picture McDowell presents of "the Kantian conception of the understanding" (M. Friedman, "Exorcising the Philosophical Tradition: Comments on John McDowell's *Mind and World*", *Philosophical Review* 105 (1996), 427–67, esp. 436). See also H. Allison, "We Can Only Act Under the Idea of Freedom", Pacific Division APA Presidential Address, *Proceedings and Addresses of the APA* 71(2) (1997), 39–50.
2. While the form of appearance is *a priori*, Kant says, the matter [*Materie*] of appearance is "given to us a posteriori only" (A20/B34). Except when otherwise indicated, I rely on the Norman Kemp-Smith translation of the *Critique*.
3. See, McDowell's preface where he describes his work as "a prolegomenon to a reading of the *Phenomenology*" (J. McDowell, *Mind and World* (Cambridge, MA: Harvard University Press, 1994), ix). I discuss the Hegelianism of *Mind and World* in S. Sedgwick, "McDowell's Hegelianism", *European Journal of Philosophy* 5(1) (1997), 21–38. In the final section of that paper, I made what I now believe was the mistake of suggesting that McDowell and Hegel have no good grounds for charging that Kant's views about the contribution of spontaneity in any way commit him to the myth of the given. I hope to correct that mistake in this chapter.
4. See also Friedman, who writes that according to McDowell's "domesticated" rendition of post-Kantian absolute idealism, Kant "embeds" his "empirical realism in a 'transcendental story' according to which appearances are the transcendental products of a non-empirical interaction between our sensibility and things in themselves, and this makes the empirical objectivity of appearances seem 'second rate'" (Friedman, "Exorcising the Philosophical Tradition", 440ff.).
5. Bird represents Kant's view as follows: "It is not that there really are two distinct realms, a natural, empirical realm and a non-natural, transcendent realm of things-in-themselves; rather there is just one realm, empirical reality, and a conceptual apparatus which tempts us to transcend it. In this account there is no suggestion that empirical reality should be demoted, or that 'absolute reality' in the shape of transcendent claims, should be regarded as superior" (G. Bird, "Kant and Naturalism", *British Journal of the History of Philosophy* 3(2) (1995), 399–408, esp. 406).
6. Kant draws our attention to the "transcendental" versus "empirical" interpretation of his distinction between appearances and things in themselves in the Phenomena and Noumena section of the *Critique* as well. See, for example, B313ff., referred to by G. Bird, "McDowell's Kant: *Mind and World*", *Philosophy* 71 (1996), 219–43, esp. 229.
7. The "critical nature of Kant's idealism ... emerges," Allison writes, "primarily through the demonstration of the inadequacy, indeed, incoherence, of the opposing transcendental realism" (Allison, "We Can Only Act", 45).
8. Kant characterizes the positions of both Locke and Leibniz as reductionist. Leibniz, he writes, "intellectualized appearances" (sensations), while Locke "sensualized the concepts of the understanding" (A271/B327). For an illuminating discussion of Kant's effort to find an alternative to the approaches of both Locke and Leibniz, see L. W. Beck, "Kant's Strategy", in *Essays on Kant and Hume*, 3–19 (New Haven, CT: Yale University Press, 1978).
9. The "receptivity of our mind", Kant writes, is its "power of receiving representations in so far as it is in any wise affected ..."; "the mind's power of producing

representations from itself" is its "spontaneity". "These two powers or capacities," he tells us further, "cannot exchange their functions. The understanding can intuit nothing, the senses can think nothing. Only through their union can knowledge arise" (B75/A51).

10. "Being," Kant writes at A598/B626, "is obviously not a real predicate ...". It is a "logical predicate" and therefore establishes at most the logical possibility of a concept. To determine whether a concept applies to an existing object, we must, he says, "go outside" the concept; we must, that is, establish that the object of our concept is given in perception according to empirical laws. See Kant's discussion "The Impossibility of an Ontological Proof of the Existence of God" (A592/B620ff.).

11. For Kant's discussion of these points, see the Transcendental Aesthetic (§§6–8). He writes: "It is ... indubitably certain, that space and time, as the necessary conditions of all outer and inner experience, are merely subjective conditions of all our intuition, and that in relation to these conditions all objects are therefore mere appearances, and not in themselves [für sich] given in this way ... For this reason ..., while much can be said a priori as regards the form of appearances, nothing whatsoever can be asserted of the thing in itself, which may underlie [zum Grunde liegen] these appearances" (B66/A49, translation modified).

12. For the transcendental realist, Allison writes: the "real world" and "purported object of human cognition" is noumenal or supersensible "in the sense that the truth conditions of claims regarding it are to be determined completely independently of any consideration of the subjective conditions of human cognition (the forms of sensibility and the schematized categories)" (Allison, "We Can Only Act", 46).

13. As Allison puts it, the thing in itself or noumenon refers not to a metaphysically distinct "non-natural realm of true being" but to a "conceptual" or "normative" space (ibid., 47). This point is argued by Bird as well. He writes that Kant's commitment to noumena is not "a material commitment to a supernatural world, but ... a commitment to its conceivability. It claims that that conceivability is required if such features as normativity, even in the moral sphere, are to be properly located" (Bird, "McDowell's Kant", 243).

14. See note 11 above.

15. He continues: "Since nature as the object of modern mathematical science is first made possible or constituted by the a priori rational structures that Kant has articulated, one cannot distance the latter from nature without making nature itself impossible" (Friedman, "Exorcising the Philosophical Tradition", 439).

16. We might identify this line of defence as the "application argument". Its general form is as follows. Kant closes the gap between mind and world because in the absence of the application of our a priori subjective forms, nature as an object of theoretical enquiry would not be possible for us. As Allison puts it, transcendental idealism with its transcendental distinction between appearances and things in themselves is required in order to "determine the conditions of empirical truth" (Allison, "We Can Only Act", 46). Bird, too, adopts this strategy of defence. He responds to McDowell's complaint about a gap between Kant's transcendental self and world, for example, by reminding us that Kant ends up with a transcendental account of subjectivity as part of the "standard procedure of abstraction", which he "deploys in identifying the a priori aspects of experience" (Bird, "McDowell's Kant", 230).

17. As Friedman puts it, "pure concepts or categories have objective meaning only when applied to the spatiotemporal world of sense. (This, for Kant, is the meaning of the

slogan 'thoughts without content are empty')" (Friedman, "Exorcising the Philosophical Tradition", 438).

18. To interpret "appearances" in a "colloquial" sense, Bird writes, is to treat them as "subjective mental states such as sensations". Those such as McDowell who interpret "appearances" in this way then go on to attribute to them "second class status" (see Bird, "McDowell's Kant", 233ff.). McDowell's mistake, Bird writes, is to ascribe to Kant an "empiricist construction programme" (*ibid.*, 240).

19. I am asserting this rather boldly and do not set out to defend this assertion here. The evidence in support of it, however, is ample. Here is a single-sentence example taken from one of Hegel's earliest essays, "Faith and Knowledge" of 1802–3: "According to Kant, all these concepts of cause and effect, succession, etc., are strictly limited to appearances; the things in which these forms are objective as well as any cognition of them are simply nothing at all in themselves" (*FK*: 101). The last part of this (difficult to translate) sentence reads: "die Dinge, in welchen diesen Formen objektiv sind, sowohl als eine Erkenntniss dieser Objekte ist schlechthin nichts an sich" (*GW* 4: 350).

20. See, for example, for Hegel's use of this language in characterizing Kant, his Jena Writings of 1802–3, in particular the section "Kantian Philosophy" in "Faith and Knowledge".

21. This is McDowell's language in *Mind and World*, but it is Hegel's language as well. In, for example, *Elements of the Philosophy of Right*, he refers to our faculties of thought and of willing as "inseparable" [*untrennbar*]: "in every activity, thinking as well as willing," Hegel writes, "we can find both moments" (*PR*: §4, my translation).

22. It would not be correct simply to say that Hegel rejects the very idea of the *a priori* (the idea of either *a priori* concepts or of *a priori* knowledge). More precisely, he rejects a particular conception of the *a priori*, a conception to which he believed Kant adhered. In the section "Kantian Philosophy" in "Faith and Knowledge", he writes that Kant "conceived of the a priori only under formal concepts of universality and necessity … [H]e turned the true a priori back into a pure unity, i.e., one that is not originally synthetic" (*FK*: 73; *GW* 4: 330). What Hegel rejects, then, is that conception of the *a priori* that presupposes the thesis of absolute opposition.

23. In contrast to Kant, both Hegel and Fichte tend to use the term "things in themselves" to pick out not merely objects independent of our subjective forms of space and time, but objects independent of our subjective forms of thought as well.

24. In "Faith and Knowledge", Hegel claims to find at least the suggestion of original identity in (for example) Kant's conception of productive imagination. The "original unity" that is implicit in the idea of productive imagination, Hegel tells us, is not a unity that presupposes the antithesis of the manifold on the one side, and self-conscious Ego on the other. It is an "original identity" precisely because it is out of this "original synthesis" that "the Ego as thinking subject, and the manifold as body and world first detach themselves" (*FK*: 71; *GW* 4: 328).

25. This claim is so central to Hegel's idealism that it appears, in some form or other, in all of his writings. Relatively accessible versions of it, however, may be found in the introduction to his *Lectures on the Philosophy of History* and in the preface to his *Philosophy of Right*.

26. See also Hegel's discussion of critique in *Encyclopaedia of the Philosophical Sciences I: Logic*: "One of the main points of the in the Critical Philosophy is the following: before we embark upon the cognition of God, or of the essence of things, etc., we

should first investigate our faculty of cognition [*Erkenntnisvermögen*] itself, to see whether it is capable of achieving this. We should first get to know the instrument, before undertaking the task that is supposed to be accomplished by means of it ... But the investigation of cognition cannot take place in any other way than cognitively ... To want to have cognition before we have any is as absurd as the wise resolve of Scholasticus to learn to swim before he ventured into the water" (*EL*: §10).

27. The theme of the "vanity" of the Kantian philosophy appears in many places in Hegel's writings; see, for example, his introduction to "Faith and Knowledge", Chapter 2 of his *Lectures on the Philosophy of World History*, and the preface to his *Elements of the Philosophy of Right*. I owe thanks to William Bristow for clarifying for me the meaning of Hegel's vanity charge against Kant.

28. Compare this with Kant's characterization of reason as "present and the same in all the actions of men and in all situations; it is not itself in time and does not fall into a new state in which it was not before" (A556/B584, translation modified).

29. McDowell is most explicit in urging us to reject, not just the idea of the "exogenous Given" but also the idea of the "endogenous Given", in Part I of his Afterword to *Mind and World*. An important insight of both Sellars and Quine, he says, is that we should find suspect "the idea that something is Given from within the very structure of the understanding" (McDowell, *Mind and World*, 135). If we fail to reject the idea of the endogenous Given or persist in presupposing (what I have been referring to here as) the "already given" nature of form, then it will not be possible for us to think of the space of concepts, McDowell points out, as "unbounded on the outside". In this way, a commitment to the endogenous Given forces on us an unbridgeable gap between mind or form and mind-independent content (or "world"). If we in other words draw a boundary around form, we of course then create for ourselves the problem of having no way to account for the relation between the forms inside the boundary and objects outside. This is a problem that, on McDowell's analysis, Kant and the coherentist such as Davidson share. Here is perhaps the place to note that although "form" for McDowell refers to the contribution of "spontaneity" (i.e. concepts), I have been identifying "form" throughout this paper with subjective form more broadly understood, that is, with Kant's forms of spontaneity and forms of intuition. This is because I understand Hegel's critique of Kantian form to be aimed at both.

30. Friedman says that he does not see how McDowell can escape the charge of coherentism either ("Exorcising the Philosophical Tradition", 444).

31. I am indebted to members of the philosophy departments at the University of Sheffield and Keele University for inviting me to present an earlier draft of this chapter to them. I am also grateful to Graham Bird for encouraging my work on this chapter and for being the ideal *Gesprächspartner*. Finally, I thank both Rolf-Peter Horstmann and the Alexander von Humboldt Foundation for the support that made possible a ten-month leave in Berlin.

CHAPTER FOUR

SUBSTANCE, SUBJECT AND INFINITY
A CASE STUDY OF THE ROLE OF LOGIC IN HEGEL'S SYSTEM

Rolf-Peter Horstmann

In recent years a number of American interpreters, and certain continental readers strongly influenced by them, have defended an emphatically neo-pragmatic appropriation of Hegel's philosophy. For these interpreters the principal contribution of Hegelian thought is to be found in a fundamental thesis advanced in Hegel's *Phenomenology*. This thesis implies that our knowledge of ourselves and of the world is socially mediated, that our knowledge of ourselves and of reality in general is dependent on, and constituted by, intrinsically social parameters. Now this is not simply to ascribe to Hegel the manifestly trivial insight that our knowledge is somehow connected with particular contexts, situations and claims, and thereby inevitably requires a certain "social space" in order to present itself as a specific cognitive attitude to states of affairs in the world. For the interpretation in question would rather seek and find in Hegel a rather more extravagant, and perhaps "deeper", insight; namely, that the concepts by means of which we speak of ourselves and the rest of reality, which we regard as the fundamental categories for describing the world and on which our understanding of reality itself is based, are already socially constituted. These concepts are socially constituted in the sense that they must be understood as the products of social practices, more precisely, of practices that reflect or express a particular way of giving and accepting reasons that is characteristic for a specific historical epoch or a specific cultural domain.

Behind this allegedly central Hegelian insight there also stands the idea, largely developed quite independently of Hegel, that the enterprise of giving and accepting reasons, as an abstract and thus extremely general feature of rationality, can be variously realized and concretized in differing contexts (historical, cultural, ideological and probably also political). The difference between these various realizations lies in what counts as a socially permissible reason for justifying a certain action or claim. And this in turn is allegedly connected with the possible character and content of the reasons in question, that is, of the concepts employed, and the sense in which they are employed, in the practice of reason-giving.

Identifying Hegel's principal philosophical contribution as the systematic articulation and elaboration of this thesis concerning the "sociality of reason" – to adopt the subtitle of a recent and rightly influential book on Hegel (Pinkard 1994) – enjoys the apparent advantage, clearly welcome to many, of suggesting a "non-metaphysical" interpretation of Hegel's project. The Hegelian idea of "absolute knowledge" at the end of the *Phenomenology* – which certainly looks suspiciously metaphysical at first sight – can therefore be interpreted from a non-metaphysical perspective as a way of expressing (of "making explicit", as Robert Brandom puts it) the insight that the totality of reality presents itself as the reflex of the way in which we understand ourselves, that is, of the way in which (given certain practices of justification) we are capable of conceptualizing ourselves. From this perspective Hegel's phenomenological talk of spirit as "the other of itself", as "being that is at home with itself in otherness" (*GW* 9: 428), can lose its apparently obscure "speculative" character and become instead an illuminating metaphor for the fundamental axiom of social constructivism. In a similar way, the neo-pragmatic approach also seems to liberate Hegel's philosophy of right and theory of the state from the traditional suspicion of providing an essentially metaphysical sanction for given social and political conditions. Hegel's social and political thought can now be interpreted as an analysis of the various conditions under which we can articulate our concepts of ourselves as social beings in the first place (as in Allen Wood's interpretation of Hegel).

Attractive and illuminating as this approach to Hegel's *Phenomenology*, and also to the *Philosophy of Right*, may be, it nonetheless entails a double disadvantage. On the one hand, it has specific difficulties in accommodating Hegel's conception of "logic" as a distinctive "science". Indeed defenders of the neo-pragmatic approach are clearly aware of this problem in so far as they are prepared either to treat the *Science of Logic* as simply obsolete (see Wood 1990) or effectively to ignore it as much as possible (see Pinkard 1994; also Honneth 2000). On the other hand, it is also extremely difficult to see how this approach can avoid the sort of epistemic relativism that Hegel himself clearly repudiated: the view not only that our knowledge claims can only be justified contextually, but also that the states of affairs to which those knowledge claims refer, what Hegel calls the "other" of the concept, can be dissolved entirely into certain epochally or culturally dependent conceptual constellations.

The following discussion is not directly concerned with the question whether such an epistemic relativism – if such a view has been defended or could indeed rigorously be defended – represents an attractive philosophical position (although I am personally sympathetic to certain aspects of this approach). Nor does it ask whether we are doing Hegel any real favours, or making him somehow more acceptable to our own time, by attempting to describe his thought in these terms. I wish rather to address the question whether such relativism is compatible with Hegel's concept of reality. I shall attempt to show that they are in fact only partly compatible with one another. Or, more precisely, I shall argue that while Hegel does indeed dissolve every identifiable state of affairs into conceptual constellations, he certainly does not regard these constellations as epochally or culturally dependent. On the contrary, he regards them as entirely coterminous with the concept of the ultimate "matter itself" [*die Sache selbst*]. The discussion will concentrate on the three related concepts of "substance", "subject" and "infinity" precisely because they all play an undeniably central role in Hegel's own conception of what could be described as the real "matter itself" or the ultimate "state of affairs". The concepts in question are therefore particularly well suited to illuminate the central issue under discussion here.

I

Hegel himself made no secret of the fact that the concepts of "substance", "subject" and "infinity" – and the related ones of "substantiality", "subjectivity", "self-consciousness", "the self" and "the infinite" – are all central concepts in his philosophy. Thus in the *Encyclopaedia of the Philosophical Sciences* Hegel attempts to explain why every true philosophy is essentially "idealism", and what this claim ultimately signifies, by explicating "the true infinite" as "the fundamental concept of philosophy" (*EL*: §95, note). And of course Hegel says something very similar about the concepts of "substance" and "subject" in a number of extremely well-known passages in his work. We need only think of the programmatic dictum from the very beginning of the preface to the *Phenomenology*, where Hegel says that the task is precisely "to grasp and to express the true not merely as *substance* but equally as *subject*" (*GW* 9: 18). We should naturally pay particular attention to the words "equally as" in the formulation here. Or then again we might think of the emphatic remarks in the introduction to the first edition of the *Science of Logic* of 1812 where he writes: "As *Science* the truth is pure self-developing self-consciousness and possesses the shape of the self, where *being in and for itself is the conscious concept, while the concept as such is being in and for itself*" (*GW* 11: 21).

Identifying the importance of these concepts for Hegel's philosophical enterprise already gives us good reason to expect that very considerable difficulties are involved in explicating the reasons that led Hegel to such formulations as these. For long experience with Hegel has surely more than confirmed the direct proportionality between central significance and profound obscurity with respect to the fundamental concepts of his work. But

71

it would also be premature and unfair to explain this simply by reference to any deficiencies attaching to Hegel's philosophical programme itself, or to the way in which he attempted adequately to realize it. There may well be many problematic aspects about the programme and its specific realization, but there is also a kind of objective reason for the real difficulty we encounter in properly explicating and appropriating Hegel's philosophy as a whole. For this difficulty is grounded in the enormous complexity of this philosophy, a complexity that Hegel himself obviously negotiated with considerable success, but that his interpreters can only approach with the greatest effort and invariably at the cost of certain omissions and simplifications. In view of this, one is well advised to begin by explaining what Hegel himself regards as the central aspect of a specific theme, before going on to interpret the theme in relation to all its other Hegelian aspects.

This necessarily self-limiting procedure certainly recommends itself if we are attempting to clarify the function and significance of the concepts of "infinity", "substance" and "subject". And that is because these terms are schematized on different levels of Hegel's system, levels whose own internal relationship is itself anything but transparent. In the first place all these terms play a key role in Hegel's logical, that is, effectively metaphysical, theory of the concept as it is developed it in the *Science of Logic*. In the second place these terms also perform a specific role in the two domains of "real philosophy" that belong to the entire system as presented in the *Encyclopaedia of the Philosophical Sciences*, namely the philosophy of nature (especially the theory of organic nature) and the philosophy of spirit. And finally, they also play a fundamental organizing role in the way the forms of consciousness are presented within the *Phenomenology*.

As far as the internal relationship between these different levels of the system is concerned, it is surely clear that Hegel is convinced that the logical–metaphysical level is conceptually basic with respect to everything else. This seems to suggest a unilateral dependency relation between the logical–xmetaphysical level and the other levels of the system. And this implies that only what can properly be grounded and demonstrated as necessary on the logical–metaphysical level can function as an explicatory element on the other levels of the system. But it seems equally the case that those elements which are conceptually legitimated on the logical–metaphysical level still require another kind of confirmation before what Kant calls "objective reality" can fully be ascribed to them. This kind of confirmation is precisely what Hegel calls "realization" and it can only be provided on the other, non-logical, levels of the system. But this in turn brings an exactly opposite dependency relation into play. For the logical–metaphysical level then becomes a reflex of relationships that have their basis in a phenomenological or real-philosophical context. Although Hegel frequently treats these (and other) relations between the different levels of the system and explicitly indicates that we cannot properly evaluate the systematic achievement of his philosophical enterprise without giving appropriate consideration to these relations, it is nonetheless hardly possible to deny that the logical–metaphysical level is the decisive one as far as the exposition of the leading concepts of the system is concerned. I shall therefore limit the following discussion to this level of Hegel's thought.

II

First of all, I should like to propose a preliminary thesis concerning the general character of Hegel's philosophical project. This thesis simply possesses a prospective orienting character and is basically intended to indicate the perspective from which Hegel is here interpreted.[1] Whatever one makes of the details of Hegel's philosophy, we should always remember that it is principally concerned with inaugurating a new conception of rationality, with grounding and elaborating a new kind of philosophical thinking. Hegel is not primarily interested in mobilizing, improving or deepening certain philosophical theories, and their logical and conceptual structures, that can already be identified within the intellectual tradition. He is essentially concerned, in a radical departure from the entire philosophical tradition of the modern period at least, with establishing a new paradigm for the proper philosophical comprehension of reality. The attempt to establish this new paradigm depends entirely for Hegel on successfully communicating a basic insight: that we require an entirely new way of conceptualizing reality, one that is grounded not in the contingent epistemic apparatus of cognitive subjects but in the very constitution of reality itself. The ultimate reasons for this claim involve a whole series of far-reaching assumptions that Hegel attempts to justify through the development and presentation of his philosophical system. These assumptions are partly ontological, partly epistemological and partly methodological in character. The most important ones are the following: (i) the conviction that we must grasp the totality of reality as a rational unity, (ii) the thesis that this rational unity is produced through the realization of its *own* concept, and must be understood therefore as the result of an essentially self-reflexive process; (iii) the claim that this process is determined by the conceptual features already contained in the (Hegelian) concept of a rational unity. Point (i) defines Hegel's project as a form of monism, (ii) commits him to an essentially reflexive concept of cognition, while (iii) articulates the project according to an organological model.

By itself, of course, this general characterization of Hegel's project amounts to little more than a series of slogans, the substantive content of which inevitably appears meagre enough. They are only intended here to suggest precisely why a so-called "theory of the concept", or indeed a "science of logic", plays a central metaphysical role in Hegel's philosophy. The essential function of Hegel's theory of the concept lies in analysing the internal constitution of what

73

alone is ultimately real or "actual", that is, of reason itself, understood here as the organized totality of reality. The internal constitution or structured character of reason must also be distinguished from its external realization in the world of nature and spirit. And that is precisely because the external realization is supposed to be determined by the internal organization of reason itself. One can visualize the basic guiding idea here by thinking of the way in which we often tend to describe the developmental process of a living organism. A fully developed living organism can be understood as produced through the successful realization of all its individual characteristics and immanent possibilities. The totality of these characteristics and possibilities can thus be described as the "concept" of the organism. In the first instance, this simply signifies the sum of everything that, in the process of development, has effectively gone to make this organism the specific individual organism that it is. In this sense the living process of any organism can be described as the realization of its concept, and the concept of the organism can be defined as the structure that determines its development in the form of the living process.

In Hegel's eyes this kind of developmental process is something that is not merely revealed in the external realization of the concept of reason in the specific forms and configurations of the world of nature and spirit. For according to Hegel, the internal organization of the concept of reason must also be understood in terms of such a process. And in this context the process is supposed to generate, in a methodically organized fashion, all the fundamental determinations, that is, the conceptual and formal elements, that in their totality go to make up the concept of reason. These formal elements also involve, in addition to what Hegel calls the determinations of being and essence, the determination of the concept itself. According to Hegel, then, the concept of reason is internally organized in such a way that it already includes its *own* concept. Since Hegel presents his theory of the concept as a "logic", he can also describe the theory of the concept developed within this logic specifically as a theory of the logical concept. In Hegel, therefore, one must distinguish between the logical theory of the concept, that is, the theory that exhibits the concept of reason in all of its aspects (including the determinations of being and essence) as logic, and the theory of the logical concept, which specifically treats the concept as a structural element of the concept of reason within the context of the logic as a whole.

But Hegel's monistic and organological model of reality involves more than the idea of an internal and an external process with regard to the realization of reason. For it also implies a further claim: both the internal and the external process are supposed to display a certain direction in the sense of progressing from simpler to ever more complex determinations of what is ultimately generated here, namely reason, that is, reality. In this connection it is further claimed that the more complex determinations cannot simply be reduced to the simpler ones that have already preceded and constituted them and that there is also something like a maximally complex determination that can function as a final determination and point of closure. Hegel describes this final determination, especially in the later formulations of the *Encyclopaedia*, as an "essential" or "over-reaching subjectivity" (see *EL*: §214 note, §215 note), and characterizes it expressly as a unique form of self-relation. For Hegel's *concept* of reason, that is, for the object of his logical theory, all of this implies that the concept in question must be both entirely determined and maximally complex. It is entirely determined in the sense that this concept must contain all the determinations that are required for an exhaustive explication of itself (or, as Hegel prefers to say, for its own "development"). It is maximally complex in the sense that this concept provides the determinations that allow us to grasp subjectivity and its unique self-relation in a non-reductive manner.

III

Whatever one may think of the details of this general sketch of Hegel's project, it serves at least to illuminate three striking features of Hegel's own conception of a science of logic:

(i) It helps to explain why Hegel was so emphatically concerned to present his logical theory as a fundamental development and elaboration of Kant's theory of the categories. Hegel shares Kant's conviction that the concept of the object is always categorially determined, although they differ on the question of how the categories are to be justified: Kant appeals to the forms of judgement as articulated in the Table of Judgements, whereas Hegel òpts for an allegedly self-generating conceptual procedure.

(ii) It also makes it possible to understand why Hegel wishes to replace "former" discipline of metaphysics, and especially ontology, with his own logical project, which is concerned with properly determining that which is "in truth".

(iii) And lastly it clarifies why Hegel should treat the kind of obscure concepts we mentioned at the beginning – those of infinity, substantiality and subjectivity – as fundamental conceptual determinations. For he interprets them all as essential, if varyingly complex, features of reason itself. But this is only marginally significant at this point since we have not as yet identified any decisive reason for expressly excluding a subjectivistic or relativistic interpretation of Hegel's overall logical project.

Now we know that Hegel himself had *one* reason for rejecting such an interpretation; namely, his firm conviction concerning the "necessity" of the logical determinations of reason. And by "necessity" in this context Hegel appears to understand at least three things, although we must also remember that these three ways of speaking about necessity are not ultimately independent of one another in Hegel's eyes. In the first place, these determinations are supposed to be necessary in the sense that the concept of reason would be underdetermined without them, and would therefore lack its full and proper development. In the second place, they are also supposed to be necessary in the sense that they, and only they, are all required to articulate the maximal complexity of self-related subjectivity and thereby the internal organization of the concept of reason. In the third place, finally, they are furthermore supposed to be necessary in the sense that each of these determinations stands in a direct constitutive dependency relation to at least one of the others. If we wish to consider the possibility of offering a non-relativistic (or non-subjectivistic) interpretation of Hegel's understanding of the concept of reason, that is, the idea of reason as something that is categorially structured within itself, then it is the third sense of necessity that is essentially significant. For if it can be shown that the categorial determinations that constitute the concept of reason are indeed ineluctably (necessarily and non-contingently) self-generating, and if we accept with Hegel that ultimately or "in truth" there is only one "reason" (or one "reality"), then one can assert the absence of any compelling alternative conception of things, and thus the non-relative status of these fundamental conceptual determinations.

Now of course, the literature on Hegel, ever since the philosopher's own lifetime, has amply shown that the idea of demonstrating necessity in this third sense involves innumerable difficulties and implausible-looking assumptions of one kind or another. The fundamental reservations that have rightly and most frequently been expressed in this connection can principally be identified under three points. The first concerns the beginning of Hegel's *Logic*, where we may well ask whether we can properly speak, in any sense, of necessity at all. The second concerns the so-called "method" of generating the logical determinations, one that clearly cannot claim necessity in the third, or any previously recognized, sense of the word. And the third, of course, concerns the conclusion of the *Logic*, where Hegel presupposes that the logical grounding of objectivity already implies something like necessity in the constitution of nature itself. For it is particularly unclear at the end of the *Logic* itself how necessity in the third sense can play any intelligible role in the transition to nature.

Quite apart from the traditional problems associated with these three issues, Hegel's claim for necessity requires elucidation in a further respect that has been much less frequently discussed. And this arises from Hegel's assumption that the specific complexity of the categorial determinations that are supposed to characterize the concept of "reason" is also itself "necessary". The possibility of a non-relativistic reading of Hegel's theory of reason also depends at least in part on how far one could succeed in making this assumption intelligible. Now since self-related subjectivity is supposed to be the maximally complex characteristic feature of the concept of reason, and since this conceptual determination of self-relation is essentially grounded in the determinations of infinity and substantiality, it is obvious that these three concepts of "infinity", "substantiality" and "subjectivity" will play a particularly central role in any attempt to justify this assumption. This in itself implies that Hegel must claim a kind of internal connection between his idea of infinity and his concepts of substantiality and self-relating subjectivity that conclusively reveals the necessity for this concept of subjectivity.

Before even attempting a general analysis of this connection, it is advisable to clarify and simplify three things. First, the claim that self-relating subjectivity represents the most complex feature of the Hegelian conception of reason simply means that it is the non-reducible feature that possesses the most (logical) presuppositions. We thus do not attempt to characterize conceptual complexity in any sense that is peculiar to Hegel. Secondly, we simply take it for granted that what ultimately matters for Hegel is to prove the necessity of the specific kind of self-relation that can legitimately be ascribed subjectivity. And this is because the important point for Hegel is precisely to reveal self-knowing or self-cognition as an integral element of his conception of reason. Here we shall therefore ignore the fact that certain other elements, such as the postulate of objectivity or objectification, for example, also play a role for Hegel's concept of subjectivity. Finally we shall also ignore everything remotely connected with the purely "technical" side of Hegel's project. This is particularly the case with regard to his concepts of identity and negation.

IV

Hegel first introduces the concept of self-relation as a structural characteristic of a specific categorial form in the so-called "logic of being". It makes its appearance there in the description of what Hegel calls "infinity". On the basis of considerations arising from the relationship between the categories of "something" and "other", Hegel attempts to show that the possibility of grasping anything as an identifiable object by ascribing qualitative character to it, or in Hegel's own terminology, the possibility of grasping anything finite at all (the red there, the roundness here), presupposes the capacity for distinguishing it from any number of other things, or, as he puts it, from the infinite. But it also presupposes that the qualitative self-presence of something can only be grasped through a concept of finitude and infinitude that does not interpret them as mutually exclusive terms. If no such conception were available, we would merely be left with a contradictory concept of infinity. And we would therefore also lack the possibility of characterizing "qualitative being" (GW 21: 144) by recourse to a concept of finitude supposedly defined in relation to that of infinitude. A tenable (non-contradictory) concept of qualitative infinitude must be articulated in such a way that it can indeed function as the counter-concept to that of (qualitative) finitude, but without thereby "negating" or excluding the latter from itself.

Hegel attempts to account for this situation by showing that infinitude cannot possibly be thought except through recourse to finitude: both concepts reciprocally elucidate one another in so far as each proves empty or contradictory unless it is related to the other. And it is this consideration, according to Hegel, that leads us to the concept of the "true infinite". This concept is supposed to result from the "sublation" of conceptually contradictory descriptive elements – elements indispensable for characterizing finitude and infinitude as opposed, that is, mutually exclusive, concepts – into a more complex structure within which these descriptive elements are indeed compatible. I think that Hegel himself reveals most clearly what his concept of infinitude is attempting to show in a specific passage from the first edition of the *Logic*:

> Neither the finite as such, nor the infinite as such, possess truth therefore. Each is intrinsically the opposite of itself and is a unity with its other. Their *determinacy over against one other* has thus vanished. What therefore emerges here is *the true infinite* in which both finitude and bad infinitude are sublated. The true infinite consists in transcending being-other, as *return-to-self*; it is the negation that is *self-relating*; it is being-other, insofar as it is no longer *immediate* being-other, but the sublation of the latter, the *re-established equality with itself*. (GW 11: 82ff.)

In the present context there are two important points about Hegel's remarks on the concept of "qualitative infinitude". In the first place, we should note that Hegel already introduces the concept of self-relation on the level of the logic of being, that is, the level that treats the categorial determinations that are supposedly constitutive for the possibility of identifying anything at all as being in some determinate way, as a (qualitatively) determined object. To put the same thing in a different, slightly less provocative manner: for Hegel the concept of self-relation is not primarily bound up with accomplishments of self-differentiation or self-identification, but is already a necessary component of the thought of objectivity in general in so far as we can only make sense of the latter by recourse to the concept of (true) infinitude. It is this Hegelian thesis that is decisive for justifying the claim that subjectivity is a feature that necessarily belongs to (Hegelian) reason. The second important point to note here is that self-relation, as a structural characteristic of "infinity" in Hegel's sense, is introduced through considerations that arise from the possibility of consistently describing the relationship between finitude and infinitude in a non-contradictory manner. The concept, or as we might better put it now, the category of infinitude, as one that implies self-relation, is introduced specifically through reflection concerning the conceptual difficulties involved in establishing a logically stable concept of finitude. It is these conceptual difficulties that motivate Hegel's claims for the necessity of a conception of infinitude essentially characterized by self-relation. If Hegel repeatedly insists on the necessity of what he calls the "determinations of thought", this derives directly from his assumption that conceptual difficulties inevitably generate a kind of logical necessity.

V

But even if we are prepared to accept the way in which Hegel introduces self-relation by explicating his concept of true infinitude, and thus to recognize the necessity that is required here, we are still far from genuinely understanding the necessity of a subjectivity conceived in terms of self-relation. For Hegel we can only come to understand this if we also endorse, among other things, a specific conception of what he terms "substantiality" or "(absolute) substance". This conception is also supposed to be a necessary one in so far as it arises immanently from the analysis of prior conceptual difficulties. Naturally I can only suggest the general import of this conception here. One could formulate it sharply in the following terms: the character of substantiality essential for any complete determination of the concept of reason requires a concept of substance that can only be conceptualized as a relationship between mutually exclusive elements that ultimately reveal themselves as structurally identical. And in so far as these elements are brought into relation through the concept of substance itself they can also be described as self-relating. The line of thought that leads Hegel to this conclusion is a reinterpretation of the Kantian categories of relation and can briefly be summarized as follows: from an analysis of the determinations that supposedly constitute the essential characteristics of the concept of substance (possibility, actuality, necessity) we see how the idea of independent substantial unity leads directly to a relationship between two independent substances in the nexus of cause and effect, and how this relationship leads to the idea of a reciprocal interaction between independent substances. Hegel interprets this nexus, already implied in the conceptual determinations of substance itself, as resulting from a process of reflection: for on closer examination the substance that was initially conceptualized as independent, or the idea of independent substantial unity, actually reveals itself as the identity of cause and effect in reciprocal interaction, that is, as an identity of opposed determinations. While independently conceived substance is nothing but, or is the same as, the identity of cause and effect in reciprocal interaction, cause and effect can still be distinguished from one another even through this process of interaction (for they too are "independent", as Hegel puts it). Thus on the one hand independent substance is its own other or, in Hegelian terms, is the "other of itself" (as cause and effect), while on the other hand substance is only what it is, is only itself in and through this other (Hegel's rather flowery way of saying that substance is nothing but this "other"). And all of this implies, for Hegel, that substance too must be interpreted as an essentially self-related structure in so far as its constitutive relation to its own other is simultaneously a relation to itself.

We should note two things here. First, Hegel conceptualizes self-relation as a relation between two structurally identical states of affairs in the context of his exposition of (true) infinity. We seem to encounter the self-relation that is characteristic of infinity – let us call this "infinite self-relation" – whenever we discover two relata that are nonetheless identical in kind. Thus the finite, in Hegel's sense, comes to stand in an infinite self-relation when it is conceptualized as related to another finite term (for this "infinite relation to itself" see *EL*: §157). Self-relation as an essential feature of substance, what in the spirit of Hegel we could describe as "substantial self-relation", clearly imposes stronger demands on the relata in question: in addition to being identical in kind, they must also be numerically identical. For, as we have seen, substance is supposed to be the same as (i.e. "nothing but") the identity of cause and effect in reciprocal interaction. Or in other words, substantial self-relation is supposed to imply infinite self-relation, although not the other way around. In this way, by specifying the demands that the relevant relata must satisfy, Hegel can attempt to distinguish different types of self-relation and to articulate the conceptual dependency relations that hold between them.[2] Secondly, Hegel's concept of substance also throws considerable light on what he understands by "unity". According to the outline I have suggested here, Hegel interprets substance as a relational structure, the characteristic relata (cause, effect) of which can only appear under two mutually exclusive descriptions that nonetheless designate the same thing (are identical with one another). The structure itself can only be a (substantial) unity in so far as it is completely determined through these specific relata and the mutually exclusive relation between them. This means that the unity of substance cannot be understood as a third term that could be identified as something somehow separate from the relata and their specific internal relationship. Although Hegel often complains that the word "unity" is not really ideal for his philosophical purposes (see *GW* 21: 78ff., 131, 139ff.; *EL*: §70, §88 note), he nonetheless uses it on many occasions and frequently in a rather misleading way. Above all, he finds it difficult to employ the concept of "the unity of opposed determinations" without suggesting the idea that some discrete third term is somehow involved here. And his sometimes rather figurative use of the expression "sublation" only served to compound the problem. Although there are certainly limits to the comparison, we can perhaps illustrate what Hegel is driving at with his "relational" descriptions of specific forms of unity by thinking of the visual puzzles familiar from Gestalt psychology, such as the famous "duck–rabbit" drawing, which can be read alternately as one or the other. To say the image represents a duck, or to say it represents a rabbit, is to describe the pictorial situation correctly in both cases, although of course the two statements are mutually exclusive. In this context we can say, in Hegelian terms, that the duck and the rabbit is "the other of itself". As "a duck that is also a rabbit" and "a rabbit that is also a duck", the forms are the indistinguishable yet mutually opposed elements of the same puzzle. In Hegelian terms they are its ideal moments, and the "unity" of the puzzle in which these elements are sublated consists precisely in the identity of both elements rather than in another third term. The unity in question can be distinguished only conceptually from that of which it is itself the unity.

VI

As far as the necessity of (self-related) subjectivity as a defining characteristic of reason is concerned, this part of Hegel's "logical" story can be fairly briefly told. It basically consists in a skilful and original transposition of the results derived from the analysis of the concept of substance into a further form of self-relation. This form of self-relation is said to be defined by the fact that its relata here relinquish the apparent independence that still characterized them under the determinations of substance. Hegel describes this form of self-relation as "subjectivity" and connects it directly with what he calls the "(logical) concept". In the first instance, therefore, the concept of subjectivity simply designates a characteristic property of the relational structure that emerges when substance is properly comprehended "in its truth". What makes this concept "necessary" in the Hegelian sense is not actually the fact that without it the concept of reason would lack the categorial resources for describing the types of phenomena that Hegel subsumes under the term "spirit" in the part of the system that he calls "real philosophy". Although this consideration must also naturally be acknowledged, it is not decisively relevant to the kind of necessity that interests Hegel here, for he is primarily concerned with conceptual necessity. And he seems to think he has successfully established such necessity in this context, for the specific form of self-relation, on which the necessary concept of (true) infinity already depends, is still only inadequately realized in the typical forms of substantiality in so far as they lack any successful "sublation of otherness" or "re-established unity with itself". If we bear this consideration in mind, we can see that the kind of self-relation that, as subjectivity, defines Hegel's "(logical) concept" is necessary in the sense that it alone exemplifies (true) infinity in a conceptually complete manner. This complete exemplification can only properly be accomplished if we find the "right" relata for this type of self-relation. And this can only successfully be done in the context of the "(logical) concept" because it is only the elements (the moments, the determinations) of the concept that constitute the relevant relational structure, one that is "capable of subjectivity", as it were. The most economical, and perhaps the most approachable, description of this structure can be found among Hegel's numerous, although rarely very clear, characterizations of what he calls "the Idea". The remarks in question constitute the main part of §215 of the *Encyclopaedia*: "[The Idea] is the course through which the concept, as the universality which is singularity, determines itself into objectivity and the opposite of this objectivity, and leads this externality, which has the concept as its substance, through its own immanent dialectic back to *subjectivity*" (*EL*: §215).

If we consider the role that Hegel's concept of (true qualitative) infinity plays in his conception of subjectivity, it is hardly surprising that throughout his life Hegel always insisted on a close connection between the concept of "infinity" and that family of concepts that also possess strong connotations of "subjectivity" for him. In the "metaphysics of subjectivity" developed in the Jena period (*Jenaer Systementwürfe II*) we already find Hegel expounding his conception of "absolute spirit" through an analysis of the concept of infinity. In the *Phenomenology* the concept of self-consciousness is also introduced via an exposition of the concept of infinity (*GW* 9: 101). In the *Science of Logic*, as early as the beginning of the chapter on "being-for-self", Hegel refers to self-consciousness as "the nearest example of the presence of infinity" (*GW* 21: 145). In the note to §215 of the *Encyclopaedia* (quoted above), Hegel asserts emphatically if obscurely that "the unity of the Idea is subjectivity, thought, infinity, and thereby essentially distinguished from the idea of substance". And in another, if less obviously central, passage of the same work (*EN*: §359 note) Hegel defines "a subject" as "that which is capable of possessing self-contradiction within itself and of *enduring* this contradiction", and goes on to add that "this is what constitutes its *infinity*".

VII

This concludes our discussion of Hegel's attempt to demonstrate the "necessity" of subjectivity. Unfortunately there is no good reason to think that we have thereby been able to render the real nature of this demonstration ultimately transparent. But this was not actually the precise intention of the foregoing discussion. We have simply tried to offer a preliminary analysis, or better a mere sketch, of the general line of argumentation with which Hegel attempts to justify his claim for the necessity of "subjectivity", where subjectivity is interpreted as the maximally complex feature of his logical concept of reason. We can formulate the result of our analysis this way: Hegel organizes his argument by articulating the implications of a specifically introduced concept of self-relation that is derived from a close examination of the concept of infinity. Although this result will probably not strike anyone as particularly surprising, it certainly makes clear once again that the concept of infinity possesses a significance for Hegel's entire logical enterprise that goes far beyond the direct context in which it is initially introduced. If, as our earlier citations indicated, Hegel expressly identifies the infinite as the fundamental concept of philosophy, he is certainly concerned with far more than simply rehabilitating the kind of unorthodox conception of infinity that is already implicit in Spinoza.[3] "Infinity" is the fundamental concept of philosophy for Hegel because it supposedly provides the structural resources necessary for adequately conceptualizing his project of describing reality as a self-realizing rational process.

But these remarks concerning certain fundamental features of Hegel's *Logic* are not really intended to add to the endless history of scarcely illuminating interpretations of his philosophy. They are presented instead as a means to a very different purpose: deciding whether the "cultural-relativist" neo-pragmatic interpretation of Hegel's project is compatible with Hegel's own systematic philosophical intentions. Against the background of the present discussion, it is hardly surprising if we encounter certain difficulties in arguing convincingly for such compatibility. These principally derive from the fact that it is far from clear how the neo-pragmatic approach could possibly accommodate Hegel's concept of logic or his theory of the concept. For if it is true, as Hegel claims, that his entire system depends on a categorial base that lays claim to conceptual (or "logical") necessity, and if it is also true, as Hegel believes, that there is no legitimate alternative to this categorial basis in so far as it essentially confirms itself (realizes itself) as reality, then there is no identifiable reason for defending the idea of a "social space" in which certain activities or practices of reason-giving could effectively constitute our categories. And Hegel would charge the neo-pragmatic interpretation with misunderstanding his own philosophical project, for this interpretation conflates the process that describes the *discovery* of the "true" categorial structure of reality through knowing and acting subjects in different historical contexts (for Hegel the phenomenological process, which certainly refers to specific social and cultural phenomena) with the process that takes the *constitution* of this "true" categorial structure as its specific object, with what one could call the "logical process". Since it is this logical process that first constitutes the overall structure within which everything real must appear (the ontological claim of the *Logic*), Hegel would find it difficult to understand, and would certainly have no systematic place in which to accommodate, the idea of an "autonomous" phenomenological process, that is, one that is independent of logic and yet constitutive of the logical categories. It is no accident, therefore, that Hegel's *Phenomenology* is primarily concerned not with generating categorial structures (although this may indeed transpire on a kind of meta-level), but with schematizing the consequences that arise from the one-sided adoption of specific paradigms and thus revealing the sceptical destruction of their claims to truth and validity (what Hegel calls "self-accomplishing scepticism").

What emerges from the previous discussion is the rather disturbing insight that once again Hegel proves too resistant to promise much hope for such well-meaning attempts to integrate his thought within a more contemporary philosophical perspective. Depending on one's intellectual temperament, this may strike us as an irritating, unfortunate or even tragic situation. But one should not assume that this conclusion necessarily represents a fatal objection to the neo-pragmatic interpretation. It may well be that the elements that cannot successfully be integrated within this kind of interpretation are ones that actually no one except Hegel himself would now find remotely convincing. It would therefore already be an achievement if we could separate these from certain other elements that might prove very fruitful for a variety of different purposes. From this perspective, the neo-pragmatic approach could be regarded less as a way of developing Hegel than, in many respects, of leaving him alone.[4]

NOTES

1. For a fuller development of the approach outlined here, see D. Emundts & R.-P. Horstmann, *Hegel: Eine Einführung* (Stuttgart: Reclam, 2002).
2. I think it is quite clear from Hegel's Jena "Metaphysics" of 1804–5 that he was attracted very early on to this way of analysing "self-relation"; see R.-P. Horstmann, *Ontologie und Relationen: Hegel, Bradley und Russell und die Kontroverse über interne und externe Beziehungen* (Königstein: Hain, 1984), 92ff.
3. In this connection see *GW* 9: 99.
4. The first version of this chapter was presented at a meeting of the *Internationale Hegel-Vereinigung* in Padua. The present version has benefited considerably from the remarks of Dina Emundts.

CHAPTER FIVE

DIALECTIC AS LOGIC OF TRANSFORMATIVE PROCESSES

Angelica Nuzzo

Unlike other parts of Hegel's philosophical system, the *Logic* raises for the interpreter not only detailed questions concerning particular arguments and the stages of its construction but also the more general, indeed preliminary problem regarding the subject as well as the overall aim and ambition of its project. Ultimately, this problem challenges the status of the *Logic* as "logic". For, it is certainly legitimate to ask whether Hegel's dialectic is really "logic" in the sense understood in the tradition preceding and following Hegel; or to ask what kind of logic dialectic is. This question has been raised time and again. Attempts to answer it include claims that Hegel's logic is an ontology that either returns to pre-Kantian metaphysics or offers a renewal of metaphysics after Kant's critique; that it provides an epistemological theory intended to guide the development of all other philosophical disciplines; that it amounts to speculative mystification of autarchic thinking, or that it is a theory of meaning or a theory regarding the pragmatic institution of norms.[1] These and analogous accounts generally stress one single aspect of Hegel's logical project leaving out the more complex constellation of reasons that he provides as justification of its overarching task. It follows that, whatever their respective merits, the explanatory potential of these readings is limited to the consequences of one single thesis: ontology versus epistemology versus theory of meaning and so forth. On all these accounts, much is left unconsidered. And the central question still remains open.

The problem of the status and thematic object of the logic is especially urgent because of the systematic position that this discipline occupies in Hegel's philosophy. At stake is its relation to the *Phenomenology* and to the *Realphilosophie* – the philosophy of nature and spirit – as well as its position within the entire system of philosophy – the logic is both the first and the last discipline of the system (see *EL*: §18; also Nuzzo 2004). In this regard as well, the status of Hegel's logic has been questioned time and again in different respects. While

Hegel presents the logic as the absolutely presuppositionless first part of the system (W 5: 68–9) it is often argued that it displays several types of presupposition that indeed influence and shape its course, thereby undermining its claim to systematic independence and its alleged formal "purity". For the logic presupposes, in some sense, the development of the *Phenomenology* (W 5: 42–3, 67); but it also presupposes, to say the very least, the successive conquests of the history of philosophy and logic as well as the determinate language in which pure thought gives expression to its forms.

My aim is to discuss the status of Hegel's dialectic logic. What kind of theory does Hegel present in the first part of his system of philosophy? What kind of logic is dialectic? What are its philosophical aims and tasks? And what is this logic *about*, that is, what kind of objects does it thematize? These questions raise the more fundamental issue of the continuing relevance of Hegel's logic. What could be the function of Hegel's dialectic for our philosophizing in the contemporary world? Other parts of Hegel's philosophy have recently received actualizing attention. The *Phenomenology* has drawn interest for its concept of recognition and more recently has been discovered by analytic pragmatists such as Robert Brandom, while the *Philosophy of Right* has not ceased to inspire debate among philosophers of the most different creed.[2] Does the *Logic* belong irretrievably to the past, to a philosophical repertoire that came alive one last time with Marx (and indeed with Lenin) but is destined to be abandoned to merely historical and philological discussions? Or instead, as I shall suggest, is dialectic logic not the most actual and lively part of Hegelian philosophy (see Žižek 1988)? Is dialectic not the instrument – the logic, as it were – that teaches us how to think and act in a lacerated, contradictory, ever-changing world? Does dialectic not display the way in which the contradictory phenomena of interdependence proper of our globalized and yet highly fragmented world come to be – the inner logic of our present time?

I shall argue for the actuality of Hegel's dialectic as logic of transformative processes.[3] The question of what Hegel's logic is *about* and hence of what kind of logic it is, is best addressed by discussing first the problematic context in which it should be placed and read. Accordingly, I begin by indicating the crucial problems that lie at the heart of the development of Hegel's dialectic. This will give us a unique perspective on the aim of Hegel's logic, and will allow us to measure its distance from the problems faced by philosophy today.[4] In a second step of the argument I shall turn to Hegel's idea of a "science" of logic, and discuss in some detail the thesis that presents dialectic as a logic of transformative processes. I shall analyse some aspects of the transformative process of Hegel's logic, and thereby provide the basis for assessing the way in which dialectic succeeds both traditional logic and metaphysics and Kant's transcendental logic.

The strategy of getting to the philosophic aim of the logic by addressing its context should not raise the expectation of a developmental history of

Hegel's idea of dialectic.[5] Rather, the claim is that Hegel's logic is configured as a logic of transformative processes precisely because it arises out of the need to give a philosophical account of and to learn how to live with some fundamental transformations of modernity, transformations that we face again in our contemporary (postmodern) world. More precisely, I contend that Hegel views transformation, transition and contradiction as the defining features of his epoch. For Hegel the crucial task of philosophy is the understanding of the historical present as it confronts the challenge of change and transformation. The aim of logic is to unravel the fundamental structures of change, to think and understand change "in and for itself", that is, to think of it not as an external event that merely happens to a certain content, subject or substrate but rather to think of change in its logical *purity* as the inner tension and dynamic impulse defining what something *truly* is (and is not at the same time).

The story that Hegel's dialectic supports – methodologically and epistemologically – the story to which the logic must be brought back as its theoretical foundation (and even justification), is not a story of unmatched success, progress and conciliation, a story whose conclusion is already predetermined at the beginning and consequently offers neither novelty nor possibility of unforeseen change and transformation. Too often we forget that dialectic is inspired by those lacerating contradictions, tragedies and uncertainties of the historical world, to which Hegel was a particularly sensitive witness. My aim is to show that this holds true not only for the young Hegel, whose interests for the "lower needs of man" (*Br* 59, Hegel to Schelling, 2 November 1800) inspire his early writings, but also for the mature Hegel, whose system begins with and is grounded in a "science of logic". As the logical process takes place in the formal – timeless and spaceless – dimension of pure thinking, the movement of contradiction that it narrates[6] is not erased in a final moment of conciliation, is never reduced to a past left forever behind or to a place abandoned once and for all. That the logic unfolds with the movement of an internal and immanent necessity does not imply that the conclusion is already set and reached from the very beginning or that the process does not know the contingency, uncertainty and vagueness of alternative decisions. The logic tells us of the ever-present and resurging contradiction that constitutes every transformation as its fundamental ingredient; it displays the nature of transition including the space of vagueness that surrounds the emergence of all new formations. To this extent, however, the logic also teaches us how to relate to such transformations *philosophically*. The logic tells us that to understand our historical present is to understand – and indeed to practise – the logic of change. Perhaps, the last of Marx's "Theses on Feuerbach" can be taken to express a similar programme.

I. THE GROWING CONTRADICTION AND ITS PHILOSOPHICAL ANSWER: DIALECTIC LOGIC

Hegel's dialectic is the philosophical answer to the "growing contradiction" of his historical world; it is both the attempt to understand such contradiction and to propose the way one can live with it.[7] This conception of logic provides the foundation of Hegel's philosophical system. Throughout his career Hegel sees the task of philosophy to be the understanding of the contemporary world. Traditional philosophy – which can be generically referred to as "logic of the understanding" – does this either by disclosing the unintelligibility of the world or, which is ultimately the same, our lack of "courage" in facing the philosophical challenges posed by it.[8] The defeat of traditional models of philosophical understanding leads Hegel to the "need"[9] for a new logic, namely, to a logic able to explain the new, unsettling features of the contemporary world.

But a difficulty seems to arise at this point concerning the relation between philosophical thinking and its contents. For, if philosophy is one's own time reflected, apprehended, expressed and finally transformed in and by thought – as the famous formula has it[10] – then philosophy cannot be separated from its contemporary world, cannot be taken in abstraction from the actuality that supports it. But what about the case of logic? Is logic not precisely the realm of abstraction, the realm of "pure" thought, that is, of thinking taken in itself without reference to any (real) content? How and why should such an abstract discipline as logic be invested of the task of comprehending the real world?[11] Indeed, on Hegel's account, the abstract and merely formal character of traditional logic is one of the principal culprits of its many failures and limitations. Hence one could infer from this that only a logic that does not make abstraction from contents, as the sterile logic of the understanding does, can fulfil the tasks that Hegel envisages for it. To be sure, Kant had already seen this point and attempted to remedy the shortcomings of formal logic by proposing a transcendental logic, namely, a logic in which contents (as contents of cognition) are introduced (see B79ff./A55ff.).[12] And yet, on Hegel's account, Kant also falls short of his task. Dialectic should be concerned not simply with contents but with a peculiar mode or method of dealing with logical forms/contents. On the other hand, Hegel continues to presents his logic as a "pure" and somehow formal science. What makes Hegel's logic pure? A few preliminary questions, however, are in order: why is the present world unintelligible both to traditional logic and philosophy and to Kant's transcendental logic and critical philosophy? And if the task of philosophy can be fulfilled only by a new logic, the explanatory link of which with the contemporary world becomes central, what can then be the purity of logical form, how shall this link be established and what makes this logic a logic? If rational thinking has to grasp "what is" in the necessity and rationality that make it "actual" (*wirklich*) (W 7: 26), this description defines for Hegel both the aim of the most abstract theory such as the doctrines of the *Phenomenology* or the *Philosophy of Right*, and the task of more concrete and occasional works such as the early essay on the "Constitution of Germany" (1799–1803) or the late pamphlet on the "English Reform Bill" (1831) (Knox 1964). In all these cases, Hegel's thematic object and philosophical objective are the same: the comprehension and explanation of the crucial features constituting the "actuality" of the present world. The apparent opposition between speculative and empirical realm yields to the solidarity of one and the same effort at comprehension. This convergence may explain, at least in part, why Hegel's occasional political writings always display a speculative inflection and interest; and why his most abstract works never lack a fundamentally political and historical motivation. As we shall see, the *Logic* provides the best case in point. To get to this claim, however, we first need to examine the characters of the present that Hegel attempts to comprehend and explain.

In 1781, Kant discloses the historical roots of the first edition of the *Critique of Pure Reason* by placing it in the "age of criticism [*Kritik*]", that is, in the period of the Enlightenment (Axi), drawing motivational and explicative force from the act of positioning the work in his historical present. The age of criticism gives rise to reason's own critique; reason's critique continues and radicalizes the criticism of the time. Kant's act was full of promise and optimism. In 1807, in the preface to the *Phenomenology*, Hegel discloses a different present as informing and indeed requiring the new work of dialectic. "It is not difficult to see," he registers:

> that our time is a time of birth and transition to a new period. Spirit has come to a break with the previous world of its existence and representation, and is about to sink this world in the past and to start the work [*Arbeit*] of its own transformation [*Umgestaltung*]. Indeed, spirit is never in a state of quiet" [as it is caught in a constant progressive movement]. (W 3: 18).[13]

Hegel wrote during the transitional period that saw Europe coming out of the turmoil of the French Revolution, prey to Napoleon's sweeping designs of conquest, the stage of new social, juridical and political experimentations, a Europe in which the industrial revolution had already begun. For Hegel the contemporary observer, the present is an open process full of uncertainties just like the work of the philosophical science at the beginning of its tasks of comprehension. We do not know anything of the new age about to begin except that it is new and different from the one we have lived in so far. If there is certainly promise and confidence in Hegel's portrait of the present time, there is also the consciousness of the effort (the movement of spirit is hard "work" – *Arbeit*; W 3: 18) of the "price" that one has to pay for every step undertaken along a path that is all but straightforward (W 3: 19). But more than anything else there is in Hegel's remark a sort of puzzlement at the task that the present world poses to philosophy. For Hegel's real focus is not so much to predict the possible contours of the new epoch about to begin, but to comprehend the transition itself – the transition that leads to it and produces the new, the process of transformation in which contemporary consciousness is caught. This is the true object of philosophical understanding; this is the chief challenge to it. How can "transition" itself (or "birth" for that matter) be understood? It can be understood not as the past nor the future, but as the changing present in its changing quality; not as the origin nor the destination of the historical process of transformation, but as the very movement of transformation, the movement in which our lives are presently immersed and engaged. Philosophy, Hegel will declare in later years, should not attempt to make predictions with regard to the future. Philosophy's task is rather the understanding of the present in situations of crisis, that is, in moments of transition and indeed of conflict and contradiction between the old and the new. But how can the contradictory tension that separates and at the same time brings together the slow continuity of growth and the sudden unexpected hiatus of birth be brought to conceptual knowledge and thereby explained?

Speaking to his contemporaries, Hegel can indeed say that "it is not difficult to see" that we live in a time of transition to a new epoch – it is not difficult to see because life provides immediate evidence for this claim as a lived uncontroversial fact. But he warns that what is known to common sense is still not conceptually grasped, is not yet philosophical knowledge.[14] On the contrary, what is easily seen, felt and lived in its immediate certainty is the hardest thing to grasp conceptually. This, however, is precisely the task to be undertaken: to give conceptual, rational form to the mere feeling or perception of change. In 1807, with the *Phenomenology*, Hegel provides a logic of change that takes consciousness as its concrete object, that is, as the place in which change occurs and become visible (*EL*: §25; *W* 5: 49).[15] Philosophical understanding of transition is the understanding of how transition takes place in and for consciousness, that being a concrete "example" or instance of the *pure* form of transition. The *Logic* will be the project of a pure staging of transition as such, the presentation of transition in and for itself, with no reference to a subject in which and for which change takes place. The logic, as presentation of the pure process of transition is itself nothing else but transition fully displayed in its inner dynamic.

A fragment, probably written between 1799 and 1800 and belonging to the work on the *Constitution of Germany*, reveals the philosophical background of Hegel's analysis of the contemporary political situation in Germany. It is, once again, a situation of deep institutional crisis and uncertain political transition in which the dangers of dissolution and self-destruction facing the German people are a felt, troubling reality. The challenge to the disillusioned philosopher[16] is the understanding of "what is". In this period (i.e. in his last Frankfurt and early Jena years), in his theoretical writings Hegel arrives at the central thought of dialectic. It has been observed that comparison between the *Constitution of Germany* and Hegel's works on political philosophy of this and the immediately successive period ("System of Ethical Life", "Essay on Natural Law") gives the impression of radically conflicting views. For, while philosophical reflection leads Hegel to an attempt at overcoming the contradictions found in the historical world, in the *Constitution of Germany* all those contradictions are left unreconciled as plain and hard facts – as facts that "should remain", as it were, in their contradictory character (Maier 1963: 340).[17] This is an important observation that supports, however, the contrary view of the fundamental continuity and solidarity between Hegel's occasional political writings and his theoretical philosophy. As the understanding of the present political situation leads to a contradiction that can neither be healed nor overcome, the effort of philosophy struggling for a comprehension of the dynamics of change leads precisely to the thought of a possible conciliation and of the conditions thereof. As logic of change, dialectic cannot be separated from the analysis of the present world. Yet, to expose the contradictory character of the present age is also, at the same time, to comprehend the ways in which contradiction develops and thereby may be overcome.

The fragment "Der immer sich vergrössernde Widerspruch ..." (*GW* 5: 16–18) placed by many editors at the beginning of the *Constitution of Germany*, offers at the same time a philosophical diagnosis of the historical crisis faced by Germany at the end of the century, and the first emergence of the fundamental terms of Hegel's logic of change. The (abstract) problem herein is: what is change? How shall the philosopher conceptualize the moment of historical transition, the unrest that everyone feels is a prevailing dimension of the present, the necessary pull (*Trieb, Drang*) towards the unknown and the new that one must grasp and embrace to be able to survive? Indeed, unlike the dead fixation of life in "positive" institutional forms and in their destructive, blocked contradictions, the contradiction that shapes transformative processes is the condition of survival – both individual and collective, both personal and national.

"Der immer sich vergrössernde Widerspruch ..." offers Hegel's philosophical diagnosis of a period of radical change, the phenomenology of a historical crisis, and the assessment of the different directions in which such crisis may develop and resolve. Significantly, however, Hegel does not point to any guaranteed solution of the "growing contradiction". Insecurity and the striving for the unknown remain the prevailing tone,[18] the predicament of the present. The fragment indicates in the "growing contradiction" and the "need" for its "sublation" (*Aufhebung*) or "refutation" (*Widerlegung*) the (logical) structure of change (*GW* 5: 16–17, 18). Herein we already meet the fundamental terms of Hegel's dialectic. Contradiction is a real force operating in history, a force moved by its own inner logic. Contradiction now defines the relation between the ideal and the real, between nature and life, between

91

what political and juridical institutions have to offer to their citizens and what individuals more or less consciously seek and desire beyond them (*GW* 5: 16, 17). Its tension is the mark of an epoch in which all certainty and security has been shattered and the only hope of survival – individual and collective – lies in the acceptance of transformation, in the capacity for facing the negativity to which life has been reduced. Knowledge in itself cannot effect transformation, although it may be a condition thereof. And not even a pure act of the "will" (individual or collective), not a social contract or mere revolutionary "violence" can bring it about. Rather, Hegel seems to suggest that transformation lies somehow in the nature of things, in the inner logic of the contradiction that animates the present time once the obstacles to its radicalization and free development are removed and contradiction is allowed to grow to its extreme consequences without being fixated into an "absolute" (*GW* 5: 16). Only "nature", the recognition and expression of real needs and desires, can lead to the articulation and thus the (dis)solution of the growing contradiction (see Bodei 1987: 19). Change takes place as contradiction gives rise to a "need", and thus to the movement of its own "refutation". For the need that contradiction be overcome – a need that arises once life has met pure negativity and recognized that it can no longer live with it and in it – is already in itself change (*GW* 5: 17).

Thus, contradiction is for Hegel the sign of historical crises; transformation and change are the development of contradiction, the movement that contradiction necessarily marshals once it is not taken as absolute, once it is not fixed within illusory limits (for those limits have been blown away once and for all by revolutionary turmoil) or repressed. Hegel's *Logic* will elaborate this seminal thought into the first, foundational part of the system of philosophy. In its basic terms, however, Hegel's dialectic logic of change is in place already in this early political work.

While the logic of change animating from within the historical present is fundamentally descriptive, it is additionally driven by a normative and evaluative impulse. We want transformation to be progress; change to be change for the better. And yet as change faces the unknown we must acknowledge that change in itself is not necessarily progressive nor has the certainty of a guaranteed end. Progress – whatever it may mean – can never be taken for granted. However, the need that accompanies change (or at least the need that refuses to take the contradiction as absolute and the limiting, suffocating conditions of the age as something irrevocably fixed) aims at radicalizing and thereby overcoming the further contradiction between the *"worse* life" of increasing human suffering and the desire for a *"better* life" (*GW* 5: 17–18, emphasis added). Such need for change, becoming an active "impulse" (*Drang*) towards a better life, is supported by all the forces of the present age: by the action of single individuals of great character, by the collective movement of entire peoples, by the depiction of poets and even by the work of metaphysics. And yet only "nature in its actual life" can attack the "worse

92

life" opposing it with the force of an effective "refutation". To leave no doubt as to the character of this refutation, Hegel clearly states that it cannot be the "object of an intentional activity" (GW 5: 18). The advancement of the growing contradiction can be countered and thereby fulfilled only by its objective, immanent resolution, not by the conscious intervention of a will. This is the thought of immanence that the *Logic* will explore in all its implications. Only in this way is the apparent change claimed by an ineffective, external violence (*Gewalt*) replaced by the real transformation brought about by the inner power (*Macht*) of contradiction. Only in this way may the "worse life" may make room for a "better life". In other words, what shall be taken as a "better" form of life is neither decided by authoritarian deed nor established by arbitrary indication of revolutionary enthusiasts. It is instead the objective, immanent result to which the (historical) movement of contradiction may lead when brought to its extreme consequences.[19] This result, however, is never guaranteed. For, the result still belongs to the realm of the "unknown" that lies beyond the process of transformation. And the philosopher, as Hegel states in the preface to the *Phenomenology*, immersed in the process, should attend only to it.

If unforeseeable change, the unrest of transition and the lacerating violence of contradiction are the prevailing dimensions of Hegel's contemporary world and the features that constitute the actuality of the historical present (and not merely contingent aspects of it), then they are also the stumbling-blocks that philosophy encounters in its attempts at a comprehension based on the logic of the understanding and on the formalism of its fixed concepts. Simply put, the present world is not understandable assuming traditional logic and metaphysics as a paradigm of comprehension because this present is contradictory, has no fixed features and, characterized by change, cannot be held fast and pinpointed by any definite concept. Therefore, on Hegel's account, it is also not surprising that in recent years traditional philosophy has yielded either scepticism or various forms of irrationalism and *Schwärmerei*. Common to all these positions is the act of confessed defeat that radically disengages philosophy from an understanding of the world and from active participation in it. Finally, Hegel contends that to the logic of *Verstand* corresponds the "dürre(s) Verstandesleben" (literally, "barren mental life") commonly experienced by the German citizen of his time – a form of life in which man's suffering and his servitude to things are rendered more acute than ever before (GW 5: 17). The need for a new method of comprehension of the real world is also, at the same time, the need for a "better life": the striving toward different conditions of life.

On Hegel's account, the fixed concepts of traditional (and Kantian) logic lay the foundation of what he calls the dead "positive". They categorize and classify a reality that is no longer actual since the movement of life has entirely abandoned it. They present a picture of the world that is indeed reassuring in its clear-cut boundaries and unambiguous classifications. It is, however, the representation of an order that has no relation to the ever-changing real, no bearing on the true needs of life, no possible application to human desires, hopes and changing values, no regard for the lessons of history. To comprehend the world according to a table of categories declared once and for all fixed and complete is indeed like trying to paint a scene from life using only two colours and only two dimensions.[20] Such procedures can yield no knowledge and no truth simply because the complexity of movement, change and transition constituting the life of the real are thereby dispensed with and utterly eliminated. The logic of the understanding engages in the analysis or dissection of what lies in front of it and proceeds by isolating the moments thereby obtained in the attempt to separate truth from falsity, the positive from the negative. To such logic, however, movement and change – the transition that lies between the terms of its dichotomies and blurs its classifications – are in principle unintelligible. For its chief assumption is that truth and falsity (as well as good and evil) must be kept separated, that their contradiction must simply be avoided and left aside. Contradiction, which is the very root of movement, is precisely that from which the fixed order of the understanding takes flight as the worst enemy of an alleged unmovable and unmoved truth.

It is easy to see, at this point, Hegel's need for a new logic that, proposing itself as a logic that has change as its object and takes contradiction as the root of change, allows for a philosophical comprehension of the peculiar predicament of the contemporary world. This logic is dialectic. Dialectic provides a worldview that is based not on fixed classifications but on structured transitions, that does not pursue the determination of objects, subjects, events or (metaphysical) substrates but presents the movement of the process of determination taken in its independence and self-sufficiency (this constitutes the "immanence" of logical development). What kind of transformative process does the logic present? And what does the idea of dialectic as logic of change imply with regard to traditional logic and metaphysics? Hegel addresses these issues both in the preface to the *Phenomenology* and in the introductory writings to his logic: in the *Encyclopaedia* as well as in the *Science of Logic*. In the following section, I shall touch on two points.

II. LOGICAL FORMS OF TRANSFORMATION

First, Hegel presents the chief difference between his speculative-dialectic logic and traditional logic by claiming that the former has the "*movement*" (*Bewegung*) of truth[21] as its object and therefore *is* itself process. The movement of truth can be presented only in and by a narrative that itself displays the form of movement; it can be grasped neither by a determinate concept nor by an intuition nor even by the rigid propositional form of judgement with its unmoved isolation of subject and predicate.[22] Discursivity implies for Hegel processuality. The logical process *is* (identical with) the movement of truth. Truth is not a concluded, fixed object, event or proposition *of which* a concept should be provided; truth is a complex movement of transformation that must be caught and expressed *in fieri* as it were, in its transforming quality and development. This movement *is* the concept of truth. Thus, dialectic logic is both the construction and the presentation of the transformative process of truth. For this reason, contradiction is promoted to the fundamental structure of dialectic. Hegel's contention is that transformation and contradiction are not only basic features of the present world ("our time is a time of birth and transition to a new period"), that is, that which constitutes "the real" (*das Wirkliche*) in its actuality and vital quality (*das in sich Lebende*) (*W* 3: 46); they also provide the defining character of pure thinking to which dialectic logic must attend as its generative centre. "The insight that the nature of thought [*Denken*] itself is dialectic, that thought as understanding must get caught in the negative of itself, in contradiction, constitutes one of the fundamental aspects of logic" (*EL*: §11 Anm). The relation between the two claims – (i) contradiction is the dimension in which the present world is experienced and comprehended in its actuality, and (ii) contradiction constitutes the nature of thought – is established by the further claim that (iii) thinking (*Nachdenken*) effects the "alteration" (*Veränderung*) of whatever it thinks as its content. If thinking discloses the form of truth, it is because thinking itself transforms its content, not because it takes it in an unmoved and fixed isolation (*EL*: §22). And since in the logic the only content of thinking is thinking itself (i.e. "pure" thinking), the logical process is the presentation of thinking's own self-transformative process. Thus, the process of transformation is both the topic of logic, the form displayed by the narrative of Hegel's logic, and that which logical thinking brings about as its immanent effect.

These considerations lead me to suggest that the transformative process staged in its complexity by dialectic logical throughout the spheres of Being, Essence and the Notion shares some essential features with the transformative and indeed self-transformative process of *labour*. Just as the present epoch announced in the preface of the *Phenomenology* sees "spirit" engaged in the hard "labour [*Arbeit*] of its own transformation [*Umgestaltung*]" (*W* 3: 18) – for this is precisely what constitutes the transformative process of historical transition (*Übergang*) – similarly, Hegel's logic is the self-transformative (and thereby also "purifying" or cathartic) process of thinking working on its own potentialities and creating the new conditions for its life in, understanding of and action on the present world. Expressions such as "the labour of reason" (*Arbeit der Vernunft*) or the "labour of the negative" (*Arbeit des Negativen*) often employed by Hegel with reference to dialectic are not metaphors, and should be taken literally (*PR*: §31 Anm.; *W* 3: 23). Set against the immediacy of an (intellectual) intuition that is effortless and provides instantaneous gratification, logical discursivity, for Hegel, is a self-transformative process that implies all the struggles, the hardship and the patience of labour. And this is the case both in the *Phenomenology*, where we follow the labour of consciousness, and in the *Logic* where at stake is the labour of the concept. This suggestion can also account for the uncomfortable and highly problematic image of creation and liberation that Hegel seems to propose at the end of the logic. If the logic is understood as the self-transformative and self-altering process of a "work" of sorts (a somehow "pure" form of labour), we can claim that in and through it logical thinking does indeed create its world as it recreates itself, thereby accomplishing its self-liberation. Such a world is precisely the world of spirit labouring on its transition to a new epoch.

I come now to the second point, which addresses the relation between dialectic and traditional logic and metaphysics, and helps clarify the type of labour that occupies pure logical thinking along the different spheres of Being, Essence and the Notion. Hegel claims that his logic, construed as the new logic that is able to grasp and express in the forms of its own process the transformative movement of the real, implies, in turn, an "alteration of the categories" (*EL*: §9) of traditional logic and metaphysics. Just as the scene of the new world arises out of preceding history as the basis on which transformation takes place, so Hegel's logic follows the logic of the tradition and radically innovates it. More precisely, Hegel's contention is that the relation of succession is a dialectic relation of "refutation" (*Widerlegung*) (W 6: 250).[23]

In the introduction to the *Science of Logic*, Hegel defines its first division, the objective logic, in relation to both traditional metaphysics and Kant's transcendental logic. With regard to the former, Hegel claims that "objective logic" "*replaces* traditional metaphysics" or "ontology"); and with regard to the latter, he observes that objective logic "*corresponds*, in part" to that which for Kant is transcendental logic (W 5: 61, 59, emphasis added). What exactly is the "alteration" of categories that allows Hegel to establish his logic as the *successor* of traditional metaphysics, general logic and transcendental logic? On Hegel's view, what makes past logic inadequate for grasping truth is not so much its alleged formality, its lack of real content. Rather, it is the way in which general logic accounts for and deals with logical forms. In traditional logic, since the logical forms or categories "as fixed determinations fall outside one another and are not held together in organic unity, they are dead forms that do not have in themselves the spirit which alone constitutes their living unity" (W 5: 41). Hegel's critique of traditional logic regards the way in which logical form is handled; it is a critique of the *method* that construes (or rather is unable to construe) logical sequences. Such logic is not only, as we have seen, useless to the comprehension of real *processes* of change; it also renders the presentation of the *unity* of logical process utterly impossible. Hegel indicates the following flaws in the way in which traditional logic treats its forms. First, logical categories are generally taken as fixed determinations: as ahistorical eternal truths or *a priori* abstractions, given to us once and for all. Secondly, they are considered in their separateness as subsisting with no relation to each other, with the consequence that apparently no contradiction is generated, no transition from one to the other is produced and no belonging to the organic unity of a common thinking process is discerned. In addition, despite all the efforts to provide a "deduction" or justification of their necessity and validity, categories of both general and transcendental logic remain merely contingent forms, randomly gathered and included in the presentation. Logical necessity, for Hegel, has to do only with the construction of the process through its internal sequences and immanent successions. The movement by which the logical process generates a successor to a determinate form provides, at the same time, the "immanent deduction" of the successive form. Such deduction is the "genesis" or "genetic exposition"[24] of the determinate form in question. Finally, on Hegel's critique, the categories of formal and transcendental logic are "dead" positive forms: they have the same status as those political and juridical institutions of the *ancien régime* from which life has forever departed. Their consecrated authority is no longer authority over men's lives or a guarantee of meaningfulness in relation to lived practices and cognition. In their dead fixity and unmoved abstract existence, they are nothing but meaningless and useless forms. Hence, in order to claim new meaning to logical form, contradiction and movement (and not merely content, as Kant contended) must be introduced in the philosophical consideration of pure thinking. Contrary to the traditional view, categories should be seen as "moments" of an ongoing, fluid process in which they are bound to modify their meaning, to interact with and contradict one another and finally to constitute the organic unity of a whole. The "spirit" that alone is able to show the living meaningfulness, that is, the "actuality" of logical thinking is the force of contradiction, the dynamism labouring on within the process (W 3: 46).

With regard to traditional metaphysics and to Kant's transcendental philosophy, Hegel presents a similar point. He claims that the new logic develops the forms of a pure determination process in such a way that in it the process – as that which determines or as that in which the dynamic of determination itself is displayed in its pure form – receives complete autonomy from any ontologically fixed substrate, from any empirically assumed thing or event and from any representation or representing subject (W 5: 55, 61). Thus, the task of Hegel's "science of logic" is to think of the process of transformation "in and for itself", that is, to consider it in its utter "purity" and autonomy. Such process, however, is not a given or assumed reality, metaphysical or empirical (W 5: 61; see also W 6: 557). It is instead a construction of thinking, when thought is engaged in the thinking of process taken in its purity (i.e. without substrates). In other words, to think of the development of determination in and for itself logically means to generate such development, to first institute it from a point of absolute indeterminateness ("being, pure being" as *beginning* of advancement; W 5: 82). Hegel's crucial claim is that the only explanation of process and processuality that can claim to be final without requiring a further foundation or justification, without postulating metaphysical or imaginary substrates (objects or subjects) is the explanation that *is* itself the process taken in its developing form – as process *in fieri*. To understand or explain transformation is to perform the transformation in question, to show what transformation is by performing it. Gianbattista Vico's aphorism *"verum et factum convertuntur"* ("the true and the made are interchangeable") is an adequate description of the programme of dialectic logic, of the movement of pure thinking.

Thus, we can conclude that the alteration of traditional categories carried out by dialectic consists in making traditional concepts fluid, in infusing in them the movement of life, in considering the movement of the "concept" as the "soul"[25] animating the logical process and driving it on from within. Thereby, Hegel indicates a fundamental task that logical thinking takes on itself, a task that can be fulfilled only by the process of self-alteration that is the labour of dialectic. In more than one passage, Hegel insists that the crucial transformation introduced by dialectic as logic of change regards the "method" by which the logical sequence is built, and consists in "calling to the life of content the dead limbs of logic through spirit" (W 5: 48). This is, to be sure, a task that Hegel fulfils not only in the first division of the logic, the objective logic. It is instead a procedure that needs to be followed in the subjective logic or "logic of the concept" as well. For the elaboration of the logic of the concept, Hegel contends, dialectic-speculative logic finds in the tradition "a material complete and ready and solidified [*festgewordenes*], one can even say ossified [*verknöchertes*], and the task consists in bringing fluidity [*Flüssigkeit*] into this material, in sparkling the life of the concept into this dead stuff" (W 6: 243). What is new and peculiar in Hegel's subjective logic in relation to the tradition is not the material of logical forms that it presents but the way in which it presents them, that is, the method. And to describe this novelty Hegel appeals, once again, to the opposition between death and life, between the unmoved fixation of a hypostatized *a priori* and the fluidity of process. Hegel's dialectic is the process in which traditional logical forms display the fluidity of movement; is the process by which *transitions* are achieved, forms are generated as *successors* of one another, and their respective meaning is determined by the position they assume within the process.[26]

In the preface to the *Phenomenology* we find a parallel claim regarding the issue of bringing "fluidity" (*Flüssigkeit*) in thinking and in the logical forms that articulate it. The task – or more precisely, as Hegel puts it, *"die Arbeit"* – consists in "realizing the universal and in infusing spirit and life [*begeisten*] in it by overcoming [*Aufheben*] fixed and determinate thoughts" (W 3: 37). The movement by which "thoughts are rendered fluid" is the "movement by which pure thoughts become *concepts*", and this is precisely dialectic as logic of change. Hegel is aware of the difficulty of the task. For one thing, it is far more challenging to spark the principle of life and movement in the ossified limbs of traditional logic than to fancy a new logic from scratch; for another, "it is much more difficult to bring fluidity into fixed thoughts than to sensible existence" (W 3: 37). The task of self-transformation that think-ing encounters in the pure "realm of shadows" (W 5: 55) that is the logic, is harder than any real challenge the world could pose to it. With these claims, Hegel touches on a crucial problem of all historical transitions. Transition, the need of change and the urge of transformation all imply a critical con-frontation (a *Widerlegung*, as it were) with the past, the tradition, the fixa-tion of the "positive". These are not so much undesired "presuppositions" of the transformative process that dialectic institutes as internal requisites and conditions structuring the process in question; they are the very beginning of the process, albeit only the negative side of it. As the "absolute method" of the logic teaches, there is no movement of advancement without a beginning. The beginning, however, is not an external, provisional or merely hypotheti-cal assumption or presupposition to be discarded as thinking moves on into a more secure territory; the beginning is instead that which proceeds driving on the movement of dialectic.

CONCLUSION

The argument of this chapter aimed at establishing the general claim that Hegel's logic is a theory of transformative processes, the thesis that dialectic is itself that self-transformative process that is the "labour" of pure thinking. To this extent, Hegel's logic of change develops in perfect solidarity with the proc-ess of historical transformation experienced by its contemporary world. At this point, however, we are not at the end of our task. First, we need to work out the details of this logic, and secondly we need to bring to light the more precise relationship that this logic entertains with the contemporary world.[27] And yet, with regard to the questions posed at the beginning and concerning the status of Hegel's logic, the following points can be established in conclusion.

Hegel's dialectic logic is not an ontological theory; if it does provide the epistemological paradigm for the understanding of the world, it does so pre-cisely because it is a theory of change with a fundamentally descriptive value. This account of Hegel's logic displays some crucial advantages over read-ings that stress its monistic, holistic or totalizing character and have fuelled so many criticisms of this part of Hegel's philosophy. While the thought of processuality does not exclude the unity/totality of the movement, it brings to the fore the fundamental character of such unity, which is dynamic and does not involve the metaphysical presence of a "substrate" of any kind (be it ontological, representative, empirical).

Finally, a brief conclusion on the most crucial issue of how Hegel's logic speaks to our own contemporary world and its challenges. I think most of us today can subscribe to Hegel's announcement in the preface to the *Phenom-enology*: "It is not difficult to see that our time is a time of birth and transition to a new period" (*W* 3: 18) – or at least we wish it were so (in which case we shall look at the disillusioned Hegel of the *Constitution of Germany*). And I believe most of us can share the feeling of uneasiness toward the uncertain possibilities that lie ahead of us as well as the more or less conscious desire for something new and unknown, which may take us out of the present geopolitical *impasse*. Despite all the "knowledge" that sciences, technologies, media and the most sophisticated information systems constantly provide us with, we still do not *know* (in the sense of the *erkannt*, not the *bekannt*) how to relate to, conceive of and live with the changes and fundamental transformations of our lives, societies, environment and, more generally, our world. Changes are happening and we do not know how to conceptualize them, how to understand them; most of the time we vaguely sense change and we do not know what it is. The information that reaches us is generally fragmented, consisting of isolated or merely juxtaposed pieces.[28] What we lack, however, is not only the unity of a systematic picture. What we are unable to see – and constitutes instead the heart of all the difficulties of our present time – is the transition, the *Übergang* that leads from one event to the other, that connects events into processes of historical development (and does not merely juxtapose them), that allows one to discern within the dynamic of change causes and effects (11 September 2001 is not and is not to be conceived of as an isolated event but is part or moment of a process).[29] Transformation catches us unprepared, not only existentially but philosophically as well. Transformation affects things, people and institutions as well as concepts (the concept of "death", the concept of "marriage" has changed).

In the present time we witness innumerable instances of the "growing contradiction" making life intolerable in many different realms. To mention only one example, a fundamental contradiction lies at the centre of current processes of globalization. Instead of binding the world in a true unity, the generalized mechanisms of economic expansion produce a world that is increasingly fragmented. Simultaneous processes of unification and fragmentation generate a growing contradiction that is visible in many parts of the world and can be felt in many lives. And yet, what seems obvious to common sense is not yet conceptually clear. In this situation the "need" for a logic of change, for a theory able to conceive contradiction and transformation in its fundamental and pure structures, arises anew. If not blocked in its inner development, the growing contradiction may lead to change. We should be ready to learn from Hegel's dialectic as logic of transformative processes.[30]

NOTES

1. For the discussion of the relation between Hegel's logic and metaphysics see H. F. Fulda, "Spekulative Logik als die 'eigentliche Metaphysik' – Zu Hegels Verwand-

lung des neuzeitlichen Metaphysikverständnisses", in *Hegels Transformation der Metaphysik*, D. Pätzhold & A. Vanderjagt (eds), 9–28 (Cologne: Dinter, 1991); for an epistemological reading of the logic see Fulda,"Hegels Logik der Idee und ihrer epistemologische Bedeutung", in *Hegels Erbe*, Ch. Halbig, M. Quante & L. Siep (eds), 78–137 (Frankfurt: Suhrkamp, 2004); for the idea of speculative mystification, consider the traditional critique of Schelling and of Marx discussed in A. Nuzzo, "Existenz 'im Begriff' und Existenz 'außer dem Begriff' – Die Objektivität von Hegels 'subjektiver Logik'", in *Die Wahrheit im Begriff*, A. Fr. Koch (ed.), 171–88 (Paderborn: Schöningh, 2003).

2. See R. R. Williams, *Hegel's Ethics of Recognition* (Berkeley, CA: University of California Press, 1997) esp. chs 1 and 15 for further bibliographical information and the most recent discussion; see also Williams, *Beyond Liberalism and Communitarianism: Studies in Hegel's Philosophy of Right* (Albany, NY: SUNY Press, 2001) and T. Nenon (ed.), *The Contemporary Relevance of Hegel's Philosophy of Right*, Supplement 39, *Southern Journal of Philosophy* (2001).

3. Transformative process is often taken as the same as change, movement, transition, development; it implies, however, a moment of "bringing to consciousness" (*zum Bewußtsein bringen*), an act of cognition and recognition. In addition, speaking of transformative process, I also indicate a moment of self-transformation (see below). To specify the different meaning of terms such as change, transition, development and so on would require the discussion of how transformative processes are differently shaped in the logic of Being, Essence and the Notion. This chapter provides the background for such research.

4. I shall return to this point briefly in my conclusion. I shall not address the issue of the ontological versus epistemological status of the logic *directly*. My aim here is to offer an account that is not necessarily exclusive of the others mentioned above but only more fundamental (in the sense of aiming at the root of the idea of the logic) and also more fruitful for our contemporary philosophizing.

5. Important work has been done in this area, and the following considerations take this work into account. See in particular the fundamental text, M. Baum, *Die Entstehung der Hegelschen Dialektik* (Bonn: Bouvier, 1986).

6. And the logic *is* this very movement; see below.

7. I use the fragment "Der immer sich vergrössernde Widerspruch …, [The ever-growing contadiction, …]" in *GW* 5: 16–18, as paradigmatic example. For information on the period of its composition and its editorial history, see the remarks by Baum and Meist in the editorial commentary in *GW* 5.

8. See Hegel's expression in the opening address at the University of Berlin, 22 October 1818: "Mut der Wahrheit" (*W* 10: 403), which comes up again in the preface to the 1827 edition of the *Encyclopaedia* (*W* 8: 13).

9. See Hegel's early considerations on the notion of "the need for philosophy" in the *Differenzschrift* (*W* 2: 20ff.): the need for philosophy refers on the one hand to the "fragmented harmony" (*zerrissene Harmonie*) and on the other to the "diremption" (*Entzweiung*) in which spirit lives.

10. Philosophy is, of course, "its time grasped in thought" (*W* 7: 26).

11. Why not art, religion, philosophy of spirit or history? As a matter of fact, neither Fichte nor Schelling sees the development of logic as a fundamental task of their philosophy. They invest other philosophical disciplines with the task of comprehending and expressing truth.

12. For Hegel's reference to Kant's transcendental logic, see *W* 5: 59.

13. See also the "Anstrengung und Bemühung" (*W* 3: 19). Translations throughout are the author's.

14. See the claim that "generally, the familiar, because it is familiar [*bekannt*] is nor understood [*erkannt*]" (*W* 3: 35).

15. In the *Phenomenology* Hegel offers an "example" of the logical method "on a more concrete object, namely, consciousness" (*W* 3: 49).

16. See this sentence from the first draft of the preface, which was cancelled from the final version: "The following pages are the voice of a mind that regretfully takes leave from the hope that Germany be lifted from its state of insignificance" (*W* 1: 452 n. 2).

17. This observation is supported by C. Cesa, "Introduzione", *Hegel: Scritti politici (1798–1831)* (Turin: Einaudi, 1972), xxii.

18. See also the "Unbekannte(s)" (*W* 3: 18).

19. To this extent, one could conclude that "better" means only "successive"; and this minimal sense is also the sense in which I take this claim at the present stage of the argument. This point is further developed below: with regard to that "pure" transformative process that is the logic, "better" is the moment that is more encompassing, more complex, richer in possibilities, that can solve the problems that a previous formation could not solve.

20. See Hegel's attacks on the "tabulating understanding" and its "monotonous formalism" in the preface to the *Phenomenology* (*W* 3: 50). Following this Hegelian account, one could argue that Kant himself has seen this problem and attempted to solve it with the theory of the reflective faculty of judgement in the third *Critique*. It is no accident that Kant indicates the specific function of teleological judgement to be that of providing an explanation of organic processes such as growth. Hegel's dialectic is the alternative to Kant's logic of the reflective faculty of judgement.

21. "Die Wahrheit ist die Bewegung ihrer an ihr selbst" (truth is its own movement taking place in itself) (*W* 3: 47). Which means there is no other truth than the movement of truth, than the movement in which truth establishes itself; hence: there is no other truth but the movement itself.

22. The famous doctrine of the "speculative proposition" is precisely the claim that unless the proposition is taken as leading to a movement in which more than one judgement is generated and a thinking process is engaged, the propositional form fails to capture the truth; see *W* 3: 59–61, 57, where Hegel opposes the view of the "*Begriff*" as "*das Werden*" of the object to the metaphysical fixation of unmoved accidents in a "subject at rest". *Begriff* is, for Hegel, "*Bewegung*" (*W* 3: 37).

23. See also the occurrence of "*Widerlegung*" in the fragment of the *Constitution of Germany* discussed above.

24. See for example *W* 3: 37–8 for "necessity", and *W* 6: 252, 245 for the "immanent deduction" of the the Notion from development of the sphere of Essence.

25. The expression "soul" is used by Hegel throughout the *Logic*; see in particular *W* 6: 551, 557 with regard to the method.

26. See A. Nuzzo, *Logica e sistema: Sull'idea hegeliana di filosofia* (Genoa: Pantograf, 1992) and "The Language of Hegel's Speculative Philosophy", in *Hegel and Language*, J. P. Surber (ed.) (Albany, NY: SUNY Press, forthcoming).

27. These two objectives occupy my forthcoming *The Actuality of Hegel's Logic*. With regard to the latter objective, however, this much should be clear from the preceding argument: to pose the problem in terms of the claim that logical process "presupposes"

real processes is to miss the point and to misunderstand the function attributed by Hegel to dialectic.

28. Is it indifferent how we come to juxtapose the many pieces? How many different versions are there of such juxtapositions?

29. I have "applied" Hegel's logic of change to the interpretation of 11 September 2001 in "Reasons for Conflict – Political Implications of a Definition of Terrorism", in *The Philosophical Challenges of September 11*, T. Rockmore, J. Margolis, A. T. Marsoobian (eds), 125–38 (Oxford: Blackwell, 2005).

30. Research for this chapter has been supported by an Alexander von Humboldt Fellowship (2005) and by a Brooklyn College Scholar Incentive Award (2005).

CHAPTER SIX

HEGEL, ETHICS AND THE LOGIC OF UNIVERSALITY
Kimberly Hutchings

It is famously difficult to understand the argument of Hegel's *Science of Logic*.[1] This difficulty is attested to by Hegel himself in the opening passages of the *Logic*, in which he draws an analogy between studying logic (the determinations of thought) in isolation from the sciences of nature and spirit, and studying grammar in isolation from knowledge of actual languages. Hegel suggests that just as the "substantial, living value" of grammar becomes evident when it is studied by those already linguistically competent across different natural languages, so the "substantial, living value" of logic will be evident to those already knowledgeable about (experienced in) the realms of nature and spirit (*L*: 57). This does not mean that logic cannot be grasped in and of itself, but Hegel suggests that any such grasp will be necessarily impoverished:

> At first, therefore, logic must indeed be learned as something which one understands and sees into quite well but in which, at the beginning, one feels the lack of scope and depth and a wider significance. It is only after profounder acquaintance with the other sciences that logic ceases to be for subjective spirit a merely abstract universal and reveals itself as the universal which embraces within itself the wealth of the particular. (*L*: 58)

Having said this, however, in seeming contradiction Hegel goes on to defend the study of logic as such as the ideal route for the education of consciousness into the power of thought itself, "remote from sensuous intuitions and aims, from feelings, from the imagined world of figurate conception" (*L*: 59). What, then, are we to make of this paradox? On the one hand, we can make sense of logic fully only in the light of knowledge of nature and spirit, and on the other, we can make sense of nature and spirit fully only in the light of knowledge of logic. But of course the paradox for Hegel is only a paradox in so far as we stick to the operations of formal thought. In formal thought opposition and contradiction are understood as mechanisms through which lack at the level of either being or consciousness is revealed, and the distinction between the subjective consciousness of the knower and objective domain of the object of knowledge is assumed to be fixed. Formal thought takes negation as a point of rest (a result), in which a particular actual or potential claim is settled; in contrast, speculative, dialectical thought identifies the negative as a principle of movement in which new possibilities are posited (including the possibility of a perspective other than that of subjective consciousness). From the formal point of view, it cannot be the case both that logic conditions the comprehension of nature and spirit and that nature and spirit condition the comprehension of logic: one element has to be origin, ground or condition. But for speculative, dialectical thought it is not the two "extremes" of the paradox but the thought of the copula "and" or "is", in other words the thought of their *relation*, that provides the key to Hegel's meaning.[2]

In the *Logic* as a whole, the reader is constantly taken through a movement of thought in which the encounter with contradiction yields an alternative direction for thought. Invariably this alternative neither embraces one or other sides of the contradiction as true, nor takes the contradiction as indicative of the inadequacies of thought; instead it offers a new synthesis. For the reader, the constant repetition of a pattern in which distinctions are drawn and then collapse to be redrawn in another form can seem exhausting and pointless. But there is more going on in the *Logic* than simply repetition. At the heart of Hegel's rethinking of thought is the putting into question of the ultimate distinction on which the idea of a logic has traditionally rested. This is the distinction between content and form, in which it is assumed that the forms of thought can be understood in abstraction from their content. But what Hegel demonstrates over and over again in his *Logic* is that the forms of thought cannot be indifferent to their content, and that the dialectical relation between content and form within thought puts into question the fixity of the distinction between logic and the other philosophical sciences of nature and spirit, and ultimately between "thinking", "being" and "doing".[3] If one thinks in this way about the interrelation of the different moments of Hegel's system, then it becomes clear both why reading the *Logic* in isolation is extraordinarily difficult, and why the way in which the argument of the *Logic* reconnects with the arguments worked through in Hegel's other texts is not self-evident. Even if one does manage to demonstrate how Hegel's arguments about logic and other aspects of his system are mutually illuminating, still there is never a neat resolution to the meaning of the copula, the "is" or "and" that binds together logic and nature or logic and spirit. It is certainly not a relation of subsumption in any direction. The logic of relation, which is ultimately what Hegel's logic is about, is always unfinished, a matter of relative rather than absolute identity, which simultaneously speaks to the necessity and the inadequacy of the determinations of thought.[4]

The sciences of logic, nature and spirit relate as links in a circular chain, in which there is no evident origin or ground (L: 842). The idea of a self-differentiating, self-mediating totality is the Absolute Idea in which the *Logic* culminates, but the ideas of "life" and "absolute cognition", endpoints of the sciences of nature and spirit respectively, are also self-differentiating, self-mediating totalities (L: 761–844; and see *EM*: §§572–7; *PhG*: 478–93). To return to the analogy with grammar and language introduced above, like different languages, the sciences of logic, nature and spirit are different but also the same. And as with the different languages, there is no meta-language that provides the external reference point for translation; the sameness and difference of the realms of thought, nature and spirit is worked out through trial and error (*Bildung*).[5]

I want to try to demonstrate the value of Hegel's argument in the *Logic* by focusing on his exploration of the logic of universality, particularity and singularity in judgement (L: 623–63). This logical exposition is illuminated and substantiated through an examination of Hegel's immanent critique of the "moral point of view" and the "beautiful soul" in the *Phenomenology* (*PhG*: 364–409). Hegel's analyses in the *Logic* and the *Phenomenology* provide resources to address the impasses inherent in the ways in which "universality" (and therefore also "particularity" and "singularity") figure in debates in contemporary moral theory. For a Hegelian ethics, universality, particularity and singularity can only be understood as mutually contaminating categories, and this necessarily problematizes any claim to settle definitively the conditions of possibility, or the truth, of moral judgement. I conclude that Judith Butler's rethinking of the ethical universal as the ongoing "difficult labor of cultural translation" (Butler *et al.* 2000: 178), provides an example of what it might mean to think about moral judgement in Hegelian terms.

I. THE LOGIC OF JUDGEMENT

In the third part of the *Logic*, Hegel moves from examining categories of thought that seek to capture the meaning of being as such (in "Doctrine of Being") and of being understood as internally differentiated between essence and appearance (in "Doctrine of Essence"), to the task of examining the categories through which thought conceptualizes itself as thought, as opposed to thought of something conceptualized as other than thought, being or essence/appearance (L: 575–844). According to Hegel, the earlier stages of his logic are inadequate in so far as they cannot be fully understood without being seen in the context of thought's comprehension of its own operations, through which categories discussed in the first two parts of the *Logic* are mobilized. "The Subjective Logic or Doctrine of the Concept" seeks to comprehend and to demonstrate thought's own operations as thought. In the first three chapters of this section of the *Logic*, Hegel's focus is on "subjectivity", that is on the meaning of conceptualization from the point of view of the thinking subject. The chapters deal with "concept", "judgement" and "syllogism", respectively. In all three of these chapters, the operations of thought are grasped as the interplay of moments of "universality", "particularity" and "singularity". And in each chapter, Hegel repeats similar moves in his argument at an ever greater level of complexity to demonstrate the fundamental error of comprehending these categories as definable and usable as mutually exclusive ideas: "Only *mere representational thinking* for which abstraction has isolated them, is capable of holding the universal, particular and individual [*Einzelne*] rigidly apart; in this way they can be counted" (*L*: 620). Hegel's greatest scorn is reserved for ways of thinking that identify universal, particular and singular with quantities, in which universal figures as "all", particular as "some" and singular as "one". To comprehend the difference between these determinations as a matter of extent, Hegel argues, is to misunderstand what the categories mean and how they are used.

Hegel's critique of quantitative thinking about universality, particularity and singularity is exemplified in his analysis of judgement in the second chapter. He introduces judgement, as opposed to any proposition in general, as a proposition that "requires the predicate to be related to the subject as one Notion [*Begriff*] determination to another, and therefore as a universal to a particular or individual [*Einzelnen*]" (*L*: 626). In other words, judgement involves claims about necessary connections between subject and predicate. He then goes on to examine different forms of judgement and the ways in which they put universality, particularity and singularity in relation to one another. An examination of Hegel's argument about the ways in which reflective judgements imply judgements of necessity, which in turn imply conceptual judgements, helps to explain Hegel's meaning.

In reflective judgements claims are made about how specific entities share in particular attributes. For example: "this man is mortal"; "some men are mortal"; "all men are mortal". Such judgements, as Hegel puts it "express an essential determination, but one which is in a *relationship* or is a *unifying* universality" (*L*: 643). However, in each case the judgement raises the question of its own ground – what is the meaning of "this", "some" and "all" as subjects and in what sense does the predicate inhere in the subject? The third judgement, the judgement of "all", may seem to make sense of the previous two, since it appears to incorporate both singular and particular within it, but how is "allness" to be understood? Hegel suggests that there are two ways of reading the "all" judgement. One is as an outcome of singular and particular judgements, the other is as their presupposition. When read as an outcome, the judgement of "all" falls into the familiar problem of induction, in which the establishment of empirical universals "rests on the tacit agreement that if only no contrary *instance* can be adduced, the *plurality* of cases shall count as *allness*" (*L*: 648). Here we find both that the universal depends on singular and particular, but also that this calls its own universality into question as a matter of principle. If the universal judgement of reflection is read as presupposition rather than outcome, then it pushes thought into reflecting on how "allness" as a starting-point is to be understood. It might be thought of, for instance, as a "common property" that is shared by all the entities under consideration. But if one is not to fall back into the problem of induction, then it needs to be more than this: not a statement of common property shared by separate entities, but an organizing principle, in which the predicate inheres in the subject as a matter of necessity. Here, Hegel argues, we move from the universal as "allness" to the universal as "genus" and its differentiation into "species". This is a different mode of configuring the relation between universal, particular and singular: the judgement of necessity (L: 648–50).

In the judgement of necessity, particular and singular are essentially connected to the universal by their nature, but it also follows that the universal is part and parcel of the particular and singular and cannot be understood in distinction from them. Hegel notes that in the judgement of necessity the dynamic of judgement effectively switches: instead of the ground of judgement being in the predicate, it is in the subject (L: 649). However, the judgement of necessity, according to Hegel, does not itself articulate the ground on which its claims as to the relation of genus to species are made. The two categories bleed into one another, yet are distinct. In what sense are we to understand the identity and difference between genus and species? And what does this tell us about the universal, particular and singular in the operations of judgement? In order to address the relations of universality, particularity and singularity in the judgement of necessity, Hegel argues that we have to examine the ways in which necessary connection between universal, particular and singular are conceivable by the thinking subject (the "judgement of the concept"). In other words, we have to focus on how the grounds of judgement are themselves judged. Hegel argues that this is not a withdrawal into "something merely *subjective*" (L: 658): "the predicates *good, bad, true, beautiful, correct*, etc. express that the thing is *measured* against its universal Notion [*Begriff*] as the simply presupposed *ought to be* and is, or is not, in *agreement* with it" (L: 657–8).

Hegel goes on to examine the "judgement of the concept" in the forms of *assertoric, problematic* and *apodeictic* judgements. Within these judgements, the question of how to justify the claim to a relation between subject and predicate in judgement is central. In these judgements he examines the inadequacy of judgements that, in judging, keep the criteria of judgement in abstraction from the matter of judgement, that is, the *combination* of the singular (subject) and the universal (predicate). In the assertoric judgement, claims such as "X is good" are rendered arbitrary by the subjectivity of the criteria through which the meaning of "good" is established. These subjectively located criteria do the work of an external "third party" judge, which "assures" the truth of the judgement, but can easily be countered by claims to an alternative set of criteria, which are equally assured by a different judge (*L*: 659–60). The assertoric judgement leaves the uncertainty of the ground of judgement in place. That is, it does not resolve the question of whether the singular (X) is good or not. In the problematic judgement, the problematic status of the singular is the focus of attention. In this case, a difficulty arises in relation to the subject (singular) and its double signification as what it is (contingent entity) and what it ought to be (the criteria by which it is defined, it constitution). This double signification suggests that the subject is both opposed to and identical with the predicate (the universal). It is only in apodeictic judgement that judgement moves forwards through the explicit articulation of its ground in the substantive identity of the subject and predicate in claims such as "the house constituted so and so is *good*, the action constituted so and so is *right*" (*L*: 661). According to Hegel, in the apodeictic judgement we can see how the "extremes" of the judgement (singular/universal) meet, not in the subsumption of "is" (singular or particular) under "ought" (universal) but in their correspondence (*L*: 662):

> If we examine the positive element of this result which effects the transition of the judgment into another form, we find, as we have seen, that subject and predicate in the apodeictic judgment are each the whole Notion [*Begriff*]. The *unity* of the Notion as the *determinateness* constituting the copula that relates them, is at the same time *distinct* from them. At first it stands only on the other side of the subject as the latter's *immediate constitution*. But since it is essentially that which *relates* subject and predicate, it is not merely such immediate constitution but the *universal* that *permeates* both subject and predicate. While subject and predicate have the same *content*, the *form relation* on the other hand, is posited through this determinateness, *determinateness as a universal or particularity*. (*L*: 663)

By the end of the chapter on judgement, Hegel claims that he has demonstrated that the identity posited by the terms of judgement (subject, copula, predicate), needs to be read as a dynamic relationality, which works through and within the "extremes". This means that universality, particularity and singularity each, as it were, contain and mediate each other as categories. Formally, however, as long as thought operates in terms of judgement, it necessarily freezes the distinction between universality and particularity in general. For this reason, Hegel argues that the syllogism, in which the relation between the universality, particularity and singularity can be expressed much more flexibly, is a more adequate way of demonstrating the logic of thought. In the syllogism, each of the terms, universal, particular and singular, can operate as the "extremes" or as the mediating term, and Hegel goes on in his chapter on "The Syllogism" to retrace the ground of judgement and show

how the meaning of the copula becomes clearer when its own status is articu-lated explicitly as a middle term in a process of reasoning, a determination of thought in its own right. In the end, even apodeictic judgement fails as long as it sticks to the form of judgement and therefore blocks the comprehension of the relation between its extremes (*L*: 664–704).

The concerns of Hegel's *Logic* are not, therefore, confined to an attempt to formalize the categories and operations of thought in argumentation in order to establish criteria to distinguish between valid and invalid inference. Instead, Hegel's project is to provide a phenomenology of thought in which the categories and operations of thought and their implications are traced rather than judged.[6] Throughout the *Logic*, this tracing of the implication of modes of thought puts into question the fixity of distinctions between categories or operations of thought. Typically, the putting into question of distinctions is accomplished in two ways. First, Hegel demonstrates that keep-ing distinctions fixed paralyses thought in significant ways. In the discussion of "universality" explored above, one example of this is how the judgement of reflection's identification of universality with "allness" stops thought in its tracks as long as "allness" is thought of both as universality (in opposi-tion to particularity) and as an empirical universal, in which case "allness" becomes identified with particularity and falls into contradiction. Secondly, Hegel demonstrates that to get beyond the stalling of thought, categories have to be rethought in a way that problematizes distinctions drawn in abstraction and focuses on the connection rather than the distinction between the catego-ries in question. We see this, for instance, in the move from the judgement of reflection to the judgement of necessity, where the nature of the connection between subject and predicate in judgement becomes central to the meaning of both subject and predicate. We also see it in the judgement of the concept, as it shifts from grounding judgement in the third party of subjective con-sciousness to grounding judgement in the singular and its double signification as both what it is and what it ought-to-be.

The upshot of Hegel's discussion of judgement and his later discussions of "syllogism", "objectivity", "life" and "cognition" in the latter part of the *Logic* is to cast doubt on the conceptual distinctions through which we keep subject and predicate, form and content, subjective and objective apart in thought. The price we pay for the loss of the certainties of abstraction is the migration of thought outside itself. The *Logic* culminates in the problem of how to follow the implications of thought within thought without spilling over into the realms of being and doing with which thought both is and is not identical. Puzzlingly, Hegel leaves the *Logic* caught forever in this paradox: on the one hand, presenting it as a self-determining, self-contained process that derives its end from its beginning and its beginning from its end, and in which one need not refer to anything outside thought in order to grasp it; on the other hand, asserting a relation (which is not a relation of identity or subsumption) between the logic (the science of thought) and the sciences of spirit and nature (*L*: 842–4). The lesson of the *Logic* is that the copula "is" is a two-way street. To the extent that the thought of thought is also the thought of being and doing, so being and doing are the being and doing of thought, its entanglement with nature and spirit. I want to go on to argue that understandings of ethical universality that are premised on the denial of this mutual contamination paralyse thought precisely because they remain limited to judgement, but that a category of universality that recognizes the limitations of judgement might still be useful in ethics.

II. THE MORAL POINT OF VIEW AND THE BEAUTIFUL SOUL

In "The Spirit of Christianity and Its Fate", Hegel explores the differences and tensions between contrasting modes of ethics under the terms "law" and "love" (*ET*: 182–301). He fleshes out the meanings of these alternative ethics by invoking the historical context of the time of Christ and associating "law" with Judaism and Roman rule (the religion of law and the commandment of the state) and "love" with the ethos taught by Jesus. According to Hegel, the logic or ethos of legality relies on the positing of a split between universal command-ment and particular act that is incapable of mediation. He explains this through the example of the relation between the law and the act of a transgressor within the framework of legalism. A crime is a particular act that contradicts the uni-versal law. Judgement is the means by which a resolution of the contradiction between the universal (law) and the particular (crime) is sought. However, in practice Hegel argues that judgement, whether of innocence or guilt, confirms universal law and particular act in their separate existences. The unification of law is purely external, freezing the particular into subordination to the uni-versal, but failing to reconcile them to one another (*ET*: 226–7). In contrast to legalism, the message of "love" resists judgement and the distinction between universal and particular on which it rests:

> Judgment is not an act of the divine, for the law, which is in the judge, is the universal opposed to the man who is to be judged, and judgment (in law) is a judgment (in logic), an assertion of likeness or unlikeness, the recognition of a conceptual unity or an irreconcilable opposition. The son of God does not judge, sunder, or divide, does not hold to an opposite in its opposition. An utter-ance, or the stirring of the divine is no lawgiving or legislation, no upholding of the mastery of the law. (*ET*: 262)

This quotation suggests that "love" counters (and perhaps conquers) "law" through the singularity of Jesus as the exemplary "beautiful soul" overrid-ing distinctions between universality and particularity. However, Hegel's argument develops in a different direction. The essay chronicles the incapacity of "law" to deal with "love", but equally that of "love" to deal with "law". At the end of the essay Jesus emerges as one who passively allows the fate of his nation to remain unassailed, a beautiful soul fleeing from rather than engaging with law, and therefore, like law, accepting a diremption of the terms of ethical life. But in the case of "love", the impossibility of reconciliation between universal and particular becomes the impossibility of reconciliation between this world and the next and therefore the decision to "render unto Caesar" (*ET*: 283).

The critique of legalism and love in Hegel's early work prefigures the much more thoroughly worked-out story of contemporary ethical thought that he tells in the *Phenomenology*. It also clearly prefigures the analysis of the categories of universality, particularity and singularity given in the *Logic*. Here, even if only in outline, we can already see how in Hegel's work arguments from logic are treated as illuminating, but also as embedded in, ethical ideas and their relation to ethical practice (the realm of spirit). In the *Phenomenology*, Hegel revisits his critiques of the figures of the "slave of law" and the "beautiful soul", but this time within the context of Kantian and post-Kantian moral theory (*PhG*: 364–409).[7] An examination of his argument casts light on both the inadequacies of particular kinds of moral thought and the understanding of categories of universality, particularity and singularity that underpin them. As I argued elsewhere (Hutchings 2003: 123), Hegel's central claim about the "moral point of view" in the *Phenomenology* is that it is self-undermining. In other words, in thinking within the terms of the moral point of view, the terms of that thinking are themselves revealed to be unsustainable. We can see this with regard both to the Kantian moral point of view, in which morality is grounded in universal reason (the universalizability of will) and in the figure of the beautiful soul, the purity of conscience of the Romantic moral subject. In the former case, moral thinking is grounded in the universal, in the latter case, it is grounded in the singular; but Hegel argues that in neither case can universality or singularity be understood consistently in the sense that is required by the moral point of view, that is to say as pure, self-subsistent categories.

Hegel reads Kant's moral philosophy as premised on the autonomy of the moral will (pure practical reason, *Wille*) in contradistinction to the heteronomy of the will influenced by natural, sensuous determination (*Willkür*). The universality inherent in moral principle is a consequence of the detachment of moral reason from nature and spirit, the realm of particularity. It is precisely because *anyone* would recognize that X or Y (for instance, telling the truth or keeping promises) is right that the moral actor can be sure that X or Y is right. The moral act, therefore, is understood as a singular event (this truth-telling or promise-keeping), or particular events (truth-tellings, promise keepings), that are subsumed under the universal and thereby detached from particularity in general (*PhG*: 379). As with Hegel's analysis of legalism in the "Spirit of Christianity", he understands the aim of moral reason to be to bring particular acts under the rule of universality, effectively wiping out their status as particular (they become instances of the universal). Moral judgement, therefore, is a matter of judging whether these acts or this act can be subsumed under the universal or not. For Hegel, this way of thinking about moral judgement raises problems of both the content and form of how the singular act or particular acts are related to the universal. The type of judgement is clearly that of the "judgement of the concept", in which acts or entities are evaluated according to universal criteria. So the first question to be raised is about how the universal is held to inhere in the singular/particular on this account of moral judgement. Is it through a "third party", which provides external criteria to bridge the gap between universal and singular/particular, as with the assertoric judgement? Is it the singular act itself that provides the bridge between universal and particular, as with the problematic judgement? And does the analysis enable shifting into apodeictic judgement, in which articulating the meaning of the copula of judgement becomes the explicit focus of attention?

Much of Hegel's critique of Kant's account of moral judgement can be understood as focused on the "content" of the copula. The argument he repeatedly makes is that the "purity" of the universal does not stand on examination of what is actually involved in Kant's account, from the insertion of concrete details into the process of universalization to the embodied and encultured (naturally and spiritually contaminated) nature of action in the world. For Hegel, Kant's argument is inadequate in so far as it does not provide the resources by which to think the interconnection of particular and universal in the singular act, which is required by Kant's own reasoning (*PhG*: 383). Ultimately, this is because of the absoluteness of the distinction between rational and natural determination in Kant's thought. In this context, Hegel argues that morality becomes a perpetual striving towards an ought-to-be, which is out of reach because it seeks to abolish the diremptions that it nevertheless requires. In effect, the apodeictic judgement becomes unintelligible in its own terms, because the universal predicate cannot be understood as connected to the subject (this act/these acts) in anything other than formal terms. Even at the level of form, however, the perpetual ought remains captured by the terms of judgement, in which universality presents itself as a determination of thought distinct and indifferent to particularity. The same message of perpetual striving is present in the form of Kantian moral judgement as well as its content.

Still engaging with the "moral point of view", Hegel moves on in the *Phenomenology* to examine an alternative account of moral reasoning, which was part of the Romantic reaction to the formalism and legalism of Kant's moral theory. According to this view, rather than being located in universal moral law, the possibility of moral judgement is grounded in conscience and purity of heart (*PhG*: 383–409). This way of thinking about morality is presented through the figure of the "beautiful soul". Although this figure is no longer identified explicitly with Jesus, there are strong echoes of Hegel's earlier argument in how the "beautiful soul" in a modern context counters the tyranny of legalism in judgement with the power of love. The beautiful soul is the romantic hero/heroine who exemplifies the perfection of moral subjectivity (the inner certainty of what it right). As such, the beautiful soul is a singularity that posits itself as the ground of connection between universality and particularity, shifting the ground of judgment from predicate to subject (*PhG*: 406–7). Although the beautiful soul, like "love" in the message of Jesus, emerges as a counter to legalism in ethics, Hegel goes on to argue that the logic of Kantian moral thinking is ultimately replicated rather than refuted from the point of view of the beautiful soul. His argument echoes his earlier case against Jesus in the "Spirit of Christianity". For the beautiful soul it is the twin distinctions between spirit and nature and between identity and difference that underpin the authority of her moral voice. The disembodied purity of the "inner self" of the beautiful soul identifies moral authority with disengagement from nature (sensuous determination), but also with a power located in an understanding of spirit as pure individuated self-legislation, disconnected from both spiritual and natural aspects of the world. In contrast to Kantian moral thought, with the beautiful soul the moral law is located within the exemplary moral subject, it is not rationally, externally accessible or knowable, and its authority derives from its singular source rather than its universal significance. Yet, Hegel argues, if we examine the content and form of this moral judgement in which the positions of singular and universal in the judgement of the moral point of view are reversed, we nevertheless find the same impossibility of grasping the interconnection between the moments of judgement except as the abolition of the terms in which it is grounded. Hegel sets out to show that there are in effect two options open to the beautiful soul, in its own terms, both of which effectively undermine her moral authority. One option is for the beautiful soul to exercise moral authority, agency and judgement. But if this option is followed, the purity and detachment of the beautiful soul immediately become compromised and mired in particularity. The other option is to withdraw into the ethereality of moral perfection, in which the beautiful soul dwells directly in the universal, and therefore also dies on Hegel's account (*PhG*: 407).[8] The option of withdrawal undermines the singularity of the beautiful soul as a bridge between universality and particularity just as much as the intervention of the beautiful soul in the world undermines it. Her fate, like that of Jesus, is that universality is held only at the expense of particularity or vice versa and, as with Jesus, Hegel suggests, the beautiful soul in its other-worldliness leaves the world as it is. This is a different story to the story of Kantian morality, but the logic of judgement, where the limitations of judgement in both content and form are not acknowledged, is at the heart of Hegel's critique in both cases.

III. TOWARDS MORAL THEORY BEYOND JUDGEMENT

The critique Hegel makes of the moral point of view and of the beautiful soul remains highly relevant to contemporary debates in ethics, where the question of how to think the meaning of, and relation between, universality, particularity and singularity is hotly contested.[9] To put Hegel's logic to work in a contemporary context, I shall move on in this section to consider three forms of moral thinking that exemplify different logics of judgement (in Hegel's sense) and show how Hegel's argument can be useful in criticizing and transforming how we think about ethics. The three forms of moral thinking are: *moral universalism*, which would include the substantive "human nature" universalisms of Aristotelianism or utilitarianism, but also procedural universalisms of a Kantian type;[10] *moral particularism*, as exemplified in versions of communitarianism in which morality is held to be relative to culture;[11] and *moral singularism*, as we find it at work in exemplary ethics, such as the feminist ethic of care and the idea of a "different voice".[12] Because of limitations of space, this discussion is necessarily somewhat schematic and focuses solely on the ways in which each of these approaches to moral theory requires the relation between the universal, particular and singular to be thought, and what the implications of those requirements are for the possibility of judgement.

Moral universalism rests on claims about the interconnection between particular attributes or acts of moral agents and a universal that either takes the form of a substantive, universally present quality (such as the human desire for happiness in utilitarianism), a universal essence that defines humanity (such as an Aristotelian account of the good life), or a universal principle, which is embedded in a universally valid procedure (as in Kantian or Habermasian moral theory). In all cases it is the universal that does the work in ethical judgement. An act or attribute is morally right or wrong in so far as it does or does not fit with or further the universal in question (happiness, human flourishing, the moral law). A Hegelian response to this way of thinking about moral judgement is to raise three sets of questions: what is the content and form of the universal? What is the content and form of the singular act? What is the content and form of the relation between universal, particular and singular in any given moral judgement of this kind? Even at the most abstract level, without a specific set of examples in mind, it is clear that these questions open up debate about the ground of judgements of the form "X is good"; "X is a good man"; "X acted rightly". The question of the content and form of the universal is the question of its empirical or formal status and how that is grounded, but also a question about how the universal is thought in its formal relation to singularity or particularity in the kinds of judgement to which specific moral universalisms give rise. In terms of content, is this a universal of "allness" as in the judgement of reflection? If it is, then it becomes caught in a problem of induction, and therefore becomes formally indistinguishable from particularity. If, alternatively, this is a universal of "genus", as in the judgement of necessity, then the universal is posited as necessarily embedded in the essence of the particular. The question then becomes how to distinguish between what is universal in the particular and particular in the universal. If the universal is an "ought to be", as in the judgement of the concept, then what are the criteria through which the relation between "is" and "ought-to-be" is to be judged? Is this relation inherent in an external set of criteria, is it inherent in the universal as a principle, or is it inherent in the subject of judgement, the singular act itself? On any of these readings, how is the singular able to participate in the universal? This question takes us back to the grounding of procedure or to the conditions of possibility of the act itself.

If we unpack these questions in the context of specific moral theories and moral judgements, we find ourselves traversing very familiar ground in debates within ethical theory. For instance, it is commonly argued by deontological thinkers that there is a problem with utilitarianism's version of the moral universal, in that it becomes a matter of "counting". The universal of "allness" collapses into the universal of "some", the "majority" rather than all. Similarly, a familiar criticism of Aristotelian accounts of the moral universal as "genus" is that it is unable to account for the claims it makes as to what counts as "genus" and what as "species", and therefore presents culturally specific virtues or attributes as generic. Yet again, a very common critique of proceduralist universalisms is that when the meaning of the universal is investigated, it turns out to be contaminated with particularity. In one sense, then, it can be argued that Hegel's account of the logic of judgement tells us nothing new: it simply traces familiar pitfalls of thinking about moral claims in certain kinds of ways. However, I would argue that Hegel is doing more than presenting us with ways of criticizing different moral perspectives in isolation. Rather, he is persistently making the point that in relation to both content and form, moral universalisms, simply in following though their own logic, are not able to sustain their own terms of judgement. The fundamental implication, for Hegel, is that those terms of judgement themselves are unstable and therefore unable to carry the weight of judgement that is assigned to them. The bearer of judgement, in this case purportedly the universal, turns out to be a restless, perpetual motion between the universal and its others.

Over the past twenty years the predominant understanding, within the Western academy, of moral thinking as inherently universalist has been challenged from a variety of directions. The most influential of these challenges has been the rise of a version of moral particularism in which the cultural relativity of morality is the crucial claim. According to communitarianism, morality is grounded in the particularity of culture (of which there is a plurality), and it is this particularity that should be seen as doing the work in moral judgement. X as the singular act or agent is good or bad, right or wrong in terms of X's identity or lack of identity with the particularity of the culture of which X is a part. In contrast to moral universalisms, in which the aim is to, as it were, assert control of the universal over the particular and singular, moral particularism seeks to banish the universal altogether and absorb particular and singular into another particular. Once again, the Hegelian response to this form of moral particularism would be to raise questions about the content and form of the "extremes" of its judgements and the copula through which those extremes are connected. What is the content and form of the particular in communitarian accounts? In terms of content, it is "culture"; in terms of form it is absolutely distinct from universality. But it is not difficult to see that here already we have a tension between content and form. How is the particular identified as a singular instance of the category of culture? Surely this has to be through the invocation of some kind of account of a universal (all cultures/culture as such), particular (cultures) and singular (this culture). The content of the particular cannot be known without reference to a universal, but this then puts its formal status as entirely distinct from the universal into question. It is a rather tired and familiar point that communitarian arguments necessarily rely on universal judgements even as they reject moral universalism. And it is an equally familiar point that the universal invoked by communitarianism has to be understood either in terms of the judgement of reflection (empirical "allness" – we know it is a culture because all cultures are x, y and z); the judgement of necessity ("genus" – we know it is a culture because it partakes of the essence of culture); or the judgement of the concept ("ought-to-be" – we know it is a culture because this is what cultures are required to be like). Moral universalists interpret the difficulties of sustaining an account of moral particularism that does not at some point rely on universal claims (which transcend the category by which such claims are intended to be confined) as an argument for a return to a focus on the universal in moral theory. For the Hegelian critic, however, the reappearance of the universal simply takes us back to another set of pitfalls and the unsustainability of fixing the terms of judgement, whether judgement is grounded in the particular or the universal.

The approach to moral theory that I call "moral singularism" emerges within feminist ethics as an alternative to both universalism and particularism, and is most familiar in the form of a feminist "ethic of care". It represents the dissatisfaction of feminist thinkers with moral universalisms premised on a particular, masculinist account of what it means to be human (in terms of substantive accounts of human nature and rationality), and with moral particularisms premised on accepting the dominant, patriarchal norms of culture as equivalent to culture itself. This form of moral thinking, in a move reminiscent of the "beautiful soul", identifies the ground of moral judgement as being in the singular: the specific voice that nevertheless carries exemplary, universal significance. On this account of morality, judgements that X is good, X is a good woman or X acted rightly are authoritative in so far as they can be grounded in the singular. That is to say, they are not authorized by universal rule or given cultural norm, but by the ways in which the singular agent has arrived at them in the context of the duties and responsibilities that are inherent in her singular being and experience. Once more we can raise the Hegelian questions as to the content and form of the extremes and copula of judgement within this approach to ethics. How are the content and form of singularity to be understood? How are the content and form of universality ("good", "right") to be understood? And how does this kind of moral thinking configure the relation between singularity, universality and particularity? Unpacking the content of singularity reveals a variety of possibilities. If singularity is that of the carer, then is it to be understood as an instance of generic virtues embedded in care as such, or as a category of persons, such as "women" or "mothers"? If the former, then singularity collapses into universality as "genus" and therefore into a form of moral universalism. If the latter, then the category of women or mothers has itself to be unpacked: is this all women/mothers, some women/mothers, a specific woman/mother? What are the criteria for what counts as woman/mother? Should woman/mother be understood as a universal or a particular? A common universalist critique of the feminist ethic of care is that it is a form of moral particularism, in which judgement, rendered context-relative, falls into contradiction because of the denial of its reliance on universal categories. From a communitarian point of view, the more likely critique is that the ethic of care is universalism masquerading as particularism, in which particular practices inherent in Western culture are illegitimately claimed to be of universal significance. Once more, Hegel's analysis of judgement prefigures familiar moves in contemporary debate over the meanings of moral claims, and once more we are brought back to the difficulty of sustaining one of the terms of judgement as the ground of connection with the other terms without transforming it into one of those other terms and thus putting the terms of judgement into question again.

The previous exploration of different perspectives on moral judgement remained within the terms of judgement. That is to say, the movement from universal to particular to singular operated abstractly, as if these were self-subsistent categories. Yet, as the discussion of each of these perspectives has illustrated, it is precisely the self-subsistence of the terms of judgement that the analysis of judgement puts into question. My aim is not to suggest that moral universalism, particularism and singularism fail as ways of formulating the meaning of moral claims, but rather that in each case it is the ways in which the categories of universality, particularity and singularity are thought that presents difficulties for judgement. Just as it is impossible to keep the terms of judgement clear and distinct within any of these perspectives, it is impossible to keep the terms of judgement clear and distinct in the comparison between them. In the light of this, it is unsurprising that much debate in moral theory is about how to find ways "between" the alternatives of moral universalism, particularism and singularism. Yet any such ways "between" that keep within the terms of judgement will end up repeating the difficulties in which moral thinking is caught.

CONCLUSION

At the end of the chapter on judgement in the *Logic*, Hegel argues that even when the instability of the terms of judgement has been fully appreciated in terms of content, there is still a problem with judgement itself as a form of thought. Formally, judgement always relies on positing universal and particular as distinct determinations (X is Y) and therefore blocks a proper grasp of the dynamic interdependence of those terms, the ways in which they both are and are not identical. In moving on to examine "syllogism" as a higher form of thought, it appears that judgement must be abandoned. In a similar way, following the above discussion, it would seem that the very idea of moral *judgement* is put into question by a Hegelian analysis, rendering us unable to make the claims X is good, X is a good woman, X acted rightly, which are both the subject matter of moral theory and part and parcel of our everyday existence. However, just as judgement survives in the terms of the syllogism so, I think, does the meaningfulness of moral judgement survive Hegel's critique of the terms of judgement. In effect, Hegel is pointing to the need for a much more careful examination of the complex conditions of possibility that underpin the intelligibility of moral claims. Any such claim cannot be seen as meaningful or valid in terms of its grounding in universal (moral law), particular (culture) or singular (beautiful soul). Instead the meaning and potential validity of moral claims is grounded in the dynamic interrelation of these three moments. An example of what this might imply for both the meaningfulness and validity of moral judgement can be found in Judith Butler's recent attempt to rethink ethical universality, building on the analysis given in Hegel's work (Butler *et al.* 2000: 15–25).[13]

In the essay "Restaging the Universal: Hegemony and the Limits of Formalism", Butler presents Hegel's account of the logic of "universality" as a critique of the ways in which it is commonly understood in ethical theory. She does this by tracing the difficulties encountered in judgement by both substantive and procedural forms of moral universalism, along the lines already discussed above. The main conclusion she draws from her discussion of Hegel's argument is that the universal is necessarily connected to the particular.[14] In practice this means that "the relation of universality to its cultural articulation is insuperable" (Butler *et al.* 2000: 24). For Butler, however, this conclusion does not imply either the embrace of moral particularism (following the communitarian move) or the abandonment of universality as a meaningful category in ethics. Instead it implies a rethinking of universality as a process of translation, that is, not as a process in which competing meanings are adjudicated in relation to a meta-language, but as a process of trial and error, in which the understanding and endorsement of moral claims depends crucially on the scope for recognition and negotiation between the authors, audiences and referents of the claims in question. According to Butler, this is a process that must allow for the possibility of mutual transformation, in which the meaning of the universal shifts across "the various rhetorical and cultural contexts in which the meaning and force of universal claims are made" (*ibid*.: 35). Butler's argument denies the possibility of definitively settling questions about the meaning and validity of claims and concepts through a process of judgement. In doing this, she repeats Hegel's lesson that the logic of universality, particularity and singularity is not ultimately a logic that can be captured in judgement's terms. The pursuit of judgement in moral theory brings us back again and again to the copula that connects the two extremes of judgement and undermines even as it confirms the terms of judgement themselves. Properly to think the copula of judgement in moral theory (as in other branches of intellectual enquiry) we must rethink the oppositions between universality, particularity and singularity in terms of both content and form.

NOTES

1. All references are to the "Greater" *Logic*, originally published in 1812, rather than to the *Encyclopaedia* Logic, which was published in various editions in Hegel's lifetime between 1817 and 1830. Departing from Miller, I render *Begriff* as "concept", where Miller uses "notion" and *Einzelne* as "singular", where Miller uses "individual". In this I follow Geraets, Suchting and Harris (*EL*).

2. See Hegel's discussion of the contrast between formal and dialectical reasoning: "formal thinking lays down for its principle that contradiction is unthinkable; but as a matter of fact the thinking of contradiction is the essential moment of the concept [*Begriff*]" (*L*: 835).

3. Catherine Malabou uses the metaphor of "plasticity" as a key to Hegel's thought; C. Malabou, *The Future of Hegel: Plasticity, Temporality and Dialectic*, L. During (trans.) (London: Routledge, 2005). This seems to me a very useful way of encapsulating the immanent dialectic of the relation between content and form in Hegel's philosophy, which works within and across the different branches of his philosophical system. For my own view on how the sciences of logic, nature and spirit (the last term covering the complex interplay between subjective self-consciousness and objective ethical life, the values, practices and institutions of culture) are distinct yet mutually dependent; see K. Hutchings, *Hegel and Feminist Philosophy* (Cambridge: Polity, 2003), 102–11.

4. This is why, for Hegel, the proposition in the form of a judgement is not suited to the expression of speculative truths: "familiarity with this fact is likely to remove many misunderstandings of speculative truths. Judgment is an *identical* relation between subject and predicate; in it we abstract from the fact that the subject has a number of determinatenesses other than that of the predicate, and also that the predicate is more extensive than the subject. Now if the content is speculative, the *non-identical* aspect

of subject and predicate is also an essential moment, but in the judgment this is not expressed" (*L*: 90–91).

5. The idea of *Bildung*, the simultaneous education of consciousness and of the reader, is foregrounded in the *Phenomenology* (*PhG*: 46–57). It is also crucial to the *Logic*, which also invites the reader to undertake the labour of thought and thereby to recognize the immanent connection between text, referent of analysis within the text and the reader/s; Hutchings, *Hegel and Feminist Philosophy*, 42–4, 104.

6. Although Hegel distinguishes between "phenomenology" and "science", the two are always intimately related, in particular in his two major texts, the *Logic* and the *Phenomenology*; Hutchings, *Hegel and Feminist Philosophy*, 32–44.

7. Hegel prefigures the application of his law/love argument in the "Spirit of Christianity" to contemporary moral theory in a passage within that text, in which he makes an explicit link between legalism and the idea of self-legislated moral law in a Kantian sense (*ET*: 211).

8. Hegel's account of the "beautiful soul" draws on Goethe's *Wilhelm Meister's Apprenticeship and Travels*, see G. Rose, *The Broken Middle: Out of Our Ancient Society* (Oxford: Blackwell, 1992), 188–92.

9. This question is clearly central to the liberal/communitarian discussion. A number of thinkers argue for forms of moral universalism that link the authority of moral claims to rational procedure in ways that clearly connect to Hegel's account of the Kantian moral point of view: J. Rawls, *A Theory of Justice* (Oxford: Oxford University Press, 1972); J. Habermas, *Moral Consciousness and Communicative Action*, C. Lenhardt & S. Weber Nicholsen (trans.) (Cambridge: Polity, 1990); O. O'Neill, *Constructions of Reason* (Cambridge: Cambridge University Press, 1989); S. Benhabib, *The Claims of Culture: Equality and Diversity in the Global Era* (Princeton, NJ: Princeton University Press, 2002). Others challenge the neo-Kantian perspective in moral theory, either by reworking the meaning of universality or by challenging the idea that moral judgement requires grounding in the universal: A. MacIntyre, *After Virtue* (London: Duckworth, 1981); M. Walzer, *Spheres of Justice* (Oxford: Martin Robertson, 1983) and *Thick and Thin: Moral Argument at Home and Abroad* (Southbend, IN: University of Notre Dame Press, 1994); M. Nussbaum, *Women and Human Development: The Capabilities Approach* (Cambridge: Cambridge University Press, 2000); R. Rorty, "Human Rights, Rationality and Sentimentality", in *On Human Rights: The Oxford Amnesty Lectures 1993*, S. Shute & S. Hurley (eds), 112–34 (New York: Basic Books, 1993). These debates gain particular resonance when applied to issues with international or global reach, such as international human rights or global distributive justice, in which theoretical perspectives are increasingly categorized either as "cosmopolitan" or as "communitarian". See T. Nardin & D. R. Mapel (eds), *Traditions of International Ethics* (Cambridge: Cambridge University Press, 1992); C. Brown, *International Relations Theory: New Normative Approaches* (Hemel Hempstead: Harvester Wheatsheaf, 1992); N. Dower, *World Ethics: The New Agenda* (Edinburgh: Edinburgh University Press, 1998); K. Hutchings, *International Political Theory: Re-thinking Ethics in a Global Era* (London: Sage, 1999); C. Brown, *Sovereignty, Rights and Justice* (Cambridge: Cambridge University Press, 2002).

10. Examples of Aristotelian universalism can be found in MacIntyre, *After Virtue*, and Nussbaum, *Women and Human Development*. Examples of utilitarian universalism can be found in P. Singer, "Famine, Affluence and Morality", *Philosophy and Public Affairs* **1** (1972), 229–43, and of procedural universalism in Rawls, *A Theory of Justice*, and Habermas, *Moral Consciousness and Communicative Action*.

11. Although communitarianism is frequently invoked as an ideal type in moral arguments, in particular concerning multicultural and international policy issues, it is a position that is far less commonly held in a strong form than the variants of moral universalism listed above. For a defence of a strong communitarian line to the effect that most moral questions can and should be answered in relation to the cultural context of the specific political community, rather than at the level of universal procedures or claims about universal human nature or human flourishing see J. Rawls, *Law of the Peoples* (Cambridge MA: Harvard University Press, 1999), and Walzer, *Spheres of Justice* and *Thick and Thin*.

12. Although "moral singularism" is less familiar as a stock position, it has deep roots in moral thought. It combines an ethics of virtue, which draws on universalist accounts of the "good'" person (and therefore on Aristotelian traditions of moral thought) with modern Protestant and romantic ideas, which insist on the uniqueness of the person and their private relation to God and/or the moral law (Goethe's and Hegel's "beautiful soul"). For moral singularists, the specificity of the person is key to the authority of their moral judgement, a perspective exemplified in contemporary feminist ethics following the work of Carol Gilligan and the idea of a women's "different voice" and a feminist ethic of care; C. Gilligan, *In a Different Voice: Psychological Theory and Women's Development* (Cambridge, MA.: Harvard University Press, 1982); S. Ruddick, *Maternal Thinking: Towards a Politics of Peace* (London: The Women's Press, 1990).

13. Butler uses the *Encyclopaedia* Logic and the *Phenomenology*.

14. "The all-encompassing trajectory of the term is necessarily undone by the exclusion of particularity on which it rests. There is no way to bring the excluded particularity into the universal without first negating that particularity. And that negation would only confirm once again that universality cannot proceed without destroying that which it purports to include" (Butler *et al.* 2000: 24).

CHAPTER SEVEN

RECOGNITION AND RECONCILIATION
ACTUALIZED AGENCY IN HEGEL'S JENA *PHENOMENOLOGY*

Robert B. Pippin

I. LIBERAL POLITICS AND THE POLITICS OF RECOGNITION

Most modern liberal versions of the state depend on a philosophically ambitious theory about the nature of human individuality and its normatively relevant implications. It is often assumed that contrasting theories about the ultimacy of inter-subjective relations and the derivative or secondary status of individuality are potentially if not actually illiberal, and Hegel's putative "organic" theory of the state is often cited as an example. A major arena for such disputes has been the claim by such neo-Hegelians as Charles Taylor and Axel Honneth that the key liberal notion of the "free and rational individual" depends for its possibility on a social condition of great political relevance: "mutual recognition". In the following, I return to the sources of this dispute (a dispute sometimes called postmodern "identity" politics) in Hegel's original arguments about "dependence" and "independence" and investigate what according to Hegel is the exact nature of the human dependence at issue and what might count as the successful satisfaction of this condition of dependence. It is, I want to argue, much easier to see what Hegel's answer is to the former question than to the latter.

We need first a general, admittedly high-altitude survey of the landscape occupied by "liberal versions of the state". This is not easy to do; versions of liberal political theory have become ever more various. There are autonomy liberals, value-neutral liberals, sceptical liberals, relativist liberals, libertarian liberals, welfarist liberals and more recently liberal or value pluralists. But it remains the case that a set of recognizable, underlying commitments characterizes the Western liberal democratic tradition, and that there are two main sorts of theoretical justifications for these commitments and their practical extensions. The common orientation has to do with the pre-eminence and in some sense the theoretical "ultimacy" of the human individual mentioned above, and so with the equality of worth of each, *qua* individual. This commitment is understood to require a limited and accountable state (accountable to the "consent of the governed"), equality before the law and, in most versions, significant and extensive property rights. The theoretical considerations advanced to support such a conception of political life amount to two different ways to claim that such arrangements are *rational*.

One set of such arguments relies on a pragmatic or a broadly consequentialist form of reasoning and is oriented from what are taken to be empirical facts and the empirical consequences of certain arrangements of power. One argues that under a liberal political arrangement, we will all simply be better off – that is, more prosperous, more secure, better able to achieve whatever ends we set for ourselves and perhaps also more likely to advance culturally. (J. S. Mill is the champion of this group.) Or one argues, somewhat less ambitiously, that in order to retain and develop what we have already achieved in any pre-civil situation, it is pragmatically reasonable to designate an umpire or sovereign, in a fiduciary relation with his subjects, with sufficient power to resolve disputes (Locke), but answerable to his clients if he fails to perform these functions. Or one argues, with something like an absolute minimum of assumptions, that we know at least that we will all be drastically worse off without an all-powerful "monster" or leviathan sovereign to enforce order (Hobbes). The idea is that no one could be presumed to want or will anything without wanting or willing what is practically necessary for the achievement of any end, and that this general interest in the success of what we attempt can be shown to yield tacit or active consent to such an arrangement, to the state or civil order. On this interest-based conception of political life, the problem of politics is a rational cooperation problem, and it has thus been given new life recently with the growing sophistication and popularity of rational choice models of reasoning. Perhaps the most influential contemporary proponent of this brand of liberalism is David Gauthier.

On the other hand, a robust theory of original *moral* entitlements – rights – is invoked to justify the moral unacceptability of a state of nature, or, said the other way around, to justify the claim that we have a duty to leave the state of nature and to establish a civil order. The state's monopoly on coercive force is justified because these claims of moral entitlement – rights claims – are justified. In this case the basic argument is that no one could be presumed to want or will anything without implicitly claiming to be entitled to such a pursuit (i.e. each has a presumptive right to non-interference), and that such an entitlement claim is not one that could be consistently denied to all others. And, the argument continues, the only possible realization of a situation wherein such equal rights claims could be secured is one where we give up the right to decide in our own case and submit to the rule of law. Such appeals to a "rational will" as the source of the state's coercive authority (by virtue of its protection of basic entitlements) is often ascribed to Rousseau and to Kant's position in his "Doctrine of Right", is quite prominent in the rhetoric of the French Revolution and its declaration of the rights of man, and is a major component, in quite different ways, in the contemporary theories of John Rawls, Ronald Dworkin, Otfried Höffe and Jürgen Habermas.

These categories are of course idealizations. In some positions there is considerable overlap and intermingling of such strategic and normative reasoning. (The cases of Locke and Rawls are the most obvious.) But the distinctions are stable enough for us to be able to identify an *alternative* modern tradition, which, by being alternative is often just thereby (and too hastily) considered non- or anti-liberal (or anti-individualist). The problem raised by this alternative tradition involve a critique of the putative "*ultimacy*" or *original* status of the individual and the implications that follow for politics if that ultimacy is denied in favour of some more complicated view of the "logic", let us say, of original relations of dependence and independence among persons. Obviously one such implication might be that the legitimacy of the state's coercive power could not be wholly defended by appeal to what an adult person would will, either in a strategic sense or, more broadly, by appeal to what such a person could be argued to be rationally committed to. The claim is that such a picture of the rational individual is a "cropped" picture, which we have arbitrarily excluded from the frame original and prior inter-subjective relations that, because these are necessary for the possible existence and exercise of any individual will, cannot be a standard subject of rational negotiation *for* individuals but that cannot be justifiably ignored. Under the influence of this distorted or cropped picture, we would falsely conclude that all relations to others are results of volition or consensus, either ex ante or post facto as a matter of reflective endorsement, and thereby we would in our theory of political life and its authority fail to acknowledge properly such pre-volitional, unavoidable, necessary ties to others (not ones we could adopt or reject as a matter of choice). As Axel Honneth (esp. 1996, 2000) has pointed out, such a fantastic, atomistic ideal of a boot-strapping, wholly self-defining and self-determining subject is bound to produce various social pathologies of a distinctly Hegelian or dialectical sort. By this I mean that we will have adopted adopt as an ideal (not just in our political lives but comprehensively) a norm of self-determination and self-authorship that cannot possibly be fulfilled and cannot even be action-guiding. It will remain formal, abstract and empty, and in trying unsuccessfully to fulfil it we will successively undermine its authority. We will, in Honneth's fine phrase, "*suffer from indeterminacy*" (Honneth 2000). (Hegel documents a number of these pathologies in his *Phenomenology*: the "frenzy of self-conceit", the "beautiful soul", and an unavoidable hypocrisy.)

By contrast, a new and different sort of claim for ultimacy in *inter-subjective relations* would form the basis of such an alternative political reflection, and the most important aspect of this relation is often a form of original, unavoidable *social dependence*. It is, so goes the claim, by ignoring or denying such original relations in a fantasy of self-reliance that we end up in those distorted or even pathological relations to others, even to ourselves.[1] As we shall see, at its most ambitiously dialectical the full claim is that acknowledging, acting in the light of, such relations of dependence is a necessary condition for the achievement of true independence, or true "self-realization", or "actualized", "concrete" freedom. And, to anticipate again, this idea amounts to what is at once one of the most noble and most abused notions of nineteenth-century European thought. The claim of such original dependence leads to a charge much more radical than one of unfairness or injustice if there is freedom for some and unfreedom for many others. The idea is that I cannot be properly said *to be free* unless others are free, that my freedom depends on theirs, reciprocally (Honneth 2000: 21). (In the version of the claim that I am interested in, being a free agent – an actual or successful agent – is said to depend on being recognized as one by others whose free bestowal of this recognition depends in turn on their being recognized as such free bestowers.)[2] This is why it is argued that an understanding of the nature of *this* sort of dependence – unavoidable dependence on recognition by others – ought to guide all reflection on both the powers and limits of sovereign authority.

This tradition is again associated with the Rousseau of *The Social Contract*. (Rousseau seems to have managed to express and defend almost all the alternatives in modern social and political theory.) This is the Rousseau who argued passionately against the enslaving effects of modern social dependence but for the creation of a new form of artificial dependence that would count as the creation of a collective independence, *the citizen* or the famous exchange of natural freedom for civil freedom. But it is most apparent in Fichte's 1796 *Grundlage* and of course in Hegel's Jena writings and his Jena *Phenomenology*, and in the left-Hegelian tradition inspired by Hegel's gripping account of "the struggle to the death for recognition" and the internal paradoxes of the master–slave dialectic. This tradition too has its contemporary resonances. The most well-known appearance of this sort of claim is in the various "communitarian" reactions to Rawls's work, and in some neo-Aristotelian work (MacIntyre), but the most worked-out and thoughtful reflections on the theme can be found in the recent work of Charles Taylor and Axel Honneth.

II. THE LIBERAL REJOINDER AND THE CORE ISSUE

This – these strands of liberal thought and this counter-strand that concedes the existence of rights-bearing, independent, self-determining individuals but denies their theoretical ultimacy – forms the context for the issue in Hegel I want eventually to raise. Of course, the thematic itself is a sprawling and barely manageable one, since it quickly spills over into claims about social psychology, developmental psychology, theories of modernity and philosophical anthropology. But the heart of the matter clearly concerns how we are to understand two issues: first, the basic claim about an "original" relation of dependence on others (what *sort* of dependence we are talking about, how it is to be related to claims for independence) and secondly in what sense we are to draw political implications from such an understanding (and I mean especially implications about the coercive use of the state's monopoly on violence). What I want to claim is that Hegel's argument for a particular sort of original dependence necessary for the possibility of individuality – recognitional dependence – is not based on a claim about human need, or derived from evidence in developmental or social psychology. It involves a distinctly philosophical claim, a shift in our understanding of individuality, from viewing it as a kind of ultimate given to regarding it as a kind of achievement, and to regarding it as a normative status, not a fact of the matter, whether empirical or metaphysical. Understanding how Hegel wants to free us from one picture and suggest another way of looking at the issue will make the relevance of this recognitional dependence much easier to see. With respect to the question of what Hegel's position is on the second issue – what political implications follow from this transformation – the issue is murkier, even somewhat mysterious, and I want only to make a few closing suggestions about what we seem to be left with.

In general, this – the status of the claim for some inter-subjective ultimacy – is the core issue because it is obviously open to a defender of some version of classical liberal theory to claim that any such putative dependence or inter-subjective bond, even if it is true that it is original and unavoidable, is irrelevant to mature political reflection. *However* "I" got to be the concrete "me" that I am, however dependent in such a process and even in the present on others in a variety of contexts, that "I" is now, *qua* adult agent, quite capable of a complete reflective detachment from any such commitments and attachments and dependencies that may have arisen. No such attachment or dependence can be counted as of value to me unless it can pass what has been called a "reflective endorsement" test *by me*,[3] unless I can "stand back" from such involvements and decide whether I ought to be so attached. And underlying such a claim is a view of the possible worth or value of my achievements to me. To be so valuable – so goes this style of thought – they must be due *to* me, must be experienced as the result of *my* will and initiative and talent. And so my claims on you and yours on me as civil beings should then be limited to what can be shown to be necessary for each of us to have a sphere of activity wherein such will might be exercised. To be a liberal in this sense is to forego "your" approval or recognition or in some large measure even your assistance. At some point in one's life giving up such dependencies, being able to act without requiring the recognition, approval or in some sense the assistance of others, is to assume the role of an adult responsible individual – to grow up, one can imagine a Thatcherite liberal insisting impatiently. For those on this side of the issue, anything less than such a commitment, especially any claim that my status or worth depends on its effective acknowledgement by others (not just on their non-interference) would be a recipe for "group think", social conformism and ultimately quite illegitimate restrictions on individual liberty in the name of what is supposed to be such originally necessary dependence.

It may be that one manifestation of such non-interference might be a callous indifference, resulting in the humiliating invisibility suffered by, say, Ralph Ellison's *Invisible Man*. But even if that is considered a wrong, our Thatcherite might concede only that it is a moral wrong, a failure of charity and not a politically correctable wrong, as if some "right" to visibility that had been violated. And it is not enough just to show that without reliance on, or trust in, the already ongoing social practices, institutions and norms into which one has been socialized there could be no determinative content to ideals such as self-determination or self-realization, or ideals at all for that matter. Establishing that might just mean that we are *worse* off philosophically, "stuck" with a contingent social content that we experience as unavoidable but reflectively unredeemable, the Heideggerean cage of *das Man* rather than the Hegelian liberation of *Sittlichkeit*. If the indeterminacy criticism holds we will also clearly need an account of the rationality of specific, modern institutions, and some way to do justice to the subjective element in our acceptance and embodiment of these norms, some explanation of how *we have made them ours* that does not revert again to the individualist reflective endorsement model and does not settle for a matter of fact habituation.

The rejoinder to all this by any proponent of "recognitional" politics clearly will turn on the argument for something like the *ultimacy* of such dependence (or a claim in social ontology) and so the *necessity* of acknowledging its indispensability in our political theory. (That is, the normative necessity of so doing, a requirement that will constitute a claim for the rationality of such acknowledgment.) It will thus rest on the claim that the sort of detachment and endorsement spoken of above is not only impossible, but is a dangerous fantasy, leading to the pathological indeterminacy already noted. However, even if this can be established, the *political* implications of such an unavoidable dependence will have to drawn carefully. After all, the language of "social harm" arising from misrecognition suggests a consequentialist form of reasoning, an argument about the weight of various social goods with, apparently, an additional claim that esteem and self-worth (and the social acknowledgement they depend on) have *more weight* than has hitherto been conceded. (Since we are talking ultimately about the use of the state's coercive force to prohibit such a harm, we will need a very *strong* argument to show that such injuries are not just unfortunate, subject to moral disapproval, but must be subject to legislative remedy, are in some way components of the common good.) That would suggest one form of an extension of the "original dependence" claim that would be consistent with, a kind of addendum to, the empirical form of liberal reasoning noted above. But the language of ultimacy and undeniability also suggests a case based on some entitlement claim, as if the wrong in question were a moral injury, of the general sort Kant argued against by denying we should ever use another as a means, should ever withhold respect for another's "incomparable" worth. This sort of claim for a kind of *right to be recognized*" implies another direction altogether, one consistent with, a kind of addendum to, the rights-based liberalism noted above. And again we would face the problem of showing some claim on others to be an entitlement requiring coercive enforcement and not just a claim that we ought, in some general moral sense, to respect.

III. THE HEGELIAN POSITION

As already noted, these sorts of doubts about the ultimacy of liberal individualism have a complex historical origin. What I want to do now is concentrate on one aspect of this pedigree – Hegel's in his Jena *Phenomenology* – not only because his account there of something like the unfolding drama of the struggle for recognition has been so independently influential, but because his account, by virtue of what Hegel says and what he does not say, raises in an interesting way both sorts of questions just noted: what *sort* of claim on others is the claim for recognition, and what, if any are its *political* dimensions?

To understand Hegel's position, we need to begin again with the fundamental issue in the difference between liberal and "recognitional" politics. (For the moment we can just let this latter stand for a conception of politics that does not tie any claim to legitimacy and justice to the interests or rights claims of sovereign rational individuals and what they have or would or must rationally will, and all this because of some claim of prior or pre-volitional dependence that requires political acknowledgement, the non-acknowledgement of which counts as a wrong.) We could put the basic problem of the independence–dependence relation in a way familiar from Kant's *Rechtslehre*· that it concerns what I can justifiably claim as mine, not yours, and the conditions under which such a distinction is possible. At this quite primary level, we should begin by noting that the basic starting-points of modern political reflection – mine, yours and ours – do not refer to empirical facts that can be read directly off the social world. They involve the establishment of normative statuses; what we mean by "mine" invokes a norm, it appeals to what is rightfully mine; we are not pointing to any empirical fact. (As Kant noted in the *Rechtslehre*, intelligible beings, beings responsive to reasons, are not limited in possession to what hey can physically hold. They can establish rational relations with others and therewith intelligible or "noumenal" possession.) And if our original dispute is about the "ultimacy of individuality", then that will have to be a dispute about the bases of such a *normative claim of content*. So, the question of my distinctness as a human individual is not the sort that can be settled by a DNA test, but concerns the extent of my (putatively) rightful exclusion of your and anyone else's interference. This seems primarily a worry about property, but, given the kind of worries about the psychology of dependence first voiced in Rousseau's *Second Discourse*, the issue is much broader. Given how materially dependent we have become (thanks to the division of labour and the growing distance between civilized life and any possible self-sufficiency), especially how dependent in the long process of human maturation, *whatever* we value in the ends we set and the views we espouse, *whatever* we "guard" as rightfully "ours", are, we come more and more to suspect, likely to be an inevitable reflection of such dependence and the conformity it enforces, however much it might feel like our own intimate self. Roussseau goes so far as to claim the following: "The Savage lives in himself; sociable man, always outside himself, is capable of living only in the opinion of others; and so to speak, derives the sentiment of his own existence solely from their judgment" (1986: 199). We can thus now see that the underlying problem pointed to – the normative status of mine in all its senses – appears as the problem of freedom, understood broadly as the ability to see myself in my own deeds, to experience such deeds as the products of my will, not the forces of social necessity; in a word *as mine*. This notion of non-alienated freedom would also involve understanding the deeds as reflections of what *I* most value, as genuine expressions of my view of the good, or whatever; as manifestations of what is rightfully and originally mine. (If I *can* experience the deeds as products of my will, but also regard them as violations of my own views of what ought to be done or never ought to be done, then I am alienated from my own deeds in another way.) Fulfilling such conditions is what amounts to practical success as a determinate agent, a free being. (All this, while conceding that there is clearly a possible difference between what I consciously take myself to value, and what in fact counts as "rightfully and originally" my commitments. In this admittedly paradoxical sense, I can be "alienated" from what I truly value, while regarding myself as free in this "expressive" sense.

And this provides the opportunity for a full if very provisional summation of what I take to be Hegel's whole claim about this matter. For it is this "success" as an agent that, according to Hegel's position in the Jena *Phenomenology*, requires as its conditions, that others: (i) recognize me as having the social status and identity I attribute to myself; (ii) recognize the deed as falling under the act-description that I invoke; and (iii) recognize me as acting on the intention I attribute to myself. In general this success requires that I am taken by others to have the intentions and commitments that I take myself to have, and so *to be doing* what I take myself to be doing.[4] (By contrast, I can claim to be a knight and to be engaging in acts of chivalry, but if the social world in which I live cannot recognize such a status or such deeds, then I am a comic imitation of a knight, a Don Quixote.) To say everything at once: Hegel's eventual claim will be that these three conditions of successful agency (or, as he often says, "actual" [*wirklich*] agency) cannot be satisfied unless individuals are understood as participants in an ethical form of life, *Sittlichkeit*, and finally in a certain historical form of ethical life, in which such relations of recognition can be genuinely mutual, where that means that the bestowers of recognition are themselves actually free, where the inter-subjective recognitional (sometimes called "communicative") relation is sustained in a reciprocal way.

But clearly this is to say so much at once as to strain the patience of any audience. But underlying the manifold of issues just presented one can still detect, I hope, what I have been calling the core or basic issue. For Hegel is clearly treating the basic notion of individuality as an *achievement*, a result of a complex inter-subjective dynamic, and not a matter of mere biological uniqueness (which he calls "particularity"). True individuals are *agents* in Hegel's account, in non-alienated relations with their deeds and commitments. (Said more precisely, they are "actual" agents, and Hegel seems to conceive of such a state as having gradations, levels.) And clearly what is driving his argument about social dependence is the claim that this status as an agent is, can be nothing other than, a social status, and a social status exists by being taken to exist by members of some community. A priest, a knight, a statesman, a citizen, are not, that is, natural kinds. One exists as such a kind by being treated as one, according to the rules of that community. And the radicality of Hegel's suggestion is that we treat being a concrete subject of a life, a free being, the same way. It is in this sense that being an individual already presupposes a complex recognitional status.

IV. HEGEL'S NARRATIVE

Why should we believe that we are dependent in just this way, that individuality, or being an individual subject, should be understood this way (as a "normative status" dependent on social recognition), and that there are both social and political conditions without which we could not become the individual subjects of our own lives?

Hegel has, when all is said and done, two main kinds of answers to this question. One is systematic and is to be found in his *Encyclopaedia*. That answer is extremely comprehensive and ranges from his treatment of relata and their relations, the logic of same and other, the category of actuality, and especially the transition in the third part, on "Geist", from a doctrine of "subjective" to a doctrine of "objective" spirit. Once that is understood, the status of the claims in "Objective Spirit" (otherwise known as his *Philosophy of Right*) can be properly assessed, especially the key claim for our purposes: "The sphere of right and that of morality cannot exist independently [*kann nicht für sich existieren*]; they must have the ethical [*das Sittliche*] as their support and foundation [*zum Träger und zur Grundlage*]" (PR: 186; SW 7: 225, §141 Addition). This is, in the language of *The Philosophy of Right*, the claim for the priority of inter-subjective relations to liberal notions of individual entitlement and responsibility.

But there is also a better-known phenomenological as well as systematic case for these claims, and that involves an unusual narrative developmental logic that is difficult to summarize economically. This narrative – surely one of the most original and exciting "accounts" ever presented in philosophy – can for our purposes be isolated as beginning with the introduction of a social conception of self-consciousness in Chapter 4 of the *Phenomenology*, especially with the introduction of the theme in the first section there, "Independence and Dependence of Self-consciousness" and the famous struggle and master–slave sections. It then extends throughout the chapter on "Reason", a good deal of which describes what are in effect attempts to avoid the messiness of such social struggle by appeal to an accessible abstract, formal status, the view from nowhere, the rational point of view. The story here is a story of various *failures* in inhabiting such a status. And Hegel then describes something like the return (in his narrative) of a beautiful version of such a social reality in the first section of the chapter about spirit (on Greek ethical life), but then that chapter too continues the *via negativa*, an account of Western cultural and political history as a history of failed sociality, misrecognition, naive assumptions of self-sufficiency and so forth ("Self-alienated Spirit", "the Terror", "dissemblance", "hypocrisy", "the beautiful soul"). (Hegel thus treats the two dominant forms of the modern Western fantasy of individual self-sufficiency: the Enlightenment and romantic notions of individual authenticity.) The Spirit narrative clearly is meant to suggest an experiential path from the one-sidedness of the ancient Greek form of a recognitive community, with a level of social integration that could not properly account for claims of individual conscience, to a modern, conversely one-sided moralism, reliant too much on the private voice of conscience, unwilling to act in a way that would subject its deed to the judgement of others, or stuck in a fierce judgemental hard-heartedness about the necessary wickedness of all actual deeds. These last are all treated as prototypical modern fantasies of normative or rational self-sufficiency. And they clearly raise the question of what would break the hold of such fantasies on the modern imagination. Quite surprisingly though we do not find in the Jena *Phenomenology* the account that played a major role in his Jena lectures on spirit – the return of a modern, successful picture of sociality, the family, labour, the modern state – successful, mutual recognition and so the achievement of a reflective, socially mediated form of subjectivity. There is no such discussion of ethical life (*Sittlichkeit*), only a fairly abstract treatment of the social and mostly philosophical dimensions of religion.

I do not propose to give a comprehensive view of this narrative here, but I shall try to isolate what seems to me to be one critical element in the answer to the question just posed (why believe any of these claims about the necessity of recognition?), and then conclude with some remarks about the relevance of the discussion of "forgiveness" to the account of spirit and ultimately to its political dimension.

To understand the fulcrum on which this account pivots – the account of practical reason in Chapter 5 – we need to reiterate that the topic of the *Phenomenology* concerns the "conditions for the possibility of normativity" in human experience. I mean that Hegel has tried to show the essential dimension of all human mindedness – consciousness – is such a normative dimension. We are being educated to see that thinking, reasoning, believing, deciding, resolving and so on should not be understood as primarily or essentially mere mental events occurring at a time. They are, but that is the wrong category with which to understand them *as practices*. As practices, activities aimed at getting something right, at finding the right course of action, their intelligibility requires attention to the rules and purpose of this practice, and the subjects of these activities should be understood as purposive rule-followers. In the Hegelian story of our mental life, what is "happening" is happening because of a subject determining that it shall; a subject taking a stand in a way, for which one is answerable. It is not simply to come to be in a state. This is what is eventually called the inherently self-conscious dimension of human mindedness. In consciousness of an object, one is not just differentially responsive to the external world, one is holding oneself to a normative claim about some object or state. (This is the clear descendent of that Kantian claim that all cognitive awareness is a judging, indeed an apperceptive judging.)[5] One is subject to any such claim only *by holding oneself to it*, and what we shall see is that also necessarily involved in "really" so being bound to such a claim – for any successful committing – is being held to it by others. This will eventually mean that it is only within some form of social relation that the inescapable phenomenological features of self-consciousness (especially the claim to normative legitimacy) can be accounted for.

This means that, in Hegel's language, in any such commitment to a claim or course of action, there is a possible gap between my own self-certainty, my subjective take on what is happening and what is called for and the "truth", often manifest when it is apparent that others attribute to me commitments and implications of commitments other than those I attribute to myself. The experience of such a gap, itself a kind of social pathology, is what Hegel appeals to as the engine for conceptual and social change, a struggle or striving for reconciliation and mutuality in such a context.[6]

This is the kind of problem that is at issue in the second half of Chapter 5, when Hegel pursues what I have been calling his critique of the ultimacy of individuality into an area where the privileged and prior status of the individual or first-person point of view seems intuitively strongest: the dependence of outer manifestations of the subject's will on the inner intentions of that subject. These passages represent the most radical of the implications that follow from what is in effect Hegel's attempt to alter that relation of priority and to argue for the reciprocal dependence of the "inner" on the "outer".

What Hegel attempts to show in a variety of contexts, against a variety of inner-oriented positions is that we cannot determine what actually *was* a subject's intention or motivating reason by relying on some sort of introspection, by somehow looking more deeply *into* the agent's soul, or by some sincerity test. "By their fruits shall ye know them" (*EL*: 199; *SW* 8: 277, §140), Hegel quotes and, Hegel would add, "*only* by their fruits or deeds". Only as manifested or expressed in a social space shared by others, subject to their "takes" on what happened, can one (*even* the subject himself) retrospectively determine what must have been intended. And of course it seems a bit paradoxical to claim that we can only know what we intended to do after we have actually acted and in a way dependent on the reactions of others, but there is little doubt that Hegel holds something like such a position. Consider: "Ethical Self-consciousness now learns *from its deed* the developed nature of what it actually did ..." (*PhG*: 283; *HW* 2: 255).

Hegel is clearly anticipating here the account of "action as expression" familiar after Wittgenstein II, von Wright's *Explanation and Understanding*, Anscombe's *Intention* and Charles Taylor's work. But the way Hegel formulates his own position, with its claim about retrospective determination and narrative logic, is quite distinctive. Formulations of that account show up frequently in a wide variety of Hegelian texts: "An individual cannot know who he is before he has made himself into actuality through action" (*PhG*: 240; *HW* 2: 218); and:

> A human being – as he is externally, i.e. in his actions, so is he inwardly; and when he is virtuous, moral, etc. only inwardly, i.e. only in intentions, dispositions and when his externalities are not identical with this, then the one is as hollow and empty as the other. (*EL*: 274; *SW* 8: 197)

However the most concentrated and richest discussion occurs in the *Phenomenology*, in the sections whose titles are already both a concise summation of Hegel's view of the nature of agency and a direct reference to our theme. After Hegel had, in "Observing Reason", demonstrated (to his satisfaction) the self-contradiction involved in the reduction of mindedness to a thing or property of things (its reduction to mere "externality"), he turns to the equally one-sided attempt to give some sort of causal and conceptual priority to "the internal" in sections called "The Actualization [*Verwirklichung*] of Rational Self-Consciousness through Itself" and "Individuality, which is Itself in and for Itself Real".[7]

What Hegel tries to show in these passages is that the actual deed negates and transcends that aspect of the intention understood as separable as cause, understood as the mere occurrence of a somatic desire or passion, as well as the idea that one's real intention can only be partly expressed in a deed, and so remains in itself inexpressible, *"unaussprechlich"*. Contrary to both views: "the individual human being *is what the deed is*". All such that if a person's deed, also called his *"Werk"*, is contrasted with the "inner possibility" then it is the work or deed that "must be regarded as his true actuality, even if he deceives himself on this point, and turning away from his action into himself, fancies that in this inner sense he is something else than what he is in the deed *(That)"* (PhG: 194; HW 2: 178–9).

Finally, there is an implication about this position that Hegel eagerly accepts, most prominently in the "die Sache selbst" section. For if there is *no* way to determine what an agent intended prior to and separate from the deed, if it is only and wholly "in the deed" that we can make such a determination, then not only are we faced with an unusual retrospective determination of intention, even for the agent, but it also follows that we cannot specify *the action* by reference to such a separate intention. What *I* take the act to be, its point, purpose and implication, now has none of the privileged authority we intuitively attribute to the agent. In such an account I do not exercise any kind of proprietary ownership of the deed, cannot unilaterally determine "what was done". This is, as it were, up for negotiation within some concrete social community, the participants of which must determine what sort of deed *"that"* would be in our practices, how our rules apply. *My intention is thus doubly "real": it is out there "in" the deed, and the deed is essentially out there "for others"*. In describing agents who pride themselves on "not caring what people think", and for "having integrity" and for "believing in themselves no matter what the critics say" and so forth, who believe that there is a *Sache selbst*, determined by my intention, Hegel notes:

> ... in doing something, and thus bringing themselves out into the light of day, they directly contradict by their deed their pretence of wanting to exclude the glare of publicity and participation by all and sundry. Actualization is, on the contrary, a display [*Ausstellung*] of what is one's own in the element of universality whereby it becomes and should become the affair [*Sache*] of everyone.
> (PhG: 251; HW 2: 227)

From the view point of such a Mr Integrity, Hegel reports, this would look like "flies" hurrying along to "freshly poured milk", busying themselves with another's business, but Hegel rejects this attitude and insists that with all action "something has been opened up that is for others as well, or is a subject-matter on its own account" (*ibid.*).

If this is so, then Hegel is claiming there to be a far deeper level of human dependence than would be claimed by mutual commitment to an ideal communicative exchange, or mutual obligation to a moral law. The content of one's status as an individual and not just the linguistic form of its expression is also taken to reflect such recognitional dependence. This has nothing to do with some sort of complete absorption of individuality into inter-subjective determinations, and Hegel's politics retains a liberal basis in determinate individuals. He may have reinterpreted *what it is* to be an individual, treating it now as the achievement of a kind of capacity, a capacity especially to negotiate successfully various boundary problems in the play of an acknowledgement of social dependence and the inevitability of individual self-assertion. But he celebrates constantly the Christian principle of subjectivity as the heart and soul of modernity's achievement and attacks only what he regards as naive and dangerous exaggerations of subjective self-sufficiency, even as he also locates the achievement of such individuality within an inter-subjective struggle. All of which just adds to the stakes involved in asking what acting in the light of such dependence would be like.

V. FORGIVENESS?

So, where *is* all this emphasis on so many modes of social dependence leading? What would be the *right* account of something like the appropriate dependence on such social recognition in the determination of what is mine, even in this deeply "inward" sense of "my own intention"? What is the political relevance of this altered sense of "mine", "yours" and "ours"?

So far, we just seem to have learned these two things: a self-image never realized in social space, never expressed in public action, a conception of individuality as socially independent and original, has to count more as a fantasy than self-knowledge, or at least as merely provisional, even though when expressed in action the public deed cannot be said to be exclusively owned by the subject, to have the meaning that the subject insists on. It is "up for grabs" in a certain sense. One's individuality becomes a social fact through action, and its meaning can then no longer be tied to the privately formulated intention or will of the agent alone.

And yet on the other hand there are clearly people whose self-image, whose practical identity, has been formed so extensively by the expectations and demands and reactions of others, that, while their own self-image does circulate successfully in society, and their view of themselves is indeed very well mirrored in how they are regarded and treated, it has to be said that one has only become the person "they" want one to be, that one does not have one's own identity, has not become who one is. As noted above, this type of slavish conformism has to count as just as much a failure to become an individual as the fantasy-indulging narcissist we just discussed. Hence the suggestion that individuality amounts to the capacity to set and maintain a boundary that is of the sort consistent with all others doing likewise and so sustainable in mutual recognition.[8]

In what amounts to the closing section of the narrative account of sociality in the *Phenomenology*, Hegel's remarks are quite elliptical and do little to help the reader draw these two insights together.[9] One could argue that the incomplete and somewhat chaotic state of the *Phenomenology* indicates that Hegel simply postponed until later his official discussion of "'objective spirit" and that, if interested in Hegelian-rational institutions as answers to such questions, we should consult those later texts, the 1817 and then later versions of the *Encyclopaedia* and the 1820 *Philosophy of Right*.

That may be but the way that Hegel, in effect, leaves his narrative "hanging" at the end of the chapter on *Geist* does not suggest any possible institutional resolution, and it is hard to imagine one with the resources he gives us. Instead of such an institutional direction, he concludes with an enigmatic discussion of something like a spiritual possibility, a quasi-religious "conversion experience", in a community: "forgiveness". Left at *that*, such a culmination might well return us again to the liberal rejoinder mentioned some time ago – we may have demonstrated the centrality, essentiality even, of forms of mutual recognition for a satisfying human life, but these are largely ethical matters that are not proper subjects for political remedy, that they lead us closer to moral and religious practices than to any programme for social reform, perhaps lead us to consider transformations in a form of life that are entirely independent of, prior to, any exercise of human will.

The last sections of the Spirit chapter present what is in effect Hegel's last treatment of what I have been calling various modern fantasies of self-sufficiency: a fanatically self-righteous conscience, a "beautiful soul" unwilling ever to act and so to sully its pure standards and the dissembler, who tries to reconcile its particularity with what could be shared by all through endless sophistical qualifications and reformulations of his maxim for action. Hegel describes this as a situation of inevitable guilt and the drama that he narrates leaves us only with the option of "confessing" such guilt to others who we hope will reciprocate in a gesture that will undermine any such pretended independence and will reaffirm in mutual forgiveness our inevitable dependence.

This moment of confession and, after an initial moment of hardhearted resistance, forgiveness, do sound very much like some moment of "release" from the grip of the ideal of self-sufficiency and fantastic independence, but there is no institutional manifestation in this account of a possible (and, it sounds like, very idealized) moral community. Moreover, there is very little in the account of modern institutions in Objective Spirit that seems in any way connected with a "hard-heart" breaking, and mutual forgiveness occurring, even in the famous supercession of morality by *Sittlichkeit*.

Let me conclude with a literary analogy in order to make this point. The situation we are left with sounds very much like the final act of *King Lear* and, frustratingly, so does the "resolution". The Hegelian elements are all in place. Lear plays the part of an "acting consciousness" with dirty hands. He is dying without a male heir and must do what he can to leave the kingdom divided in ways that will not invite invasion by Burgundy, France and others. He enacts in the division of his kingdom the dependence of his personal and familial life on a shared political world. Cordelia is the initially hardhearted moralist or even beautiful soul, who finds her father's intermingling of these acts of private love with the public demands of this recognitive community unforgivable. (Lear seems to think of speech as inherently duplicitous: the price we pay for our dependence and vulnerability. Cordelia, rashly, thinks speech, the public enactments of dependence, is dispensable; that *silent* love is love enough.) We all know the catastrophe that ensues from these two fixed positions. In finally losing his status as king, in learning that his social status is not absolute, that it cannot obliterate the bonds of private love, Lear becomes a father again, the true nature of our manifold dependences revealed to him; and with the "breaking of Cordelia's hard heart, she becomes again his loving daughter and they can both express mutual forgiveness in lines as heartbreaking as any in literature. *But there is nowhere for any of this to go.* Lear's famous words evoke the exclusively personal moments of conversion and redemption possible within the cage of social necessity.

> No, no, no, no! Come, let's away to prison:
> We two alone will sing like birds i' the cage:
> When thou dost ask me blessing, I'll kneel down,
> And ask of thee forgiveness: so we'll live,
> And pray, and sing, and tell old tales, and laugh
> At gilded butterflies, ...[10]

And when Kent begins the political restoration at the end of the play, we are left with the same feeling of unsatisfactory tidying up that, I would suggest, we experience when we turn from the *Phenomenology* to the account of modern institutions in the account of Objective Spirit. The conversion and transformation that occur, as figures in general for collapse of the aspiration to self-sufficient individuality, seem to present something profoundly transforming and pre-institutional. But what?

Some see all this as evidence of the "tragic nature of all social action" for Hegel, comprising both a universal dimension and an inevitable transgression of such a law. But that is Hegel read through Adorno, in my view.[11] The aspiration for a culminating reconciliation is everywhere in Hegel, but everywhere elusive. The solution to the problem he presents us with is not to abandon that hope, but to try to understand what he meant, and especially to try to find the links between that aspiration and his theory of the state, both because the relation seems mysterious and because what Hegel has written about it has inspired some of the most intense criticism of his position. Here is a frequent image that testifies to the depth of the problem as Hegel saw it and that he invoked throughout his career, early and late. In his *Lectures on Aesthetics*, Hegel claims that Spirit, human being itself, *is* a "wound" that

Spirit inflicts on itself, but which it can heal itself (*A* 1: 98), and in doing so reiterates what he had claimed at the end of this chapter of the *Phenomenology*, many years before, when he had promised us even more: "The wounds of spirit heal, and leave no scars behind" (*PhG*: 407; *HW* 2: 360).

NOTES

1. The implication that follows from putting together these two claims about "suffering from indeterminacy" and the priority of original inter-subjective relations of dependence is that it is such relations that provide the determinate content for modern ideals of equality, individual dignity, mutual respect and the like. (It must always be in terms of such dependence that we understand what it is to respect each other, acknowledge dignity and so forth.) This is a consequence Honneth accepts (*Suffering from Indeterminacy: An Attempt at a Reactivation of Hegel's Philosophy of Right*, J. Ben-Levi (trans.) (Assen: Van Gorcum, 2000)), but it opens the door to the question about how we evaluate such social communities once we have eliminated all reliance on methodological individualism, on "what rational individuals would will". I discuss this issue further below.

2. I defend this at greater length in R. B. Pippin, "What is the Question for Which Hegel's 'Theory of Recognition' is the Answer?", *European Journal of Philosophy* 8(2) (2000), 155–72, and in a different way in *Henry James and Modern Moral Life* (Cambridge: Cambridge University Press, 2000).

3. See the use of this phrase in C. Korsgaard's work, especially in *The Sources of Normativity* (Cambridge: Cambridge University Press, 1996).

4. Such a subject "perceives itself just as it is experienced by others, and the perceiving is just existence which has become a self" (*PhG*: 395; *HW* 2: 351).

5. This is admittedly a controversial reading. For a defence of it, see R. B. Pippin, *Hegel's Idealism: The Satisfactions of Self-Consciousness* (Cambridge: Cambridge University Press, 1989).

6. Indeed this gap helps one understand what would otherwise be somewhat paradoxical in the whole account given thus far of the priority of recognitional dependence in the possibility of true individuality. The question would be: must I not *already be* a free, self-determining being to be properly responsive to any such inter-subjective exchange with another, and to be capable of bestowing the kind of recognition that would count for another as constitutive of his or her individuality? And the answer would be that such a self-ascription must always be *provisional*, mere self-certainty, something challengeable and correctable "socially". I develop this claim more fully in a forthcoming book, *Hegel's Practical Philosophy: Rational Agency as Ethical Life*.

7. Miller's translation rightly captures Hegel's suspicion about such a possible position, "Individuality which takes itself to be real in and for itself", but there is no "takes itself" in the German.

8. Why there has to be *that* sort of constraint is clearly an independent and arguable issue.

9. The succeeding account of religion treats it much more as philosophically "representative" than as the social phenomenon that interested the young Hegel.

10. ... and hear poor rogues
    Talk of court news; and we'll talk with them too,
    Who loses and who wins; who's in, who's out;
    And take upon's the mystery of things,
    As if we were God's spies: and we'll wear out,
    In a walled prison, packs and sects of great ones,
    That ebb and flow by the moon.   (Shakespeare, *King Lear*: Act V, Scene III)
11. I am here disagreeing with J. Bernstein, "Confession and Forgiveness: Hegel's Poetics of Action", in *Beyond Representation: Philosophy and Poetic Imagination*, R. Eldridge (ed.), 34–65 (Cambridge: Cambridge University Press, 1996).

CHAPTER EIGHT

THE CONTEMPORARY RELEVANCE OF HEGEL'S PRACTICAL PHILOSOPHY

Ludwig Siep

The question concerning the contemporary relevance of Hegel's practical philosophy has many different aspects to it. Some commentators see Hegel's thought as an anticipation of the debate between liberalism and communitarianism, others interpret it as a critical diagnosis of society from the normative perspective of communicative freedom (Honneth 2000), while others regard it as an attempt to develop a kind of collective self-reflection on the relevant criteria of truth and justice (Pinkard 1994; Brandom 2001). In the following discussion, I should like to defend three theses:

(I) Hegel presents us with a theory of social differentiation, or rather of "full differentiation" [*Ausdifferenzierung*], that does not simply abandon the claim of "practical philosophy" to be a normative science.

(II) Hegel distinguishes different levels within a unified concept of right that involves all the "generations" of fundamental rights, as they have recently been called, and simultaneously thematizes the question concerning their historical realization.

(III) Hegel's philosophy of right contains a concept of the political that is critically relevant to contemporary discussions concerning the appropriate role of the state.

I

For Hegel, the principle of "actuality", and of its "scientific" comprehension through philosophy, implies a process of self-differentiation, or an immanent differentiation into independent systems that obey their own internal "logic", that is to say, display an inner coherence of their own. Both the kind of differentiation and the inner logic involved vary according to whether we

143

are considering the realm of nature, society, culture or pure thought. For instance, the way in which the concept and reality of life determine organic nature, concretely specifying and revealing its internal structure and development, is different from the way in which freedom is realized in society, or absolute spirit is realized in religion and philosophy.

Diversity also applies to the development of systems and structures within the social world. In his Jena writings, Hegel sought to combine the aspects of integration and differentiation familiar from classical political philosophy: the traditional Aristotelian account of the formation of families, towns and city-states and the Platonic doctrine of the social classes, with the conception of society that is reflected in modern theories of natural law and modern political economy. In this regard, he was essentially responding to the effective dissolution of the old European system of classes or "estates" and articulating the political and social implications of the fundamental change of perspective that now regarded the free choice of profession, rather than rank and occupation as defined by birth, as the crucial factor in determining the individual's social status. Hegel interpreted the political and social importance of the classes of civil society, structured through the economic activities of the market, in the light of the failure of the abstract social contract theory that in his view characterized the pre-Napoleonic phase of the French Revolution.

In his mature philosophy of objective spirit, Hegel presents the family, civil society with its classes and professions and their various agencies of self-organization, and the state itself in its administrative and more specifically political character, not merely as distinct forms of organization with specific purposes of their own, but also as distinct forms of "ethical life" (Sittlichkeit). These structures provide a diversity of social goods and allow their respective members to develop a different mentality and self-image, a differentiated understanding of their own freedom and social position, of the appropriate recognition they deserve and of their own "dignity" within society.

Above all, it was through his analysis of "the system of needs" that Hegel grasped the dynamic of the modern world of labour, with its sudden transformations and its growing trend towards specialization, and the globalizing tendencies of increasingly trans-national markets. My aim here, however, is not to discuss how Hegel anticipated subsequent theories of economic crisis, class-structure or colonialism and so on. Rather, it seems to me that the greatest interest of his political philosophy from the contemporary perspective lies primarily in the way in which he explicitly combines the concept of social differentiation with that of normative integration. In this respect Hegel's position differs significantly from many recent theorists of modernity and social differentiation, ranging from Weber to thinkers such as Luhmann, for whom the structure of modern society can no longer be described as "integrated by reference to norms".

In modern social philosophy, the theory of "full differentiation", that is, of the functional specialization of social spheres with specific structures of their own, has acquired almost unchallenged dominance. The distinctions between and the reciprocal dependence of different social worlds can be interpreted in phenomenological terms, in terms of systems theory, or in terms of the theory of rational communication. Luhmann's system theory actually combines aspects of all three approaches. There are both interesting similarities and differences between the social philosophies of Luhmann and Hegel. They share a comparable understanding of the inner coherence of specific systems, and of their capacity to represent other systems in their own language and from their own particular standpoint. And they also share the idea that "subjectivity" cannot properly be grasped solely from a first-person perspective or be interpreted exclusively within the context of the human individual alone: natural, social and conceptual entities and processes also display structures of subjectivity and reflexivity (Siep 2000).

However, the two theories of self-differentiation and reflexivity diverge crucially in their treatment of the relation between differentiation and integration. For Luhmann, the integration of particular systems and of society as a whole is an open-ended process of ongoing communication. As in the case of natural evolution, there is no turning back to less differentiated and less complex states of affairs. That is why any appeal to the "old European" conception of the autonomy of the person, or of the intrinsic self-sufficiency of the social order, is simply a backward-looking form of self-deception.

Despite its developmental direction, the process of differentiation itself has no aim over and beyond its own self-perpetuation. For Luhmann, any attempt to interpret social systems with reference to governing norms or principles is theoretically impossible and practically undesirable. For Hegel, on the other hand, a process of social differentiation that cannot ultimately be grasped as a form of self-differentiation, that is, one that possesses no immanent norm and cannot conceptualize itself in such terms, would merely represent a case of what he calls "bad infinity".

As a normative theory of full differentiation, Michael Walzer's (1983) conception of the different spheres of justice comes much closer to Hegel's philosophy of objective spirit. For Walzer, as for Hegel, full differentiation is more than a simply functional feature of society precisely because it also generates specific forms of justice. According to Walzer, each specific sphere ("money and trade", "education and culture", "security and well-being", etc.), depending on the particular goods specific to each, involves a different way of determining fair distribution and raising legitimate claims. To transfer a system of distribution appropriate in one sphere over to other spheres would not simply violate the differentiation of the relevant spheres and bestow undue power on one sphere in particular. It would also damage the individual rights if arrangements appropriate to one sphere allowed us to raise equal claims in the context of another (for instance a politician claiming financial rewards). If, on the other hand, the boundaries of the different spheres are reciprocally respected and the particular structures for the distribution of goods are properly protected, then it is possible to actualize both freedom and justice within the social system as a whole.

Judged from the perspective of Hegel's concept of self-differentiation, however, there is still something unsatisfactory about the way in which Walzer's theory specifies the different forms of justice. For Walzer is unable to show how the various senses of justice arise intelligibly from a common core. Instead, each form of justice is based on the given kind of social good that is distributed in each sphere. The differentiation in question is not presented as the systematic development of a common idea of justice.

For Hegel, by contrast, the full differentiation of social spheres is essentially governed by a normative concept: the idea of freedom that permits the development of the individual's particular abilities and the pursuit of one's particular interests within the overall context of a just social order. Thus the family, the different professions and classes, the corporations, the administrative sectors and the constitutional powers of the state are all different levels and stages of a single development.

The family recognizes the natural particularity and the specific physical and emotional needs of the individual. The individual likewise responds to the demands of the other members and of the "institution" of the family, in a way that cannot be grasped in strictly contractual terms. On entering civil society as an adult, on the other hand, the individual now acquires specific rights and incurs specific obligations. This enables him to affirm the right to property and to pursue his life and career in his own way. But this freedom only acquires substance and permanence in so far as the individual develops a specific competence within a certain profession and pursues this profession to the benefit of society with an appropriate mentality and sense of "social standing". This outlook recognizes duties that are beyond the letter of the law, such as diligence, reliability and similar virtues, but that are nonetheless properly expected of people in specific professions, such as businessmen, doctors, teachers and so on. And to this day such expectations have always exceeded what is "strictly stipulated" as such.

In return for his honesty, the individual can also expect a certain "material justice" that protects his property, and thus the general security of his life, from the contingencies of individual circumstance and the processes of the market. On Hegel's account, material justice goes beyond the kind of social security that derives from membership in a particular professional group, or from the task of the "corporations", to promote labour policies that can combine a free choice of trades and professions with high levels of employment. Some of what according to Hegel are the "familial tasks" of civil society must actually be discharged by the state in its secondary function of stabilizing the processes of civil society.

As far as the mediation between individual freedom and justice is concerned, it is quite true that the genuine tasks of the state lie elsewhere: the state must be able to identify and to realize communal ends and purposes in the domain of law and cultural policy in a way that is truly independent of purely private interests. For freedom can only properly be fulfilled in a state where individuals are able to participate in the "communicative" identification and realization of collectively shared tasks. But this process of "will-formation", at the political level of the state, should also involve what Hegel calls the "essential spheres" or "larger interests" of society (PR: §311). The domains of agriculture, commerce, the trades and professions, knowledge and scholarship, the military and so on, cannot, however, simply be considered as so many closed systems. For although they develop their own distinctive perspectives concerning the welfare and justice of society as a whole, these perspectives can nonetheless be successfully integrated with one another.

Hegel's model for the full differentiation and integration of social systems is, of course, based on his own conviction that the structure of social organization and the relationship between the different groups and classes can ultimately be reconstructed and articulated in a conceptually "necessary" manner. Each chosen occupation and social position is not merely necessary for the prosperity of society as a whole, but can also be derived from the conceptual relation between universality, particularity and individuality. While this conceptual order may not apply to the particular branches of trade and commerce, it is applicable to the distinction between the agricultural, commercial and administrative classes in general. Furthermore, on Hegel's account, the relevant level of self-reflection that belongs to these classes, from the unreflective trust of the agrarian class through the utilitarian perspective of trade and commerce to the self-conscious insight into the common good among the intellectually educated officials and civil servants, can be said to follow the immanent logic of spirit.

Clearly, this sets certain limits on one's freedom to choose a specific profession and on civic equality in general. This is because membership of the different classes depends on faculties and education and also because the political judgement of the members of the agricultural class has less impact on the political process than that of the other classes. There is also a further problem with the contemporary application of this model. In a technological society where immediate human labour is becoming increasingly redundant and the domain of the leisure and entertainment industry is becoming increasingly important, we cannot deny that socially necessary occupations and professions are also becoming rarer.[1] The production of goods and the supply of services, and the way in which they are distributed through the operation of the market, is effectively turning into a relationship between "private" individuals. In this respect "recognition" now consists almost entirely in relevant financial rewards or other forms of personal "gratification". From the contemporary perspective, Hegel's idea of a conceptually necessary structure of social classes binds social recognition much too closely to stable conditions of socially necessary labour.

147

Hegel's *Philosophy of Right* may not offer a relevant solution to the problems of today. But it can certainly offer contemporary social philosophy some food for thought as an interesting attempt to combine the concept of social differentiation with that of normative integration. And despite the criticisms that have commonly been levelled against it, we can also say the same of Hegel's concept of right itself, as I shall now attempt to show.

II

The concept of right that Hegel presented in his *Philosophy of Right* has long been a principal target of criticism. This concept encompasses a range of claims extending from the defence of the individual's right to property and to freedom of conscience, through the state's right to ask the citizen to sacrifice life and property in the extreme case, to the right of the historically most progressive states to impose their own political constitution and culture on other states. But does this not simply evacuate the very content of the concept of right entirely? Does it not relinquish all of the gains that had originally been acquired by the Enlightenment discourse of rights?

There is no doubt that Hegel's conception of right harbours certain dangers. They are connected with questions concerning the delimitation of the rights of the state in relation to individual rights, and with the "legalization" of expansionist policies since the nineteenth century. However, I should simply like to draw attention here to the fruitfulness of a concept of right that involves several dimensions and explicitly thematizes the progressive development and realization of these dimensions. For a similarly multidimensional concept of right has also come to represent a topical issue and priority in contemporary legal and political philosophy.

We have become accustomed in recent political philosophy to speak of first, second and third "generations" of basic rights (Waldron 1993).[2] The first generation of rights designates the sort of protective and participatory rights formulated by and enshrined in the revolutions of the eighteenth century and the democratic reforms of the nineteenth century. These include civil rights that protect the citizen against the power of the state, such as the right to property and the right to freedom of conscience and moral conviction, as well as rights that allow active participation in the political process in a republic or a constitutional monarchy, and above all the right to vote.

The second generation of rights includes claims to social support or assistance in the case of individual or collective disaster. They have been institutionalized incrementally from the nineteenth century onwards and especially in the period following the Second World War. This process has transpired in varying degrees and has involved a continuous debate concerning the status and character of such rights.

The third generation of rights are rights to collective goods such as peace, education, a clean environment, measures promoting economic and social development, and sometimes specific cultural goods such as languages and religions, especially those of minorities. It was these last questions in particular that served to ignite the debate between liberals and communitarians. But the character and status of these third-generation rights, in so far as they are interpreted as a matter of individual rights, has remained a controversial subject in legal and political philosophy.

Of course, it is equally controversial whether these successive generations of rights effectively follow a progressive or indeed teleological course. Some authors such as T. H. Marshall (1963: 73ff.) and, more recently, Axel Honneth (1996) have explicitly defended this view. Legal theorists and economists within the liberal tradition, on the other hand, suspect that overtaxing and extending the role of the state in this way can only lead to a reduction of individual rights. From the liberal perspective, the welfare state could hardly avoid becoming paternalistic, and even tyrannical, if it attempted to meet all the demands placed on it by such putative rights.

On the other hand, the state has certain ends and obligations, such as provision of social assistance or the protection of the natural environment, that it cannot possibly relinquish without violating the concept of basic rights. But these obligations do not always conform to the model of individual claims-rights sanctioned by the state. Authors such as Jeremy Waldron (1993: 353ff.) have pointed out that we are confronted here with a combination of individual interests, individual needs for shared social goods and often also specific group-rights.

I believe that it is a strength of Hegel's concept of right that it is capable of conceptualizing and articulating what we have here called the "generations" of right precisely as an internal development of the idea of right as the very "embodiment of freedom". A number of authors have clearly pointed out, against his liberal critics, that Hegel does indeed maintain a positive conception of basic rights. However, he is less interested in the general declaration of basic rights than in seeing them concretely incorporated in the actual legislation, customs and way of life of the community as a whole (Lübbe-Wolff 1986; Siep 1992: 294). In addition, one must concede that as far as the "first generation" of rights is concerned, Hegel does not really do full justice to the rights that protect the citizen in relation to the state. But at every level of the *Philosophy of Right* Hegel addresses, implicitly or explicitly, the kinds of legitimate claims that effectively correspond to "basic rights" in the modern sense.

As is generally recognized, the first part of the *Philosophy of Right*, under the title of "Abstract Right", presents a systematic developmental account of the way in which the free will is able to appropriate or alienate things and accomplishments in accordance with universal rules that are free of any personal or political coercion. For this, according to Hegel, is how the freedom of the will is developed independently of natural determinations and is recognized by other rights-bearing individuals and by a community governed by law. But this freedom must also be secured where necessary against the purely particular usurpation of the general will – the very nature of conscious criminality according to Hegel – through the coercive and penal response on the part of the violated general will.

In the second part of the *Philosophy of Right*, under the title of "Morality", the individual's right to realize what is right and good in accordance with his own insight is certainly circumscribed by the limits that a law-governed community necessarily imposes on anyone who justifies his actions exclusively on the basis of inner conviction or conscience. But the freedom to *judge* in accordance with one's own conscience is recognized as something beyond the reach of the state, as a "sanctum" that the state can neither scrutinize nor coerce. The chapter on morality broadens the concept of right not only with respect to the free cultural and educational development of the individual and the expression of personal conviction, but also to general welfare over and beyond the sphere of property and contractual law. Welfare is therefore not merely a matter of private benevolence, but something that must also be secured through the institutions of a just community independent of the vagaries of subjective disposition.

Welfare in the broad sense involves more than the protection of the essential conditions for life, as already mentioned, in the case of disasters that physically or materially threaten people's capacity to earn a living or to maintain themselves. It also includes affective aspects such as the self-respect that the individual acquires as a recognized member of the "bourgeois family", and as a competent and conscientious member of society who participates in the processes of production, exchange and administration in general.

These forms of ethical life extend individual freedom not only through the elements of welfare, but also through the specifically ethical form of freedom that comes from uniting with other individuals in the social institutions that are required for the proper fulfilment of shared collective tasks. The highest level of this unification is achieved in a state where the individual rational will can recognize and promote constitutionally regulated political freedom, can develop a self-image and cultural identity of its own, and can contribute to the intellectual quest for truth. I shall return to this in the final part of this chapter. But it is already important to note here that individual rights for Hegel also involve claims to participate in a specific political culture.

This extension of the concept of right to embrace ideas of welfare and ethical freedom is particularly interesting from the perspective of contemporary debate. Even before the development of the modern welfare state or of modern theories of social justice, Hegel had already shown that in order to think of themselves as free citizens and bearers of rights individuals must also be able to trust in a reliable basis for the conduct of their life in society. This presupposes institutions that can provide security for the basic conditions of

150

life, something that is accomplished partly by the family and partly by professional associations and other social institutions. These claims can and should be satisfied in a variety of ways, ranging from the formation of cooperatives and the establishment of occupational forms of insurance and financial assistance through to state-supported institutions of public health and the relevant regulation of trade and commerce and so on.

Such claims may not always be mounted or enforced in strictly "legal terms". For Hegel, unlike Fichte, there is no absolute right to work, but merely a general obligation, especially on the part of the corporations, to influence the labour market "gently" without eliminating its basic rules. Such rights are best seen as social goods that must be provided through the joint effort of different agencies and organizations. And failure to satisfy these demands in general terms not only undermines individual rights, but also threatens to destroy common goods such as social peace and respect for the law by encouraging class entrenchment and class conflict.

Ahead of any further issues of ethical freedom and active membership in a political community, such goods and the claims associated with them must already be described as "communal" ones in Waldron's sense (1993). Such goods, such as military security or clean air, must be secured collectively and cannot be enjoyed in a personal or exclusive sense. Goods such as friendship, good humour, cultural attainment and so forth can clearly only be realized through mutual participation in a community. From Waldron's perspective, it is groups and communities, and not just individuals, who can rightfully make claims on such goods. But this certainly does not mean that we have to posit some collective subject or invoke some supra-personal conception of the "spirit of the people", something that is also entirely inappropriate where the Hegelian concept of spirit is concerned.

Hegel interprets this development and enrichment of the concept of right as a kind of historical teleology, as a genuinely rational process revealing itself in modern constitutional and social history. The development of individual freedom certainly requires the establishment of a system of civil rights – and in this respect of course Hegel regarded the Napoleonic "Code Civil" as the rational outcome of the French Revolution. But the development of individual personality also requires both the market economy with its "professional" groups and classes and the effective stabilization of the market through corporations and other social institutions. In Hegel's time these processes were only beginning to emerge at all clearly and they certainly did not entirely follow the path he had anticipated. But Hegel considered the stabilization of civil society and the attenuation of its crises as a necessary condition if the rights of individuals and groups are not to remain abstract and ineffective.

This immanent differentiation and enrichment of the concept of right does not merely exemplify a historical teleology. It also represents a *substantive* teleology that explicates the internal organization and differentiation of society and the state itself. It is based on the principle of inner differentiation and integration of social and political systems and subsystems, as already discussed in the first part of the essay. But not all of the goods and rights we have mentioned are defined or secured in the form of claims that can be strictly enforced or guaranteed by the state. There are different sorts of legitimate claims or goods, which must also be guaranteed and fulfilled in different ways.

The argument for the contemporary relevance of Hegel's practical and political philosophy that I have defended here appears to come at a certain cost. For it only seems plausible if we also repudiate the core of Hegel's *Philosophy of Right*: the idea of the political state as an absolute end in itself, one whose power and existence represents the highest "right" that ultimately takes precedence over all individual rights. Is there any sense, therefore, in which we can still speak of the contemporary relevance of Hegel's *political* conception of the state? In the last part of this essay, I shall attempt to show the contemporary relevance of his conception of civic political life, an idea that Hegel, following the tradition of classical political philosophy, undertakes to revive under the modern conditions of a fully differentiated and increasingly emancipated society.

III

In his *Philosophy of Right*, Hegel recognized the demands that are placed on the state by a fully differentiated but nonetheless unstable form of society. The market economy, with its increasing capacity to satisfy actual needs and to produce new ones, facilitates the development of the most varied talents and abilities. It not only increases the level of material comfort and well-being – something that in Hegel's view "has no qualitative limits" (*PR*: §195) – but also permits the self-definition and self-differentiation of individuals in the first place. But the crises that unavoidably afflict the market can also produce disastrous consequences for the individual and serve to exacerbate class conflict. This must be remedied as much as possible by the "police" and the "corporations", that is, by the agencies of state administration and the corporate structures of class representation.

However, the various activities through which the state successfully stabilizes civil society are only subsidiary tasks of the state in Hegel's view. They represent the social rather than the truly political side of the state. The latter consists essentially in the institutions of constitutional monarchy, in the organized division of powers within the state that have the sovereign at their "summit". Reason demands the existence of such a state as a kind of end in itself. Many interpreters have emphasized the strong "institutionalism" of Hegel's *Philosophy of Right* (Henrich 1982), and many have strongly criticized it (Honneth 2000: 102–27).[3]

On the one hand, Hegel justifies this institutionalism through his conception of objective spirit. The latter is embodied in the state as the "unmoved" end in relation to the action and knowledge of individuals. In Hegel's view this end no more instrumentalizes the individuals that serve it than marriage and the family instrumentalize their individual members. For in both cases the individuals themselves, whether as "familial" or as political beings, equally represent the "end" of the institution in question. The individuals find their own realization or ultimate vocation in these institutions.

On the other hand, Hegel's theory of the state also involves a conception of man as a political being that represents a new version of this traditional doctrine under the conditions of modern civil society. One might be tempted, with Luhmann (1997: II 841, 912ff.), to interpret this approach as another version of the traditional European idea of a hierarchically and teleologically organized social totality with the state as its final all-embracing *telos*. One could also ask, however, which aspects of Hegel's account of political life might still be relevant today (Siep 2002).

For Hegel, the freedom of the individual and the community is only properly realized through political life in a state whose institutions promote the formation of a rational general will. In the *Philosophy of Right* we read that individuals should recognize "the universal" embodied in the political constitution and the genuine political activities of the state "as their own spirit" and "act on its behalf as their own final end" (*PR*: §260). It is precisely this combination of the political life of individuals with their private and particular interests that Hegel calls "concrete freedom".

The state must do more than preserve and support the differentiation between the spheres of family and society, as well as the differentiation between distinct economic sectors and the occupational classes involved in them within society itself. It must also offer individuals the opportunity for public action, for serving, preserving and participating in the constitutional order and political culture of the community. To be a spiritual being in Hegel's sense is necessarily to be a political being, just as for Aristotle the rational animal – the *zoon logon echon* is essentially a political animal. It is through reason that we decide, through public speech and decision, what is just or unjust, what is useful or harmful, for all.

As the "actualization of concrete freedom", the Hegelian state must acknowledge the personal interests of individuals and particular groups in the independent spheres of family and the market. Through the economic laws of "the invisible hand" and the normative laws based on the idea of the general will, the personal will must "pass over of its own accord into the interest of the universal" (*PR*: §260). However, this process is not something that can simply be entrusted to experts or specialists. Rather, it must be integrated with the conscious will and conduct of the citizens. This double mediation of the personal and the political constitutes the very principle of the modern state for Hegel.

Hegel explicitly recognizes the political dimension of human life in its own right, even though he clearly interprets political participation in an obviously pre-democratic way.[4] He rejects the idea of popular sovereignty, of universal suffrage and of the primacy of the legislature, because they would render the state dependent on quite contingent constellations of majorities that are effectively coalitions of various private and group interests: "election is ... reduced to a trivial play of opinion and caprice" (*PR*: §311).

Nevertheless, Hegel believes that it is an essential task of the deputies to draw on their own specific areas of competence and to articulate the specific interests of the different classes and professional groups where legislative consultation is concerned. The deputies ought therefore to "include representatives of each particular main branch of society (e.g. trade, manufacture, etc.) – representatives who are thoroughly conversant with it and who themselves belong to it" (*PR*: §311). Thus the determination of the common good must not be produced through the mere aggregate of particular interests and opinions, but must explicitly take into consideration the "larger interests" and "essential branches of society" that are important to the common good (*PR*: §311).

One may ask here whether modern democracies have not found their own ways of allowing the "larger interests" to influence legislation, either through representation of important groups within parliamentary parties themselves or through the comments of professional associations on particular legislative proposals prepared by the ministerial bureaucracy. In this respect, not every voice possesses an equal value even in a parliamentary system. Furthermore, the participation of political parties in the formation of the public will has now become an important way of "mediating" the will of the voters. The issue here, however, is not the historical development of modern democracies, which Hegel did not really anticipate and whose beginnings he viewed with considerable scepticism in any case.

With respect to the fundamental question, however, whether the right to active participation in shaping the life of the state is essential for the self-realization of the individual, Hegel's position is still highly relevant. The same can be said for the question whether the state must restrict itself to sustaining the conditions of the private well-being of individuals, or whether it also has a duty to concern itself with public goods, with collective aims and forms of social life.

In the first place, we should recognize that Hegel essentially retains the Rousseauean and Kantian idea that one cannot properly be described as free or as a person unless one is able to participate in some sense in the legislative process. However, Hegel does not regard formal participation in the legislature as decisive here, and the legislature is no longer the highest authority on his version of the division of powers anyway (Siep 1992: 240–69). What is decisive for Hegel is rather the opportunity for participating in public life in general, either directly through one's professional life as a government employee, like the educated class of academic teachers or civil servants, or indirectly in the case of the other occupations and professions and their self-governing agencies and bodies. Individuals can only realize their own rational and political nature by leading their life in conscious political "union" with others.

But this also involves meaningful communal activities such as active participation in the formation of law, of intellectual life, of aesthetic and religious culture. In this respect Hegel can certainly be regarded as a forerunner of the modern communitarians, although he also emphasizes the importance of liberal individual rights and the freedoms associated with the free choice of profession, with the activities of trade and commerce and the market in general.[5]

The attempt to restrict the function of the state to securing the conditions for the pursuit of individual well-being has surely become a paradoxical aim in any case. In order to sustain the international competitiveness of the economy of a country or locality, the state takes specific structural measures in areas such as energy, transport, communications, education and science, and public health that can have far-reaching effects both on the private life of individuals and collective forms of behaviour. The alleged neutrality of the state in relation to individual conceptions of happiness and the conduct of life has now become largely illusory even in liberal states.

Rather than setting marginal constraints on the private pursuit of happiness, properly political decisions concern fundamental social choices on which both shared forms of life and individual life plans equally depend. We are here involved with decisions about specific values, decisions that must be openly addressed in the context of our "political life".

In the contemporary debate concerning the authentic tasks of the state it seems to me that the Hegelian conception of the ethico-political vocation of man is of lasting significance. Which of these tasks can be implemented through governmental agencies alone and which can appropriately be delegated to private ones? Can public tasks and functions simply be left to experts or do they require the participation of citizens in determining policy and choosing the relevant political "personnel"?

If the self-realization of the individual depends on participation in a political "union" of the kind described, then politics is not a matter for experts alone and the tasks of the state cannot all be assumed by private agencies. Hegel's conception of the political state is therefore not merely an obsolete example of "state worship". The idea of the state as an end in itself may well possess an overly strong metaphysical core. However, Hegel's claim that citizens can only find their necessary ethical fulfilment in the domain of public and political life is a significant contribution to political anthropology and contemporary discussions concerning the tasks and limits of the state.

The same can be said for Hegel's conception of right as a form of concrete freedom that is not simply limited to the unhindered pursuit of an individual life-plan within the parameters of law. For it implies a social and political dimension of recognition with regard to particular social functions and a civic union in a genuinely political, autonomous community.

In contrast to Rousseau, and also the early Hölderlin, Hegel did not regard the modern form of the division of labour, of specialization, of the market, simply as forces of dislocation, atomization and alienation. Rather, he saw them as necessary processes that effectively allowed individuals to form and to develop particular talents and abilities. Self-objectification is certainly a phase in this process of formation, but not its principal end or result. For when these economic processes are socially and politically balanced, they transform these specialized individuals through various economic and cultural processes into active moments within an autonomous whole. To achieve this, however, the different social domains with their various customary outlooks and mentalities must be integrated within a political whole with shared values, norms and aims.

It is true, of course, that various contemporary developments, such as the growth of trans-national organizations and the relativization of the family unit through looser and more temporary forms of personal partnership, challenge Hegel's conception of the way in which particular interests can successfully be mediated with the tasks of the community as a whole. The priority that he accords to the nation-state, one characterized by a relatively homogeneous culture at that, and his rudimentary conception of international law, have obviously become deeply problematic. But if my three theses can indeed claim some support in Hegel's text, then despite the historical limits of his model of the nation-state, of constitutional monarchy and of a society structured through estates and corporations, his conception of social differentiation, of concrete freedom, of political life in its own right, are not simply hopeless, pre-modern throwbacks to an old European idea, but continue to speak to central questions of contemporary political philosophy.

NOTES

1. On the dissolution of the traditional classes or estates and the concept of "honour" defined in terms of social position, see A. Honneth, *The Struggle for Recognition: The Moral Grammar of Social Conflicts*, J. Anderson (trans.) (Cambridge, MA: MIT Press, 1996).
2. A slightly different form of this triple articulation can be found in Honneth, *The Struggle for Recognition*.
3. For Henrich this "institutionalism" is a problem that afflicts the *Philosophy of Right* rather than Hegel's philosophy of objective spirit as a whole.
4. Emundts and Horstmann emphasize the "anti-democratic" features of the Hegelian conception of legislation in so far as both chambers effectively subsist "without any direct political involvement of the people"; see D. Emundts & R.-P. Horstmann,

Hegel: Eine Einführung (Stuttgart: Reclam, 2002), 105. Despite the fact that the estates delegate through the corporations and are summoned through the authority of the monarch (*PR*: §308), they do permit the indirect involvement of the citizens in the legislative process and in the formation of public opinion, which is essential for their political life (*PR*: §315).

5. On the communitarianism debate see A. Honneth (ed.), *Kommunitarismus: Eine Debatte über die moralischen Grundlagen moderner Gesellschaften* (Frankfurt: Campus, 1993) and M. Brumlik & H. Brunkhorst (eds), *Gemeinschaft und Gerechtigkeit* (Frankfurt: Fischer, 1993).

CHAPTER NINE

CATCHING UP WITH HISTORY
HEGEL AND ABSTRACT PAINTING
Jason Gaiger

Are Hegel's aesthetics of merely retrospective interest, a melancholy tour through the fossilized remains of past cultural greatness, as one author has recently claimed (Wyss 1997, 1999)? Or is it possible to establish the relevance of Hegel's ideas to subsequent art practice, even though art has developed in ways that Hegel himself could not possibly have anticipated? Beat Wyss's seductive but highly misleading picture of the philosopher wandering through a vast imaginary museum of his own construction, bathed in the glow of sunset and confident that history had reached its end in the task of philosophical comprehension, enacts the very ossification of Hegel's thought that it purports to criticize. Nonetheless, the enormous changes that the practice of art has undergone since Hegel's death in 1831 make the task of connecting his views to later art highly problematic. In this paper I analyse contrasting arguments for the contemporary relevance of Hegel's aesthetics that have been put forward by two of the foremost Hegel scholars working today: Stephen Houlgate and Robert Pippin. Both take the emergence of fully abstract painting in the early years of the twentieth century as an important test case, yet they reach diametrically opposed conclusions as to how abstract art should be understood from a Hegelian point of view.

It is a striking feature of contemporary debates in aesthetics, particularly in Anglo-American analytic philosophy, that whereas Kant's *Critique of Judgement* remains an indispensable and highly productive point of reference, Hegel's *Lectures on Aesthetics* are rarely, if ever, mined for enduring insights into aesthetic experience or the role of art in modern society. Although this has much to do with the reception history of the two philosophers in the English-speaking world, it may also be connected to the fact that Kant's aesthetics is not linked to the discussion of specific art works (with the single exception of some lines from a poem by Frederick the Great), whereas Hegel's aesthetics is grounded in a detailed historical account of the development of art up to and including his own time. The explanatory potential of Kant's theory is not tied to particular forms of art. Rather, his goal is to provide an account of aesthetic experience that is sufficiently broad to encompass our responses to both natural beauty and to art. The very abstraction of Kant's account, including his celebrated attempt to locate the ultimate ground of our pleasure in the beautiful in a dynamic attunement or free play between the faculties of imagination and understanding, allows his ideas to be related to almost any object of aesthetic attention. By contrast, Hegel's analysis of the changing functions that art has fulfilled at different stages of human social and historical development gives his aesthetics a retrospective character, making it difficult to extricate more general claims that might have application beyond their original context. Hegel's sensitivity to the historical character of art, and his willingness to recognize the transitory status of the various forms in which it has been produced, prevents the straightforward extension of his ideas to later art practice.

A second obstacle is presented by Hegel's much-discussed thesis of the "end of art". If Hegel held that the development of art had come to an end, and that art had been superseded by religion and philosophy, he would appear to have little to offer that could help us to understand the different ways in which art has continued to change in the century and a half that has elapsed since his death. However, as both Houlgate and Pippin emphasize (Houlgate 2005; Pippin 2003), Hegel should not be misconstrued as putting forward a grandiose claim about the "death" of art. They both interpret Hegel's thesis as a means of drawing attention to a fundamental alteration in the way in which art matters to us, that is to say, as a claim about art's changed social and cultural function rather than its exhaustion or lack of significance. The second obstacle is thus closely related to the first. Hegel's thesis of the end of art cannot be dismissed either as an aberration or as extraneous to the substance of his thought. Rather, a proper understanding of what he means by this provocative observation goes to the very heart of his aesthetics. It is *in* Hegel's account of the historicality of art that his contemporary relevance is to be found, although, as we shall see, Houlgate and Pippin differ in the way in which they understand this claim.

At stake in this dispute is not simply the "application" of Hegel's aesthetics to later art practice, but how we are to interpret his views on art in the first place. Both Houlgate and Pippin base their accounts on H. G. Hotho's posthumous three-volume edition of the lectures on aesthetics, which they continue to describe as the "standard edition".[1] As the work of Annemarie Gethmann-Siefert, Helmut Schneider and others has shown, however, there are grounds for serious reservations about the reliability of Hotho's text, which was not published until 1835, four years after Hegel's death.[2] A new basis for the study of Hegel's aesthetics is provided by the ongoing discovery and publication of the surviving sets of transcripts and lecture notes that were made by students who were present at Hegel's lectures. These notes and transcripts, some of which are astonishingly detailed and well-written, were clearly held to be valuable since many were expensively bound and kept in private libraries. Not only do they provide a vivid picture of Hegel's activity as a lecturer, but, unlike Hotho's edition, which fuses Hegel's different lecture courses into a single work, they allow us to trace the evolution of his views over time. Although it is not possible to give a full account of these important discoveries here, I begin with a brief discussion of the current state of scholarship. I provide a survey of the available primary sources and then consider the charges that have been raised against Hotho's editorial procedure in producing his posthumous edition. I then return to the central concern of this paper and assess in turn Houlgate's and Pippin's account of abstract art from a Hegelian perspective.

I. THE TEXTUAL BASIS FOR STUDYING HEGEL'S LECTURES ON AESTHETICS

Between 1818 and 1829 Hegel gave five separate series of lectures on aesthetics. The first series, the content and structure of which is closely connected to the systematic position allocated to art in the *Encyclopaedia* of 1817, was given in Heidelberg in 1818. Hegel lectured on art and religion together, treating them separately for the first time in Berlin. For the delivery of the lectures, he used a notebook in which he formulated his ideas in short, condensed paragraphs supplemented by extensive explanatory notes, much as he did in the *Encyclopaedia* and the *Philosophy of Right*. This information is related by Hotho, who still had access to Hegel's notebook when he prepared his edition. There are no extant transcripts or student notes from the Heidelberg lectures and Hegel's own notebook is lost.

Hegel first lectured on aesthetics in Berlin in the winter semester of 1820–21 to an audience of around fifty students, which included Heinrich Heine. For these lectures Hegel began a new notebook, which he continued to use for all the later lectures with ever more extensive supplements and modifications. Again, this notebook was available to Hotho, who used it in the preparation of his edition. Once his edition was published, he broke up the notebook, sending parts of it to friends and other interested parties. Only a few fragments have since been recovered (see e.g. Sziborsky 1983; Schneider 1984). There is just one extant set of student notes to this lecture series, by Wilhelm von Ascheberg. These were published under the editorship of Helmut Schneider in 1995.

Hegel next lectured on aesthetics in Berlin in the summer semester of 1823. The lectures were announced under the title, "Aestheticen sive philosophiam artis". The sole surviving transcript, by Hotho, was published under the editorship of Gethmann-Siefert in 1998.[3] This is the most accessible and readable of the transcripts that have so far been published. Hotho left his notes as he took them down during the lectures, rather than writing them up afterwards, although he subsequently added a number of marginal additions, which are clearly marked in the published version.[4] Hegel held a third series of lectures in the summer semester of 1826, once again announced under the title "Aestheticen sive philosophiam artis", for which there are four surviving sets of notes of variable quality. Two of these have now been published.[5] Hegel gave a final set of lectures in the winter semester of 1828–29, for which there are three extant sets of student notes, none of which have been published at the time of writing. Whereas in the first three series of Berlin lectures Hegel adopted a two-part structure in which the first section is devoted to the "universal" and the second to the "particular", in the final series of lectures he adopted a three-part structure, divided into the "universal", the "particular" and the "individual".

When Hotho started work on his edition of the aesthetics he had access not only to both of Hegel's notebooks and to his own detailed notes from the last three lecture series, but also to a large number of other sets of student notes, most of which are now lost. He had been a student of Hegel's since 1822 and he was able to base his edition on first-hand knowledge of Hegel's lectures as well as a variety of important primary sources that are no longer available to us. Why, then, should there be doubts about the reliability of his edition? Questions about Hotho's editorial practice were first raised as long ago as 1931 by Georg Lasson (1931).[6] However, it is principally due to the work of Gethmann-Siefert that these questions have now started to receive proper attention. On the basis of a close comparison of Hotho's text with the available transcripts and notes she argues that:

> Even if for many years no one was aware it, the debate about Hegel's *Aesthetics* has always at the same time been a dispute about the relevance (*Aktualität*) of the view of art that Hotho surreptitiously wove into Hegel's philosophy of art by reworking his sources in the published version of the aesthetics. In the process many of Hegel's ideas were enfeebled, made unclear, and, above all, given a substantially different emphasis. (*Hotho*: xv)

As Gethmann-Siefert points out, Hotho's account of his editorial procedure in the preface to his edition should already have led to a more circumspect attitude to the published text. Hotho states his conviction that the manuscripts and lecture notes represent little more than "sketches and observations". His task had been to restore the "animating inner life" (*jenes erquickendes innere Leben*) through the "structuring of the whole" (*Gliederung des Ganzen*), the addition of missing "dialectical transitions" (*dialektische Übergänge*), the tightening up of "loose connections" (*lose Zusammenhangenden*) and an increase in the "introduction of examples" (*Anführung von Kunstbeispielen*) (see Hotho's "Vorrede", xiv, cited in Gethmann-Siefert 1991: 93). Hotho spent nearly three years carrying out this work. The result was a massive three-volume edifice, the text of which in the modern German edition runs to nearly 1600 pages. By comparison, the surviving transcripts and lecture notes are much more modest in scale. The printed version of Hotho's own transcript of the 1823 lecture series is just over 300 pages. It now seems beyond doubt that the unwieldy size of the *Lectures on Aesthetics*, the frequent repetitions of the same material and, perhaps more importantly, the existence of numerous discrepancies between different parts of the text, can be attributed to Hotho's editorial labours.

Equally significant is Hotho's insistence on the need to demonstrate the superiority of Hegel's aesthetics in face of the rival systems that had been presented by F. W. J. Schelling and K. W. F. Solger. He laments the lack of systematic completeness in the material Hegel had left behind and insists that in order to organize and give structure to the lectures he was obliged to "complete" Hegel's system. Displaying the characteristic over-identification of the student with his teacher, Hotho strives to be more Hegelian than Hegel. Unlike Hotho's edition, the lecture transcripts reveal the frequently tentative character of Hegel's observations on art, his willingness to revise his ideas in the light of new experiences and a continuous assimilation of new ideas and materials. Conspicuously absent are the strongly normative pronouncements on the success or failure of individual artworks from the standpoint of the system, which have rightly troubled later readers, as well as the forced "dialectical transitions" from one art form to another. We know from Hegel's correspondence that although he hoped to publish a work on the philosophy of art he was not yet ready to do so. Gethmann-Siefert has urged that we should see his aesthetics as a "work in progress", subject to continual revision and rewriting over the different lecture series. Hotho's monumental edition of the *Lectures on Aesthetics* not only obscures these differences by amalgamating the various series into a single, systematic work, it also gives the mistaken impression that Hegel's thought on the subject had reached definitive form.

It is now almost impossible to work out exactly what belongs to Hegel and what was introduced by Hotho.[7] As Lasson was the first to point out, the description of art as the "sensuous appearance of the idea" (*das sinnliche Scheinen der Idee*) is nowhere to be found in any of the surviving sets of notes. Yet this formulation is still taken to encapsulate Hegel's view and is treated as such by both Houlgate and Pippin. Hotho does, of course, have his defenders on grounds of both style and content. Brigitte Hilmer, for example, while readily admitting the extent of Hotho's textual interventions, claims that close study of the *Logic* alongside the surviving transcripts "reveals him to have been perhaps Hegel's most brilliant interpreter" in so far as his ordering of the material is based not on his own subjective preferences but on Hegel's "logic of the concept" (Hilmer 1997: 213). It seems wisest, however, to treat Hotho's edition with a degree of circumspection and, where possible, to look for guidance and corroboration from the transcripts and lecture notes. As more of these are published and studied, we will gain a fuller picture of Hegel's lectures on aesthetics. Hotho's edition remains a fascinating document, but it can no longer be treated as the "standard text"; at the time of publication it already belonged to the reception history of Hegel's ideas.

II. A CRITIQUE OF ABSTRACT PAINTING
FROM A HEGELIAN PERSPECTIVE

With these reflections in mind, I now want to turn to the specific question addressed by this chapter: how should abstract painting be understood from a Hegelian point of view? I begin with Houlgate's ambitious attempt to show that Hegel's aesthetics provide us with the resources not only to understand the emergence of fully abstract art but also to *criticize* this development. Houlgate's arguments form part of a more comprehensive project, the aim of which is to show "the great value and relevance [of Hegel's ideas] to current social, political, aesthetic, theological and philosophical discussions" (Houlgate 1991: 2).[8] His interpretation of Hegel's philosophy of art is deeply bound up with his interpretation of other areas of Hegel's thought, including his logic, philosophy of history and philosophy of religion, to mention just some of the topics that are given equal prominence in his account. In a recent essay entitled "Hegel and the Art of Painting" he has drawn together his thoughts on the subject and presented in an even more pointed form an argument that he first put forward in *Freedom, Truth and History*:

> Hegel's account … provides an important way of understanding – and of criticizing – certain developments that have taken place in painting since his death. For it suggests that during the last one hundred and fifty years painting has increasingly lost sight of its distinctive nature and function. (Houlgate 2000: 61)

Houlgate's strongly normative interpretation of Hegel's aesthetics depends on identifying certain indispensable conditions that a painting must fulfil if it is to be successful as a work of art. He argues that Hegel provides an "account of the nature of painting *as such*" and that it is this "philosophical account – not just historically contingent prejudice – that leads Hegel to esteem so highly the paintings of the Italian Renaissance and of the Dutch seventeenth century" (*ibid.*). Houlgate contends that Hegel first determines the *concept* of a given phenomenon, be it freedom, religion or art, and then examines the extent to which this concept has been exemplified in history. On this view, conceptual determination not only precedes the task of historical analysis, it also provides a normative basis for establishing the legitimacy or otherwise of actual historical developments since there are limits to the permissible range of "deviation".

It is open to question whether this essentialist project is compatible with Hegel's thoroughly historical conception of the meaning and significance of art. The very attempt to identify "the nature of painting *as such*" would appear to depend on treating one particular stage in the development of painting as normative and then employing this as a measure by which to criticize subsequent developments. In response to this objection Houlgate might argue that although the practice of painting develops over time, and is thus historical, the essence of painting, what he terms its "distinctive nature and function", is progressively revealed, and that once this is understood we come to recognize it as valid for the art of other times and places.[9] However, the claim that the standpoint of philosophy enables us to deliver a verdict on art and to evaluate its success or failure in terms of some progressively revealed normative standard is at odds with Hegel's emphasis on the philosophical task of comprehending art's changing social and cultural function. I have already observed that Hotho's incorporation of strong normative judgements into his edition of the *Aesthetics* appears to have little basis in Hegel's actual lectures. The surviving notes and transcripts reveal that Hegel was interested in *understanding* a work of art as a manifestation of human culture rather than in *evaluating* its success or failure, something that arguably belongs to the domain of connoisseurship or art-appreciation rather than philosophy.

Hegel's lectures on aesthetics contain numerous transitions between different forms and stages of art. Although there is an element of "overcoming" in every transition, this does not mean that one stage of art is necessarily to be ranked any higher than any other. The relative superiority of a particular stage is dependent on the standpoint from which the development is described. To take just one example, in the 1823 lectures Hegel states unequivocally that "The concept of beauty is realized in classical art: nothing can be more beautiful" (*Hotho*: 179). However, he goes on to argue that in comparison to Romantic or Christian art, classical art lacks "inwardness" (*Innigkeit*), which is only fully realized in romantic art.[10] Hegel's goal is not to weigh artworks against each other in some sort of vast world-historical project of evaluation, but to grasp the inner connection between the form and content of art and its changing social, political and religious contexts. To take any one aspect of Hegel's account as normative for the rest is to arrest the movement of his thought and to lose sight of the dynamic tensions that keep the lectures on aesthetics in perpetual motion.

I now want to consider Houlgate's argument more closely and to examine the grounds on which he believes it is possible to provide a normative interpretation of Hegel's treatment of painting. In all the published sets of notes, as well as Hotho's edition, Hegel devotes the final section of the lectures to the individual arts of architecture, sculpture, painting, music and poetry. Having already established the special relation in which each of these forms of art stands to a particular stage in humanity's historical development, he is now in a position to examine the resources and possibilities inherent in the different media of art. Hegel is, of course, aware that no one art form is the exclusive preserve of a particular epoch or society. His claim, rather, is that each form of art occupies a privileged position as the appropriate vehicle for the expression of the highest thoughts and ideas of a society at just one, extended period in human history. For example, although he acknowledges that the ancient Greeks also possessed great painters, he contends that the visual arts in Greece reached their fullest expression in the art of sculpture (*Pfordten*: 205; see also W 3: 19ff.; A 2: 799ff.).[11] In the 1826 lectures the transition from sculpture to painting is identified with the mystery of transubstantiation and the entering of the divine directly into the community of worshippers. However such claims are to be understood, it is clear that for Hegel the subsequent prominence given to painting is closely connected to the Christian emphasis on inward reflection. Although he concedes that other peoples – including the Chinese, the Indians and the Egyptians – also excelled in the art of painting, he asserts unequivocally: "The ideal of painting is Romantic, in which subjectivity, which is for itself, gives painting its fundamental determination: spiritual inwardness" (*Hotho*: 253; cf. *Ascheberg*: 244ff.).

What is it, then, that makes painting rather than sculpture the appropriate vehicle for expressing the spiritual inwardness that Hegel identifies as the characteristic feature of the Romantic era? Hegel's argument is based on the claim that different artistic media possess different resources and limitations and that each art form has its own proper mode of representation. Whereas sculpture, as an art of three dimensions, inhabits the same spatial environment as the viewer, painting, which is produced on a flat surface, creates an illusory world that belongs to the domain of appearance or semblance (*Schein*). In the 1826 lectures, Hegel declares that "Painting *is* the art of semblance" (*Die Malerei ist die Kunst des Scheins überhaupt*) (*Pfordten*: 206).[12] Like a work of sculpture or architecture, a painting is also a physical object, consisting in pigment on a ground; but in so far as it creates a new, imaginative space that exists only for the viewer it is discontinuous with the physical world. Hegel maintains that the transition from the objective substantiality of sculpture to the creation of semblance on a plane allows "responsive subjectivity to be set free" (*Hotho*: 249). What we see in a painting is produced by the mind for the mind and is the result of the artist's own, free activity.

On the one hand, anything and everything can be represented in painting, from the most humble domestic utensils to dramatic historical events. As Hegel puts it, "free subjectivity enters into the particular, whose sphere is infinitely extended" (*Hotho*: 249). On the other hand, since everything is created by, and depicted from, the standpoint of the artist, the interest we take in painting is not merely in its subject matter but also in the artist's response to what he or she has depicted. Hegel claims that painting allows subjective inwardness to be made visible even through the depiction of insignificant objects or trivial events, such as a quarrel in a tavern. In such cases, "The entire interest resides in the harmony [of the artwork] rather than in the object [represented]" (*Hotho*: 256). Hegel clearly has in mind here the work of Dutch seventeenth-century still-life and genre painters. However, he suggests that the most telling example of works in which we are interested in the artist's response rather than the object depicted is given by landscape painting. It is consistent with the diminished significance that he places on natural beauty that he should consider landscape painting primarily in terms of its capacity for representing the mood or feeling (*Stimmung*) of the artist. In the 1823 lectures he observes that "Landscape painting apprehends nature through the soul and mind, and orders its subject matter in accordance with the goal of expressing a mood. For this reason it cannot be or become a mere imitation of nature" (*Hotho*: 255–6).[13]

These considerations prepare us for the transition to the art of music, in which the subjective element that had first come to the fore in painting achieves independent expression.[14] Just as painting shares with sculpture the capacity to depict concrete objects and events, so it shares with music the capacity to represent the inner motions of the soul through the formal arrangement of its constituent elements. Houlgate concedes that:

> The parallel drawn by Hegel between painting and music (which of course is a non-representational art) suggests that part of the pleasure we derive from painting stems from the purely formal play and harmony of color as such, in abstraction from the constitution of visual illusion. (Houlgate 2000: 70)

Houlgate's question, however, is how these ideas might relate to a type of painting that lay nearly a century in the future in which the abstract elements of line, form and colour are treated as fully independent of figurative representation. He is in no doubt that "Hegel would have had very little sympathy for twentieth-century abstract art", and maintains that he would have rejected it not out of "personal conservatism" but for "clear philosophical reasons" (*ibid.*: 73). He puts forward two separate arguments in support of this view. The first rests on the claim that for painting to fulfil its "distinctive nature and function" it must continue to occupy the middle ground between sculpture and music that is allotted to it by Hegel:

> In Hegel's view, sculpture remains too external, spatial and solidly material to express adequately the concentrated inwardness of spirit, whereas music withdraws from the external and spatial altogether into the sphere of time and sound. Painting avoids both extremes of sculptural materiality and musical inwardness and links the external *and* the internal together… That, indeed, is what specifically distinguishes painting as an art. (*Ibid.*: 75)

Two related questions are raised by this argument. First, is Houlgate right to claim that Hegel has identified once and for all those characteristics that are specific to painting *as such* or should we accept the more modest claim that Hegel sought to explicate the types of painting with which he was familiar? And secondly, does Hegel's treatment of painting allow for the emergence of new possibilities? We have seen that he assimilated into his aesthetics the Romantic conception of landscape painting as an expression of the inner mood of the artist. It seems plausible to suggest (historical considerations aside) that abstract painting could also be identified as a further stage in the transition from the merely imitative depiction of the external world to greater "inwardness of spirit". The residual orientation towards recognizable subject matter that is found in the work of early abstract artists such as Wassily Kandinsky and Piet Mondrian would fit coherently into this account, as would the progressive "emancipation" of form, line and colour for purely expressive purposes. Since the overall tendency of Hegel's analysis of Romantic art is towards the gradual dematerialization of art, leading from painting through music to poetry, non-figurative art would appear to have a place already marked out for it. I should like to suggest, however, that we should not place too much weight on the so-called "dialectical transitions" that link the various elements of Hegel's account. As we have seen, these transitions are given greater prominence in Hotho's edition than in Hegel's own lectures. Painting is no more defined by its relation to sculpture and music than it is by its relation to any other art form; this simply happens to be the order in which Hegel treated his subject matter.

Houlgate's second argument is more difficult to represent in a compressed form since it is intimately bound up with his reading of Hegel's philosophy as a whole. He begins the chapter on aesthetics in *Freedom, Truth and History* by reminding us that for Hegel the highest truth resides in "the activity of dialectical reason in the world, unifying and reconciling what is distinct, contrary or contradictory". Since art, religion and philosophy represent three different forms in which this highest truth is given expression, albeit at a different level of clarity and understanding, he concludes that "The appropriate content for art is thus unity, reconciliation and harmony, the 'resting with oneself' (*Beruhen auf sich*), which constitutes aesthetic freedom" (Houlgate 2005: 211).[15] He follows Hegel in arguing that the high value we place on art cannot be explained in terms of art's capacity to imitate external reality. However, he gives prominence to his own concerns when he asserts that "The purpose of art is not to replicate what we see in the world about us, but to reveal the unity and wholeness which in our everyday experience we often overlook" (*ibid.*: 213). Houlgate's identification of reconciliation, unity and harmony as the "truth" of art leads him to reject the historical phenomenon of avant-garde art, with its exploration of fragmentation, discontinuity, juxtaposition and dissonance as appropriate modes of response to modern social existence. He criticizes some of the foremost artists and writers of the twentieth century, including Kafka, Picasso and Georg Grosz, on the grounds that their work serves to reinforce and deepen the wounds it exposes rather than helping to heal them. Artworks that "bring us face to face with the unredeemed darkness or the prosaic drabness of life" represent "an impoverishment of aesthetic experience" (*ibid.*: 215). Instead of seeking to "unsettle, sometimes even to destroy, the coherence and integrity of human character and identity" (*ibid.*: 225), art "must give expression to a sense of freedom and unity which enables us to feel reconciled with the world and made whole by the aesthetic experience" (*ibid.*: 215). This argument, which seems calculated to drive the reader into the arms of Adorno, shares much in common with other anti-modernist polemics, including those put forward from both left- and right-wing perspectives. Houlgate may be entitled suggest that such positions represent a distortion of Hegel's views, but given the ends to which the attack on the avant-garde art was put in the twentieth century it seems historically insensitive not to distinguish his argument from its apparent forebears.

Houlgate's central charge against abstract art is expressed in the following quotation:

> from a Hegelian point of view, whatever we may have gained through this "emancipation" of art – especially painting – from traditional representational methods, whatever experimental "freedom" we might have acquired, the effect has been to deprive us of the means to give sensuous, bodily expression to the richness and wholeness of human life. (*Ibid.*: 217)

Houlgate maintains that abstract painting is an impoverished form of art in so far as it relinquishes painting's richest resource: the capacity to depict in concrete, sensuous form the external manifestation of human inwardness and freedom. In "Hegel and the Art of Painting" (2000), he presents a second, and more radical version of this argument. There he contends that "human freedom can only be rendered concretely visible by means of the created image of the human face and body ... at least in so far as it is an art, painting must be 'representational'" (*ibid.*: 64). This second argument should, I believe, be rejected. Houlgate's insistence that the representation of human freedom in painting can only be achieved through figuration is difficult to reconcile with Hegel's claim that freedom can also be articulated in non-representational art forms such as architecture and music. Rather than insisting on a literal depiction of human freedom, Hegel explores with great subtlety the way in which different art forms can serve as a vehicle for humanity's "highest" thoughts and ideas.

The weaker form of Houlgate's argument is more difficult to counter. The question remains as to why some twentieth-century artists believed it was necessary to relinquish the possibilities afforded by figurative painting, thereby breaking with a pictorial tradition that reaches back through the Renaissance to the art of antiquity. Houlgate's answer is that abstract art reflects a conception of freedom that is itself wholly abstract. Modern aesthetic sensibility has been overwhelmed by *Verstand* – abstract understanding – leading artists to revert to forms of art that are more appropriate to the Symbolic stage of art. From this perspective, it is the avant-garde that is conservative or reactionary since it embraces only an "abstract" idea of human freedom. Consideration of Robert Pippin's article "What Was Abstract Art? (From the Point of View of Hegel)" (2002) will enable me to examine this question in more detail.[16] For, in contrast to Houlgate, Pippin claims that the basic premises of Hegel's aesthetics are consistent with the trajectory of modernism and that it is abstract rather than representational art that is most adequate to Hegel's account of the historical realization of subjectivity in the modern world.

III. A DEFENCE OF ABSTRACT PAINTING
FROM A HEGELIAN PERSPECTIVE

The difference between Pippin's approach and that pursued by Houlgate is clearly marked by Pippin's claim that a contemporary interpretation of Hegel's aesthetics needs to acknowledge "the historical experience of the inadequacy of traditional representational art" (Pippin 2002: 7). He recognizes that the emergence of abstract art was accompanied by a "great shift in aesthetic standards and taste" that is "unprecedented in its radicality" (*ibid.*: 1). Like Houlgate, he approaches this development from a Hegelian perspective. However, instead of rejecting abstraction he contends that it is continuous with the underlying tendency of Hegel's lectures on aesthetics:

> the basic narrative direction in Hegel's history of art is towards what could be called something like greater abstraction in means of representation – from architecture and sculpture, towards painting, music, and finally poetry – and greater reflexivity in aesthetic themes… the cluster of topics raised by the question of the meaning of abstraction naturally invites an extension of Hegel's narrative. (*Ibid.*: 3)

Pippin is aware that in the wake of the historical decline of modernism any such narrative is likely to be treated with suspicion and that claims for an internal logical development of art no longer hold much attraction. He therefore pursues the more fruitful strategy of establishing a link between abstract painting and the social and ethical structures of the societies out of which it emerged. This involves drawing a connection between his own conception of a normativity without foundations – the self-authorizing, self-legislative capacity to establish the validity of the norms by which (he claims) we regulate our lives – and the freedom from obligating conventions that he takes to characterize abstract painting.[17]

Pippin's defence of abstract art from a Hegelian perspective contains two central components. The first consists in a demonstration of the inadequacy of traditional, representational art to the self-understanding of modern society; the second consists in a demonstration of abstract painting's greater adequacy to this purpose. Pippin addresses directly a question that Houlgate leaves unresolved, asking why at a particular stage in European modernization representational art came to be seen as inadequate, "a kind of historical relic rather than a living presence" (*ibid.*: 7).[18] A full answer this question would need to address a wide range of developments, including the emergence of new technologies of reproduction (such as photography and film), the separation of art from the patronage of the Church and the state, the establishment of an independent art market, the exhaustion of the traditional genres of painting and their perceived inability to capture salient features of modern, predominantly urban experience and the increasing self-consciousness of artists about the historical conditions of their own practice.

Although Pippin is surely aware of these phenomena, his goal is to identify what he terms the "specifically Hegelian" answer to his question. This leads him to a reconsideration of Hegel's theory of the end of art, which, as I have already indicated, he interprets not as a claim about the death of art but as describing a fundamental change in the way in which art can and does matter to us. This relatively uncontroversial interpretation is supported by two highly contentious claims. First, despite the high praise that Hegel bestows on Dutch realist painting of the seventeenth and eighteenth centuries, Pippin maintains that for Hegel the unheroic and prosaic character of the modern bourgeois world makes it unsuited for "aesthetic presentation". Secondly, he claims that under the conditions of modern ethical life, in which "norms get their grip on us without primary reference to the sensible", we no longer need to articulate our self-understanding in the sensuous form of art. Instead, "our sensual lives have themselves been rationalized, transformed into habits, practices and institutions with some sort of rational transparency to themselves" (*ibid.*: 14). Such arguments are unlikely to convince anyone who is not already persuaded that we live under conditions of rational transparency rather than thickening layers of opacity. However, Pippin seeks to establish a connection between his account of the "full subjectivity of experience", including what he terms the "self-legislating, self-authorizing status of the norms that constitute such subjectivity", and the perceived inadequacy of traditional representational art. Since what "unavoidably must matter now is the realization of a kind of freedom, autonomy", he concludes that "It is the historical realization of subjectivity in the modern world (especially the greater realization of freedom in philosophical and political life) that makes representational art … matter less for us than it once did and had to" (*ibid.*: 20).

The second stage of Pippin's argument is no less problematic than the first, but as he readily admits, it is far more difficult to articulate since it requires showing how abstract painting is somehow better equipped than figurative art to represent human freedom. Describing his position as "no more than a pro-legomenon to a full Hegelian case for modernism in general and for abstrac-tion in particular" (*ibid.*: 21), he shies clear of any concrete examples of how this actually works out in practice. We are offered, instead, some rather gnomic pronouncements on post-impressionism, in which "the constituent elements of painterly meaning begin to come apart, or perhaps they come to seem more and more a result of having been actively put together" (*ibid.*: 22). He then suggests that the ability to make sense of these independent compo-nents as a painting can be identified with Kant's account of the active role of the subject in synthesizing the data given through the senses. Kant's observa-tion in the *Critique of Pure Reason* that reason does not "beg" from nature, it "commands" (A653/B681), according to Pippin, "already sounds the deepest theme of what would become modernism in the arts: freedom" (Pippin 2002: 17). Many things are run together here, but the basic argument is clear: the emergence of fully abstract painting is identified with freedom from depend-ence on sensual immediacy and so "a kind of enactment of the modernist take on normativity since Kant: *self-legislation*" (*ibid.*: 23). Pippin acknowledges that what "a kind of self-authored normativity or human freedom might *be* is a terribly difficult question", but he concludes that "over the last hundred years, and especially in the experiments of abstraction, we now have some sense of what it *looks* like" (*ibid.*: 24).

This is undeniably a highly suggestive, if somewhat indeterminate, defence of abstract painting from a Hegelian point of view. Pippin's argument is, however, exposed to a number of objections. It is a long way from Kant's epistemological account of the spontaneity of the mind, the transcendental status of which means that (if correct) it necessarily holds true of human cognition in all times and places, to the claim that abstract painting is the appropriate form of expression for the historical realization of subjectivity in the modern world. The principal stumbling block, however, lies in the conflict between Pippin's affirmative account of a fully self-legislating, self-authorized subjectivity and the concrete historical experiences out of which abstract painting emerged. Although the exact dates remain a matter of con-troversy, it is broadly accepted that fully abstract art first appeared around the time of the First World War and that it was a product of the European avant-garde movements of the early twentieth century, including both Cubism and Expressionism. All three of the acknowledged innovators of abstract art, Kandinsky, Kasimir Malevich and Mondrian, were motivated by a sense of crisis in Western society. In numerous writings they affirmed their belief that abstract painting could help to bring about the "spiritual renewal" of humanity.[19] A similar sense of historical crisis underpinned the second wave of abstract painting in the period during and immediately after the Second

World War. The key figures of American abstract expressionism, including Mark Rothko, Jackson Pollock, Barnett Newman and Clyfford Still, developed their own "signature style" out of a close engagement with Surrealism and a self-consciously heroic attempt to overcome a suppression of individuality, which they saw as taking place not only in European totalitarian states but also in modern American consumer culture. Pippin's identification of abstract painting with the achievement of greater "rational transparency" in our habits, practices and institutions is profoundly at odds with the oppositional character of modernist art and the attempt by avant-garde artists to develop a form of art that could offer a means of resistance to the dominant values of bourgeois society.

Given that abstract painting is itself a historical phenomenon, now fully assimilated into the history of art and long since displaced as an ambitious art form by minimalism, conceptual art and the myriad forms of installation, site-specific and multimedia work that have emerged since the 1960s, the claim that abstraction provides a test case for the *contemporary* relevance of Hegel's aesthetics is also open to question. Although abstract painting does continue to be produced, the period in which it could claim to be at the forefront of ambitious art practice is surely past. Michael Fried has argued that the world out of which modernism arose, including, above all, the utopian belief in the transformative power of art, is more remote to us today than the civilizations of a distant age.[20] Neither of the approaches considered here engages with recent art practice or the consequences of post-1960s art for our understanding of abstract painting. Pippin introduces an added level of complexity in so far as he seeks to comprehend – from a Hegelian standpoint – our own modernist history, casting his account in the past tense while at the same time projecting his account forwards into the future. However, his resistance to the various forms of art that helped to precipitate the crisis of modernism is revealed by his defensive insistence that "there was no failure of modernism, no exhaustion by the end of abstract expressionism .... The aftermath – minimalism, 'literalism', op and pop art, postmodernism – can better be understood as evasions and regressions rather than alternatives" (Pippin 2002: 20). Although Houlgate's cultural conservatism is more readily visible, Pippin's account is equally closed to the new forms and practices of art that have dominated the art world for the past fifty years. A proper understanding of abstract painting requires not only that we struggle to comprehend the development of a form of art of which Hegel had no historical knowledge, but also that we seek to comprehend the reasons for its *loss* of critical potential.[21]

In the first part of this chapter I argued that to take any one aspect of Hegel's account as normative is to lose sight of the dynamic tensions that keep his lectures on aesthetics in motion. The ongoing publication of the notes and transcripts of Hegel's lectures offers further confirmation that these tensions are central to his aesthetics. To give just a few examples: he treats art both as a distinctive mode of disclosure of the highest truth and as just one of three different modes in which this truth is disclosed; he maintains that art's specific mode of presentation is sensuous and material and yet he describes the historical development of art in terms of its progressive emancipation from dependence on sensuous immediacy; he divides the history of art into three consecutive stages, and yet he readily admits that the distinctive features of any one stage are also to be found in the others; he identifies the classical stage as the "highest" realization of beauty, and thus adheres to the classicism of the late eighteenth century, which measured all prior and later art against the unsurpassed achievements of the ancient Greeks; but he is equally interested in what is *not* classical, in the breakdown and discontinuities of form and content that characterize both Symbolic and Romantic art; finally, and most tellingly, he argues both for a thoroughly historical account of art and for the "end" of art's historical role. By sustaining these tensions Hegel never allows art to be treated simply as an instantiation of concepts and ideas that can be analysed independently of their concrete historical realization. It is in the demand that we to come to terms with art's constantly changing character rather than in a separable set of normative commitments that the contemporary relevance of Hegel's aesthetics resides.

NOTES

1. No direct criticism is intended here, since most writers on Hegel's aesthetics, including the present author, have long relied on Hotho's edition. Nonetheless, it is important to note that Annemarie Gethmann-Siefert published an account of her reservations concerning Hotho's edition, based on a detailed study of the extant transcripts, as early as 1991; A. Gethmann-Siefert, "Ästhetik oder Philosophie der Kunst: Die Nachschriften und Zeugnisse zu Hegels Berliner Vorlesungen", *Hegel-Studien* 26 (1991), 92–110. The same volume of *Hegel-Studien* also contains Helmut Schneider's report on Wilhelm von Ascheberg's lecture notes based on Hegel's 1820/21 lecture series in Berlin. This was the first of the transcripts to be published (see note 3 below), and both Houlgate and Pippin make reference to it. To date, there are a total of twelve surviving transcripts.

2. Hotho's edition was published in three volumes in 1835 as part of the posthumous publication of Hegel's *Werke*, which appeared between 1832 and 1845. A second edition, with minor changes, was published in 1842. This text has provided the basis for all subsequent editions, including the English translation by T. M. Knox and the Suhrkamp edition of Hegel's *Werke*, which contains the *Vorlesungen über Ästhetik* in vols 13–15.

3. I use "transcript" to translate the German *Mitschrift* and "student notes" to translated the German *Nachschrift*. The term *Mitschrift* is used to describe notes taken during the course of a lecture, while the term *Nachschrift* is used to describe notes that were written up into a clean version afterwards. It goes without saying that a *Mitschrift* is likely to offer a more reliable guide.

4. By comparing Hotho's transcript of Hegel's lectures on the philosophy of history with the surviving part of Hegel's own notebook to those lectures as a "control", Gethmann-Siefert has shown that Hotho was an excellent note-taker. In the era before tape recorders, note-taking was a much prized and highly practised skill, and competent note-takers were in great demand by other students.

5. See *Pfordten*. The notes by C. H. V. von Kehler are published in A. Gethmann-Siefert & B. Collenberg-Plotnikow (eds), *Philosophie der Kunst oder Aesthetik: Nach Hegel. Im Sommer 1826* (Munich: Wilhelm Fink, 2004).

6. As Gethmann-Siefert notes, Hegel scholarship has until recently paid little attention to Lasson's research.

7. After Hegel's death, Hotho took over his lectures on aesthetics at Berlin University. In 1832 he was offered a post in the paintings section of the new Berlin Kunstmuseum and published his first book on art, *Vorstudien für Leben und Kunst* (Stuttgart: Cotta, 1835). He became an important member of the so-called "Berlin School" of art historians. See U. Kulturmann, *Geschichte der Kunstgeschichte: Der Weg einer Wissenschaft* (Berlin: Ullstein, 1981), 171ff.

8. The second edition of this book, published under the title *An Introduction to Hegel: Freedom, Truth and History* (Oxford: Blackwell, 2005), contains a substantial amount of new material, but the chapter "Art and Human Wholeness" is left unaltered. All further quotations will be from this second edition.

9. An argument along these lines has been put forward by Arthur Danto, who describes his own theory of art as both essentialist and historicist. Danto maintains that "The concept of art, as essentialist, is timeless. But the extension of the term is historically indexed – it really is as if the essence reveals itself through history"; see A. Danto, *After the End of Art: Contemporary Art and the Pale of History* (Princeton, NJ: Princeton University Press, 1997), 196. For a discussion of Danto's ideas in relation to Hegel's aesthetics, see J. Gaiger, "Art as Made and Sensuous: Hegel, Danto and the 'End of Art'", *Bulletin of the Hegel Society of Great Britain* 41/42 (2000), 104–19.

10. Hegel compares the inwardness and pathos of the suffering of the Virgin Mary as represented in Christian painting with the suffering of Niobe or Laocöon as represented in Greek sculpture; see *Ascheberg*: 260ff.; *Pfordten*: 209ff.; *Hotho*: 254ff., W 3: 53ff.; A 2: 825ff.

11. Hegel does take into account the fact that very few paintings have survived from antiquity and that those that have survived, principally wall-paintings from provincial towns, may not be representative. However, it is hard to avoid the conclusion that Hegel's conclusions are based on the works that were available to him rather than consideration of the role that painting actually played in ancient Greek and Roman societies.

12. Compare too *Ascheberg*: 243, where Hegel claims that "semblance is the central concern of painting" (*das Scheinen [ist] die Hauptsache der Malerei*).

13. The claim that landscape painting can be interpreted as an expression of the inner life of the artist is a standard feature of Romantic theories of art. For a discussion of this idea in relation to Schiller's theory of landscape depiction, see J. Gaiger, "Schiller's Theory of Landscape Depiction", *Journal of the History of Ideas* 61(3) (2000), 115–32.

14. In the 1820–21 lecture series, in order to effect the transition from a representational to a non-representational art form, Hegel speaks explicitly of "the music of painting" (*die Musik der Malerei*); see *Ascheberg*: 251.

15. Houlgate goes on to argue that "Like philosophy, art expresses the truth that lies in the dissolution of opposites and in the emergence of unity and reconciliation. But art does not express this truth in its clearest and most determinate form. Art is not the logical articulation of the idea of unity as an *idea*; it is, rather, the mere *appearance* of the truth" (Houlgate, *An Introduction to Hegel*, 213).

16. A slightly modified version of this article appears in R. B. Pippin, "Hegel on the Historicity of Art: Abstract Art and the Hegelian Narrative", in *Geschichtsphilosophie und Kulturkritik: Historische und systematische Studien*, J. Rohbeck & H. Nagl-Docekal (eds), 202–28 (Darmstadt: Wissenschaftliche Buchgesellschaft, 2003).

17. Pippin has given a fuller account of what he means by "normativity without foundations" elsewhere. See, for example, *Idealism as Modernism: Hegelian Variations* (Cambridge: Cambridge University Press, 1997).

18. Traditional forms of representational art did, of course, continue to be produced but, with rare exceptions, it ceased to be a vehicle for the expression of new thoughts and ideas. Compare, for example, Alex Potts's discussion of the exhaustion of classical models of the nude in late-nineteenth-century figurative sculpture: "the classicising figure ceased to be a viable model for any even remotely critical sculptural practice because it presented itself so blatantly as a reassuringly consumable commodity. It had become the reification of a fixed subjective ideal, rather than a stimulus to think subjectivity anew. If it was to sustain an imaginative response, a sculptural object had in some way to resist being projected as a familiar and gratifying image of the self" (A. Potts, *The Sculptural Imagination: Figurative, Modernist, Minimalist* (New Haven, CT: Yale University Press, 2000), 17).

19. For an illuminating discussion of the goals of early abstract artists, see P. Wood, "The Idea of an Abstract Art", in *Art of the Avant-Gardes*, S. Edwards & P. Wood (eds) (New Haven, CT: Yale University Press, 2004).

20. "This is a world, and a vision of history, more lost to us than Uxmal or Annaradapu-rah or Neuilly-en-Donjon. We warm more readily to the Romanesque puppets on God's string, or the kings ripping blood-sacrifice from their tongues, than to workers being read to from *Izvestia* or *El Machete*" (M. Fried, *Farewell to an Idea: Episodes from a History of Modernism* (New Haven, CT: Yale University Press, 1999), 6). Pippin's account of modernism is strongly influenced by Fried's work, which, in turn, incorporates a number of Hegelian motifs, including most prominently the idea of the "unhappy consciousness".

21. For an attempt to make good this claim, see J. Gaiger, "Post-Conceptual Painting: Gerhard Richter's Extended Leave-Taking", in *Themes in Contemporary Art*, G. Perry & P. Wood (eds), 89–135 (New Haven, CT: Yale University Press, 2004).

CHAPTER TEN

NEW DIRECTIONS IN HEGEL'S PHILOSOPHY OF NATURE

John Burbidge

If any part of Hegel's philosophy is dated, lacking relevance to the modern world, it is his philosophy of nature. In developing its argument, and when lecturing on its various paragraphs, he refers to the science of his time. Because physics, chemistry, geology and biology have all made giant strides since then, however, the confident claims of 1830 now look rather like superstitious misunderstandings.

Indeed, Karl Popper, relying on Hegel's dissertation of 1801, claims that in his own day Hegel ignored the most recent discoveries of science, confidently arguing that there was no planet between Mars and Jupiter, even after the then classified as a planet Ceres had been discovered. As well, "Hegel's bombastic and mystifying cant" is so pretentious and full of fancies that it need never be taken seriously (see Popper 1966: 27–9).

Not surprisingly, this part of Hegel's philosophy has been little read and studied over the past two centuries. It was not translated into English until 1970, although it then appeared in two forms, in Arnold Miller's *Hegel's Philosophy of Nature* (1970) and in Michael J. Petry's three-volume edition of the same name (1970). Petry, however, did more. In his notes he cited the scientific texts and journals of Hegel's time, showing that Hegel was aware of contemporary theories and experimentation, and incorporated their results into his text and lectures.[1] Far from presuming to tell nature what it should be like, we discovered, Hegel was interested in the most recent discoveries scientists had made.[2]

Most of the references to contemporary science occur either in remarks Hegel himself appended to his basic paragraphs, or in his lectures. These latter are available either as supplementary notes added to each paragraph by his editors, or now published in full transcript from some of his students' lecture notes.[3] Much more problematic are the core paragraphs, in which Hegel sets down the systematic structure of his thought. As Popper suggests, they are obscure, and filled with an abstract jargon that has little connection to the world of nature we encounter either casually or in controlled experiments. Is it his way of bluffing, by suggesting that nature can be given some kind of abstract but meaningless description, in the same way that Molière's imaginary invalid assumes that it is the soporific powers of a sleeping potion that make it effective?[4]

Certainly it is the main text of the *Philosophy of Nature* that makes it most resistant to appropriation by recent philosophers. What is Hegel trying to do? How does this text relate to what science is in fact doing? Is he just playing a game to ensure that he can claim systematic completeness?

Edward Halper and Stephen Houlgate maintain that Hegel simply extends his logic into the realm of nature. In the *Science of Logic*, thought works through the meaning of a concept, and so arrives at a new term; it offers, as Halper puts it, "a self-generating conceptual development that does not draw on anything outside the system" (2002–3: 23). This self-generating process, he says, continues into the philosophy of nature. For Halper, even though the Absolute Idea is already complete in itself, it rehearses its logical development again, this time adding the various logical categories to its own completeness. Thus each stage produces a complex of several categories in which the originals remain irreducibly diverse (*ibid.*: 27).[5] Since the additional categories are taken from those already developed within the logic, the philosophy of nature and the philosophy of spirit follow the same order from being through essence to concept, even though these terms are now being coupled with the completeness of the Absolute Idea in a complex.

Houlgate takes a different tack. There is, he says, a "distinctive logic of nature" that is "generated by the natural-logical structure of externality" (Houlgate 2002–3: 118).[6] This leads into a very strong claim:

> If an empirical phenomenon does not appear to us to manifest the conceptual determination that has been shown to be rationally necessary, then either the logic is telling us something about the empirical phenomena which we have not yet seen, or Hegel has matched up the wrong empirical phenomenon with the logical determination. In neither case, however, do we have any proof that the logical determination concerned has been falsely derived or that it is not manifested in the natural world at all.
>
> (Houlgate 1986: 126)

For all of Houlgate's confidence that Hegel's *a priori* deductions must be true, whether our actual experience confirms them or not, the approach taken by Halper and Houlgate offers grist to Popper's mill. For if the philosophy of nature is strictly the work of self-generating thought, and if what Hegel concludes concerning astronomy, physics, chemistry, geology, botany and zoology has been disconfirmed by experiment, then, using the normal standards of scientific research, that system has been proved false. Elective affinity, for example, no longer provides the key to chemical change in the way that Torbern Bergmann claimed in the late eighteenth century in "De attractionibus electivis" (1782). Biology is now built around the evolution of new species, even though Hegel said that there are no metamorphoses in nature. Months after Hegel died, Michael Faraday proved that the changes produced in the galvanic cell are primarily the product of electrical currents, not of chemical interactions, as Hegel had so vigorously maintained.[7]

In other words, if Hegel's philosophy of nature is a logical construction that purports to tell us what nature is all about, it remains simply a curiosity – evidence for the overweening presumption of this German Idealist. It would then be hard to mine it for new directions of Hegelian research. Rather, it would continue to be – what it was for over a century and a half – an embarrassment for all serious students of Hegel's thought.

There is, however, another way of reading Hegel's dense prose that can open up more promising perspectives, and even suggest how his philosophy of nature might contribute to the advance of scientific thinking. To develop this alternative we need to move forwards cautiously and circumspectly. I shall first outline what I understand to be the core of Hegel's logical method. Then I shall indicate what role it plays in the philosophy of nature: organizing the material systematically but not presuming to tell nature what it must be like. Finally I shall explore how this method would operate once we accept from biology the evidence for evolution, and how it might completely alter the way a philosophy of nature might function.[8]

I

In the introduction to his *Encyclopaedia* Logic Hegel offers a "more precise conception" of his logical method. "Formally," he says, "the logical has three sides: the abstract or understanding side, the dialectical or negatively rational side, and the speculative or positively rational side" (*EL*: §79). That schema needs to be fleshed out in more detail.

Hegel takes over from Kant his conception of understanding. For Kant, understanding introduces a uniting function, where a synthesis generated by the imagination is integrated into a single concept (A76–9/B102–4). As a result this concept can be taken on its own, quite apart from any intellectual operation that led to it, and its distinctive meaning analysed.

The next move is more specifically Hegelian. For when we thoroughly analyse a concept we find that we are led to contrary and opposite conceptions. Just as Socrates used dialectic to show his interlocutors that their assumptions produced the exact opposite of what they intended, dialectical reason shows that a specific meaning requires its antithesis.

This kind of shift, however, is not in one direction only. For when we analyse the antithetical term we are led back to its opposite – the concept with which we began. There is a double transition, a feature, Hegel says, of utmost importance.[9]

It is this double transition that brings together the two concepts into a synthesis, so that thought can consider them as a totality. This new move is the work of speculation, or positive reason. Now we notice not simply the negative differences, but also the positive bonds that hold the two terms together. We have a sense of the whole.

However, as Kant suggested, any synthetic totality of this sort can be integrated into a single term. Understanding's uniting function collapses the reciprocal dynamic into a simple unity, which can then be abstracted and analysed on its own. The cycle begins again. To illustrate how this works in the *Logic*, we shall review its familiar first chapter. Once we isolate the meaning of pure being as indeterminacy simply equivalent to itself, we find we are thinking "nothing". Dialectic has led us to its exact opposite. Yet when we isolate the thought of "nothing" we find that it, too, is simple indeterminacy that is nonetheless equivalent to itself. Its definition dialectically turns out to be the same as that of "being". We have a double transition.

So we speculatively consider the whole pattern and find that its key is the movement or transition from one thought to its antithesis and back again. The implicit positive that makes the whole thing work is this dynamic, to which we give the name "becoming". And there is not just one kind of becoming; for when we move from "being" to "nothing" we have a "ceasing to be"; and when we go from "nothing" to "being" we have a "coming to be". Putting these two movements together we have a cycle that can continue without end: a progress into infinity.

This cycle is completely self-contained, and so can be considered as a simple unity. The whole dynamic is collapsed by understanding into a single thought: a being that comes to be and passes away. To this new concept we give the name "a being" or "determinate being".

In this first chapter of the *Logic*, then, we see how understanding an abstracted concept on its own ("being" or "nothing") leads dialectically over to its opposite; how the return from the opposite to the point from which we began creates a double transition that can be considered speculatively; and how the speculative totality itself becomes a self-contained dynamic that can be collapsed into a single term to be abstracted and understood in its turn.

II

What happens when we turn from the *Logic* to the philosophy of nature? At the end of his discussion of the Absolute Idea or method, Hegel says that pure thought makes itself redundant.[10] Yet it can anticipate that whatever we discover in nature will be amenable to being described in logical terms. For in the logic's dialectical moments, we have learned that "difference", "externality", "contingency", "particularity" and many other such terms are required whenever we want to do justice to "being", "internality", "necessity" and "universality". Now we can apply the former set as independent terms whenever they fit the world we in fact experience.

More than this, we can clarify what to expect in this world where thought is redundant. It will be a complete realm; and it will be characterized by the fact that things are externally related to each other: there is no implicit meaning that leads from one term to another.

How, then, does Hegel propose to produce a philosophy of nature? For philosophy requires that we think; and in fact think about nature. Schematically, it seems to me, it happens this way: thought thinks about what would be quite other than thought – its most general and basic characteristics. Then it looks to experience to see what in fact fits that description. Next it sees what happens in that realm once we distinguish its various moments. We analyse and abstract the phenomena that match our original projections, and we notice the significance of what happens. Finally we take our original thought and incorporate into it the results that in fact have emerged. We create a speculative synthesis, and from this we can generate a new concept that integrates the various elements into a single thought. Once we have that thought, we then turn back to nature to see what fits this new template.[11]

I shall illustrate this pattern by entering into dialogue with Houlgate. As we have seen, he claims that there is a distinctive logic of nature, which provides "a logical deduction or derivation of the basic determinations of nature". "We begin," he goes on to say, citing Hegel's lectures of 1823–4, "with the determination of externality. … We then ask, 'If we look around in nature, what do we call that which in our representation corresponds to this thought?' and we see that this is space." From this Houlgate concludes "that, strictly speaking, the philosophy does not deduce the necessity of *space* as such. It deduces the necessity of *externality*, and we find in experience that space is what most obviously corresponds to such externality" (2002–3: 115).[12]

To this point we agree. Thought looks in nature for abstract externality and finds that space corresponds to its concept. Further, thought looks for what would be the negation of pure space and finds that that is a *point*. When we then ask what would be other than a point, we discover a *line*, and if we repeat the question, we come to a *plane*, and then an *enclosing surface*, which separates off a single complete bit of space. At each stage thought has asked its question, and finds in experience an answer to that question. In other words, Houlgate and I agree in saying that thought does not logically derive space, or point or surface. Rather, it asks the question to which these are the answers.

The place where we disagree, however, is in the next move. How does thought generate its next question? If we are to have a thoroughly *a priori* procedure any new concept should emerge simply by reflecting further on externality and negation, not on anything that might chance to correspond with those concepts. Yet this is not what Houlgate says: "Hegel goes on to argue that the negativity of *space* considered 'for itself' is time. and that the unity of *space and time* is place" (*ibid.*: 119, emphasis added). I have introduced emphasis into that quotation to show that even for Houlgate the next move does not happen using pure logic, but includes that which initially only *corresponds* to our thought, and that (according to Hegel's lectures) is not required by that thought.[13]

In the paragraph where Hegel introduces time, he does start with negativity. But not with negativity pure and simple: it is the negative relation between *point* and pure *space*; it is the negativity that develops its determinations as *line* and *plane*, all terms that have come from our experience, not our thinking. The question philosophy asks at this point, then, is: what happens when *this kind* of external negativity exists on its own account ("for itself") and is indifferent to the peaceful juxtaposition of *space*? To this question, philosophy finds in experience that the corresponding answer is *time* (EN: §257).[14]

The critical move, then, is the move from one stage of the philosophy of nature to the next. Houlgate and I agree that we start a stage by developing a conceptual framework, and we then look to experience to see what corresponds to that framework in nature. We agree that the aspects of that stage worth noticing are those that respond to particular expectations of thought (in the case of space, simple externality). Where we disagree is in the move that Hegel makes once this is done. For all that Houlgate mentions space and time as he moves on to the next stages, he claims that this is a distinctive kind of "logic of nature", which develops its new concepts *a priori*.[15] I hold that at this point thought reflects on what it has in fact discovered and, building on this, formulates a new conceptual perspective. We can certainly call this "logic of nature", but it is not strictly *a priori*. At each transition thought takes into account what it has in fact discovered in the previous stage.

As in the logic, thought is required to analyse the starting-point for any stage in the philosophy of nature. We need to understand what we are looking for. And thought is required to integrate the results of its investigation to produce a new kind of concept. There needs to be a speculative synthesis. The two disciplines, however, differ in the intermediate stage. In the logic, dialectic passes over to an antithesis or contrary in the very process of understanding its initial concept. In the philosophy of nature, in contrast, thought "declares itself redundant", looks to see what in nature corresponds with its analysed starting-point and then incorporates the results of these observations into its final reflections.

On my reading of the philosophy of nature, then, new experimental evidence would introduce complications into the systematic story. Galvanism would need to be moved back from the section on chemical process to that on electricity, once Faraday's research was published and confirmed.[16] And the conclusions drawn by Charles Darwin and Alfred Wallace on the evolution of the species would require a significant rethinking of how the whole philosophy of nature functions. To this question we now turn.

III

In his introduction to the *Philosophy of Nature* Hegel notes that nature is to be regarded as a system of stages, where one follows another with a kind of necessity. This would suggest that he advocates some kind of natural evolution. But he immediately goes on to say that this is not to be understood as if each stage is generated by a *natural* process. It happens rather within the implicit, internal idea that constitutes the ground of nature. In other words, metamorphosis does not occur in nature, but only in that conceptual thinking which grasps the underlying rationality of the universe (*EN:* §249).

In his written remark, Hegel makes his rejection of evolution explicit: "Any thinking consideration must completely reject such nebulous, in principle sensuous, conceptions as (in particular) the so-called *emergence* of (for example) plants and animals from water and then the *emergence* of more developed animal forms from lower forms, and so on" (*EN:* §249 Remark). And in his lectures he expands further:

> The way of evolution, which starts from the imperfect and formless, is as follows: at first there was the liquid element and aqueous forms of life, and from the water there evolved plants, polyps, molluscs, and finally fishes; then from the fishes were evolved the land animals, and finally from the land animals came man. This gradual alteration is called an explanation and an understanding; it is a conception which comes from the Philosophy of Nature, and it still flourishes. But though this quantitative difference is of all theories the easiest to understand, it does not really explain anything at all. (*Ibid.*)

> It is important to hold fast to identity; but to hold fast to difference is no less important, and this gets pushed into the background when a change is conceived only quantitatively. This makes the mere idea of metamorphosis inadequate. (*EN:* §249 Addition)[17]

We can clarify the point Hegel makes by recalling the critical synthetic move identified in the previous section. The negativity involved in the point, line, plane and encompassing surface does not of itself convert into time. Rather, thought notices this negativity, builds it into its concept of "self-externality" and thereby develops the template to which time corresponds.

183

All of this is the work of conceptual thought. The fact that experience does offer something that matches the template offers evidence that nature is ultimately grounded in reason. But there is no evidence that nature itself manifests any development from space to time. Nor does the situation change as we advance through the philosophy of nature. It is conceptual thought that justifies the move from geology to botany, from botany to zoology, and from zoology to the human sciences.

For Hegel, the prevailing conceptions of evolution involve simply adding new features to simpler elements. It is, he says, a "quantitative" procedure. In some way or other lungs get added to molluscs, wings and legs to fish and wombs to land animals. On his view, a fully scientific explanation should introduce negativity: a dialectic whereby opposites appear. And that negativity in which contraries interact by distinguishing one from the other must be incorporated into any more complicated succeeding stage. The process in which negativity or non-union is integrated with union or identity does not happen in nature, except within individual living organisms.

At this point it is instructive to compare Hegel's philosophy of nature with his philosophy of spirit. Unlike nature, spirit can dwell with death and incorporate that negativity into its life. This means that experience never presents us with the most basic forms of spiritual life in isolation, or with abstracted capabilities.[18] The philosophy of spirit must learn to distinguish carefully the various constituent moments of our human existence, as well as the way they interact, moving through failure and negativity on the way to more comprehensive forms. Immediate intuitions disappear into the dark pit of the subconscious before resurfacing as conventional ideas; the conscious conjunction of meaning and sign becomes mechanical and unthinking before liberating pure thought; abstract right leads to fraud and crime before we can begin to talk about social structures; nation-states call on their young to sacrifice themselves in war before we can talk about international relations. It is this interaction between the positive and the negative that generates history's progress towards freedom. As the negatives that frustrate life gradually emerge and are then incorporated into a more overreaching spiritual dynamic, human beings become better able to determine themselves and their own future.

Nature is unable to do this. Its genera and species are fixed. To be sure, living organisms can interact with their environment to maintain themselves, and indeed pass through the metamorphosis of egg to caterpillar to chrysalis to butterfly. A dog can learn to tend sheep or guide the blind. But that development stops once the animal dies, and it has to start once again from the beginning with each new egg and each new puppy. What is learned by the individual does not get passed on to the species.

Darwin challenged that whole conception of nature. This was because his explanation of evolution was more successful than those of Hegel's day in incorporating negativity. Consider Darwin's theory of natural selection. Morton O. Beckner summarizes it this way:

(1) Populations of animals and plants exhibit variations. (2) Some variations provide the organisms with an advantage over the rest of the population in the struggle for life. (3) Favourable variants will transmit their advantageous characteristics to their progeny. (4) Since populations tend to produce more progeny than the environment will support, the proportion of favourable variants that survive and produce progeny will be larger than the proportion of unfavourable variants. (5) Thus, a population may undergo continuous evolutionary change that can result in the origin of new variants, species, genera, or indeed new populations at any taxonomic level. Darwinian natural selection may accordingly be defined as a differential *death rate* between two variant subclasses of a population, the lesser death rate characterizing the better-adapted subclass. (Beckner 1967: 297–8)

In this summary there are tendencies that capture elements of Hegel's rational method. First, overpopulation is the result of a successful species pushing its inherent potential for life to the utmost. This then produces the opposite of what is intended, for in the struggle for survival, death overwhelms those variants least able to acquire food or produce offspring. The interplay of positive overproduction and the negative struggle for survival on the level of the species resembles the way each organic individual appropriates and resists incursions from its setting in maintaining its singular existence.[19]

What Darwin's theory did not easily explain was why successful variations develop in the first place. It was not until the twentieth century that biologists realized that genetic material could remain recessive throughout generations, and then emerge once it was combined in a new way with other genetic material through sexual reproduction. This makes a second aspect of Darwin's theory of interest; for he suggested that, in the competition for a mate, certain features might be more successful in attracting desirable partners and so come to predominate, as less endowed individuals die without progeny.

The theory advanced by Darwin makes evolution fit more easily into a Hegelian framework because it incorporates negativity. But it has more radical implications. For now we can say that metamorphoses *do* happen in nature, not by simple quantitative addition but by the interaction of positive and negative forces. Once a new stage emerges from the struggle for survival, it becomes a successful, integrated species in its turn, producing a more complicated stage simply through natural processes on their own.

Evolution, however, remains a theory. While gradually evidence has accumulated to provide both confirmation and revision, the overall picture is a construction of thought. And as such it retains many presuppositions, in particular an understanding of cause as linear and mechanical, rather than a conception of development as the work of reciprocal interaction. Evolution is understood as a progressive accumulation of more complex characteristics,

185

not as a process where creative contingencies and established habits enter into a struggle where much is lost even though there are inevitable gains.

Theory determines where one looks for evidence, and what kinds of things one identifies as causally effective. It is always underdetermined by the evidence. That is to say, alternative explanations that take account of all the data are always possible. But this means that reflective thought has a critical role to play in examining basic presuppositions. Philosophy, once it is sensitive to the evidence that scientific investigation discovers, may contribute to the development, and criticism, of such presuppositions.

In other words, there is a reciprocal relationship between philosophy (or reflective thought) and science. On the one hand, philosophy must listen to and take account of the discoveries of science. Even if thought might ultimately question theoretical presuppositions, the results of conscientious investigation tell us about what nature is like. At such points thought must declare itself redundant. On the other hand, philosophy can explore the way thought functions in developing and determining its concepts, showing implicit connections that are frequently overlooked in the heat of the hunt, and identifying operations that have disappeared from view under a blanket of custom and tradition. Conflict can result.

We can see how this happens by constructing a dialogue between a Hegelian philosophy of nature and evolutionary science. First, the fact that evolution had an explanatory model that fits with evidence discovered in the Galapagos and the Indonesian archipelago opens up a wider understanding of the way nature functions than Hegel himself had allowed. The critical shift from one stage to the next need not happen simply in the realm of pure thought, whenever philosophy integrates the results of experience with its conceptual arsenal to produce a new template. Nature itself makes such transitions, not always successfully, but nonetheless significantly. As a result, not only do we need to make thought redundant whenever we observe what nature is like at a particular stage, but we need to observe carefully the way new forms emerge in fact.

Secondly, however, reflective thought can suggest other conceptual models of explanation that may show how such development takes place, models more successful than the conception of a linear causal sequence that has carried over from mechanics. When evidence places the theory of a progressive, accumulative advance in question,[20] then a reconsideration of the concepts being used, their presuppositions and their implications may well turn out to be productive.

Unfortunately, science has advanced exponentially since Hegel's day. No longer is it possible for a single person, even one with as much natural curiosity as Hegel,[21] to be up to date on the most recent work in all its many subdisciplines. And it would be presumptuous for a mere philosopher to tell science *a priori* how to proceed and how to organize its experimental observations. Nonetheless it may be possible to suggest some ways by which

Hegel's philosophical method could play a role in developing a comprehensive understanding of nature, not by anticipating what may be the result of future investigation in biochemistry or astrophysics but by suggesting how all the data can fit together within a complete picture.

IV

Evolution introduces the concept of history into nature. Indeed, since Darwin's time, explanation using natural development has been extended far beyond the realm of the living to include not only the formation of rocks and shifting of continents but also the emergence of matter from energy after the Big Bang. There is no self-conscious appropriation of events in natural processes as there is in historical ones. Nonetheless, past events become incorporated into later bodies and states, serving as a form of petrified memory. And the remnants of this past from time to time rise to the surface to produce, along with other contingencies, new elements, new compounds and new organisms. To indicate how a contemporary Hegelian might apply his logical insights to the world of nature, then, we could do worse than draw some analogies with what Hegel has to say about the historical dialectic.

The significant developments in history happen behind the back, so to speak, of the actors and agents. The primary engine of historical development is our human passions: immediate reactions to emergent events. "It is," says Hegel, "what we may call the *cunning of reason* that it sets the passions to work in its service, so that the agents by which it gives itself existence must pay the penalty and suffer loss" (*LPW*: 89). His comments leading up to this remark are also worth noting:

> The particular interests of the passions cannot therefore be separated from the realization of the universal; for the universal arises out of the particular and determinate and its negation. The particular has its own interests in world history; it is of a finite nature, and as such, it must perish. Particular interests contend with one another, and some are destroyed in the process. But it is from this very conflict and destruction of particular things that the universal emerges, and it remains unscathed itself. For it is not the universal idea which enters into opposition, conflict, and danger; it keeps itself in the background, untouched and unharmed, and sends forth the particular interests of passion to fight and wear each other out in its stead. (*Ibid.*)

That last phrase is interesting, for it has been taken over from Hegel's logical discussion of teleology. Any ultimate goal, he has suggested, is reached by allowing the particular means to "abrade" each other (the German is *sich aneinander abreiben*). That is, they rub against each other, wearing each other down, rather like the rocks on a pebble beach, which continue to be tumbled around by the surf until they become smooth and round and perhaps, in the long run, particles of sand.

There is much negativity here. The various particulars attack and injure each other. In addition, however, there is reciprocity. There is a double transition as each one, following through with its own immediate impetus, impacts on another, which responds in accordance with its own inherent drive. It is, in fact, this double transition that sets the stage for the next act. A *modus vivendi* develops that begins to institutionalize the conflict and its resolution; as that becomes normal and accepted there emerges the structure of a new social order, the basis for a new kind of freedom. Freedom, suggests Hegel, simply results from releasing the destructive forces contained in the passions from their leashes. It is a synthesis of violent reciprocal interaction, which becomes integrated into an accepted order.

All of this happens on its own, not because human beings consciously intend it to work out that way. The significant developments, although initiated by conscious reactions to hurts and insults, emerge from what goes on behind the agents' backs. They result from the interplay of passionate action in ways that no participant anticipates. In other words, the progress of history is indifferent to the suffering of its protagonists. But this is no different to what happens in nature. Natural forces expand and push for dominance, only to be frustrated and restricted by other forces. Whatever results is simply the product of that interaction, embodying the creative responses that each side has had to make within the conflict. History does not develop according to any overarching plan or strategy.

Certainly Hegel applied the same logic to the philosophy of nature. But there the reconciling and integrating moment does not emerge directly from the interaction of mechanical, physical or chemical processes. It is the work of an independent reason that reflects on what it has observed. The underlying rationality of the universe – "God as he is in his eternal essence before the creation of nature and a finite mind" (*L*: 30) – provides the connecting link from stage to stage.

Now, however, we can ask whether we may not learn something from applying the logic of history to the realm of nature. For natural forces do not necessarily have a linear, mechanical progression. They interact, and that interaction produces results quite different from whatever would have happened had each force been allowed to proceed on its own. Only if there is this possibility of novelty emerging from conflict can we make sense of the early development of the universe, or of the strange forms animals take once a species is isolated on an island or removed to another continent. There is a kind of teleology present, a movement towards ever greater complexity and adaptability. It is as if nature is taking the first, incipient steps on the way to freedom. If a long-lasting and successful species suddenly disappears from the scene, if a particular creative sport leads nowhere, it is not removed by some *deus ex machina* who has a transcendent plan in mind. Rather, that venture simply cannot withstand the rough and tumble of the "abrading" torrent. What survives is what adapts within that struggle. And so adaptation, ever more complex and comprehensive, is the goal of nature's historical development.

How, then, can contemporary philosophers of nature who want to remain heirs of Hegel proceed? They cannot presume to predict what nature will offer as evidence. Nor can they prescribe how scientists should organize their investigations. Like Hegel, they must recognize that thought makes itself redundant in order to listen to what nature, and its scientific investigation is telling us. But they will ask certain questions. At each stage they ask: are there identifiable processes where forces interact in a dynamic reciprocity – where there is a form of "double transition"? Can we find an interplay between matter and anti-matter? Can we see two chemicals reacting to each other in peculiar ways? Is there a significant interaction between a family of plants or animals and its environment where each does violence to the other? This question is different from that posed by Hegel. He asks: what in nature conforms to our logical expectations – of abstract externality, for example, or its negation? We are now looking for a double process in which two natural tendencies come into conflict and "wear each other down".

But there is another difference. For, rather than gathering together all the evidence and reflecting on what kind of concept this might suggest, we turn back to nature and ask a second question: are there stages, not present before, that emerge from this interaction and not only incorporate the distinctive features of the previous dynamic, but also acquire a stability that gives them permanence? These new integrated entities will have their own distinctive character, quite different from anything that has gone on before, yet derived from the preceding "struggle of the passions".

It is tempting to go further and apply this template to contemporary science. But only fools would rush into such a venture. For the answers to those questions have to be discerned by careful observation. And developing ever more sophisticated techniques to do that is the prerogative of disciplined and sensitive scientists. Here I must be content with suggesting this new approach to the philosophy of nature. Whether it in fact will provide new insights is for others to discover.[22]

NOTES

1. Dietrich von Engelhardt did the same for chemistry in *Hegel und die Chemie: Studien zur Philosophie und Wissenschaft der Natur um 1800* (Wiesbaden: Pressler, 1976).

2. On the title page of the first edition of *Phenomenology*, Hegel was introduced not only as Doctor and Professor of Philosophy at Jena, but also as Assessor of the Ducal Mineralogical Society of Jena and member of other learned societies, among which was the Physics Society of Heidelberg.

3. The edited additions are included in both English translations. Notes from single lecture courses can be found in *Bernhardy, Ringier, Uexküll, Griesheim* and *Bonsiepen*.

4. In Act 1, Scene i of *Le Malade Imaginaire*. In her challenging study, *Petrified Intelligence: Nature in Hegel's Philosophy* (Albany, NY: SUNY Press, 2005), Alison Stone argues that the obscure vocabulary of the key paragraphs is not just an abstract description of experienced facts, but an *a priori* metaphysical derivation of certain concepts, into which are fitted "scientific claims on a merely provisional and interpretive basis" (*ibid.*, 27).

5. What is puzzling about Halper's thesis is why the concepts of mechanism, chemism and life, which come late in the *Logic*, are to be correlated with abstract right, morality and art, and have nothing directly to do with mechanics, chemistry or biology. Confronted with the fact that Hegel refers back to the section on chemism in his discussion of chemical process, Harper does allow that the combination of Absolute Idea with the concept of real measure provides "an instance of chemism" (E. Halper, "The Idealism of Hegel's System", *The Owl of Minerva* 34(1) (2002–3), 46. One would have thought, however, that Hegel intended chemism to be a central part of any conceptual mix and not just a casual reference.

6. We shall return to this argument later.

7. The implications of this *a priori* reading become quite serious. For it is not simply the philosophy of nature that is proved false. Since it uses methods developed in the logic, and since these methods have led to conclusions that are patently false, the whole framework of Hegel's philosophy is put in question. This certainly is the inference that Popper draws.

8. While Alison Stone allows that my *a posteriori* method is philosophically viable, she nonetheless advocates an *a priori* reading; Stone, *Petrified Intelligence*, 19. For her, however, Hegel in the *Science of Logic* does not simply derive concepts analytically, but is rather "describing really existing ontological structures", which "must exist as structures *of* matter" (*ibid.*, 102). As a result, "the *Logic* only describes [the forms of thought] in *abstraction* from the material world" (*ibid.*, 104), and is thus derivative from a primary encounter with that world. This move calls into question the "strength" of her *a priori* reading. Overall she claims her reading has the advantage of fecundity, yet has to admit that none of the arguments she constructs in defence of it (by bringing together passages widely dispersed throughout his writing) are ultimately reliable. I hope to show in the sequel that my "*a posteriori*" interpretation may be more fruitful.

9. This doubling of the dialectic is not mentioned in the *Encyclopaedia* (EL: §81), but it was introduced into the discussion of method in the second edition of the *Encyclopaedia*: "The development of this sphere becomes a return into the first just as the development of the first is a transition into the second; only through this doubled movement does the difference receive its due, in that each of the two differentiated [terms], considered on its own, reaches completion in the totality, and thereby occupies itself in becoming one with the other" (*EL*: §241). This same point is made in the second edition of the *Science of Logic*: "The *positing* of the totality requires the *double* transition, not only of the determinateness into its other, but equally the transition of this other, its return,

into the first ... This observation on the necessity of the *double* transition is of great importance throughout the whole compass of scientific method" (*L*: 323).

10. Hegel's term in both texts is "*sich entlassen*".

11. As I understand it, Hegel came to this approach towards the end of his years at Jena. Initially he followed Schelling and Kant (in his *Metaphysical Foundations of Natural Science*) in constructing an *a priori* framework (much in the way the Pythagorean theorem constructs triangles around a right-angled triangle) and then proving its validity by showing that nature fits the schema.

12. Houlgate is referring to *Uexküll*: 104.

13. See: "If space is not in fact the appropriate representation, this does not harm the thought, which still remains true" (S. Houlgate, "Logic and Nature in Hegel's Philosophy: A Response to John W. Burbidge", *The Owl of Minerva* 34(1) (2002–3), 115.

14. The passage reads: "Negativity, as point, relates itself to space, in which it develops its determinations as line and plane; but in the sphere of self-externality, negativity is equally *for itself* and so are its determinations; but at the same time, these are posited in the sphere of self-externality, and negativity, in so doing, appears as indifferent to the inert side-by-sidedness of space. Negativity, thus posited for itself, is Time" (*EN*: §257).

15. It is unfortunate that Houlgate does not spend as much time in articulating this transition as he does in developing the initial discussion of space. Nor, in his analysis of my discussion of chemical process, does he consider the critical paragraphs §§335–6, which prepare the move to organic physics.

16. Hegel was quite prepared to resist scientific developments if they did not fit his theories, however. Because the atomism of his time talked of indivisible elementary particles, he refused to accept the position of John Dalton and Johan Berzelius, in which basic chemicals were made up of discrete units. He preferred the questionable experiments of his colleague Georg Friedrich Pohl concerning the chemistry of the galvanic process to Berzelius's suggestion that the process was primarily electrical. And he refused to call all basic chemical substances "elements", limiting this term to oxygen, hydrogen, carbon and nitrogen. See J. Burbidge, "Hegel on Galvinism", in *Hegel on the Modern World*, A. Collins (ed.), 111–24 (Albany, NY: SUNY Press, 1995), and "Hegel und die Chemie: Drei Auseinandersetzungen mit der chemischen Orthodoxie, In *Hegel und die Lebenswissenschaften*, O. Breidbach & D. von Engelhardt (eds), 43–53 (Berlin: Verlag für Wissenschaft und Bildung, 2002).

17. The "Philosophy of Nature" to which Hegel refers is that espoused by Schelling and his associates.

18. Hegel does allow that some of the most primitive anthropological forms emerge into prominence in certain forms of madness.

19. Another place where negativity enters into evolution is in the area of mass extinctions. Palaeontologists have identified a number of such occurrences over geological time, and after each one there is a flourishing of new genera and new species. "Along comes a mass extinction, with its 'differential rules' for survival. Under the new regulations, the very best of your traits, the source of your previous flourishing, may now be your death knell. A trait with no previous significance, one that has just hitchhiked along for the developmental ride as a side consequence of another adaption, may hold the key to your survival" (S. J. Gould, *Wonderful Life* (New York: Norton, 1989), 307).

20. This is what Gould, in his book on the Burgess Shale, *Wonderful Life*, suggests has happened to the traditional model of evolutionary theory.

21. Mind-boggling is the way in which Hegel is able to bring extensive contemporary information into his lectures not only on nature and psychology, but also on politics, history, art and religion.

22. An earlier draft of this paper was sent to two colleagues in physics, both of whom had, as undergraduates, studied nineteenth-century philosophy and German Idealism. Their responses are of interest. Professor Ian Affleck, Professor of Physics and University Killam Professor at the University of British Columbia, writes: "I think there may be something to your idea (or Hegel's idea) about conflicting natural forces. That seems to be the way physicists (and I presume other scientists) often think about phenomena. Other examples come to mind besides the ones which you give: – the variation of air density with altitude can be simply modelled in terms of balancing the gravitational force on a layer of air against the net upward force resulting from the pressure of the layer below and (the lesser) pressure from the layer above; – the thermal equilibrium state of a system is determined by balancing he tendency to minimize the energy against the tendency to maximize the entropy (or randomness); – the formation of galaxies in the early universe is modelled in terms of a competition between the overall expansion of the universe, which makes objects in it (like small grains of matter) move apart from each other, and the gravitational force which pulls objects together. It often seems to be balance between conflicting "forces" which makes things the way they are. Whether this is something fundamental about nature or just about the way people think about nature is not so clear to me."

Dr Ranpal Dosanjh, formerly a postdoctoral researcher in physics and currently in the doctoral programme in philosophy at the University of Toronto writes: "One example I was thinking of: the nuclear structure of the elements is determined to a large extent by a negotiated equilibrium between the strong force and the electromagnetic force. On their own, a bunch of protons do not want to form a nucleus together, since the electromagnetic force drives them apart (all being positively charged). However, they are also subject to strong interactions, which are (fittingly) very strong but short range. There is not enough of a pull from the strong force arising from the protons themselves to keep a pair of them together. However, the addition of neutrons provides extra strong force attraction without additional electromagnetic effects. Thus as the size of the nucleus increases, new equilibria are achieved, resulting in different proton/neutron ratios."

192

CHAPTER ELEVEN

HEGEL AND THE GOSPEL ACCORDING TO IMMANUEL
Nicholas Walker

Some time during his last few months at the Tübingen *Stift*, the theological seminary, or possibly just after moving to take up a post as house-tutor in Berne in October 1793, Hegel penned the short essay *Religion ist eine*, or the "Tübingen Fragment", as it used to be known.[1] Whenever this relatively brief text was composed, it basically represents Hegel's first piece of independent work, written entirely for his own purposes and definitely not intended for the eyes of his teachers. It merits careful examination in so far as it is thematically linked with all the subsequent writings of the Berne period (1793–98). For the first time in many years Hegel was finally able to express his own developing views on Christian theology and religion directly, to speak "the truth that can stand forth freely and openly before all", as he put it with coded Enlightened pathos in one of the "Sermons" with which he was periodically obliged to regale his fellow students at the *Stift* (D: 181). In a similar spirit he wrote to Schelling in 1794 shortly after escaping the suffocating physical and intellectual confines of the seminary: "I believe the time has come when one should speak out more freely in general, as indeed in part people already can and do" (*Br* 1: 11). The result is an acerbic settling of accounts with all the "rubbish" and "verbal junk" of the pseudo-Kantian theologians of Tübingen and the copious "troop of parrots and scribblers devoid of every thought or higher interest" (*Br* 1: 16–17) associated with them. The essay adumbrates an incipient programme of intellectual enlightenment and religious reform. Despite its tentative character the text provides a kind of design for most of what follows from Hegel's hand during the next two or three years, and may even shed some illumination on the vexed question of Hegel's authorship of, or potential contribution to, the so-called "Earliest System Program of German Idealism". It also gives a fair indication of the full range of influences working on Hegel's thought when he parted company with Hölderlin and Schelling and began to write down his own ideas in earnest. The piece presents a fusion of some of the most heterogeneous elements in the cultural heritage of the period. This apparent syncretism on the part of the young Hegel partly explains the radically divergent interpretations that have been proffered even of this early phase of his intellectual development.

What is the purpose and overall structure of the essay? Hermann Nohl placed it first in his pioneering edition of Hegel's "Early Theological Writings" under the general title "Fragments on Folk Religion and Christianity", although even this essay should perhaps cast some doubt on the appropriateness of Nohl's rather tendentious description of Hegel's early manuscripts as "theological". We can summarize the fundamental problem, or cluster of related problems, with which Hegel is principally concerned in terms of an eminently *practical* threefold question: how must a religion be constituted if it is to be rational rather than dogmatic or superstitious on the level of doctrinal content, to be subjective rather than objective on the level of individual belief and motivation, and finally to be public rather than merely private on the level of social and political life? Providing an answer to this complex but, in Hegel's eyes, ultimately single question means presenting a normative concept of religion in its most concrete desirable form, a standard by which Hegel can measure the orthodox theology and practical religion of his own age. The difficulty of the text, as well as its exceptional interest, arises from the way in which Hegel adopts a broadly Kantian model of pure rational religion, the essence of which lies exclusively in the exercise of morality, as the paradigm for assessing the claims of (allegedly) orthodox doctrine (i.e. for articulating everything that was fundamentally *wrong* with the thought of his first teachers, such as Johann Friedrich Flatt and Gottlieb Christian Storr, and emphasizing the self-determining character of morality proper). Yet, on the other hand, it is equally clear that his concrete ideal of what an optimally functioning *"Volksreligion"* would look like, in its affirmative rather than merely critical aspect, is drawn from very different sources. Close examination of Hegel's period of study at the *Stift* suggests that his pragmatically motivated interest in Kant did not necessarily imply the same kind of outright discipleship that could be observed among a number of other "enlightened" seminarians, and that his well-attested enthusiasm for Rousseau itself implies a number of possible contrasts with the strict letter of Kantian moral theory. Nevertheless, Hegel's Kantian starting-point is clearly announced in the following passage:

> Since the difference between pure rational religion, which worships God in spirit and in truth, and makes his service consist only in virtue, and the fetish faith that believes it can procure God's love through something other than a will that is good in itself, is so great that the latter has absolutely no worth as against the former, and the two of them are of quite distinct species; and it is crucial for mankind to be led ever closer to rational religion and that fet-

> ish faith be rejected ... the question arises as to how a folk religion must be set up in order a) negatively, to give as little occasion as possible for cleaving to the letter and the ceremonial observance, and b) positively, that the people be led to rational religion and become receptive to it. (W 1: 28–9)

But the specific purpose of his present investigation is to determine precisely how to make this pure rational religion existentially effective or "*lebendig*", and to distinguish it from dead theoretical or would-be metaphysical knowledge of God as an infinite supernatural object and so on. To facilitate this Hegel introduces a direct contrast between "subjective" and "objective" religion, one that parallels but is not formally identical with Kant's distinction between a practical religion of pure subjective morality and a merely "statuary" faith. Hegel wishes to investigate:

> what institutions are requisite in order that the doctrines and power of religion should enter into the web of human feelings, become associated with human impulses to action, and prove living and active in them, in order that religion become wholly subjective. When it is subjective it does not reveal its presence merely by putting the hands together, bending the knees, abasing the heart before the sacred, but rather spreads out into very budding branch of human impulse. (W 1: 16–17)

What Hegel means by "subjective" religion is best understood by considering its opposite, which Hegel characterizes with little echoes of G. E. Lessing:

> Objective religion is *fides quae creditur*, the understanding and the memory are the powers involved here ... Practical evidences may also form part of objective religion, but then they are only dead capital – objective religion can be arranged in the mind, organized as a system, set forth in a book, expounded in discourse; subjective religion expresses itself only in feelings and actions. (W 1: 13–14)

Or as he puts it most simply in terms reminiscent of Fichte, theology is a "matter of the memory and the understanding", whereas religion is a "matter of the heart" (W 1: 17). How can we make the pure principles of morality "actual" and ensure that they are properly planted in the human soul, woven into the texture of our affective life, "the holy web of human feelings" as he calls it with a favourite Platonic metaphor that recurs throughout the text (W 1: 16, 31, 43). When Hegel comes to sum up the course of his argument, he famously specifies three major conditions that must be fulfilled in a living *Volksreligion*: "I. Its doctrines must be based upon universal reason./ II . Fancy, heart and sensibility must not thereby go away empty-handed. / III. It must be so constituted that all the needs of life – the public affairs of the state are connected with it" (W 1: 33).

The first, most obviously Kant-inspired, condition here is clearly qualified by the different tone and emphasis of the second. Hegel's approach to the question of sensibility is doubtless marked by his early reading of Rousseau, and probably of Schiller. What had impressed Kant about Rousseau was the primacy of practice and the emphasis on the irreducible self-certainty of moral experience. And this was fundamental for the young Hegel too and in perfect harmony with his earliest convictions, shared with Lessing, concerning the indubitable universal principles of "natural religion". Yet an equally striking feature of Rousseau's thought was the great significance ascribed to moral sentiments such as altruism and sympathy, an approach more consonant with the general spirit of Enlightenment and its emphasis on cultivating the seeds of human goodness and its tendency to identify human happiness with the exercise of the good.

The legalistic-rigoristic dimension of Kantian ethics in its strict form clearly did not recommend itself to the young Hegel even when the direct influence of Kant was in some way at its strongest. The rather eclectic character of this early essay, the relatively external coordination of its different elements and the lack of convincing mediation between them, is reflected at a significant juncture where Kantian and un-Kantian paths of thought are abruptly juxtaposed with some terminological confusion. The task of religion is to awaken:

> feelings which are more susceptible to the influence of reason, and approach more closely to morality, ... allowing moral feelings to germinate ... feelings which, although they are not moral, that is, do not spring from respect for the law, ... are nonetheless worthy of love, and inhibit evil inclinations and further the highest development of human beings – of this kind are all benign inclinations, compassion, benevolence, friendship. (W 1: 29–30)

Hegel's appeal to "inclinations" is a concession to the realm of non-moral motivation from the Kantian perspective. Although Hegel does not doubt that respect for the moral law is the crucially determining categorial moment, his principal concern is the question of making this law effective by anchoring, if not precisely grounding, it firmly in the rich texture of human sensibility in the broadest sense. Hegel's concept of "subjective" religion is thus not simply coterminous with the concept of Kant's "rational" religion, although it is equally opposed to the positive extra-moral content of "objective" religion. The appeal to the subjective dimension concerns the practical problem often discussed in this period as a conflict between the "head" and the "understanding" on the one hand, and the "feeling" and the "heart" on the other.

Hegel is often regarded, especially in the light of his later polemics against the partisans of "immediacy", as entirely unsympathetic to the claims of feeling in relation to those of reason, and to every trace of Pietism and "*Empfindsamkeit*". But as we ought to expect of an avid reader of Rousseau and a "devotee of Lessing" (*Br* 1: 21), the matter is not nearly so simple. This is naturally not to claim that Hegel's thought, whether now or subsequently, can be subsumed under a counter-Enlightenment tradition of German culture that supposedly began to make itself felt before the last decade of the eighteenth century was out in response to the "abstract" rationalism of philosophy and the upheaval of the French Revolution. It was Hegel's overriding practical concern to try to improve on the Critical Philosophy at what seemed to many of its sympathetic critics to be its weakest point, namely its account of psychological motivation, its rigoristic conception of morality, and its apparent devaluation of the sensible and affective dimension of moral experience. Hegel's equivocations with respect to Kant are further revealed in one of the most interesting passages of his essay:

> the fundamental principle of the empirical character is love – which has something analogous to reason in it in this respect – and just as love finds itself in others, or rather by forgetting itself, transcends its own existence and, as it were, lives, feels, and acts in others, thus reason as the principle of universally valid laws recognizes itself in every rational being as a fellow citizen of the intelligible world. (W 1: 30)

Even as he concedes that it is a "pathological principle of action", Hegel invokes love as the exemplary case of "benevolent inclinations". If in Rousseau and in the moral sense tradition the higher sentiments of sympathy and friendship already imply an extension of the individual self, Hegel articulates this thought explicitly as a self-finding of oneself in and through the other. He is visibly struggling to vindicate the central role of altruistic feelings and rescue them from the moral limbo to which Kant had seemingly relegated them.

The idea of constructing, or encouraging, an alternative to the otherworldly and life-denying religiosity of the present is transparently modelled on the aesthetic Greek religion of the *polis*. Given that a *Volksreligion* is not simply directed, as modern private religion allegedly is, to the cultivation of specifically personal morality or to securing individual salvation for the believer in the hereafter, it is capable of exercising a social and political effect on the "spirit of the people" (W 1: 37). The Herderian overtones of Hegel's educative conception of religion, of his emphasis on the internal relations between the political, ethical, artistic and religious elements for the "formation of the spirit of the people" (W 1: 34) are unmistakable, although Hegel's broad conception of *paideia* also recalls Rousseau's concept of a "*religion civile*". The unusually lyrical and effusive depiction of the Greek spirit towards the very end of the essay is particularly reminiscent of Johann Gottfried Herder (see W 1: 42–3).

The Greek idea, or idealization, that Hegel evokes here is his retrospective utopia, the first explicit statement of what he later called "the ideal of his youth" (Br 1: 59): a paradigm of integrated wholeness that vouchsafes a glimpse of an ideal that is more than an "infinite task". But the intensity with which this living ideal is evoked only serves to underline the wretchedness of the present and the radical contrast between two historical worlds: one in which "the festivals of the people ... were all religious festivals, dedicated to the honor of a god, or of some human being deified for his services to the state", where "everything, even the excesses of the Bacchants, were consecrated to a god", and one in which "the joys and pleasures of men must stand ashamed in the eyes of a religion" which presents "too dismal an appearance" to encourage happy participation (W 1: 49). As Hegel acidly remarks in the spirit of Rousseau:

> Our religion would educate men to become citizens of heaven, whose gaze is ever directed thither, who have become alien to human feelings. In our greatest public festival, one draws near to enjoy the heavenly gifts in colors of mourning and with lowered gaze – at the festival which ought to be the feast of universal brotherhood! (W 1:42)

And what of the alternative spirit embodied in the Greek ideal? "We know of this Genius only by hearsay, we can only gaze in love and wonder upon a few traits of his character ... Which merely awaken a sorrowful yearning for the original ... It has flown from the earth" (W 1: 44). But for Hegel the profound contrast between past and present that he has so accentuated in the closing pages of this text does not terminate in a futile exercise in nostalgic longing, but provides an immediate incentive to further constructive reflection. It spurs him on to pursue a deeper historical understanding of the problem of establishing a rational form of religion that will effectively fulfil his original canons and conditions. The task to be undertaken now presents itself as essentially twofold: the diagnostic task of explaining the historical failure of traditional Christianity in so far as it has degenerated into an "objective" faith grounded not in reason but in special authority, and thus infected with fetishism and superstition, and the parallel constructive task of radically reforming the body of Christian belief and excluding the "positive" elements of the inherited "Christian religion" to reveal the rational core of the "religion of Christ" as conceived in the spirit of Lessing and Kant.

It is to this dual task that Hegel turns in his reconstructed gospel account or "Life of Jesus" and in the extended essay on "The Positivity of the Christian Religion". The former composition (N: 75–136) is arguably Hegel's only properly self-contained and completed text among the early writings and dates from the middle of 1795. The title by which it is now generally known was supplied by his first editor and biographer Karl Rosenkranz and inevitably suggests a comparison with David Friedrich Strauss's seminal work of 1835, *The Life of Jesus Critically Examined*. Although Hegel's piece has no significance as a specimen of historical scholarship or biblical criticism, it represents a very interesting early example of a genre that would proliferate in the first half of the nineteenth century as traditional theological doctrines continued to lose their hold on Protestant intellectual life in particular, as increasingly urgent attempts were made to rescue the central ethical or humanistic significance of Jesus's teaching from the dogmatic interpretations of the Church on the one hand and from the sceptical and relativistic implications of the "higher" criticism (see Schweitzer 1913).

But Hegel's "Life of Jesus", which is a *philosophically* reworked account, shows no interest in ascertaining by critical or philological methods how much of the gospel story can be authenticated as an "accurate" record. He is solely concerned with fulfilling the demands set by Kant's philosophy of religion, namely to provide a moral interpretation of the truth-content of "Christianity" in so far as it is capable of being reconstructed accordingly. The austere character of Hegel's drastic recomposition results from this single overriding aim and the image of Christ that emerges from this purifying process represents the sharpest possible contrast with the theological orthodoxy to which he had been exposed in the *Stift*. But it is also instructive to note how far Hegel's first independent confrontation with the Christological question prepares the way for his interpretation of the incarnation in the Frankfurt years (1797–1800) and in many crucial respects remains determinative for *all* of his subsequent reflections on the Christian religion.

In the Tübingen Fragment Hegel had already presented an outline of a form of life in which moral, aesthetic, religious and political dimensions are concretely interrelated with one another. And it is clear that the early ideal of the *Volksreligion* represents the embryonic shape of Hegel's life-long concern with a comprehensive concept of ethical life or *Sittlichkeit*.[2] But his immediate starting-point in contemporary life is precisely the stark contradiction between this ideal and the reality of established religion in an all too obvious alliance with the despotic spirit of paternalistic authority. Since Hegel does not expect nor advocate an ahistorical and impossible return to the organic wholeness of Greek social life (and the young Hegel systematically ignores the obviously problematic unacceptable features of such a pre-modern social order), his most important task must be to show how his own inherited religious tradition can in principle be purified of its irrational dogmatic content to exhibit the universally acceptable rational substance paradoxically *concealed* within allegedly *revealed* religion, to liberate the latent content from its reified and suffocating form. And in conjunction with this he will also need to provide a convincing account of how the rational "essence of Christianity" – to adopt a suspect and subsequent expression – was so obscured and

199

radically misunderstood as to become the very type of a religion of unfreedom and superstition.

In Hegel's "Life of Jesus", which Schweitzer describes as a "Kantian-rationalistic paraphrase" of the gospels, Hegel pursues the first of these inter-related problems. Hegel's letter to Schelling of 16 April 1795, shortly before he began working on the present text, provides an excellent indication of the specific purpose of Hegel's *Religionskritik* at this period:

> I believe there is no better sign of the times than this, that human-ity is presented as so intrinsically worthy of respect – a proof that the nimbus around the heads of the oppressors and gods of the earth is now vanishing. The philosophers will demonstrate this dignity and the peoples will learn to feel it, and they will not merely demand their rights which have been trodden into the dust, but once again assume them and appropriate them for them-selves [*sich aneignen*]. Religion and politics have acted in league with one another, the former has taught what despotism required: contempt for the human race and its incapacity to achieve any-thing good, to be something through its own efforts [*durch sich selbst*]. (Br: 24)

The letter reveals a precise grasp of the logic of estrangement that Hegel sees at work within "positive" or unreformed religion. The conceptual antithesis between the autonomous self-appropriation of the human essence and a het-eronymous self-disownment in thrall to an alien being structures much of Hegel's discussion of theological orthodoxy in the early writings (and largely governs his interpretation of the medieval world and of Catholic thought in general throughout his mature writings). It hardly seems anachronistic to recognize the explicit schema of "ideological" projection and compensation in texts such as the following, where the young Hegel already speaks rather like a "young Hegelian" who would reclaim what is our own (*unser Eigen-tum*), "take back the beauty of human nature, which we ourselves deposited within an alien individual while retaining for ourselves only the most repul-sive things of which it is capable, joyfully recognize the former once again as our own work [*unser eigenes Werk*]" (W 1: 100–101). The fundamental bur-den of Hegel's complaint against traditional Christianity is that it ultimately makes us "*fremd*" in one way or another: alien to society and our fellow human beings through preoccupation with the question of personal salva-tion, alien to nature both within and without through morbid asceticism and otherworldliness, alien to the divine through emphasis on the total otherness and transcendence of God in external relation to humanity as the passive recipient of grace from above.[3]

In radical contrast to the supernatural figure miraculously incarnated in human form presented by his theology teachers, Hegel's Jesus is a man who claims no special authority for himself since he is simply "the Teacher of the Gospel" that we find in Kant's *Religion within the Bounds of Reason Alone*. Hegel takes it for granted that all the supernatural elements in the gospels are simply superstitious accretions whenever they cannot be treated as symbolic presentations of moral truth. Ultimately all historical claims are irrelevant in principle to our spontaneous assent to whatever truth is contained in Christ's teaching since as any close student of Lessing would know, without the added stimulus of reading Kant or Fichte, there can be no legitimate passage from the contingent and merely "probable" realm of historical belief to necessary practical or theoretical truths of any kind. To make our belief in any way *dependent* on specific historical claims, whether transmitted by fallible human recorders or allegedly by means of "special revelation", would be to embrace the theological "innovation" bitterly contested by Lessing (attempting "to hang eternity upon a spider's thread"). It is worth emphasizing that Hegel's own attitude to the "historical" foundations of religious belief, and his consequent indifference to textual-critical problems concerning the scriptures, remained largely unchanged in the entire course of his development. In this respect the influence of Lessing, which is explicitly acknowledged in Hegel's earliest manuscripts, can still easily be identified *between* the lines of his Berlin lectures on the philosophy of religion in the 1820s. As far as the reconstruction of Christian doctrine is concerned Hegel boldly follows Kant's recommendations for a rational hermeneutic of scripture.[4] Consequently Hegel is quite untroubled by the thought that his exegesis might seem anachronistic and it would be something an understatement to describe it as "forced".

Thus, in Hegel's drastically re-edited Sermon on the Mount, Jesus declares: "That which you are capable of willing as a universal law amongst men, binding also upon yourselves – act according to such a maxim: for that is the fundamental law of morality." And adds, in words that would not seem out of place in the mouth of Mozart's Sarastro: "Enter through these portals of justice into the temple of virtue. Morality is the sole standard for a life well-pleasing to God" (N: 87). Jesus proclaims the gospel of autonomy to those who have lost all sense of their own spontaneity as rational beings, and are burdened by a wholly statutory religion administered in a spirit of external legalism. He is compelled to employ existing religious ideas to communicate with his hearers, such as the idea of the Messiah, even though he thereby exposes his teaching to the danger of perversion and misinterpretation. In this text, as in all his other early manuscripts, Hegel clearly shares Kant's disparaging view of Judaic "religion" as little but ceremonialized "fetishism". For both of them these strictures also apply with equal, if not stronger, force to most of historical Christianity, which only intensifies the most problematic features of the religious culture in which it first arose. Hegel stresses that Jesus strives to prevent men from ascribing any absolute or special status to his own person instead of harkening to his universal message:

201

> Do I demand respect for my own person? Or belief in me? Do I
> desire to impose a standard for judging and evaluating men that
> I have myself invented? No! – It is rather respect for yourselves,
> belief in the holy law of your reason, attention to the inner judge
> in your breast, to conscience as a standard that is also the standard
> of divinity, that I desired to rouse within you.   (N: 119)

John the Baptist had already prepared the way for this gospel of autonomy in preaching that none should expect any exclusive marks of favour ("by descent and lineage") but should solely strive to "develop the divine spark that has been imparted to them, that bears witness to the fact that in a more sublime sense they descend from divinity itself" (N: 75). Hegel is clearly attempting to exploit the concept of autonomy in semi-platonic language and integrate it with the Johannine imagery of the spirit.[5] The Stoic rhetoric of the human soul as a "*scintilla dei*" is hardly one that recommended itself to Kant himself for a number of reasons, but Hegel is bent on reclaiming it to interpret the indwelling of the "holy" spirit in a way that specifically dissolves the qualitative distinction between Christ and those who "believe" in him. Drawing freely on the fourth gospel (cf. John 15:1–14), Hegel lets Jesus say to his disciples in language that invokes both Kant and Lessing:

> I behold you around me like shoots of a vine who bear the fruit it
> has nourished, and now, detached from the vine, bring the good
> to fulfillment through your *own* living power, … you have grown
> into the freedom of your *own* will, you will bear fruit through the
> power of your *own* virtue, if indeed the spirit of love, the power
> which inspires both you and me, is one and the same.
>
> (N: 126, emphasis added)

Despite the undeniable Kantian rhetoric of much of Hegel's text, the overall tone is also subtly different from Kant's religious writings in a number of telling respects. In the programmatic opening passage of his "Life of Jesus" Hegel reformulates the beginning of the fourth gospel thus:

> Pure Reason – incapable of any limits [*sic*] – is the Divinity itself
> … It is Reason which teaches us to know the vocation of man and
> the unconditional end and purpose of life. Reason is often indeed
> darkened, but has never utterly been extinguished. Reason is the
> sole source of truth and contentment which all human beings can
> open up within themselves.   (N: 75)

It is the unconditional claim of *practical* reason that is here described as absolutely unlimited, but the identification with reason itself with God (with whatever we can legitimately mean by that word) is a striking deviation from the letter of Kant's doctrine and clearly reveals the influence of Schelling's endorsement of Fichte on Hegel's mind at this time (cf. *Br* 1: 22). Hegel's conspicuous silence about the apparently "sceptical" epistemological context in which Kant's philosophy of religion is embedded, especially the character-istic rhetoric of divine unknowability, inevitably lends a different appearance to his work. It is already noteworthy that nowhere in his early writings is Hegel prepared to speak of the scope and reach of "our" reason. For Hegel the normative moral order is "above us" only in the sense that it represents an unconditional principle that has the right to govern our behaviour as sen-sible beings (and indeed he characteristically avoids the Kantian "rhetoric of height" even in this early text). As in the early Fichte and Schelling, the divine is not as such "personal". In so far as we incarnate the divine principle effec-tively within our own lives and spontaneously recognize it as the law of our own rational nature, we can legitimately be said to participate in the divine itself. Hölderlin expressed this crucial motif of participative recognition in a poem composed a couple of years later: "They alone believe in the divine / Who share in it themselves" ("Menschenbeifall", 1798).

Thus Hegel may appear *more* orthodox than Kant when he describes Jesus explicitly in divine terms, whereas for a religion within the bounds of mere reason the idea that this individual "Son of Man" should also be the "Son of God" must remain a "holy mystery". But this appearance is deceptive since there is in principle nothing uniquely divine about Christ as opposed to other human beings. That is why Hegel's gospel simply omits the traditional mys-tery of the resurrection, the very "copestone of the Christian faith" accord-ing to one of the sermons at the *Stift* in which Hegel had dutifully echoed his theology teachers (D: 182). Yet here too the respective attitudes of Kant and Hegel to the resurrection narratives are significantly different, although they concur completely in rejecting such "miracles" as irrelevant to the autono-mous moral life. Hegel does not repudiate the idea of a physical resurrection because it implies a too grossly materialistic conception of the human soul, as Kant appears to do in a highly involved footnote on the subject.[6] Hegel objects to it as a miracle that prevents living individuals who are a concrete union of soul and body from discovering the true spiritual principle here and now within themselves. Jesus had to "leave" his disciples if they were to tran-scend absolute reliance on *his* sensible presence and spiritual dependence on *his* personal authority: "Be not distressed, therefore, that I must be parted from you – but honor the spirit which dwells in you and hearken to its uncor-rupted voice. We may be separate and different from one another in person, but we are one in essence" (N: 125).[7]

Hegel is so taken here with the task of eliminating all miraculous non-moral and non-spiritual incentives as a superstitious obstacle to genuine self-determination that he does not yet think of linking the idea of death and resurrection symbolically to the Pentecostal descent of the spirit as the advent or inauguration of spiritual *"Mündigkeit"*. But the final exhortation of Jesus, full of obvious Kantian echoes as it is, is particularly suggestive for Hegel's subsequent development in this respect:

> I will not leave you orphaned – for I leave a leader within your-selves. ... You have become men who can finally trust in your-selves without the leading strings of another – if I am no longer amongst you, may the ethical life you have developed be your guide – the holy spirit of virtue will preserve you from the ways of error.   (N: 125)

With the conclusion to his "Life of Jesus" the young Hegel stands at a criti-cal point of transition where his originally Kantian starting-point will be transformed, sublated but not abstractly negated, as he develops the concept of autonomous and self-authenticating "spirit" within an essentially inter-subjective context. It is thus ultimately more appropriate to Hegel's rational hermeneutic of religion than it is to Kant's if the hallowed name of Immanuel originally signified the "God who is amongst us" (Isaiah 7:14) and would subsequently be read as a prophecy of the divine–human incarnation itself (Matthew 1:23).

NOTES

1. Modern commentators often avoid the various "titles" that previous editors have ascribed to many of Hegel's early manuscripts and identify them by the relevant "incipit". W 1 (*Frühschriften*), which is largely based on the *Werke* of 1832–45, con-tains a broad selection of texts from 1793–1802. For a chronological list of Hegel's early manuscripts see G. Schüler, "Zur Chronologie von Hegels Jugensdhriften", *Hegel-Studien* 2 (1963), 91–118, and H. S. Harris, *Hegel's Development: Towards the Sunlight* (Oxford: Oxford University Press, 1972), 517–27. For *Religion ist eine* see W 1: 9–44, and Harris, *Hegel's Development*, 481–507.

2. In his Berlin lectures on the philosophy of history, Hegel still formulates his pre-eminently social conception of religion in terms of an expanded concept of the moral life: "Philosophy alone comprehends the Kingdom of God and the ethical world [*die sittliche Welt*] as a single idea, and recognises how time has worked towards the reali-zation of this unity" (W 12: 457).

3. It is no exaggeration to claim that Hegel's early writings are centrally concerned with the thematic of "alienation". That the young Hegel never uses a single identifiable term such as "*Entfremdung*" is less significant than the logic of "self-possession" and "dispossession" that animates them. Hegel operates continually with the opposition of "*fremd*" and "*eigen*", along with a host of associated terms such as "scission" or "sep-aration" [*Trennung*], "laceration" [*Zerreissung*] and "opposition" [*Entgegensetzung*]. Building explicitly on Kant's theory of autonomy, Fichte had already used the concept of "*Enteignung*" to characterize the self-disowning of positive faith in his *Attempt at a Critique of All Revelation*, G. Green (trans.) (Cambridge: Cambridge University

Press, [1792] 1978). To recognize that the principal theme of all Hegel's writings is the possibility of authentic *"Aneignung"*, of the material and spiritual reappropriation of externality in every form is to acknowledge the significant continuity between Hegel's early "critique" of religion and his later "sublation" of it: *Kritik* remains an ineliminable moment of *Aufhebung*. In this sense Hegel's work is no more marked by a fundamental "coupure" than is Marx's. I have argued this with reference to the Frankfurt writings in "Hegel's Encounter with the Christian Tradition", in *Hegel and the Tradition: Essays in Honour of H. S. Harris*, M. Baur & J. Russon (eds), 190–211 (Toronto: University of Toronto Press, 1997).

4. Kant appeals to the idea of an allegorical deciphering and therefore privileges the "interpreter of scripture" over the "scholar of scripture": "Such interpretation may well seem forced [*gezwungen*] with respect to the text (of revelation), and often indeed be so, and yet must be preferred ... to a literal one" (I. Kant, *Werke, vol. 8: Religion innerhalb der Grenzen der blossen Vernunft*, W. Weischedl (ed.) (Frankfurt: Suhrkamp, 1968), 771 ff.

5. Hegel's Jesus says explicitly: "Man as man ... is not merely a wholly sensuous being – there is also spirit in him, also a spark of the divine essence, the heritage of every rational being ..." (*N*: 79). Kant is reticent about employing the language of "spirit" at all, although he does identify rational faith with "the spirit of God which leads us in all truth" (Kant, *Werke, vol. 8*, 773–4).

6. Kant is concerned to reject what he calls "materialism with respect to personality" (ibid., 793–4).

7. Hegel's early animus against the idea of spiritual dependence on authority, doubtless intensified by personal experience at the *Stift*, partly explains his later antipathy to Friedrich Schleiermacher's concept of "the feeling of absolute dependency" as the essence of the religious relationship. Hegel insists throughout his early writings that we recognise the *shared* spirit of our spirit in our fellow human beings ("*unseregleichen*") (see W 1: 96).

CHAPTER TWELVE

WHAT IS CONCEPTUAL HISTORY?

Iain Macdonald

I. PHILOSOPHY AND HISTORY

In the final lines of the *Phenomenology*, Hegel makes the complex claim that the contingency of history and the science of knowing in the sphere of appearance together constitute a "conceptual history" (*begriffene Geschichte*): a "conceptually comprehended" history (*PhG*: 493; W 3: 591). What is this suggestive but frustratingly obscure formula meant to convey? The question is vexing, not least because the *Phenomenology* itself is neither a philosophy of history nor a philosophical history in any traditional sense; it rather takes the form of a quasi-historical narrative that picks up on the difficult problem of philosophy's relation to history.[1] For this reason, the attempt to understand what Hegel means by the term may be helped along by a critical analysis of selected aspects of his philosophy of history.[2] The limits of the question therefore go beyond the specific project of the *Phenomenology*, although answering the question will involve returning to one of the central themes of that book, namely, the concept of experience (*Erfahrung*). In any event, the aim here is not so much to evaluate Hegel's theory of world history as it is to gain a better understanding of how in general he understands historical knowledge in relation to philosophical knowledge of the absolute, a central concern throughout his career.

Consequently, clarifying the meaning of conceptual history may help to resolve a problem that frequently arises in reading Hegel: how exactly does Hegel reconcile the concrete, contingent events of history with the universal demands of reason? In its most acute form, this problem takes the form of a dilemma: neither wanting to accept a merely empirical or pragmatic view of history, nor wanting to see reason as an abstract universal force that inescapably determines historical existence. In order to deal with the problem, two sets of issues will be discussed here, representing the two horns of the dilemma: first, Hegel's critique of the pragmatic and conjectural historians of the eighteenth century, which brings into focus his own view of history in relation to philosophical thinking;[3] and secondly, Theodor W. Adorno's critique of Hegel's philosophical account of history, which provides an opportunity to test the cogency and limits of Hegel's view. The guiding question is: how is Hegel's *conceptual* account also a *history* of sorts?

In a first moment, then, the issue can be approached by way of Hegel's later philosophy of history. Obviously, the expression "philosophy of history" covers a wide range of works, authors and concerns, although for Hegel these can be reduced to: (i) reflection on various possible subjective "arrangements" of what we call historical "facts" or "chains of events"; and (ii) reflection on universal features of human experience in the great diversity of individuals and peoples to whose histories we have access. More specifically, the philosophy of history is for Hegel an attempt to make intelligible the rational structure of experience manifest in the wealth of concrete practices and individual interests in history. As one might expect, this entails a certain critical stance towards the contingency of history:

> The sole aim of philosophical enquiry is *to eliminate the contingent* [*das Zufällige zu entfernen*]. Contingency is the same as external necessity, that is, a necessity which originates in causes which are themselves no more than external circumstances. In history, we must look for a general design, the ultimate end of the world, and not a particular end of the subjective spirit.
>
> (*LPW*: 28; *VPW* 1: 29)

Clearly, this "elimination" of the contingent will be problematic for more materialistic readers (such as Adorno, as we shall see), but Hegel's approach is more nuanced than it may seem at first glance. At the very least, the philosophy of history requires us to examine and take seriously the point of contact between what is individual and what is universal as both of these moments manifest themselves in history. As such, the historiographical "handling" of the individual or of the contingent is of paramount significance.

II. PRAGMATIC HISTORY

Hegel's typology of historiographical approaches is laid out in the introduction to the 1822–28 *Lectures on the Philosophy of World History*.[4] He begins with what he calls *original* history, which requires more or less direct or "intuitive" (*anschaulich*) acquaintance with the events recounted. Herodotus and Thucydides are prime examples of this class of historians. However, this mode of writing is limited by its very strength: original history does not transcend its own present, the epoch represented. Because the original historian writes about more or less contemporaneous events, their broader import and spiritual significance cannot be made apparent, at least not in the context of what is actually presented in such works.

In contrast to original history, which relies primarily on a direct acquaintance with events, *reflective* history deals with what is *"present in spirit* [im Geiste gegenwärtig]" (*LPW*: 16; *VPW* 1: 10), whereby a connection is forged between the past and the spiritual concerns of the present day. Here, Hegel says, we are in the domain of "those whom we generally call *historians*" (*LPW*: 16; *VPW* 1: 10). There are, according to the lectures, four modes of reflective history: general histories of eras, nations or of the world (e.g. Livy, Gibbon); so-called pragmatic history, to which we shall return in a moment; critical history, or the meta-historical investigation of the authenticity and credibility of historical narratives; and specialized history, such as the history of art, of law, or of religion. In Hegel's ordering of these reflective models, he says that the last of these, specialized history, is the one that is most closely related to his own endeavour, the highest in the typology of histories: the *philosophical* history of the world. Presumably, this is because the specialized histories of art, of law, of religion and so on achieve a general perspective that national histories, for example, do not typically aim for. But although this general perspective may naturally seem to be more closely related to the philosophical perspective than the history of a specific nation, the sheer generality of specialized histories (as compared with histories of a somewhat narrower focus) is not in and of itself the full reason to privilege them. In fact, in order to understand Hegel's philosophical approach to history we might profit from turning back to pragmatic history (*pragmatische Geschichte*) for insight into what philosophical history inherits from reflective history, in the first instance because pragmatic history makes manifest "the end to which historians generally aspire" (*LPW*: 19; *VPW* 1: 16).

To be sure, in Hegel's time pragmatic histories were usually seen as histories with a moral or political programme: to instruct and edify the reader through the lessons of the past. However, Hegel not only doubts that history has ever taught anyone anything, he also criticizes the *"petty psychologist"* and the *"moralising* pragmatist, who misuse history for external ends (*LPW*: 20; *VPW* 1: 17).[5] It is therefore crucially important to add that, for Hegel, pragmatic history is not reducible to historiography with specific moral or political agendas. He understands it as a broad and general rubric, defined in the main by its attempts to make the past present to us, whether this is taken instrumentally (didactically) or more generally reflectively (more philosophically). Philosophical historians such as Hume and Voltaire should therefore figure prominently on a list of more adept pragmatic-reflective historians; and in fact, in the text Hegel explicitly mentions is Montesquieu's *De l'esprit des lois*, which, he thinks, evinces "a thorough, open-minded, comprehensive view of historical situations and a profound sense for the Idea in history" (*LPW*: 22; *VPW* 1: 20). In his criticisms of *narrow* pragmatism, then, Hegel is really defining a *broader* pragmatism, or what we should really call the philosophical moment of pragmatic history. By rejecting historians who preach, he praises those who *think* and know how to pick out what is true and pertinent from the general morass of historical particulars.[6]

Essentially, for Hegel, "pragmatic" means dealing with history as a living totality, in terms of reasons, trends, motivations, causes and effects, rather than merely chronicling events or holding up individuals as exemplars. In short, it means perceiving the general in the particular or, as Voltaire sardonically puts it: "If you have nothing to say other than that it was just one barbarian after another on the banks of the Oxus and Jaxartes rivers, then in what way are you useful to the public?" [*Si vous n'avez autre chose à nous dire, sinon qu'un barbare a succédé à un autre barbare sur les bords de l'Oxus et de l'Iaxarte, en quoi êtes-vous utile au public?*] (Voltaire 1829: XXX: 223). Pragmatic history thereby discovers the vital actuality behind the events it presents: "The events are various, but their general significance, their inner quality and coherence, are *one*. This sublates the past and raises the event into the present" (*LPW*: 20, translation modified; *VPW* 1: 18). We should see in these statements the general achievement of reflective history as a whole, understood along pragmatic lines: the facts and events recounted in reflective history are *organized* and presented *systematically* for us in such a way as to vivify the past and bring out what in it speaks to us as relevant (as defined by the subjective spirit of the historian). Ideally, the principle of organization is not external, is not contaminated by extraneous edifying purposes; it is rather developed out of the spiritual material of the facts themselves such that they take on a more universal cast: "In every advance which the object makes, [there is] not only an external coherence and necessary continuity; there is also a necessity at work within the *object itself*, within the *concept*. This [is] the true substance of history" (*LPW*: 20; *VPW* 1: 17). Thus, if pragmatic history gives us access to the "true substance" of history, then it can only be because in pragmatic reflection the activity of spirit discovers a living present within a wealth of contingent details. Consequently, the question posed by pragmatic history is formally very similar to the question posed by philosophy: what force is driving the contingent from within; what unifies historical experience and makes it a spiritual whole?

Given Hegel's presentation of the general significance of pragmatic histories, it should come as no surprise that in the Jena period he was struck by Fichte's description of the transcendental philosopher as a "pragmatic historian of the human mind" (Fichte 1982: 198–9).[7] In fact, however, Hegel's interest in the philosophical import of pragmatic history goes back to his youth. The young Hegel was thoroughly fascinated by pragmatic histories of nations, peoples and religion, which sought to unify events and to bring out what is universal in them. In an early diary entry, a fourteen-year-old Hegel wrote of a popular pragmatic world history, probably Johann Matthias Schröckh's *Allgemeine Weltgeschichte für Kinder* (1779–84):

[The author] relates all the principal events while yet wisely leaving aside the numerous kings and wars in which frequently only a couple of hundred men scrap it out; he remains with what is admirable and instructive in history. In this manner he carefully and consistently conveys the state of learning and science.

(Rosenkranz [1844] 1977: 431)

A few days later, Hegel continues the thought:

I've wondered for a long time what pragmatic history might be. Well, today I finally found out, though it's still an obscure and one-sided notion. Pragmatic history is, I think, when one goes beyond relating mere facts by developing the character of a famous man, of a whole nation, its ethical life, customs, religion and diverse variations and deviations of these as compared with other peoples.

(*Ibid.*: 433)

Pragmatic philosophical histories (better represented by authors such as Hume and Voltaire than the instructive Schröckh), then, provide us with the general perspective necessary to make the move to the perspective of conceptual history by exemplifying the development of the universal out of the particular. But such pragmatic histories – in spite of their implicit development of the particular in the direction of the general – do not achieve a universal enough perspective; they are still too contingent, too rooted in particular concerns, as the young Hegel already recognized. Another brand of generally pragmatic history, so-called "conjectural history", will take us one step further.[8]

III. CONJECTURAL HISTORY

The moralizing pragmatist that Hegel mentions in the *Lectures on the Philosophy of World History* is doubtless a reference to minor authors such as Schröckh rather than the great eighteenth-century philosophical historians, but it is important to add that even the most philosophical of pragmatic histories still frequently took a moral (or political) tone, without necessarily becoming the organs of special agendas. Thus in the case of figures such as David Hume, Adam Smith or Adam Ferguson, the aim of "bringing a present into the past" (*LPW*: 23; *VPW* 1: 21) was often mixed in with that of seeking insight into our moral character. Such histories often relied on the twin assumptions that what is natural (i.e. natural for the moral beings we are) is discernible in history, and that therefore history has a quasi-universal content that can bring us to an understanding of our moral human nature.[9] From

211

these assumptions numerous consequences follow that bring reflective history closer to speculative insight. For example, conjectural history expands beyond national boundaries, bringing into play sources from a variety of cultures and periods in order to bolster the claim that human nature is uniform or that the course of social development follows certain general principles. The contingent is thereby contextualized within a broader framework of natural (universal) development. Such an approach was of interest to Hegel for obvious reasons. His philosophical perspective on history can thus be brought out more fully by including here the specifically moral and philosophical subbranch of pragmatic history generally called conjectural history.

The expression "conjectural history" was coined by the Scottish Enlightenment philosopher Dugald Stewart in his 1793 *Account of the Life and Writings of Adam Smith, LL.D* (Stewart 1858). The expression, he says, is meant to refer to Smith's *Theory of Moral Sentiments*, Hume's *Natural History of Religion* and similar works. Bluntly put, in seeking to understand our moral sense, we are naturally brought to reflect on the historical development of the human race before the advent both of writing and of history as a discipline. However, this leads us into the embarrassing situation of dwindling supporting documents and testimony. In this case, in want of direct evidence, says Stewart, when recounting how history seemingly presents us with a natural progression of peoples and cultures, all with similar passions and interests:

> we are under a necessity of supplying the place of fact by conjecture; and when we are unable to ascertain how men have actually conducted themselves upon particular occasions, of considering in what manner they are likely to have proceeded, from the principles of their nature, and the circumstances of their external situation. (Stewart 1858: X, 33–4)

Referring especially to Smith's *Dissertation on the Origin of Languages,* Stewart further emphasizes that we can expect satisfying results from such a conjectural approach on the basis of a justified assumption about the uniformity of human nature:

> although it is impossible to determine with certainty what the steps were by which any particular language was formed, yet if we can shew, from the known principles of human nature, how all its various parts might gradually have arisen, the mind is not only to a certain degree satisfied, but a check is given to that indolent philosophy, which refers to a miracle, whatever appearances, both in the natural and moral worlds, it is unable to explain. (*Ibid.*: X, 34)

The emphasis in conjectural history, then, is on the natural progression of human moral and social life from so-called "rude tribes" to modern peoples, projected on the basis of general characteristics of human nature, which are derived from observation and a broad acquaintance with history.

Adam Ferguson gives us even sharper insight into the relation of history to human nature. In his *Essay on the History of Civil Society* ([1767] 1995), he too insists on the uniformity of human nature as the basis on which it is possible to develop a plausible history of society. But it is important to emphasize that for Ferguson and the other conjectural historians, human nature is neither an essence nor a rationally derived principle. On the contrary, says Ferguson:

> in what manner the faculties of thought or reason remain, when they are not exerted, or by what difference in the frame they are unequal in different persons, are questions we cannot resolve. Their operations alone discover them: when unapplied, they lie hid even from the person to whom they pertain, and their action is so much a part of their nature, that the faculty itself, in many cases, is scarcely to be distinguished from a habit acquired in its frequent exertion. (*Ibid.*: 30)

Thus writing a history of human progress based on the observed uniformity of human nature is not to posit an abstract essence of what it is to be human, rational and so on, but rather to immerse oneself in the study of customs and habits, travel narratives, economic relations, a whole miscellany of cultural documents and, in short, in a multiplicity of particulars in order to bring out the regularity and uniformity that is implicit in the intersecting accounts of human practices and cultures through the ages. Obviously, then, the metaphysical question of an unadulterated essence or of a timeless absolute is meaningless on the view of these empirically minded thinkers; we can only look for answers in history. There is no *a priori* that is not reducibly *a posteriori*. Or as Ferguson so forcefully puts it: "If we are asked, therefore, Where the state of nature is to be found? We may answer, It is here" (*ibid.*: 14). In short, then, conjectural histories try to gain insight into our moral character; and while the uniformity of human nature that they try to explain requires them to leave the limited terrain of traditional historical analysis by adopting a conjectural approach where necessary, they nevertheless remain committed to the history of facts as the locus of the unfolding of our uniform human nature.

From another angle, however, it should be clear that the conjectural historians were asking more metaphysical questions than historians who do not engage in conjecture about the prehistorical development of our moral character. By departing from documentary evidence, if only briefly, in order to lay out necessary stages of economic development (e.g. Ferguson) or the evolution of religion (e.g. Hume), they make claims about what *must* have been the case given all that we know about history and human nature. And such claims have a quasi-universal status relative to the contingencies of facts and events that could have been otherwise. This too is a way of bringing out what is present in spirit in the past; present, that is, not as fact *per se*, but as a relative necessity that helps us make sense of the facts.

Now, the terrain of reflective history is no doubt theoretically very rich and one would certainly be justified in thinking that Hegel learned fundamental lessons from the pragmatic and conjectural historians; for example, that the universal must be developed out of the particular; that history is a continuity of discontinuities; that it holds universal meaning for us through the exertions of a coherent human nature or spirit that pushes us forward because it is anchored in our past; that the *a priori* is not to be abstractly opposed to the *a posteriori* and so on. Indeed, to go a step further and conclude that Hegel's *Phenomenology* and his philosophy of history developed directly out of pragmatic and conjectural historiography is a tantalizing prospect. But as already intimated, the textual evidence shows that the mature Hegel took a strongly critical stand against pragmatic and conjectural historical writing, although the severity of his critique has to be seen in the light of his attempt to define true philosophical history against the backdrop of its reflective relatives. In one passage from the *Encyclopaedia*, for example, he condemns pragmatic history for its "failure to appreciate" the role of world-historical individuals by putting the emphasis on their personal idiosyncrasies and motivations. To focus on the peculiarities of human nature (on what Hegel calls *Menschenkenntnis*) in this way is to reduce history to a mere "game of contentless activity and contingent events" (*EM*: §377 Addition 2; *W* 10: 10–11; see also *LPW*: 44–5; *VPW* 1: 51–2). In another passage, aimed specifically at Stewart, his compatriots and the idea of the uniformity of human nature, he says:

> these thinkers sought an *a priori* philosophy, but not in the speculative sense. The universal representation of their principle is given by the notion of sound common sense [*der gesunde Menschenverstand*]. To this they've added benevolent desires, sympathy, and a moral sense; and on such a basis they have produced admirable moral writings. That's all very well if all one is aiming for is an approximate degree of knowledge and learning about what universal thoughts [*die allgemeine Gedanken*] are, in order to talk about them historically, appealing to examples and explaining them.   (*LHP* 378–9, translation modified; *W* 20: 286)

Hegel strikes out here at Scottish philosophy and by extension pragmatic–conjectural historiography, which derives its claims about human nature from "sound common sense" (one of Hegel's known bugbears) instead of from what must universally be the case for experience to be possible. Thus what allows us definitively to separate Hegel's philosophy of history from conjectural and pragmatic histories is the role of the universal in relation to the particular. In other words, Hegel gives a philosophical definition of history that rules out the very methods adopted by the conjectural and pragmatic approaches: "In history we must look for a general design, the ultimate end of the world, and not a particular end of the subjective spirit or mind; and we must comprehend it by means of reason, which cannot concern itself with particular or finite ends, but only with the absolute" (*LPW*: 28; *VPW* 1: 29).[10]

In contrast to pragmatic and conjectural approaches, then, Hegel argues that history's rationality transcends the rough estimate of a relatively uniform human nature; and instead of remaining with vestigially contingent similarities distilled by reflection, the conceptual historian must aim at the general structure of reason, an eternal constant, although one that is always susceptible to self-misunderstanding in concrete instances. In short, Hegel wants to unfold the universal dimension of thought and so put paid to the pragmatic–conjectural reduction of reason to what merely *seems* universal because it is deemed to be natural. It is for these reasons that he sees the need for a truly philosophical history, that is, history conceptually comprehended and understood as a process of the self-development of the absolute concept. While reflective history, informed by pragmatic and conjectural principles, seeks the universal, the latter is at best a pseudo-universal if it remains enmeshed with happenstance. Thus, in agreement with the most philosophical of reflective historians, Hegel thinks that human nature (spirit) is necessarily expressed historically, but *contra* them, he thinks that we can free the universal from the grittiness of historical events; that is, we have to see the universal *in* the historical without reducing it *to* the historical. After all, as cited above, "the sole aim of philosophical enquiry is *to eliminate the contingent*" (*LPW*: 28; *VPW* 1: 29).

IV. HEGEL'S LACK OF SYMPATHY FOR THE PARTICULAR

The trouble (if trouble it is) is that Hegel sometimes seems to suggest that absolute cognition is not so much about the reciprocal mediation of concept and history, but rather about the move from history as contingent to logic as necessary, or from one-sided cognition of the particular to total cognition of the universal: "the True is the whole" (*PhG*: 11; *W* 3: 24). So while it is clear that Hegel attempts to preserve what is true in the conjectural-pragmatic approach (the development of the universal out of the particular), while dispensing with what is false or at any rate insufficient (the pseudo-universal of a uniform human nature), he comes down firmly on the side of the absolute. The relation of the universal to the individual is precisely one in which the contingent, and so the individual, is negated. The universal is supposed to be the development of the individual, of what is true in the individual, but it is not the individual as such. Or in other words, the identity of *a priori* and *a posteriori* is one in which the individual (a person, an object, an event) must shed its idiosyncrasies in order to align itself with the whole, the absolute.

It is when he is defending this point that Hegel sometimes goes so far as to deride the contingent and the individual in the name of the universal. For example:

> Individuals often have their own peculiar opinions of themselves, of their lofty intentions, of the splendid deeds they hope to per-form, and of their own supposed importance from which the world, as they think, must assuredly benefit. Be that as it may, such ideas merit no further attention here. ... Furthermore, the indi-vidual may well be treated unjustly; but this is a matter of indiffer-ence to world history, which uses individuals only as instruments [*Mittel*] to further its own progress.   (*LPW*: 65; *VPW* 1: 76)

This idea, that the individual is nothing but a mere instrument or agent, is also contentiously (and infamously) described as the cunning of reason:

> it is not the universal idea which enters into opposition, con-flict, and danger; it keeps itself in the background, untouched and unharmed, and sends forth the particular interests of passion to fight and wear themselves out in its stead. It is what we may call *the cunning of reason* that it sets the passions to work in its serv-ice, so that the agents by which it gives itself existence must pay the penalty and suffer the loss.   (*LPW*: 89; *VPW* 1: 105)

So on the one hand, Hegel's philosophy of history seeks to correct what he sees as the one-sided pragmatic–conjectural emphasis on empirical obser-vation and historical similarities, and to that end he attempts to show how history is to be comprehended conceptually, whereby the true goes beyond any "average estimation" of human nature. But on the other hand, he seems to impute objectivity to the absolute and has it standing back cunningly while expendable individuals fight it out. In short, if the conjectural-pragmatic approach is all too empirical, then in these passages Hegel seems to be over-stating the project of a philosophy of world history or making it sound too transcendental or too isolated from real concerns. In other words, in spite of what he claims, there might at the end of the day be nothing truly historical about conceptual history.

This is, of course, one of Adorno's principal critiques of Hegel. "In the midst of history", as he says, Hegel always "sides with its immutable element, with the ever-same, the identity of the process whose totality is said to be pristine [*heil*]" (Adorno 1973: 357; 1886: VI, 350; see also Adorno 1973: 326–9; 1997: VI, 320–22, 350). Or more specifically:

> Hegel distorts the facts of the matter by misconstruing the negativity of the universal and by affirming identity, even while admitting that non-identity is also necessary. He lacks sympathy for the submerged utopia of the particular and for the non-identical which might come to be, if only realized reason could leave the particular reason of the universal behind.
>
> (Adorno 1973: 318; 1997: VI, 312, translation modified)

It would appear, then, that whereas Hegel pushes us to eliminate the contingent in order to grasp the absolute, Adorno takes up the cause of the downtrodden, non-identical, contingent particulars who allegedly play out a script that reason has written for them in advance. But to see things in this way would be to miss the point of Adorno's complaint entirely, which is far more Hegelian than it appears. For Adorno's remarks should be read as an internal correction of Hegel, or as a valuable reminder that the absolute cannot maintain its distance from the contingencies of history. In this way, Adorno's critique may help us to understand more clearly the nub of Hegel's position, which does not in fact commit him to an extreme anti-individualism.

It is important to note at the outset that Adorno's defence of "the nonidentical" does not merely take up the cause of the particular or the suffering individual in abstract opposition to Hegel's universalism. His rejection of any isolation of world spirit from its individual "agents", spirit keeping itself in the background untouched and unharmed, does not mean that he is defending a garden-variety anti-metaphysical materialism. Indeed, Adorno recognizes that we need the universal for the particular to be rescued from its debasement: "A true priority of the particular would only be achievable by virtue of a transformation of the universal. Simply bringing it into existence is a complementary ideology" (1973: 313, translation modified; 1997: VI, 307). The point is not that we need to protect the particular from the ravages of the universal. It is rather that we need to rethink and redeploy the dialectical relationship between the particular and the universal in such a way that the particular is given its due by the universals that subsume it, in such a way that the universal is always marked (transformed) by the particular. The "transformation of the universal" will thereby be nothing other than a return to dialectical development, a refusal of the stasis that metaphysics courts.

Adorno's main complaint is thus that Hegel seems to abandon the dialectic where it must be rigorously maintained: at the moment where absolute knowing breaks away from history (see Adorno 1973: 334–8; 1997: VI, 328–31). The correct response is to reactivate the dialectic, to negate the impediment and restart the self-corrective mechanisms of thought. This is the submerged utopia that Adorno has in mind. As he puts it, utopian thinking is simply "thinking that thinks difference [*Differenz*] in relation to what exists now" (1973: 313; 1997: VI, 308). The utopia of the particular is not for that reason a real state of affairs; it is the open-ended ideal of reason as a self-corrective power (although of course Adorno knows well enough not to be overly optimistic about this power's real manifestations). Thus Adorno's response to Hegel must not be read as promoting a counter-dialectic, one that would seek to return us from the arrogance of the universal to the plurality of sensuous particulars. What he is aiming at in his talk of utopian thinking is a method, praxis essentially, that is able to reactivate a stalled dialectic. Unsurprisingly, the philosophy of history is the site for this struggle as it is most obviously there that the universal emerges from the chrysalis of the contingent, in a context where subjective spirit (the historian, the philosopher, but also the political agent) must reflect on this very process.

In other words, if it is possible to "rescue" (as Adorno puts it) the dialectic through a critical return to its own resources, then we must be able to show how the contingent and the necessary, the individual and the universal, or the historical and the immutable are necessarily enmeshed in Hegel's own thought (1993: 83; 1997: V, 320). The parameters for a successful rescue are obviously somewhat limited, for if Hegel concedes too much ground to the contingent, conceptual history would return to mere conjecture, while on the other hand, siding with the universal and the immutable would inevitably belie the historicality of conceptual history.

V. THE HISTORICALITY OF EXPERIENCE

As mentioned at the outset, the expression "conceptual history" occurs at the end of the *Phenomenology,* in a passage where Hegel is attempting precisely to show how contingent historical events and the absolute fit together. "The *goal,*" he says, is "absolute knowing, or spirit that knows itself as spirit, [which] has for its path the recollection of diverse spirits as they are in themselves and as they accomplish the organization of their realm" (*PhG*: 493; *W* 3: 591). From the point of view of preserving the mere contingent existence of diverse forms of spirit – their coming-to-be and passing-away – these "diverse spirits" constitute history as such, while from the point of view of preserving their conceptually comprehended organization (*nach der Seite ihrer begriffenen Organisation*), they articulate the science of knowing as it takes place in the sphere of appearance. Taken together, these two perspectives constitute conceptual history, or absolute knowing. History is therefore the history of contingent events and peoples, but it is also and essentially the concrete event of conceptual comprehension: a relation of particular to universal that comes to know itself *as* this structural relation of particular to universal. Conceptual history therefore demands that we see history from the perspective of the concept, while still insisting that the absolute universal, the concept as such, emerges within this history, instead of being rationalistically imposed from outside. Conceptual history, on this view, would be the inner truth of history.[11]

Such is a possible, perhaps orthodox, response to Adorno's challenge. But for evident reasons, the challenge remains intact: logical transitions garbed in the dress of the particular do not constitute history, nor do they account for the failures of reason as well as they do the successes. The pseudo-historicality of conceptual self-development is no better than the pseudo-universality of the conjectural historians. Does Hegel then succumb to Adorno's critique? The concept of experience as developed in the *Phenomenology* may help us to see why not.

In essence, experience designates a "reversal of consciousness [*eine Umkehrung des Bewußtseins*]" (*PhG*: 55; W 3: 79), that is, an enactment of rational self-correction. For Hegel, experience is not something passively acquired and synthesized; it already designates an historical praxis, the activity of individual consciousness putting itself at odds with its passively accepted cognitive norms and beliefs in order to adjust them as and when this becomes necessary: "this *dialectical* movement which consciousness exercises on itself and which affects both knowledge and its object, is precisely what is called *experience*" (*PhG*: 55; W 3: 78). Put differently, the act of rational self-correction is both a necessary possibility of reason *and*, simultaneously, an *act* necessarily carried out by particular individuals in history; it cannot remain abstract and still be *experienced*. However, because consciousness is usually caught up in the real details of its decisions and actions, it does not usually grasp the general pattern of experience (which Hegel calls "determinate negation"); it does not see the forest for the trees:

> it is just this necessity itself [i.e. the necessity attaching to dialectical progression], or the *origination* of the new object, that presents itself to consciousness without its understanding how this happens, which proceeds for us [i.e. philosophical consciousness], as it were, behind the back of consciousness.   (*PhG*: 56; W 3: 80)

With this in mind, the aim of the *Phenomenology*, of Hegel's "science of the experience of consciousness" (*PhG*: 56; W 3. 80), is just the presentation of possible shapes of experience (individual, ethical, moral, scientific, aesthetic, religious, ultimately spiritual) from the standpoint of the general pattern of experience. Hegel thereby shows us the side of experience we do not generally see: the patterns according to which experience brings about the transformation of self and world.

It is in this way that Hegel manages to bind together the universal (the pattern of experience as stemming from the structure of consciousness) and the particular (the gritty, historical "stuff" with which individual consciousness struggles): he describes the development of generic natural consciousness through its moments of real crisis and decision. The key is that reason *only* "happens" when the mere possibility of self-correction becomes a reality for and by historical consciousness. Only fully historical consciousness can decide to refuse sense-certainty, the hopeless reductionism of desire, the misunderstood yearning of the unhappy consciousness, the ridiculous claim that "the being of Spirit is a bone" (*PhG*: 208; *W* 3: 260) and so on. (This is perhaps one reason why Hegel's historical references in the *Phenomenology* are so ambiguous or multi-referential: the reader is thereby forced to make the connection to real circumstances.) It is only in the experienced moment of rational insight that reason exerts itself *as* reason: "what I thought before cannot be the case and so I must adjust my conception of myself and the world accordingly". This moment, although described *generically,* can only be *specified* historically, of course, since the determinations that define it are just the individual and social concerns that impose themselves in history.

With this in mind, the cunning of reason can now be understood as a particularly maladroit way of expressing a real concern that Hegel expresses better elsewhere: the fact that individual, historical consciousness is not always ready to undertake the act of self-correction. Natural consciousness "is always … learning from experience what is true in it; but equally it is always forgetting it and starting the movement all over again" (*PhG*: 64; *W* 3: 90). In other words, individual consciousness is not always up to the task, for various reasons: cultural (e.g. Antigone), ideological (e.g. Robespierre) or personal (e.g. plain cowardice). Consciousness is nothing but the capacity to determine and surpass limitations, as Hegel says, but he also readily admits that individual consciousness cannot always muster the strength required:

> anxiety may well make [consciousness] retreat from the truth, and strive to hold onto what it is in danger of losing. But it can find no peace. If it wishes to remain in a state of unthinking inertia, then thought troubles its thoughtlessness, and its own unrest disturbs its inertia.　　　　　　　　　　　　　　　　(*PhG*: 51; *W* 3: 74–5)

Individual consciousness can certainly cling dogmatically to obsolete truths, but it also has the inbuilt capacity to redetermine the true, and so transform itself and the world. There is, of course, a certain optimism at work here: wherever there is conflict or tension, in principle *some* individual consciousness will be able to confront it and undertake to negate it, although in fact this or that individual may not manage it.[12]

VI. WHAT IS CONCEPTUAL HISTORY?

Now we are in a position to see that against the pragmatic–conjectural historians, Hegel's claim is that we have the right, grounded in experience, to lay claim to a truly universal structure: that of reason itself. One way of summing this up would be to say that while conjectural-pragmatic history attempts to clarify *actual* experience in relation to human nature, conceptual history attempts to relate actual experience to (necessarily) *possible* experiences of consciousness in general, although to grasp the structure of experience, we must pay a certain price: we must "eliminate the contingent.

However, "eliminating the contingent" can be understood in two quite distinct ways, each corresponding to one of the two ways outlined above in which Hegel tends to speak of the particular–universal dynamic. If we put the emphasis on the negative reading of the cunning of reason, then to "eliminate" the contingent would mean discounting or even sacrificing individuals who do not correspond to world-historical spirit; particular human beings would be no more than the unwitting agents of a process of reason that outstrips them. On the other hand, if we put the emphasis on the concept of experience, we thereby stress that reason is *only* active in particular human beings and in the critical, evaluative power that is at their disposal as a universal function of consciousness. While it may seem at first blush that we have to decide on which perspective is the "correct" view, the interpretation of the cunning of reason given in the previous section should go some way towards dispelling this abstract opposition. The cunning of reason is just the idea that while this or that individual may not be willing or able to put in the work required to change things, nothing in principle can bring a halt to the self-corrective activity of reason.

Of course, Adorno's critique of Hegel conveys a strong message to the reader: we cannot – must not – opt for an understanding of reason and history that shows contempt for suffering individuals and, moreover, we cannot justify being unequivocally optimistic about the power of reason. But in fact, if we limit ourselves to the core of the project of the *Phenomenology*, the concept of experience, we can perhaps secure a valuable resource for replying to Adorno's initial challenge. In experience (in the Hegelian sense), we witness a struggle in which reason indeed emerges victorious, but only as the result of ongoing historical acts of self-correction. It is only if we take the concept of experience out of the picture that something like the so-called cunning of reason can proclaim the priority of the universal over the particular. In the concrete, the historical struggle between the universal and the particular is precisely the substance of experience: the real movement of natural (individual, historical) consciousness in its evaluative rapport with what is for-itself and what is deemed to be in-itself.[13]

By emphasizing experience, then, it becomes clearer how to interpret the demand that philosophy "eliminate the contingent" (*das Zufällige zu entfernen*). Contingency is not "extirpated" by the concept; on the contrary, it is the historical moment of self-evaluation and self-correction prompted by doubt or suffering. Contingency is for that reason *required* for consciousness to recognize itself in the concept, for consciousness to redetermine and transform the universal as a result of contradictions that surge up in experience.[14] Were contingency not so required, the concept would be nothing more than a point-like and self-absorbed *nunc stans*, "a lifeless solitude [*das leblose Einsame*]" (*PhG*: 493; *W* 3: 591), as Hegel himself admits.

Of course, philosophy aims at the general and so thought must "distance" itself from the contingent, as the German verb "*entfernen*" suggests (too narrowly translated as "to eliminate"). We must be "at a certain remove" from the contingent in order to grasp what is necessary within it, in order to see that our search for truth and justice are always shaped by the experience of determinate negation. What is first and foremost necessary and universal is experience *qua* the necessary possibility of self-correction; but what experience designates is nothing other than the *particular* moment of self-reflection in which self-correction happens. This arch-philosophical operation, this "standing at a remove from the contingent" thus need not be considered the callous act of sacrificing the individual to the universal dictates of reason. On the contrary, the necessary possibility of self-correction forces us to reconceive reason as the generic act of self-correction that can only be realized concretely, when circumstances align and false consciousness is left behind, not once and for all, but in a given set of circumstances.

What is conceptual history, then? It is the ordered recapitulation of the possible experiences of consciousness that makes manifest the general definition of experience outlined here. It is conceptual to the extent that it aims at basic forms; but it is no less historical to the extent that it stresses real, experienced needs – felt by the individual or by a community – to transform our self-conception and our conception of the world. The critical point is that sublation never takes place by itself. Reason is and requires "purposive activity" (*PhG*: 12; *W* 3: 20) on the part of individuals who respond to historical reality. Experience is Hegel's name for the real individual's historically contingent but conceptually necessary relation to the absolute: it is the universal praxis that formally guarantees that reason can attempt to correct false consciousness. Conceptual history is thus a recapitulation of the diverse forms taken by experience. It is the philosophical template for a process that is ineliminably historical, or a general demonstration of the concrete self-corrective power of reason.[15]

NOTES

1. Of course, the question of the relation of the *Phenomenology* to real history is perennial, but little has been written on the subject of conceptual history as such. On the general question of the historical nature of the *Phenomenology*, most commentators understandably stress the logical dimension over the phenomenal dimension. History is thereby subordinated to its rigorous conceptualization. And yet it is also generally acknowledged that Hegel's absolute requires its manifestation in history. Stephen Houlgate argues forcefully for the view that history and absolute truth are "inseparable" (*An Introduction to Hegel: Freedom, Truth and History* (Oxford: Blackwell,

2005), 17), while at the same time claiming that the *Phenomenology* "does not describe the historical transformation of one shape of consciousness into another. It traces the experience that each shape *logically* must undergo" (*ibid.*, 101). This does not necessarily lead to a contradiction, but it does suggest that we need to get clear on what conceptual history is, as opposed to real history and logic.

While putting much emphasis on historical detail, H. S. Harris's monumental commentary, *Hegel's Ladder*, 2 vols (Indianapolis, IN: Hackett, 1997) pays little attention to conceptual history *per se*. Harris shows himself to be quite uninterested in the specific import of the term, and seems to assimilate it to conceptual *science* at the end of his book. With respect to the general question of history, Harris merely says that Hegel's "task is to set what everyone knows about the history of culture – or what every educated person agrees one ought to know – into an order that reveals its philosophical significance *for us*" (*ibid.*, II, 749). In a note, Harris adds that "we do not need to worry about the different sorts of history that Hegel distinguished in his maturity" (*ibid.*, I, 104 n.125). Yet in an earlier passage he insists on the importance for Hegel of Fichte's conception of philosophy as a pragmatic history of the human mind, which suggests that Hegel would almost certainly have thought about the philosophical merits of pragmatic historiography in relation to his own project (*ibid.*, I, 16). Werner Marx, whose short book on the *Phenomenology* Harris cites approvingly on this point, does not offer an argument for leaving the meaning of conceptual history undiscussed. This is perhaps understandable given the limited scope of his book, but it cannot serve as a general justification for avoiding the issue; W. Marx, *Hegel's Phenomenology of Spirit: Its Point and Purpose: A Commentary on the Preface and Introduction*, P. Heath (trans.) (New York: Harper & Row, 1975), 61.

Falke's full-length commentary on the *Phenomenology* focuses on how the various shapes of consciousness and spirit relate to the system as a whole. Drawing on Hegel's preface and the final chapter on absolute knowing, Falke writes: "Philosophy has become reflexive. It no longer deals with existent being, but rather with its abbreviations. The *Phenomenology,* understood as the conceptual organization of history or as the systematic reconstruction of historically received shapes of consciousness, assembles these abbreviations under the sign of Mnemosyne into a 'gallery of images' or a *musée imaginaire*" (G.-H. Falke, *Begriffne Geschichte: Das historische Substrat und die systematische Anordnung der Bewußtseinsgestalten in Hegels Phänomenologie des Geistes. Interpretation und Kommentar* (Berlin: Lukas, 1996), 68–9). For Falke too, then, conceptual history has less to do with empirical history than with the interrelation of the spiritual positions that develop out of empirical history. Perhaps – but the question still arises as to how Hegel understands the production of these abbreviations and their relation to traditional historiographical methods (*ibid.*, passim). The aim of the present essay is to sketch a preliminary answer to some of the questions posed by the expression "conceptual history" without favouring the logical over the historical dimension of the term.

2. Jean Hyppolite is among the few who see the closing lines of the *Phenomenology* as dependent on an implicit philosophy of history; J. Hyppolite, *Genesis and Structure of Hegel's Phenomenology of Spirit*, S. Cherniak & J. Heckman (trans.) (Evanston, IL: Northwestern University Press, 1974), 605–6, and *Introduction à la philosophie de l'histoire de Hegel* (Paris: Seuil/Points Essais, 1983). Joseph McCarney makes a similar suggestion, emphasizing that Hegel's later philosophy of history depends on "a general logic or dialectic of consciousness" of the sort worked out in the *Phenomenology*; but

the focus of his book is such that the meaning of conceptual history is not analysed in depth; J. McCarney, *Hegel on History* (London: Routledge, 2000), 87, 165–6.

Although most commentators who deal with Hegel's lecture courses on the philosophy of history make some mention of the *Phenomenology,* the specific problems it raises are most often seen as secondary in relation to the historical evolution of the state, which is taken to be the principal actor in world history. But as Walter Jaeschke points out, this view depends on the mediation of metaphysics and history and therefore on an understanding of spirit in time: "granted that world history for Hegel is closely tied to the existence of states, nevertheless it is not, in the last analysis, the state in which history is grounded, but rather in the concept of spirit. The only reason why there is a history of states is that there are forms of spirit in time." Jaeschke goes on to stress that, on its own, this in no way entitles us to view Hegel's entire system as a philosophy of history; W. Jaeschke, "World History and the History of the Absolute Spirit", in *History and System: Hegel's Philosophy of History*, R. L. Perkins (ed.), 101–15 (Albany, NY: SUNY Press, 1984), 103.

3. O'Brien discusses some of these issues from the standpoint of the later philosophy of history. However, he anachronistically emphasizes latter-day pragmatism in explaining what Hegel calls pragmatic history and so overlooks the relation of Hegel's thought to the pragmatic and conjectural approaches of his time; G. D. O'Brien, *Hegel on Reason and History: A Contemporary Interpretation* (Chicago, IL: University of Chicago Press, 1975), 22–3.

4. Hegel lectured on this subject four times between 1822–23 and 1828–29. The introduction to the fifth and final 1830–31 lecture course differs substantially from the earlier introduction. Hegel's manuscript lecture notes, which were available to the first editors, have not survived, apart from the 1830 introduction and a portion of the introduction to the 1822 lectures. Moreover, some student notes that were available to the first editors are no longer extant. For these and other reasons, the historical editions of these lecture courses have all been quite distinctive. For present purposes, Hoffmeister's edition, first published in 1955 (*VPW*), has been used. Nisbet's English translation of the introduction, cited here, is based on Hoffmeister. For a brief overview of the main editions and their sources, see F. Hespe, "Hegels Vorlesungen zur 'Philosophie der Weltgeschichte'", *Hegel-Studien* 26 (1991), 78–87. The extant manuscripts are published in *GW*: vol. 18. Student notes of the 1822–23 lectures taken by Griesheim, Hotho and Kehler are published in *Vorlesungen*: vol. 12. Substantial editorial commentary is included in each of these volumes. For a more detailed analysis of Hegel's typology, see L. Pompa, *Human Nature and Historical Knowledge: Hume, Hegel and Vico* (Cambridge: Cambridge University Press, 1990), 72ff.

5. Hegel famously remarks that "Rulers, statesmen and nations are often advised to learn the lesson of historical experience. But what experience and history teach is this – that nations and governments have never learned anything from history or acted upon any lessons they might have drawn from it" (*LPW*: 21; *VPW* 1: 19).

6. In some respects, Hegel's view echoes that of the *Popularphilosoph* Thomas Abbt, who in 1761 outlined "the true concept of pragmatic history". For Abbt, as for Hegel, the specifically pragmatic character of pragmatic history had little to do with sprinkling historical writing with edifying maxims. Rather, the pragmatic historian "seeks to direct the reader's eye regularly towards universal philosophical causes, for he can presume that setting them side by side against historical reality will produce the liveliest impression"; T. Abbt, "Hundert und ein und funfzigster Brief. Anmerkungen über

den wahren Begriff einer pragmatischen Geschichte", in *Briefe, die neueste Litteratur betreffend*, vol. 9, 118–25 (Berlin and Stettin: Nicolai, 1761), 123.

7. On this question, see D. Breazeale, "Fichte's Conception of Philosophy as a 'Pragmatic History of the Human Mind' and the Contributions of Kant, Platner, and Maimon", *Journal of the History of Ideas* 62(4) (2001), 685–703. However, Breazeale focuses mainly on the philosophical use of the term "pragmatic", which is derivative of the historical use of the word. Hegel's early interest in Fichte's notion of pragmatic history is made clear in a well-known entry from the so-called waste book (predating the *Phenomenology*): "Only by way of the history of consciousness *does one know what these abstractions are* that one has through the concept: *Fichte's* merit" (W 2: 559).

8. Hegel doesn't distinguish rigorously between pragmatic and conjectural histories.

9. Abbt too claims that "as a philosopher, [the historian] must investigate the most natural connection" obtaining between the events he recounts; Abbt, "Hundert und ein und funfzigster Brief, 120. See also Humboldt's "Über Göthes Herrmann und Dorothea": "The stricter pragmatic notion of truth … straightforwardly demands what is natural, and even if it doesn't exclude the extraordinary and the unusual, they must always perfectly accord with the course of nature taken as a whole, that is, with the species-concept of humanity, even if it rises above it" (W. von Humboldt, *Aesthetische Versuche, erster Theil* (Braunschweig: Vieweg, 1799), 319).

10. Of course, Hegel is not dismissing these thinkers out of hand, not least because his social and political philosophy bears a debt to Scottish Enlightenment thought. See in particular Waszek 1988. For an analysis of Hegel and Hume on the question of history, especially with regard to the uniformity of human nature, see Pompa 1990.

11. With a tweak or two, any number of commentators could fit the bill here; see for instance B. Bourgeois, "Hegel et la déraison dans l'histoire", in *Logik und Geschichte in Hegels System*, H.-C. Lucas & G. Planty-Bonjour (eds), 57–79 (Stuttgart: Frommann-Holzboog, 1989), 59.

12. For example, Kepler claimed that Mars's elliptical orbit nearly drove him to madness because he expected it to be circular. Ultimately, he chose to transform the received view of planetary motion. However, it would have been entirely consistent with the conservative tendencies of natural consciousness for Kepler to have refused the possibility of elliptical orbits. In that case nothing *in principle* would have prevented someone else from overcoming Kepler's "anxiety" over elliptical orbits; he would merely have missed his chance, as it were. This is not due to reason itself understood as an objective force. It is because a given individual was unable to take the steps required to sublate the specific tensions that plagued determinate knowledge in a specific context. The key is that it is always natural consciousness, the historical individual, who is so plagued and called upon to act. Reason, or the dialectical deployment of contradiction and decision, is fully historical and rationality always rests on the shoulders of real individuals.

Bourgeois appears to be making the same point when he writes: "It is of course essential that someone dot the 'i' but when it comes to realizing *universal* structures of objective spirit, the domain of historical rationality, there will always be someone there to do it" (Bourgeois, "Hegel et la déraison dans l'histoire", 61). There is, however, a gaping chasm between an unspecified "singular will" that will "sooner or later" appear and do what is necessary and the specific world-historical individual who here and now gives timely voice to reason. For one thing, waiting for someone to come along to dot an "i" could rapidly disintegrate into the most delusional form of hope

    – a kind of jobsworth messianism that puts too strong an accent on individuality, as opposed to the individual. Individuality does not act; individuals do.

13. See "The Experiential Content of Hegel's Philosophy" in T. W. Adorno, *Hegel: Three Studies*, S. Weber Nicholsen (trans.), 53–88 (Cambridge, MA: MIT Press, 1993). It should be noted that Adorno's reading of Hegel in this essay is more generous than in *Negative Dialectics*, E. B. Ashton (trans.) (London: Routledge, 1973).

14. In his classic essay "Hegels Theorie über den Zufall", Dieter Henrich says that according to Hegel "it is contingency [*der Zufall*], not the contingent [*das Zufällige*], that is necessary, and so the determinate contingent object cannot be of substantial interest" (D. Henrich, *Hegel im Kontext* (Frankfurt: Suhrkamp, 1975), 168). This is one way of explaining what it means to eliminate the contingent. However, it should be specified that absent the contingent, contingency is an idle concept – never one without the other, even if philosophy can only deal with the *concept* of contingency.

15. This chapter grew into its present form over the course of many discussions with D. Perinetti about Hegel and the philosophy of history. In particular, his knowledge of the Scottish conjectural historians, which he was so willing to share, was of great help to me. I should also like to thank N. Walker and especially K. Deligiorgi for their very helpful and generous comments.

CHAPTER THIRTEEN

HEGEL'S INTERPRETATION OF ARISTOTLE'S *PSYCHE*
A QUALIFIED DEFENCE

Allegra de Laurentiis

In the chapter on "Plato and Aristotle" in the *Lectures on the History of Philosophy*, Hegel praises Aristotle's work for displaying a principle of "pure subjectivity" that, by contrast, he considers largely absent from the Platonic *corpus*:

> In general, Platonic thinking [*das Platonische*] represents objectivity, but it lacks a principle of life, a principle of subjectivity; and this principle of life, of subjectivity, not in the sense of a contingent, merely particular subjectivity, but in the sense of pure subjectivity, is proper to Aristotle.   (W 19: 153)[1]

Elsewhere and repeatedly, Hegel refers to Aristotelian conceptions of organic life and of thinking – especially from the *Metaphysics* and the *De Anima* – as the first speculative insights to be found in the history of (Western) philosophy.

A "speculative insight" in Hegel's sense may be characterized in a general way as grasp of the thinking subject's theoretical and practical relation to itself, that is, as theoretical self-knowing and practical self-will.[2] "Speculative" is any concept that grasps (holds together intelligibly) what other kinds of cognition keep asunder, for example, the subjective and objective dimensions of a phenomenon or a state of affairs.[3] But even independently of a detailed analysis of the meaning of speculative insight or a speculative principle, one is struck by the apparent inconsistency of these claims on Aristotle with Hegel's overall view of the logically necessary stages of philosophical thinking in history. This view is synthetically expressed in an 1820 introduction to the *Lectures on the History of Philosophy* in the following way:

> According to this idea I now maintain that the succession of the systems of philosophy in *history* is *the same* as the *succession in the* logical *derivation* of the conceptual determinations of the Idea.

> I maintain that if one strips the fundamental concepts [*Grund-begriffe*] of the systems that have appeared in the history of philosophy of what concerns their exterior shape, their application to the particular and similar features, one obtains the various stages of determination of the Idea itself in its logical concept.
>
> (*GW* 18: 49–50)[4]

Coupled with Hegel's well-known understanding of philosophy as fulfilment of the Delphic command "know thyself",[5] whose outcome is *"reason that knows itself"* [*die sich wissende Vernunft*] (*EM*: §577), this claim on the history of philosophy appears to contradict quite bluntly his enthusiastic appraisals of the Stagirite. The claim seems to exclude the possibility of early forms of knowledge that logically belong to later stages of spirit's development, including, of course, spirit's self-reflection in philosophy. Indeed, the theory of the history of philosophy[6] expounded in (among other places) the 1820 introduction and at work in the lectures themselves is quite in agreement with the theory of the *"self-thinking* Idea" from the last sections of the *Encyclopaedia*. According to this text, although "know thyself" is the first explicit formulation of philosophy's goal, it still marks as such only the abstract beginning of philosophic science. The implicitly speculative nature of thinking can only be recognized over time and can experience a fully fledged realization only in the individual self-conceptions and politically free (or "self-willed") institutions of modernity.

In addition, Hegel's praise of Aristotle contrasts sharply with his own sweeping judgements (in the body of the same lectures) on the stunted achievements of ancient philosophy precisely with regards to grasping self-reflexive subjectivity, in both theoretical and practical perspectives. The following brief excerpt from the 1820 introduction is quite representative of what Hegel says elsewhere on the same topic:

> In order to bring a *concrete example* of the *slowness* … with which *spirit* comes to *grasp* itself, I need only refer to *the concept of its freedom* … The Greeks and the Romans – not to mention the Asiatics – knew nothing of this concept – namely that *man as man* is born free, that he is free. – Neither Plato nor Aristotle – nor Cicero and the Roman jurists, let alone the [ancient] peoples, knew this concept, although it alone is *the source of right.* They did know of course that an *Athenian, a Roman* citizen, an *ingenuus*, is free – that there are the free *and* the un-free – and exactly for this reason they did not know that man *as* man is *free* …, that is, … man as apprehended in thought and as he apprehends himself in thought. (*GW* 18: 56–7)

These inconsistencies in Hegel's appraisal of ancient philosophy's achievements have been highlighted and criticized both by scholars interested in

Hegel's conceptions of thinking, subjectivity or freedom, and by those whose concern is rather with protecting the spirit and the letter of Greek philosophy from what they perceive as biased, if not exploitative, interpretations on the part of nineteenth-century philosophers.

And yet, even scholars of ancient philosophy sometimes seem to be at a loss when facing conceptually pivotal parts of the texts under their scrutiny. A strategy sometimes pursued in the reconstruction and interpretation of puzzling (or unorthodox) texts by Plato is that of attributing to them ironic or parodic intent. An example of this strategy is Harold Cherniss's vastly influential 1932 interpretation of the second part of Plato's *Parmenides*, a text in which contradiction is discussed in ways that, since Cherniss's contribution, many have felt to be simply abstruse and, worse perhaps, inconsistent with more standard views of Plato's on logic and predication. In the *Republic* (and elsewhere), Plato rejects contradictory descriptions of physical as well as psychological phenomena (for example, of motion and of "mastery of self") as unintelligible.[7] In the *Parmenides*, however, a subject matter defined as "the one itself" ("*to hen autos*"; generally taken to refer to Parmenides' poem *About Nature*), is proved to be neither continuous nor discrete, neither finite nor infinite, neither moving nor at rest, neither similar nor dissimilar to itself nor to others, and so forth (*Parmenides* 137d–141d). Because of its inconsistency with other Plato texts, Cherniss declared the dizzying discussion of the "one itself" in the second part of this dialogue to be a parody of sophistic argumentation, rather than a subversive attempt at thinking through the logical and ontological implications of Plato's concept of "idea", possibly in order to expose its internal dialectical structure.

As for commentaries on Aristotelian texts, one often finds in them abrupt condemnations of original passages as unintelligible, sometimes followed by their rejection as "spurious", "interpolated" or at the very least so obscure as to merit separate treatment. The latter strategy is being used whenever particular portions of an otherwise coherent text appear to contradict the overall line of interpretation pursued. A recent example of this separation strategy is Stephen Menn's remarkable exegesis of the first two books of *De Anima*. One of his main claims is that Aristotle's theory of the soul in the overall plan of the treatise, which Menn understands principally as a "program for reforming natural philosophy" (2002: 115) *vis-à-vis* its pre-Socratic and Platonic precedents, stands and falls with Aristotle's conception of an (absolutely) *unmoved* mover,[8] a conception intended to exclude the idea of a *self-moving*, and thus in a peculiar sense *moved*, mover. Menn stresses that Aristotle's choice of analogy for *psyche* as principle of organic life is that of an "art" rather than an "artisan". "Art" would denote a static, non-subjective set of immutable principles prescribing and enabling the artisan's activities, while "artisan" would suggest a subjective agency that may or may not be capable (or willing) to put the art into practice. According to this interpretation, there is no place in Aristotle's *De Anima* for the ethically tainted analogy of the soul with the artisan as a subjective agent – an allegory used instead by Plato in the *Timaeus* (compare in particular *Timaeus* 35 a1–b3). According to Menn, Aristotle would reject such an analogy as "a relapse into mythology" because "the underlying nature and causality of such an 'artisan' would be obscure" (Menn 2002: 115–16). In this reading of *De Anima* as a treatise of natural philosophy the natural soul does not metamorphose into a self-moved mover. Thus, there is no transformation of "substance" (*ousia*) or subject matter (*hypokeimenon*) into a "subject" whose thinking activity (*noein*) may well escape strictly causal accounts.

The naturalistic character of the soul in *De Anima*'s account of its reproductive and perceiving functions is uncontroversial. However, this character does not suffice to explain the soul's further functions: *phantasia* and (passive and active) *nous*. Indeed, Menn limits explicitly his interpretation of *psyche* to the text of the treatise up to, but not including, the pivotal chapters on *nous* (*De Anima* III, Chs 4, 5). In a specially formulated footnote, he acknowledges that Aristotle's full theory of soul would actually require the artist analogy, which is to say, some form of a principle of subjectivity. This would be necessary in order to explain, in addition to the feeding, reproductive, sensing and perceiving functions, the soul's rational, properly speaking thinking function. Given, however, the objective philosophical difficulties (one is tempted to say, the speculative character) of *De Anima*'s chapters on *nous*, Menn maintains that Aristotle is "in aporia about how to describe" the rational soul (Menn 2002: 116 n. 45). He claims that the philosopher's predicament is epitomized by the famous characterization of the thinking soul as being "in a manner potentially all objects of thought, but … actually nothing until it thinks" or also "nothing at all in actuality before it thinks" (*De Anima* III, Ch. 4, 429b 30–1, 429a 22–4). Menn seems to consider these characterizations as bordering on the nonsensical when he describes them as an "odd mixture" of the *Timaeus*' receptacle and Anaxagoras' *nous*. Although he insists that the notion of an absolutely unmoved mover may ultimately prove useful even as an explanation of *nous*, he concludes by avowing "I shall stay away from these extremely controversial chapters in this paper" (Menn 2002: 116 n. 45).[9]

Despite Hegel's idiosyncratic formulations and his occasionally questionable translations of Greek texts, I find that his interpretation of fundamental principles of Greek philosophy sheds light precisely on the meaning and rigour of texts that others feel compelled to view as inauthentic, of questionable attribution, or simply as hopelessly controversial. My claim implies neither that Hegel gives the most accurate account of the individual philosopher's self-understanding, nor that he provides us with the best literal paraphrases of textual passages. Indeed, Hegel is interested in doing neither. In the 1820 introduction he declares his strategy quite explicitly: "The history of philosophy must itself be philosophical" (*GW* 18: 39). On the one hand, philological and historiographical skills are required of the philosopher in order to convey, as much as possible, the original meaning of concepts and arguments in the epochal context of their formation. As a philosopher, however, who is engaged in uncovering the logical succession of philosophic principles (*Grundbegriffe*) through history, his interpretation of concepts and arguments must go beyond their epochal meaning. Hegel announces his lectures not as "*Historie*" but as "*Geschichte*" of philosophy. He aims at reconstructing the objective logical consequents and historical successors of the principles of each philosophical system of the past.

Two recent interpreters of Hegel's reading of Aristotle represent well opposite attitudes on the topic. On the one hand, Alfredo Ferrarin's *Hegel and Aristotle* (2001) is both deeply knowledgeable and highly critical of Hegel's reading; on the other hand, Michael Wolff's *Das Koerper-Seele-Problem* (1992), of equal scholarly depth, presents in decidedly sympathetic terms Hegel's resolution of the so-called mind–body problem as resulting precisely from Hegel's interpretation of Aristotelian *psyche*. Focusing on one aspect of Aristotle's and Hegel's notions of soul, namely its classification as substance, I want to argue that already Aristotle's "substance" (*ousia*) as applied to soul (*psyche*) carries two different connotations depending on the term in relation to which soul is said to be substance. Although these two senses are implicit in the Aristotelian use of soul-as-substance, only the first is developed systematically and with remarkable detail in the *De Anima*, while the second is given a largely dogmatic exposition, but no systematic account, in the famous chapters of Book III dedicated to the passive and active intellect. The first is a conception of soul as internal principle of organic nature (*physis*); the second is a conception of soul as the ground of thinking mind (*nous*). The distinction between these two basic connotations of the same concept seems to me to lie at the core of the continuity of and difference between Aristotle's and Hegel's theories, a relationship that continues to be a source of puzzlement in the contemporary literature. Hegel understands his philosophy of "Subjective Spirit"[10] as providing the systematic completion of Aristotle's incomplete theory of soul or, more precisely, his incomplete theory of the relation between natural soul and intellect. After a brief sketch of Ferrarin's and Wolff's readings, I argue in favour of the plausibility and meaningfulness of Hegel's interpretation. One result of my analysis is that the inconsistencies in Hegel's judgement about Aristotle mentioned at the beginning of this chapter are more apparent than real.

As it is impossible here to give an adequate summary of the two books, I limit myself to indicating what I take to be representative claims of their respective theses. I hope my selective presentation is fair, although I am aware that it cannot do justice to the painstakingly in-depth accounts of Hegel's reading of Aristotle provided by the two authors.

Despite Ferrarin's highly nuanced criticism of Hegel, it ultimately amounts to a radical rejection of his reading of the *De Anima*. His book focuses on Hegel's interpretation of Aristotle's notion of *energeia* (or, as applied to the natural soul, *entelecheia*) in terms of a principle of subjectivity, an interpretation

Ferrarin judges to be "arbitrary". He stresses the one-sidedness of Hegel's projection of "pure subjectivity" (quoted at the start of this chapter) onto Aristotle's attempt to make sense of "forms" that are not only combined with, but actually internal to, "matter". He underlines the exaggerated nature of Hegel's claim that we can find in the *De Anima* a programme of unification between the natural soul and the self-thinking thought of the *Metaphysics*: not accidentally, just the programme of Hegel's own Philosophy of Spirit in the *Encyclopaedia* (Ferrarin 2001: 10–11). Ferrarin chastises Hegel for translating *energeia* as "activity" (*Tätigkeit*, or also *Wirklichkeit*), intended not just as an objective process but as the activity of a subject (whether "man" or "god" shall be left aside here). Yet he also acknowledges the usefulness of this interpretation of *energeia* for bridging the gap between nature and thought (especially self-thinking thought) in Aristotle's philosophy. He is fully aware that the concept of "subjectivity" in Hegel is not the same as that of "individual subject", in that "subjectivity" simply denotes the activity of (inward, independent) actualization of a potentiality, while "subject" implies more. (To state this complex matter briefly, being-subject implies the particularization of the abstract universality of subjectivity *tout-court*, a particularization that results in "universal singularity"; see *EL:* §163.) Thus Ferrarin understands why Hegel can both praise Aristotle's philosophy for containing a principle of subjectivity and deny him any awareness of the "absolute value" of individual subjectivity (see *PR:* §124 Addition, §185 Addition; Ferrarin 2001: 18) in metaphysical as well as ethical and political terms. He even judges Hegel's explanation of the irreducibility of thinking to the thinker to be "ingenious" (Ferrarin 2001: 315) and appears to consider Hegel's reading of Aristotle more accurate than Neoplatonic ones. Overall however, he presents Hegel's reading as a distortion and misrepresentation of Aristotle's philosophy, guided by the intent of making it into a more or less direct precursor of his own. This judgement is best understood in the light of Ferrarin's implicit assumptions about the project and systematic character of the *De Anima*. He writes, for example, that "the *De Anima* ... for Aristotle is the culmination of the philosophy of nature *from which the chapters on* nous *alone are excluded*" (*ibid.:* 255, emphasis added); he criticizes Hegel for judging "philosophers more for their intentions than for the realization of those intentions" and for reading Aristotle in particular with the aim of "explaining what Aristotle left unexplained" (e.g. the relation between human and divine intellect) (*ibid.:* 15, 315). I hope to show that Hegel would not disagree with these characterizations of his historical approach to philosophic theories, given his conviction that any other approach would lead to endless repetition without grasp of the productive principles of past philosophies.

Wolff's book consists of a line-by-line commentary of §389 and Remark of the 1830 Anthropology (W 10) and a "corollary" to the commentary. This is the only text in the *Encyclopaedia* in which Hegel treats the so-called mind–body problem in a systematic way. From his exhaustive analysis Wolff draws conclusions that are, if not opposite, very different in substance from

Ferrarin's. Wolff believes that Hegel's reception and assimilation of Aristotle's theory of *psyche* is precisely what allows him to resolve the mind–body problem by showing that it is a false problem to begin with (Wolff 1992: 13). In arguing against modern pre-critical philosophy's many versions of dualism, mentalism and reductive materialism, Hegel would find in Aristotle's work the vantage point of a theory of "soul" and "living body" that precedes the emergence of a metaphysical and logical split between the two (*ibid.*: 14). Thus, by assimilating Aristotle's theory, showing its limitations and developing it further to meet the challenges of nineteenth-century psychology and physiology, Hegel is able to prove that two obstinate questions of modern philosophy derive from unsupported metaphysical presuppositions rather than from inevitable paradoxes. These are the questions (a) of the immateriality *versus* materiality of the soul (treated in part 2 of Wolff's "corollary") and (b) of the interaction (*Gemeinschaft* or *commercium*) between soul and body (part 3). With regards to this latter question (a topic that I shall not cover in this chapter, except obliquely), Wolff shows how Hegel's understanding of "soul" as *the concept* of "living bodies" eliminates the conundrums of their alleged "interaction". In the Addition to the section from the Anthropology that forms the basis of Wolff's discussion, Hegel writes: "In truth, however, the [so-called] immaterial relates to the [so-called] material not like a particular relates to another particular, but rather like the genuinely universal, subsuming particularity under itself, relates to the particular" (*W* 10: §389 Addition). In other words, the relation between soul and body is neither an unsolvable mystery (as assumed by natural scientists whose experience compels them to reject materialist reductionism), nor an unintelligible fact attributable only to divine intervention (as for Malebranche). It is rather the same relation as holds between the adequate concept of a phenomenon and the experiences, representations or intuitions connected to the phenomenon *per se*. As for (a), Wolff points out the two related but distinct connotations of Hegel's (Aristotelian) talk of soul-as-substance that I have briefly mentioned above, that is, soul as principle of nature and as ground of mind. Hegel, whose principal conception of soul is, as just stated, that it is the adequate ("true") concept of the living body, concedes that one may well adopt a classification of soul as substance, as Aristotle does, as long as one is ready to grasp that one and the same substance may be form of one entity and matter of another. Since my chapter is largely in agreement with Wolff's thesis, further consequences of this latter, all-important distinction will become clear in the course of the analysis.

Between the two approaches just sketched there appears to be little controversy about the legitimacy, on Hegel's part, of presenting Aristotle's soul in terms of an essence (*ousia*), in so far, that is, as the latter means the intrinsic *form* of organisms: *ousia* as *eidos* or, as Aristotle more often says, *logos*. Aristotle characterizes the soul clearly and repeatedly as essence in-forming living nature:

It must follow, then, that soul is substance [*ousia*] in the sense that it is the form [*eidos*] of a natural body having in it the capacity [*dynamei*] of life. Such substance is actuality [*entelecheia*].

(*De Anima* II 1, 412a 19–21) [11]

It has now been stated in general terms what soul is, namely, substance as notion or form [*kata ton logon*]. And this is the quiddity [*to ti en einai*] of such and such a body.

(*De Anima* II 1, 412b 10–11)

Now the soul is cause and origin [*aitia kai arche*] of the living body … For the soul is the cause of animate bodies [*empsychon somaton*] as being in itself the origin of motion, as final cause and as substance. Clearly it is so as substance, substance being the cause of all existence. And for living things existence means life, and it is the soul that is the cause and origin of life. Furthermore, actuality is the notion or form [*logos*] of that which has potential existence.

(*De Anima* II 4, 415b 8–15)

Hegel's sharing this characterization of *psyche* does not imply that the entire meaning of *Seele* in Hegel's system is exhausted by the Aristotelian concept of *psyche* as substantial *logos* of natural organisms. Nor does it imply that Hegel reads Aristotle as providing a complete and definitive account of soul. On the one hand, the soul of Hegel's Anthropology is indeed the internal formal principle by which living nature distinguishes itself (self-differentiates) from non-living nature; on the other hand, soul is also the "stuff, "material" or "substantiality" away from which spirit develops towards ever increasing "subjectivity", namely through its phases as consciousness, self-consciousness and reason to mind or subjective spirit proper.

While the last sections of the *Philosophy of Nature* present "soul" in relation to nature, the very first section of the Anthropology defines it in relation to spirit. Soul, Hegel states, is a self-presupposition of spirit:

Spirit has *become* as the truth of nature. … In the Idea this result has the significance of … [being] the first over against what precedes it … Spirit that has become has therefore the meaning that nature sublates itself by itself as the un-true and that in this way spirit presupposes itself … as *simple* universality in which it is *soul*, not yet spirit [proper]. (W 10: §388)

In itself, soul can be represented (*vorgestellt*) and understood (*verstanden*) as soon as reflective thinking makes its appearance. Its concept, however, can only be grasped (*begriffen*) from the perspective of an advanced stage of spirit. It is from the perspective of concrete spirit ("spirit become") that its own

234

origins in and differentiation from nature can be explained, as the Anthropology is about to do, in terms of its development from merely living, to feeling, self-feeling and finally actual (human) soul. The next section in the Anthropology specifies further the dynamic relation of soul to more complex forms of spirit (that is, the relation of early to later modes of the latter): "The soul ... is the *substance*, the absolute ground of all particularization and singularization [*Besonderung und Vereinzelung*] of spirit to the effect that *spirit* has in soul all the material [*Stoff*] of its determination while soul remains the identical ideality of these determinations" (W 10: §389). To illustrate the primitive, "abstract" character of spirit's phase as natural soul Hegel then borrows psychological and metaphysical features of *psyche* from the *De Anima*: "But in this as yet still abstract determination, soul is only the *sleep* of spirit; – the passive *nous* of Aristotle which is *potentially* everything" (*ibid.*).

Thus, Hegel here identifies soul, defined abstractly (and this means also "in a preliminary way"), with the sleeping state of Aristotelian *psyche* and the passivity and pure potentiality of *nous*. He does this precisely because he intends to go beyond the *De Anima*. He intends to develop the "concrete determination" of spirit by providing a systematic treatment of the science of thought thinking itself. While soul is indeed a principle of nature, its full actualization lies elsewhere. Already soul itself, if compared with the matter of which it is the principle, is a negation of corporeal nature: "*In itself*, matter has no truth within the soul; as being-for-self, soul divides itself [*scheidet sich*] from its immediate being and posits it over against itself as a corporeity incapable of resisting its own formative power [*Einbilden*]" (*EM*: §412). But it is in spirit proper that this negativity of matter finds its full manifestation: "Spirit is the existent truth of matter, namely, that matter itself has no truth" (W 10: §389 Remark).

Since Hegel goes along with Aristotle's classification of soul as a substance, the double character of soul's logical–metaphysical status (to repeat: its functions as immaterial principle of corporeity and as ground of spirit) can perhaps be better grasped in the light of the logical features exhibited by the category of essence in Hegel's *Logic*. Hegel's "soul" appears to be as much a relational concept as that of "essence": its precise meaning depends on other notions it is related to, that is, on *notions with respect to which* it is soul or, in the terminology of the "Doctrine of Essence", notions "through which it shines". Categories grouped under "essence" are relational concepts *par excellence*. The general category of Essence itself denotes the mediation performed by thinking between two poles: Being (its primary object or immediate content) on the one hand, and itself as the Notion (*der Begriff*), on the other. The two poles in relation to which the soul has different functions, and thus "soul" different meanings, are nature and spirit. In particular, soul relates to nature as a formal principle but to spirit as a material ground. Since nature and spirit form a continuum (namely one *Wirklichkeit*), the same constellation is described by stating that the living body relates to soul as soul relates to spirit. In relation to the natural organism, soul is its organizational principle, that is, its internal logical *eidos* or *logos*; in relation to spirit, soul is its "stuff", its ground of existence ("*Stoff*" or "*Grundlage des Geistes*"), its *hyle* as *hypokeimenon*.[12] In this sense, it is legitimate for Hegel to characterize the soul as both a formal and a material principle.

A twofold metaphysical determination of soul surfaces indeed repeatedly, if indirectly, in Aristotle's text. For example, affections of the soul (anger, fear, pity) are said to be immaterial although always already embodied (see *De Anima* I 1, 403a 3 and subsequent discussion). Although necessarily coincident with affections of the body, affections of the soul are not logically identical with them – or the two kinds would not be distinguishable in judgement. And since we deduce the existence and capacities of soul from our acquaintance with bodily affections and manifestations,[13] the characterization of affections as *logoi enuloi* – enmattered forms – (*De Anima* I 1, 403a 25)[14] may well be applied to the soul as a whole. The latter is the immaterial dimension of the body it in-forms, all the while this body is soul's only mode of existence.

The double metaphysical status of *psyche* is one important reason for Hegel to attribute "speculative insight" to Aristotle. Aristotle himself does not develop this ambivalence, nor does Hegel credit him with having done so. But the ambivalence is objectively contained in the Aristotelian doctrines of soul's sleeping and waking states, of thought's potentiality and actuality, and of the passive and active *nous*. Hegel considers these speculative insights to be in need of systematic development. Thus, he stresses the character of soul as a middle term between materiality and immateriality. Soul is immaterial in so far as it negates nature (soul is "Nature ... as the un-true"; W 10: §388); it is material in so far as it is negated by spirit proper (it is "*soul*, not yet spirit"; *ibid.*). Philosophical science must go beyond Aristotle's conception of soul and its affections as enmattered forms while preserving the dialectical character of this very conception. It must show that, and in what sense, soul is also the material for spirit's self-differentiation from nature.

Soul's double status implies that the contradictory concepts of materiality and immateriality are related dialectically. Common sense tends to associate nature with materiality, spirit (and thus soul) with immateriality. But the physical sciences themselves deny the concept of matter a univocal referent. Speaking about the physicality of nature, Hegel remarks that "in recent times matter has been thinning out even in the hands of the physicists", who find themselves compelled to study "*imponderable* matters [*Stoffe*] such as heat, light and so forth" (W 10: §389 Remark). These so-called matters lack all properties that common sense attributes to matter as such: gravity, extension, impenetrability. Thus, even for the physicist (not just for the "idealist" philosopher!) the term "matter" might well refer to a highly "immaterial" content. And what is true of the matter of inert bodies must apply *a fortiori* to the corporeity of living ones. Mindful of Aristotle's classification of the many senses of being-substance, according to which matter without form and form without matter are nothing, so that all existents must be "of both" (*De Anima* II 1, 412a 9), Hegel stresses that any rational account of actuality will have to take into consideration the dialectical nature of matter and form. The actuality of the soul or reality of the living body can be no exception.

If "matter" refers to modes of existence ranging from the extended and impenetrable to the incorporeal, then it will come as no surprise that spirit itself is articulated in shapes that relate to one another as matters to forms. Soul, for example, is matter for consciousness proper, while consciousness proper is matter for spirit; or natural consciousness (*das natürliche Bewusst-sein*) – articulated in sensibility, perception and understanding – is the matter of self-consciousness (*Selbstbewusstsein*) and reason (*Vernunft*); or, to take an example of the same relation in objective spirit, the customs and traditions of each generation are "the soul, spiritual substance ... the *material* present" to the next (*GW* 18: 37).

To sum up this point: for Hegel, body is to soul as soul is to spirit. Regarding the first of these two relations, he does embrace Aristotle's characterization of soul as substance in its eidetic meaning: soul is the formal, immaterial essence of an organized natural substratum. But Hegel then goes further: soul is, in turn, the natural substratum of an organized spiritual substance. In so far as Aristotle does not develop a philosophy of subjective spirit, the speculative core of his conception of soul remains merely implicit. Still, by acknowledging the dialectic character of matter and form or of potency and actualization with regards to organic bodies, states of consciousness, and – last but not least – thought itself (in the discussion of *nous*) Aristotelian theory implicitly acknowledges also the existence of a non-natural realm of actuality: *Geist*. This is objectively (and that means for Hegel logically) implied by Aristotle's notions of soul as at once natural and divine, of intellect as passive and active, and of *nous* as thinking and as self-thinking thought. Thus, *De Anima* Book III, Chapters 4 and 5, adumbrate a theory of spirit that only modern philosophy would be able to disclose as a "second nature".

Accordingly, Ferrarin is right in imputing to Hegel several "departures" (Ferrarin 2001: 254) from the Aristotelian text, except that such departures need not be grounds for rejecting his interpretation. In the light of Hegel's own understanding of the history of philosophy, implying as it does an objective logical development of *Grundbegriffe* in historical time, it would be peculiar indeed if he did *not* depart from his predecessors, or if his interpretations were limited to their explicit self-understanding (assuming that a reliable method to identify the latter were possible in principle).

Despite the lack of development of the idea of soul as ground of spirit in Aristotle's work, non-natural aspects and functions of *psyche* inform much of his reflection in the last book of the *De Anima*, to say nothing of the *Nicomachean Ethics*. Equally, though, methodological reflections from the first book of *De Anima* show that a non-naturalistic account of the soul is actually *required* by Aristotle's own epistemological criteria of a "true account".

By applying these criteria to the principal subject matter of the treatise, it is possible to show that *psyche* must be explained in a twofold manner.

In the passages in question (*De Anima* I 1, 403a 25), Aristotle explains that only a double account of the affections (*pathe*) of life-endowed bodies can do justice of their complex nature. The competent philosopher will not define anger as being either a "boiling of the blood, [a] heat about the heart" or a "desire for retaliation". Rather, the truth of anger is that it concerns body and soul simultaneously. Neither bodily temperature without aggressive desire, nor desire without bodily temperature give the meaning of "anger" its due. Thus, the true philosopher will account for all affections from the perspective of the natural scientist (as *physikos*) as well as from that of the logician (as *dialektikos*). He will have to provide both the physical description *and* the meaning carried by the phenomenon for its underlying subject (*hypokeimenon*): the angry man. The philosopher will provide "the matter" as well as "the form or account (*logos*)" because "the account is the form of the thing, but this account, if it is to be, must be realized in matter of a particular kind" (*De Anima* I 1, 403b). In order for "heat about the heart" and retaliatory desire to be aptly identified as anger, they must be grasped as a unity, just as all existing beings must be grasped as unities of matter and form.

It should be added that, from a purely epistemological perspective, Aristotle applies these criteria for true philosophizing to non-living teleological objects of investigation as well: just as "anger" is ill defined by temperature or desire alone, so "house" is ill defined as "stones, bricks and timber" or as "sheltering device" alone. Only a specific configuration of certain materials, one that aims at fulfilling a specific end (*telos*), is appropriately defined as house (compare *De Anima* I 1, 403b 5).

From these reflections on method it follows that *psyche* cannot be truthfully accounted for from the perspective of the *physikos* alone. Whatever the complex operations of the reproductive and sensitive functions of soul, they all turn out to be directed by and towards a non-reproductive and non-sensible, "formal" or "eidetic" principle of soul. This is the topic of the chapters on *nous*, the province of the logician and metaphysician of soul. The Aristotelian criterion of the double account is contained in Hegel's doctrine that philosophic truth can only have systematic form: the true is the whole. The key to the arguments developed in the *Realphilosophie* – including spirit in its subjective dimension: as soul, as consciousness and as mind – is to be found in the *Science of Logic*. Vice versa, the *Science of Logic* taken alone is a merely abstract account of what the *Realphilosophie* is about, namely the Idea in its actuality.

Despite Aristotle's explicit rejection of "merely physical" and "merely dialectical" accounts, commentators still like to think of the *De Anima* as attempting a purely naturalistic explanation of life, of sensibility and, despite the obvious difficulties, of thought. Criticisms of Hegel's reading as biased and textually unwarranted seem to derive from a rejection of the dialectic intrinsic to the concept of *psyche* and from a neglect of the implicit role of *nous* in the explanation of the functions of *psyche* that precede it in the exposition.

That observation could of course only be proved by a detailed reconstruction of the entire trajectory of the *De Anima* from sensibility through perception and imagination to passive and active thought. Since this cannot be provided here, I only offer one additional consideration in support of my defence of Hegel's reading. This consideration is relatively independent of an assessment of the systematic nature of the *De Anima* as a whole. Aristotle's talk of soul as substance of natural bodies leads one to the question whether this substance can or must itself be natural. Speaking for many commentators, Ferrarin's answer to this question is a straightforward "yes": "Aristotle's naturalistic approach ... is rooted ... in the soul being a natural thing [*sic.*] which is known like any other natural thing, as a form-in-matter" (Ferrarin 2001: 258). But this statement leads inevitably to further, seemingly unanswerable questions: if soul is a "thing" or form-in-matter, what is, in turn, its form? What is its matter? And if soul is a "natural thing" as much as body is, how do they differ? Further, how will the *physikos* alone or, for that matter, the *dialektikos*, explain their distinction? It seems that the problem of a natural versus non-natural status of the soul cannot be resolved by embracing only one of these alternatives. The problem is analogous to the Kantian one pertaining to whether the principle of the unity of appearances could itself be an appearance. It obviously cannot, or such appearance would in turn require another principle of its unity and so on into infinite regress. Similarly, if the Aristotelian *arche* of organisms were natural, it would have to be a natural organism (an animalcule, perhaps, something explicitly rejected in Aristotle's criticism of his predecessors), which in turn would require its own *arche* and so on to infinity. The similarity of Aristotle's reasoning with that of Kant in this matter ends here, of course. For Kant, as is well known, the teleology of natural organisms is a necessary but "problematic' concept. More generally, the purposiveness of nature is "inexplicable" because it can be considered critically "only in relation to our cognitive power, and hence in relation to the subjective conditions under which we think them" (*Critique of Judgement*, §74). By contrast, Aristotle's immaterial principle (which is nothing less than a principle of immateriality) is not a merely methodological necessity for explaining our experience of living corporeity. It is intended as an objectively truthful account, provided by the *dialektikos*, of organic bodies as described by the *physikos*. Despite being an immaterial principle, the *eidos* we call soul is as real as the *hyle* whose principle of organization it is. The soul is the real *logos* (Hegel: the actual concept) of the equally real living body. Consistently with Hegel's view, for Aristotle the best (that is, true to reality) principle of explanation of living organisms is not a merely epistemological, "subjective" device. In the explanation of life, subjectivity and objectivity coincide.[15]

The closeness of Hegel's conception of truth to Aristotle's "true account" can be fleshed out further. If soul is to body as form is to matter, then the meanings of "soul" and "body" will depend on their mutual relation, just as is the case with form and matter. But mutual dependency does not imply semantic or formal logical identity. Understanding both the *dialektikos*' and the *physikos*' accounts to be true does not engender an identity philosophy's cognitive "night in which all cows are black". The two passages of the Anthropology already quoted (*W* 10: §389 Remark and §412) concisely clarify this point. Hegel's assertion that the "truth of matter" is "that matter has no truth" because its truth is spirit, is not an immaterialist rejection of the independent existence of material things, but *a realist rejection of the irrational belief in the independent existence of matter*. It is a rejection of the naive assumption that the abstract concept of "matter" has a material object (*Gegenstand*) (or even a shared material element of objects) for referent. In the case of organisms, this translates into a rejection of the independent existence of their corporeity. Being-matter is one aspect of organisms; being-non-matter is the other. Both are necessary but neither is the sufficient condition of being-organism. Neither condition can be experienced, thus neither can be verified, independently of the other. What can be experienced and verified is always already a matter–form "compound" or rather, in Hegel's preferred terminology, a *unity* of matter and form.[16] Starting out from our pre-philosophical acquaintance (*Bekanntschaft*) with organisms as units, we come to distinguish (*ur-teilen*, Hegel's term for Aristotle's *krinein*) their components, judging organisms to be not simple but internally differentiated units, eventually achieving knowledge (*Erkenntnis*) of what organisms truly are: "the separation of the material from the immaterial [can be] explained only from the foundation of the original unity of both" (*EM*: §389 Addition). In the same way in which "matter" is not a thing, "soul" is not a thing either. It is rather the particular form of a particular kind of things – living things. The question so popular among modern philosophers, "Is soul a material or immaterial thing?", is as ill-posed as a question that no modern philosopher asks: "Is matter a material or immaterial thing?" It is analogous to a Kantian antinomy of reason: whether the world is finite or infinite cannot be settled by proving the thesis true and the antithesis false or *vice versa*. While Hegel agrees with Kant that such oppositions inhere in reason on account of its dialectical nature, he argues against Kant, as is well known, that the conflicts generated can be resolved precisely by reason itself. With regards to the so-called mind–body problem, a first step towards this resolution is represented by Aristotle's emphasis on the twofold ontological status of living bodies and their affections.

"Body", then, is the receptive or passive (so-called material) aspect of being-organism; "soul" is its causative or active (so-called immaterial) aspect. The one is not reducible to the other, but neither is it accurate to say that they "interact", because they are never separate to begin with. Neither monism (materialist or mentalist) nor dualism (as commonly if somewhat improperly attributed to Plato or Descartes) is an adequate metaphysical foundation for the explanation of living things. In Michael Wolff's words:

Between the psychic and the somatic, as long as we understand them not as things but as processes, activities and aims (like tasting, listening, blinking, walking, eating and breathing), there is *with regards to their materiality* no specific difference: both the psychic and the somatic are related to an internal end of the organism ... and are equally rooted in material presuppositions.

(Wolff 1992: 155, emphasis added)

Hegel's rejection of monism and dualism as one-sided metaphysical theories for the explanation of realities in process such as living bodies or souls is the modern equivalent of Aristotle's rejection of the one-sided accounts of the *physikos* and *dialektikos*. Aristotle scholars have even forged a technical term to capture the metaphysical position they find inscrutable: "hylemorphism".[17] But without an analysis of the dialectical relation of *hyle* and *morphe*, this word does nothing to solve the "mystery" of Aristotelian theory's imperviousness to being classified as naturalistic or idealistic, monistic or dualistic, empiricist or rationalist. "Hylemorphism" seems rather to fulfil the same function as that of "original sin" (as once remarked by Marx) in theologians' explanations of the existence of evil in God's excellent creation: it presupposes what it is supposed to explain.

NOTES

1. Although all translations are my own, I have consulted *LHP*.
2. See, for example, the formulation given to the as yet only "abstract" form of speculative subjectivity in the practical sphere in the *Philosophy of Right*: "*der freie Wille, der den freien Willen will*" ("the free will which wills the free will") (*PR*: §27).
3. Other important features belong to the meaning of "speculative" in Hegel, including a going beyond what is given, as well as a making objective of what is originally understood as being merely subjective; see M. Inwood, *A Hegel Dictionary* (Oxford: Blackwell, 1992). A treatment of the relation of speculation and absolute Idealism exceeds the scope of this chapter.
4. *Vorlesungsmanuskripte II (1816–1831)*. Hegel attributes "speculative content" to Aristotelian philosophy at several junctures in the *Logic* and in the *Encyclopaedia*. In the 1830 edition, he calls the *De Anima* "the best or even only work of speculative interest ever written on the philosophy of spirit" (*W* 10: §378).
5. "*Know thyself*, this absolute command ... means knowledge of the true in man [*Mensch*] as well as of the true in and for itself, – of essence itself as spirit" (*W* 10: §377).
6. The expression "theory of the history of philosophy" is from K. Düsing, *Hegel und die Geschichte der Philosophie: Ontologie und Dialektik in Antike und Neuzeit* (Darmstadt: Wissenschaftliche Buchgesellschaft, 1983), 7.
7. See Plato: "Yet isn't the expression 'self-control' ridiculous?" (*Republic* 430e–431) and the subsequent "solution" of this paradox in terms of an "interactive" model, that is, a

relation between different parts of the soul, a "better" or "stronger" and a "weaker" or "worse" part.

8. In reading *"to proton kinoun akineton"* in this way, Menn belongs to a long and honourable tradition including, among others, Friedrich Schelling and, more recently, A. Ferrarin, *Hegel and Aristotle* (Cambridge: Cambridge University Press, 2001).

9. A similar approach characterizes Ferrarin's chapter dedicated to Hegel's interpretation of the Aristotelian *nous*. Here, the central interpretive problems of the relation between active intellect and unmoved mover, between the transcendence and/or immanence of *nous*, and between *nous* and body are declared to be questions that must "always remain open". Despite his criticism of Hegel's attempt to disclose precisely these relations, Ferrarin adds: "I focus on what is relevant for the Hegelian exegesis without taking a stand on the endless disputes about the nature of the intellect" (Ferrarin, *Hegel and Aristotle*, 309–10 n. 65). It seems to me, however, that a criticism of Hegel's reading would have to be supported by an alternative interpretation of Aristotle.

10. See W 10: §§388–412 (Anthropology); W 10: §§413–39 (Phenomenology); W 10: §§440–82 (Psychology).

11. This definition is repeated at 412a 27–8 with the specification that soul is the *first* actuality of a living body, implying that there is a further one (or further ones).

12. M. Wolff, *Das Körper-Seele-Problem: Kommentar zu Hegel, Enzyklopädie* (Frankfurt: Klostermann, 1992), 126, makes the same point.

13. See *De Anima*: "For activities and functions are *logically* prior to faculties" (II 4, 415a 18–20, emphasis added).

14. In this instance, I replace Hicks's rendering of *logoi enuloi* as "forms or notions realized in matter" with "enmattered forms". Although Hick's formulation is very close to Hegel's understanding of *Begriffe* of the objects that realize them, and is thus in my view a very perceptive rendition of Aristotle's thinking, still I prefer here "forms" for *logoi*. A truly literal translation, "enmattered reasons", would strike too many readers as a Hegelian outrage.

15. For a very different perspective see Ferrarin, *Hegel and Aristotle*, 258ff.

16. By pointing to this important terminological difference I do not mean to suggest that Aristotle's "compound" and Hegel's "unity" differ *only* terminologically. It is actually an intrinsic part of Hegel's critique of Aristotle that he is ultimately incapable of conceiving an *internally differentiated* unity, as opposed to an aggregate or compound of differences.

17. Menn writes accurately that "hylomorphism of itself does not explain Aristotle's conception of the teleological relation of soul and body, or his explanatory programme" ("Aristotle's Definition of Soul and the Programme of the *De Anima*", *Oxford Studies in Ancient Philosophy* 22 (2002), 114). Wolff calls "hylemorphism" a *"Verlegenheitswort"* (Wolff, *Das Körper-Seele-Problem*, 154), that is, a word intended to help one out of embarrassment.

BIBLIOGRAPHY

The bibliography is divided into three sections: the first contains the German editions of Hegel's works cited in this volume; the second contains the English translations cited or consulted by the authors or given for the reader's convenience; the third contains references to works cited in the text together with some additional material on Hegel. References are given to the page numbers or paragraph numbers of the English editions cited below. References to German editions are given to volume and page, paragraph or page number alone, as appropriate in each case.

GERMAN EDITIONS OF HEGEL'S WORKS

Bonsiepen, W. "Hegels Raum-Zeit-Lehre" (Berlin 1821/22, Nachschriften by von Uexküll and an anonymous student). *Hegel-Studien* 20 (1985), 9–78.

Briefe von und an Hegel, vol. I, J. Hoffmeister (ed.). Hamburg: Meiner, 1969.

Dokumente zu Hegels Entwicklung, J. Hoffmeister (ed.) (Stuttgart: Frommans, [1936] 1974).

Gesammelte Werke, H. Buchner & O. Pöggler (eds). In association with the Deutschen Forschungsgemeinschaft hrsg, v. der Reinisch-Westfälischen Akademie der Wissenschaften. Hamburg: Felix Meiner, 1968.

Hauptwerke in sechs Bänden. Hamburg: Felix Meiner, 1999.

Hegels theologische Jugendschriften, H. Nohl (ed.). Tübingen: Mohr, [1907] 1971.

Naturphilosophie: Band I: Die Vorlesungen von 1819/20 (Bernhardy Nachschrift), M. Gies (ed.). Naples: Bibliopolis, 1982.

Phänomenologie des Geistes, H.-F. Wessels & H. Clairmont (eds). Hamburg: Felix Meiner, 1988.

Philosophie der Kunst oder Aesthetik: Nach Hegel. Im Sommer 1826, A. Gethmann-Siefert & B. Collenberg-Plotnikow (eds). Munich: Wilhelm Fink, 2004.

Philosophie der Kunst: Vorlesung von 1826, A. Gethmann-Siefert, J.-I. Kwon & K. Berr (eds). Frankfurt: Suhrkamp, 2005.

Sämtliche Werke: Jubiläumsausgabe in zwanzig Bänden, H. Glockner (ed.). Stuttgart: Frommann, 1941.

Vorlesung über Ästhetik, H. Schneider (ed.). Frankfurt: Peter Lang, 1995.

Vorlesungen über die Philosophie der Natur: Berlin 1819/1920 (Ringier Nachschrift), M. Bondeli & Hoo Nam Seelmann (ed.). Hamburg: Felix Meiner, 2002.

Vorlesungen über Naturphilosophie Berlin 1821/22 (von Uexküll Nachschrift), G. Marmasse & T. Posch (eds). Frankfurt: Peter Lang, 2002.

Vorlesungen über Naturphilosophie Berlin 1823/24 (Griesheim Nachschrift), G. Marmasse (ed.). Frankfurt: Peter Lang, 2000.

Vorlesung über die Philosophie der Kunst, A. Gethmann-Siefert (ed.). Hamburg: Felix Meiner, 1998; student edition, 2003.

Vorlesungen über die Philosophie der Weltgeschichte, 4 vols, J. Hoffmeister (ed.). Hamburg: Felix Meiner, 1955.

Vorlesungen: Ausgewählte Nachschriften und Manuskripte, 13 vols, Nordrhein-Westfälichen Akademie der Wissenschaften (ed.). Hamburg: Felix Meiner, 1983.

Werke in zwanzig Bänden, E. Moldenauer & K.-M. Michel (eds). Frankfurt: Suhrkamp, 1986.

ENGLISH TRANSLATIONS OF HEGEL'S WORKS

Early Theological Writings, T. M. Knox (trans.). Introduction and Fragments translated by R. Kroner. Chicago, IL: University of Chicago Press, 1948.

Elements of the Philosophy of Right, A. W. Wood (ed.), H. B. Nisbet (trans.). Cambridge: Cambridge University Press, 1991.

Encyclopaedia of the Philosophical Sciences I: Logic [1830]. Reprinted as *The Encyclopaedia Logic: Part I of the Encyclopaedia of Philosophical Sciences*, T. F. Geraets, W. A. Suchting & H. S. Harris (trans.). Indianapolis, IN, Hackett, 1991.

Encyclopaedia of the Philosophical Sciences II: Philosophy of Nature [1817]. Reprinted as *Hegel's Philosophy of Nature: Being Part Two of the Encyclopaedia of the Philosophical Sciences, 1830*, A. V. Miller (trans.). Oxford: Clarendon Press, 1970.

Encyclopaedia of the Philosophical Sciences III: Philosophy of Mind [1830]. Reprinted as *Hegel's Philosophy of Mind: Being Part Three of the Encyclopaedia of the Philosophical Sciences, 1830*, W. Wallace (trans.), together with the *Zusätze* in Boumann's text (1845), A. V. Miller (trans.). Oxford: Clarendon Press, 1971.

Faith and Knowledge, W. Cerf & H. S. Harris (trans.). Albany, NY: SUNY Press, 1977.

Hegel's Aesthetics: Lectures on Fine Art, 2 vols, T. M. Knox (trans.). Oxford: Clarendon Press, 1975.

Lectures on the History of Philosophy, E. S. Haldane & F. H. Simson (trans.). London: Kegan Paul, Trench, Trübner, 1892–96. Reprinted in facsimile (Lincoln, NE: University of Nebraska Press, 1995).

Lectures on the Philosophy of World History: Introduction, H. B. Nisbet (trans.). Cambridge: Cambridge University Press, 1975.

Phenomenology of Spirit, A. V. Miller (trans.). Oxford: Oxford University Press, 1977.

The Philosophy of History, J. Sibree (trans.). New York: Dover, 1956.

Science of Logic, A. V. Miller (trans.). New York: Humanities Press, 1976. Originally published (London: Allen & Unwin, 1969).

GENERAL BIBLIOGRAPHY

Abbt, T. 1761. "Hundert und ein und funfzigster Brief. Anmerkungen über den wahren Begriff einer pragmatischen Geschichte". In *Briefe, die neueste Litteratur betreffend*, vol. 9, 118–25. Berlin and Stettin: Nicolai.

Adorno, T. W. 1973. *Negative Dialectics*, E. B. Ashton (trans.). London: Routledge.

Adorno, T. W. 1993. *Hegel: Three Studies*, S. Weber Nicholsen (trans.). Cambridge, MA: MIT Press.

Adorno, T. 1997. *Gesammelte Schriften*, 20 vols, R. Tiedemann (ed.). Frankfurt: Suhrkamp.

Allison, H. 1983. *Kant's Transcendental Idealism: An Interpretation and Defense*. New Haven, CT: Yale University Press.

Allison, H. 1997. "We Can Only Act Under the Idea of Freedom", Pacific Division APA Presidential Address. *Proceedings and Addresses of the APA* 71(2), 39–50.

Ameriks, K. 2000a. *Kant and the Fate of Autonomy: Problems in the Appropriation of the Critical Philosophy*. Cambridge: Cambridge University Press.

Ameriks, K. ed. 2000b. *The Cambridge Companion to German Idealism*. Cambridge: Cambridge University Press.

Andrew, E. G. 2001. *Conscience and Its Critics: Protestant Conscience, Enlightenment Reason and Modern Subjectivity*. Toronto: University of Toronto Press.

Apel, K.-O. 1994. *Selected Essays*, E. Mendieta (ed.). Atlantic Highlands, NJ: Humanities Press.

Aquila, R. E. 1989. *Matter in Mind: A Study of Kant's Transcendental Deduction*. Bloomington, IN: Indiana University Press.

Aristotle 1966. *Metaphysics. A Revised Text*, W. D. Ross (ed.) Oxford: Clarendon Press.

Aristotle 1984. *Metaphysics*, W. D. Ross (trans.). In *The Complete Works of Aristotle*, vol. 2, J. Barnes (ed.). Princeton, NJ: Princeton University Press.

Aristotle 1961. *De Anima*, W. D. Ross (ed.).Oxford: Clarendon Press.

Aristotle [1907] 1991. *De Anima*, R. D. Hicks (trans.). Cambridge: Cambridge University Press.

Bauch, B. 1993. "Limiting Reason's Empire: The Early Reception of Hegel in France". *Journal of the History of Philosophy* 31(2), 259–75.

Baum, M. 1986. *Die Entstehung der Hegelschen Dialektik*. Bonn: Bouvier.

Baylor, M. G. 1977. *Action and Person: Conscience in Late Scholasticism and the Young Luther*. Leiden: E. J. Brill.

Beaney, M. 1990. *The Bonds of Sense: An Essay in the History of Analytic Philosophy*. Oxford: Oxford University Press.

Beck, L. W. 1978. "Kant's Strategy". In *Essays on Kant and Hume*, 3–19. New Haven, CT: Yale University Press.

Beckner, M. O. 1967. "Darwinism". In *The Encyclopedia of Philosophy*, vol. I, P. Edwards (ed.), 297–8. New York: Macmillan.

Beiser, F. 1987. *The Fate of Reason: German Philosophy from Kant to Fichte*. Cambridge, MA: Harvard University Press.

Beiser, F. 1992. *Enlightenment, Revolution and Romanticism: The Genesis of Modern Political Thought 1790–1800*. Cambridge, MA: Harvard University Press.

Beiser, F. C. (ed.) 1993. *The Cambridge Companion to Hegel*. Cambridge: Cambridge University Press.

Benhabib, S. 2002. *The Claims of Culture: Equality and Diversity in the Global Era*. Princeton, NJ: Princeton University Press.

Bernasconi, R. 1986. "Hegel and Lévinas: The Possibility of Forgiveness and Reconciliation". *Archivio di Filosofia* **54**, 325–46.

Bernstein, J. 1996. "Confession and Forgiveness: Hegel's Poetics of Action". In *Beyond Representation: Philosophy and Poetic Imagination*, R. Eldridge (ed.), 34–65. Cambridge: Cambridge University Press.

Bird, G. 1995. "Kant and Naturalism". *British Journal of the History of Philosophy* **3**(2), 399–408.

Bird, G. 1996. "McDowell's Kant: *Mind and World*". *Philosophy* **71**, 219–43.

Blumenberg, H. 1983. *The Legitimacy of the Modern Age*, R. M. Wallace (trans.). Cambridge, MA: MIT Press.

Bodei, R. 1987. *Scomposizioni. Forme dell'individuo moderno*. Torino: Einaudi.

Bourgeois, B. 1989. "Hegel et la déraison dans l'histoire". In *Logik und Geschichte in Hegels System*, H.-C. Lucas & G. Planty-Bonjour (eds), 57–79. Stuttgart: Frommann-Holzboog.

Bowie, A. 2003. *Aesthetics and Subjectivity from Kant to Nietzsche*, 2nd edn. Manchester: Manchester University Press.

Brandom, R. 1979. "Freedom and Constraint by Norms". *American Philosophical Quarterly* **16**(3), 187–96.

Brandom, R. 2001. "Holism and Idealism in Hegel's *Phenomenology*". *Hegel-Studien* **36**, 57–92.

Brandom, R. 2002. *Tales of the Mighty Dead: Historical Essays in the Metaphysics of Intentionality*. Cambridge, MA: Harvard University Press.

Breazeale, D. 2001. "Fichte's Conception of Philosophy as a 'Pragmatic History of the Human Mind' and the Contributions of Kant, Platner, and Maimon". *Journal of the History of Ideas* **62**(4), 685–703.

Brinkmann, K. 2003. "Hegel on Forgiveness". In *Hegel's Phenomenology of Spirit: New Critical Essays*, A. Denker & M. Vater (eds). Amherst, NY: Humanity Books.

Brown, C. 1992. *International Relations Theory: New Normative Approaches*. Hemel Hempstead: Harvester Wheatsheaf.

Brown, C. 2002. *Sovereignty, Rights and Justice*. Cambridge: Cambridge University Press.

Brumlik, M. & H. Brunkhorst (eds) 1993. *Gemeinschaft und Gerechtigkeit*. Frankfurt: Fischer.

Burbidge, J. 1995. "Hegel on Galvinism". In *Hegel on the Modern World*, A. Collins (ed.), 111–24. Albany, NY: SUNY Press.

Burbidge, J. 2002. "Hegel und die Chemie: Drei Auseinandersetzungen mit der chemischen Orthodoxie". In *Hegel und die Lebenswissenschaften*, O. Breidbach & D. von Engelhardt (eds), 43–53. Berlin: Verlag für Wissenschaft und Bildung.

Butler, J. 1988. *Subjects of Desire: Hegelian Reflections in Twentieth Century France*. Ithaca, NY: Cornell University Press.

Butler, J., E. Laclau & S. Žižek 2000. *Contingency, Hegemony, Universality: Contemporary Dialogues of the Left*. London: Verso.

Caird, E. [1883] 1886. *Hegel*. Edinburgh & London: William Blackwood and Sons.

Campbell, R. 2001. "The Covert Metaphysics of the Clash between 'Analytic' and 'Continental' Philosophy". *British Journal for the History of Philosophy* **9**(2), 341–59.

Cesa, C. 1972. "Introduzione". *Hegel: Scritti politici (1798–1831)*. Turin: Einaudi.

Cherniss, H. 1932. "Parmenides and the 'Parmenides' of Plato". *American Journal of Philology* 53, 122–58.

Coffa, J. A. 1991. *The Semantic Tradition from Kant to Carnap to the Vienna Station*. Cambridge: Cambridge University Press.

Collins, A. (ed.) 1995. *Hegel on the Modern World*. Albany, NY: SUNY Press.

Dahlstrom, D. 1993. "The Dialectic of Conscience and the Necessity of Morality in Hegel's *Philosophy of Right*". *The Owl of Minerva* 24(2), 181–9.

Danto, A. 1997a. *After the End of Art: Contemporary Art and the Pale of History*. Princeton, NJ: Princeton University Press.

Danto, A. 1997b. *Connections to the World*. Berkeley, CA: University of California Press.

D'Arcy, E. 1961. *Conscience and Its Right to Freedom*. New York: Sheed & Ward.

Davidson, D. [1974] 1984. "On the Very Idea of a Conceptual Scheme". In *Inquiries into Truth and Interpretation*, 183–98. Oxford: Clarendon Press.

De Laurentiis, A. 2005. *Subjects in the Ancient and Modern World: On Hegel's Theory of Subjectivity*. Basingstoke: Palgrave Macmillan.

Deligiorgi, K. 2002. "Kant, Hegel, and the Bounds of Thought". *Bulletin of the Hegel Society of Great Britain* 45/46, 56–71.

D'Hondt, J. 1982. *Hegel et hégélianisme*. Paris: Presses Universitaires de France.

Di Giovanni, G. (ed.) 1990. *Essays on Hegel's Logic*. Albany, NY: SUNY Press.

Di Giovanni, G. 1995. "Hegel, Jacobi and 'Crypto-Catholicism' or Hegel in Dialogue with the Enlightenment". In *Hegel on the Modern World*, A. Collins (ed.), 53–72. Albany, NY: SUNY Press.

Düsing, K. 1983. *Hegel und die Geschichte der Philosophie: Ontologie und Dialektik in Antike und Neuzeit*. Darmstadt: Wissenschaftliche Buchgesellschaft.

Dummett, M. 1993. *The Origins of Analytic Philosophy*. London: Duckworth.

Dower, N. 1998. *World Ethics: The New Agenda*. Edinburgh: Edinburgh University Press.

Doz, A. 2001. *Parcours Philosophique. Tome 1: Avec Hegel*. Paris: L'Harmattan.

Eldridge, R. 1989. *On Moral Personhood: Philosophy, Literature, Criticism, and Self-Understanding*. Chicago, IL: University of Chicago Press.

Emundts, D. & R.-P. Horstmann 2002. *Hegel: Eine Einführung*. Stuttgart: Reclam.

Engelhardt, D. von 1976. *Hegel und die Chemie: Studien zur Philosophie und Wissenschaft der Natur um 1800*. Wiesbaden: Pressler.

Falke, G.-H. 1996. *Begriffne Geschichte: Das historische Substrat und die systematische Anordnung der Bewußtseinsgestalten in Hegels Phänomenologie des Geistes. Interpretation und Kommentar*. Berlin: Lukas.

Ferguson, A. [1767] 1995. *An Essay on the History of Civil Society*, F. Oz-Salzberger (ed.). Cambridge: Cambridge University Press.

Ferrarin, A. 2001. *Hegel and Aristotle*. Cambridge: Cambridge University Press.

Fichte, J. G. [1792] 1978. *Attempt at a Critique of All Revelation*, G. Green (trans.). Cambridge: Cambridge University Press.

Fichte, J. G. 1982. *The Science of Knowledge*, P. Heath & J. Lachs (ed. and trans.). Cambridge: Cambridge University Press.

Findlay, J. N. 1955–56. "Some Merits of Hegelianism. The Presidential Address". *Aristotelean Society Proceedings* 56, 1–24.

Finlayson, G. 1988. "Does Hegel's Critique of Kant's Moral Theory Apply to Discourse Ethics?". *Bulletin of the Hegel Society of Great Britain* 37/38, 17–34.

Flay, J. 1984. *Hegel's Quest for Certainty*. Albany, NY: SUNY Press.

Flay, J. 1990. "Hegel's *Science of Logic*: Ironies of the Understanding". In *Essays on Hegel's Logic*, G. di Giovanni (ed.), 153–69. Albany, NY: SUNY Press.

Fried, M. 1999. *Farewell to an Idea: Episodes from a History of Modernism*. New Haven, CT: Yale University Press.

Friedman, M. 1996. "Exorcising the Philosophical Tradition: Comments on John McDowell's *Mind and World*". *Philosophical Review* 105, 427–67.

Fulda, H. F. 1991. "Spekulative Logik als die 'eigentliche Metaphysik' – Zu Hegels Verwandlung des neuzeitlichen Metaphysikverständnisses". In *Hegels Transformation der Metaphysik*, D. Pätzhold & A. Vanderjagt (eds), 9–28. Cologne: Dinter.

Fulda, H. F. 2004. "Hegels Logik der Idee und ihrer epistemologische Bedeutung". In *Hegels Erbe*, Ch. Halbig, M. Quante & L. Siep (eds), 78–137. Frankfurt: Suhrkamp.

Gadamer, H.-G. 1976. "Hegel's Dialectic of Self-Consciousness". In *Hegel's Dialectic: Five Hermeneutical Studies*, P. Christopher Smith (trans.), 54–74. New Haven, CT: Yale University Press.

Gaiger, J. 2000a. "Art as Made and Sensuous: Hegel, Danto and the 'End of Art'". *Bulletin of the Hegel Society of Great Britain* 41/42, 104–19.

Gaiger, J. 2000b. "Schiller's Theory of Landscape Depiction". *Journal of the History of Ideas* 61(3), 115–32.

Gaiger, J. 2004. "Post-Conceptual Painting: Gerhard Richter's Extended Leave-Taking". In *Themes in Contemporary Art*, G. Perry & P. Wood (eds), 89–135. New Haven, CT: Yale University Press.

Gethmann-Siefert, A. 1991. "Ästhetik oder Philosophie der Kunst: Die Nachschriften und Zeugnisse zu Hegels Berliner Vorlesungen". *Hegel-Studien* 26, 92–110.

Gethmann-Siefert, A. & B. Collenberg-Plotnikow (eds) 2004. *Philosophie der Kunst oder Aesthetik: Nach Hegel. Im Sommer 1826*. Munich: Wilhelm Fink.

Gilligan, C. 1982. *In a Different Voice: Psychological Theory and Women's Development*. Cambridge, MA.: Harvard University Press.

Gould, S. J. 1989. *Wonderful Life*. New York: Norton.

Habermas, J. 1984/1987. *The Theory of Communicative Action*, 2 vols, T. McCarthy (trans.). Cambridge: Polity.

Habermas, J. 1987. *The Philosophical Discourse of Modernity*, F. Lawrence (trans.). Cambridge: Polity.

Habermas, J. 1990. *Moral Consciousness and Communicative Action*, C. Lenhardt & S. Weber Nicholsen (trans.). Cambridge: Polity.

Halper, E. 2002–3. "The Idealism of Hegel's System". *The Owl of Minerva* 34(1), 19–58.

Harris, H. S. 1972. *Hegel's Development: Towards the Sunlight*. Oxford: Oxford University Press.

Harris, H. S. 1997. *Hegel's Ladder*, 2 vols. Indianapolis, IN: Hackett.

Hartmann, K. 1972. "Hegel: A non-Metaphysiscal View". In *Hegel: A Collection of Essays*, A. McIntyre (ed.), 101–23. New York: Anchor.

Henrich, D. 1975. *Hegel im Kontext*. Frankfurt: Suhrkamp.

Henrich, D. 1982. "Logische Form und reale Totalität. Über die Begriffform von Hegels eigentlichem Staatsbegriff". In *Hegels Philosophie des Rechts: Die Theorie der Rechtsformen und ihre Logik*, D. Henrich & R.-P. Horstmann (eds), 428–50. Stuttgart: Cotta.

Henrich, D. (ed.) 1983. *Kant oder Hegel? Über Formen des Begrundung in der Philosophie*. Stuttgart: Cotta.

Hespe, F. 1991. "Hegels Vorlesungen zur 'Philosophie der Weltgeschichte'". *Hegel-Studien* 26, 78–87.

Hilmer, B. 1997. *Scheinen des Begriffs: Hegels Logik der Kunst*. Hamburg: Felix Meiner.

Hirsch, E. 1954. *Lutherstudien*. Gütersloh: Bertelsmann.

Honneth, A. 1991. *The Critique of Power: Reflective Stages in a Critical Social Theory*, K. Baynes (trans.). Cambridge, MA: MIT Press.

Honneth, A. (ed.) 1993. *Kommunitarismus: Eine Debatte über die moralischen Grundlagen moderner Gesellschaften*. Frankfurt: Campus.

Honneth, A. 1996. *The Struggle for Recognition: The Moral Grammar of Social Conflicts*, J. Anderson (trans.). Cambridge, MA: MIT Press.

Honneth, A. 2000. *Suffering from Indeterminacy: An Attempt at a Reactivation of Hegel's Philosophy of Right*, J. Ben-Levi (trans.). Assen: Van Gorcum.

Horstmann, R.-P. 1984. *Ontologie und Relationen: Hegel, Bradley und Russell und die Kontroverse über interne und externe Beziehungen*. Königstein: Hain.

Hösle, V. 1987. *Hegels System: Der Idealismus der Subjektivität und das Problem der Intersubjektivität*. Hamburg: Felix Meiner.

Hotho, H. G. 1835. *Vorstudien für Leben und Kunst*. Stuttgart: Cotta.

Houlgate, S. 1985. "Some Notes on Rosen's *Hegel's Dialectic and its Criticism*". *Hegel-Studien* **20**, 213–19.

Houlgate, S. 1986. *Hegel, Nietzsche, and the Criticism of Metaphysics*. Cambridge: Cambridge University Press.

Houlgate, S. 1991. *Freedom, Truth and History: An Introduction to Hegel*. London: Routledge.

Houlgate, S. (ed.) 1995. *Hegel and British Idealism. Bulletin of the Hegel Society of Great Britain* **31**.

Houlgate, S. 2000. "Hegel and the Art of Painting". In *Hegel and Aesthetics*, W. Maker (ed.), 61–82. Albany, NY: SUNY Press.

Houlgate, S. 2002–3. "Logic and Nature in Hegel's Philosophy: A Response to John W. Burbidge". *The Owl of Minerva* **34**(1), 107–25.

Houlgate, S. 2005. *An Introduction to Hegel: Freedom, Truth and History*. Oxford: Blackwell.

Humboldt, W. von 1799. *Aesthetische Versuche, erster Theil*. Braunschweig: Vieweg.

Hume, D. [1777] 1989. *Enquiries Concerning Human Understanding and Concerning the Principles of Morals*, L. A. Selby-Bigge (ed.). Oxford: Clarendon Press.

Husserl, E. 1988. *Cartesian Meditations: An Introduction to Phenomenology*, D. Cairns (trans.). Dordrecht: Martinus Nijhoff

Hutchings, K. 1999. *International Political Theory: Re-thinking Ethics in a Global Era*. London: Sage.

Hutchings, K. 2003. *Hegel and Feminist Philosophy*. Cambridge: Polity.

Hyppolite, J. 1974. *Genesis and Structure of Hegel's Phenomenology of Spirit*, S. Cherniak & J. Heckman (trans.). Evanston, IL: Northwestern University Press.

Hyppolite, J. 1983. *Introduction à la philosophie de l'histoire de Hegel*. Paris: Seuil/Points Essais.

Inwood, B. 1985. *Ethics and Human Action in Early Stoicism*. Oxford: Clarendon Press.

Inwood, M. 1992. *A Hegel Dictionary*. Oxford: Blackwell.

Jaeschke, W. 1984. "World History and the History of the Absolute Spirit". In *History and System: Hegel's Philosophy of History*, R. L. Perkins (ed.), 101–15. Albany, NY: SUNY Press.

Jarczyk, G. 1980. *Système et Liberté dans la Logique de Hegel*. Paris: Aubier.

Kant, I. 1902. *Kants gesammelte Schriften*, 29 vols, Königlich-Preussische Akademie der Wissenschaften (ed.). Berlin: Walter de Gruyter.

Kant, I. 1968. *Werke, vol. 8: Religion innerhalb der Grenzen der blossen Vernunft*, W. Weischedl (ed.). Frankfurt: Suhrkamp.

Kant, I. 1980. *Critique of Pure Reason*, N. Kemp-Smith (trans.). London: Macmillan.

Kant, I. 1996. *Metaphysics of Morals*, M. Gregor (trans.). Cambridge: Cambridge University Press.

Kelly, G. A. 1998. "Notes on Hegel's 'Lordship and Bondage'". In *The Phenomenology of Spirit Reader*, J. Stewart (ed.), 172–91. Albany, NY: SUNY Press.

Kersting, W. 1982. "Sittengesetz und Rechtsgesetz – Die Begründung des Rechts bei Kant und den frühen Kantianern". In *Rechtsphilosophie der Aufklärung*, R. Brandt (ed.), 148–77. Berlin: Walter de Gruyter.

Knox, T. M. (ed. and trans.) 1964. *Hegel's Political Writings*, intro. by Z. A. Pelczynski. Oxford: Clarendon Press.

Köhnke, K. C. 1991. *The Rise of Neo-Kantianism: German Academic Philosophy between Idealism and Positivism*, R. J. Hollingdale (trans.). Cambridge: Cambridge University Press.

Korsgaard, C. 1996. *The Sources of Normativity*. Cambridge: Cambridge University Press.

Kukathas, C. & P. Pettit 1995. *Rawls: A Theory of Justice and Its Critics*. Cambridge: Polity.

Kulturmann, U. 1981. *Geschichte der Kunstgeschichte: Der Weg einer Wissenschaft*. Berlin: Ullstein.

Lasson, G. (ed.) 1931. *G. W. F. Hegel Die Idee und das Ideal: Nach den erhaltenen Quellen neu herausgegeben*. Leipzig: Felix Meiner.

Lewis, C. S. 1960. "Conscience and Conscious". In *Studies in Words*, 181–213. Cambridge: Cambridge University Press.

Löwith, K. 1953. *Weltgeschichte und heilgeschehen: Die theologischen Voraussetzungen der Geschichtsphilosophie*. Stuttgart: Lohlammer.

Longuenesse, B. 1981. *Hegel et la Critique de la Metaphysique*. Paris: Vrin.

Lübbe-Wolff, G. 1986. "Über das Fehlen von Grundrechten in Hegels Rechtsphilosophie". In *Hegels Rechtsphilosophie im Zusammenhang der europäischen Verfassungsgeschichte*, H. Ch. Lucas & Otto Pöggeler (eds), 421–66. Stuttgart: Frommann Holzboog.

Luhmann, N. 1997. *Die Gesellschaft der Gesellschaft*. Frankfurt: Suhrkamp.

Lukács, G. [1938] 1975. *The Young Hegel*. London: Merlin Press.

MacIntyre, A. 1981. *After Virtue*. London: Duckworth.

Maier, H. "Hegels Schrift über die Rechtsverfassung". *Politische Vierteljahrsschrift* (1963), 323–58.

Malabou, C. 2005. *The Future of Hegel: Plasticity, Temporality and Dialectic*, L. During (trans.). London: Routledge.

Malabou, C. 1996. *L'Avenir de Hegel: Plasticité, Temporalité, Dialectique*. Paris: Vrin.

Marcuse, H. 1987. *Hegel's Ontology and the Theory of Historicity*, S. Benhabib (trans.). Cambridge, MA: MIT Press.

Marshall, T. H. 1963. "Citizenship and Social Class". In *Sociology at the Crossroads*, 67–127. London: Heinemann.

Marx, K. 1978. "Contribution to the Critique of Hegel's Philosophy of Right". In *The Marx–Engels Reader*, R. C. Tucker (ed.), 16–25. New York: Norton.

Marx, W. 1975. *Hegel's Phenomenology of Spirit: Its Point and Purpose: A Commentary on the Preface and Introduction*, P. Heath (trans.). New York: Harper & Row.

McCarney, J. 2000. *Hegel on History*. London: Routledge.

McDowell, J. 1994. *Mind and World*. Cambridge, MA: Harvard University Press.

McDowell, J. 1996. "Reply to Gibson, Byrne, and Brandom". In *Philosophical Issues 7: Perception*, E. Villanueva (ed.), 283–300. Atascadero, CA: Ridgeview Publishing.

McDowell, J. 2001. "L'idealismo di Hegel come radicalizazzione di Kant". *Iride* 34, 527–48.

McDowell, J. 2003. "Hegel's Idealism as Radicalisation of Kant". In *Hegel contemporaneo: La ricezione americana di Hegel a confronto con la tradizione europea*, L. Ruggiu & I. Testa (eds), 451–77. Milan: Guerini e Associati.

Menke, C. 2005. "Innere Natur und soziale Normativität: die Idee der Selbstverwicklichung". In *Forum für Verantwortung: Die kulturellen Werte Europas*, H. Joas & K. Wiegandt (eds), 304–52. Frankfurt: Fischer.

Menn, S. 2002. "Aristotle's Definition of Soul and the Programme of the *De Anima*". *Oxford Studies in Ancient Philosophy* 22, 83–139.

Nardin, T. & D. R. Mapel (eds) 1992. *Traditions of International Ethics*. Cambridge: Cambridge University Press.

Negri, A. 1962. "La Tragedia nell'Etico". *Giornale Critico della Filosofia Italiana* 41, 65–86.

Nenon, T. (ed.) 2001. *The Contemporary Relevance of Hegel's Philosophy of Right*, Supplement 39, *Southern Journal of Philosophy*.

Neuhouser, F. 2000. *Foundations of Hegel's Social Theory*. Cambridge, MA: Harvard University Press.

Nussbaum, M. 2000. *Women and Human Development: The Capabilities Approach*. Cambridge: Cambridge University Press.

Nuzzo, A. 1992. *Logica e sistema: Sull'idea hegeliana di filosofia*. Genoa: Pantograf.

Nuzzo, A. 2003. "Existenz 'im Begriff' und Existenz 'außer dem Begriff' – Die Objektivität von Hegels 'subjektiver Logik'". In *Die Wahrheit im Begriff*, A. Fr. Koch (ed.), 171–88. Paderborn: Schöningh.

Nuzzo, A. 2004 "Hegels Auffassung der Philosophie als System und die drei Schlüsse der Enzyklopädie". In *Hegels enzyklopädisches System der Philosophie*, B. Tuschling & U. Volgel (eds), 459–80. Stuttgart: Frommann Holzboog.

Nuzzo, A. 2005. "Reasons for Conflict – Political Implications of a Definition of Terrorism". In *The Philosophical Challenges of September 11*, T. Rockmore, J. Margolis, A. T. Marsoobian (eds), 125–38. Oxford: Blackwell.

Nuzzo, A. forthcoming. "The Language of Hegel's Speculative Philosophy". In *Hegel and Language*, J. P. Surber (ed.). Albany, NY: SUNY Press.

O'Brien, G. D. 1975. *Hegel on Reason and History: A Contemporary Interpretation*. Chicago, IL: University of Chicago Press.

O'Neill, O. 1989. *Constructions of Reason*. Cambridge: Cambridge University Press.

Paton, H. J. 1979. "Conscience and Kant". *Kant-Studien* 70(3), 239–51.

Patten, A. 1999. *Hegel's Idea of Freedom*. Oxford: Oxford University Press.

Petry, M. J. (ed. and trans.) 1970. *Hegel's Philosophy of Nature*, 3 vols. London: Allen & Unwin.

Plato 1997. *Timaeus*, D. J. Zeyl (trans.). In *Plato: Complete Works*, J. M. Cooper (ed.). Indianapolis, IN: Hackett.

Pinkard, T. 1994. *Hegel's Phenomenology: The Sociality of Reason*. Cambridge: Cambridge University Press.

Pinkard, T. 2000. *Hegel: A Biography*. Cambridge: Cambridge University Press.

Pinkard, T. 2002. *German Philosophy 1760–1860: The Legacy of Idealism*. Cambridge: Cambridge University Press.

Pippin, R. B. 1989. *Hegel's Idealism: The Satisfactions of Self-Consciousness*. Cambridge: Cambridge University Press.

Pippin, R. B. 1995. "Hegel on the Rationality and Priority of Ethical Life". *Neue Hefte für Philosophie* 35, 95–126.

Pippin, R. B. 1997. *Idealism as Modernism: Hegelian Variations*. Cambridge: Cambridge University Press.

Pippin, R. B. 2000a. "What is the Question for Which Hegel's 'Theory of Recognition' is the Answer?". *European Journal of Philosophy* 8(2), 155–72.

Pippin, R. B. 2000b. *Henry James and Modern Moral Life*. Cambridge: Cambridge University Press.

Pippin, R. B. 2002. "What Was Abstract Art? (From the Point of View of Hegel)". *Critical Inquiry* 29(1), 1–24.

Pippin, R. B. 2003. "Hegel on the Historicity of Art: Abstract Art and the Hegelian Narrative". In *Geschichtsphilosophie und Kulturkritik: Historische und systematische Studien*, J. Rohbeck & H. Nagl-Docekal (eds), 202–28. Darmstadt: Wissenschaftliche Buchgesellschaft.

Pippin, R. B. forthcoming. *Hegel's Practical Philosophy: Rational Agency as Ethical Life*.

Pompa, L. 1990. *Human Nature and Historical Knowledge: Hume, Hegel and Vico*. Cambridge: Cambridge University Press.

Popper, K. 1966. *The Open Society and its Enemies*, II, 5th edn. Princeton, NJ: Princeton University Press.

Potts, A. 2000. *The Sculptural Imagination: Figurative, Modernist, Minimalist*. New Haven, CT: Yale University Press.

Potts, T. C. 1980. *Conscience in Medieval Philosophy*. Cambridge: Cambridge University Press.

Quante, M. 1993. *Hegels Begriff der Handlung*. Stuttgart: Frommann-Holzboog.

Rawls, J. 1972. *A Theory of Justice*. Oxford: Oxford University Press.

Rawls, J. 1999. *Law of the Peoples*. Cambridge MA: Harvard University Press.

Rorty, R. 1993. "Human Rights, Rationality and Sentimentality". In *On Human Rights: the Oxford Amnesty Lectures 1993*, S. Shute & S. Hurley (eds), 112–34. New York: Basic Books.

Rose, G. 1981. *Hegel contra Sociology*. London: Athlone.

Rose, G. 1992. *The Broken Middle: Out of Our Ancient Society*. Oxford, Blackwell.

Rosen, M. 1982. *Hegel's Dialectic and its Criticism*. Cambridge: Cambridge University Press.

Rosenkranz, K. [1844] 1977. *Georg Wilhelm Friedrich Hegels Leben*. Darmstadt: Wissenschaftliche Buchgesellschaft.

Rousseau, J.-J. 1986. *The First and Second Discourses*, V. Gourevitch (ed. and trans.). New York: Harper & Row

Ruddick, S. 1990. *Maternal Thinking: Towards a Politics of Peace*. London: Women's Press.

Schneewind, J. B. 1998. *The Invention of Autonomy*. Cambridge: Cambridge University Press.

Schneider, H. 1984. "Neue Quellen zu Hegels Ästhetik". *Hegel-Studien* 19, 9–46.

Schröckh, J. M. 1779–84. *Allgemeine Weltgeschichte für Kinder*, 4 vols. Leipzig: Weidmann.

Schüler, G. 1963. "Zur Chronologie von Hegels Jugensdhriften". *Hegel-Studien* **2**, 91–118.

Schweitzer, A. [1905] 1913. *Geschichte der Leben-Jesu-Forschung*. Tübingen: Mohr.

Sedgwick, S. 1997. "McDowell's Hegelianism". *European Journal of Philosophy* **5**(1), 21–38.

Sedgwick, S. 1998. "Metaphysics and Morality in Kant and Hegel". *Bulletin of the Hegel Society of Great Britain* **37/38**, 1–16.

Sedgwick, S. (ed.) 2000. *The Reception of Kant's Critical Philosophy: Fichte, Schelling and Hegel*. Cambridge: Cambridge University Press.

Sellars, W. 1956. "Empiricism and the Philosophy of Mind". In *Minnesota Studies in the Philosophy of Science, vol. I: The Foundations of Science and the Concepts of Psychology and Psychoanalysis*, H. Feigl & M. Scriven (eds), 253–329. Minneapolis, MN: University of Minnesota Press.

Siep, L. 1983. "The *Aufhebung* of Morality in Ethical Life". In *Hegel's Philosophy of Action*, L. Stepelevich & D. Lamb (eds), 137–55. Atlantic Highlands, NJ: Humanities Press.

Siep, L. 1992. *Praktische Philosophie im Deutschen Idealismus*. Frankfurt: Suhrkamp.

Siep, L. 2000. "Esprit objectif et évolution sociale". In *Dans quelle mesure la philosophie est pratique*, M. Beinenstock & M. Crampe-Casnabet (eds), 245–63. Fontenay aux Roses: ENS Éditions.

Siep, L. 2002. "Selbstverwirklichung, Anerkennung und politische Existenz: Zur Aktualität der politischen Philosophie Hegels". In *Gerechtigkeit und Politik: Philosophische Perspektiven* R. Schmücker and U. Steinvorth (eds.), *Deutsche Zeitschrift für Philosophie*, Special Volume 3.

Singer, P. 1972. "Famine, Affluence and Morality". *Philosophy and Public Affairs* **1**, 229–43.

Speight, A. 1997. "The *Metaphysics of Morals* and Hegel's Critique of Kantian Ethics". *History of Philosophy Quarterly* **14**(4), 379–402.

Speight, A. 2001. *Hegel, Literature and the Problem of Agency*. Cambridge: Cambridge University Press.

Speight, A. 2005. "Butler and Hegel on Forgiveness and Agency". *Southern Journal of Philosophy* **43**(2), 299–316.

Stepelevich, L. S. 1987. *The Young Hegelians*. Cambridge: Cambridge University Press.

Stern, R. 1993a. "James and Bradley on Understanding". *Philosophy* **68**, 193–209.

Stern, R. (ed.) 1993b. *G. W. F. Hegel: Critical Assessments*, 4 vols. London: Routledge.

Stern, R. 2002. *Hegel and the Phenomenology of Spirit*. London: Routledge.

Stern, R. & N. Walker 2000. "Hegelianism". *Routledge Encyclopaedia of Philosophy*. London: Routledge.

Stewart, D. 1858. *The Collected Works of Dugald Stewart*, 11 vols, W. Hamilton (ed.). Edinburgh: T. Constable.

Stone, A. 2005. *Petrified Intelligence: Nature in Hegel's Philosophy*. Albany, NY: SUNY Press.

Sziborsky, L. 1983. "Hegel über die Objektivität des Kunstwerks: Ein Eigenhändiges Blatt zur Ästhetik". *Hegel-Studien* **18**, 9–22.

Taylor, C. 1975. *Hegel*. Cambridge: Cambridge University Press.

Taylor, C. 1984. "Philosophy and its History". In *Philosophy in History*, R. Rorty, J. B. Schneewind, Q. Skinner (eds), 17–30. Cambridge: Cambridge University Press.

Taylor, C. [1979] 1992. *Hegel and Modern Society*. Cambridge: Cambridge University Press.

Theunissen, M. 1978. *Sein und Schein*. Frankfurt: Suhrkamp.

Toews, J. 1980. *Hegelianism: The Path Toward Dialectical Humanism 1805–1841*. Cambridge: Cambridge University Press.

Van der Zande, J. & R. H. Popkin (eds) 1998. *The Skeptical Tradition Around 1800: Skepticism in Philosophy, Science, and Society*. Dordrecht: Kluwer.

Voltaire, J. M. A. 1829. *Œuvres de Voltaire*, A. J. Q. Beuchot (ed.). Paris: Lefèvre, Werdet et Lequien Fils.

Von Engelhardt, D. 1976. *Hegel und die Chemie: Studien zur Philosophie und Wissenschaft der Natur um 1800*. Wiesbaden: Pressler.

Waldron, J. 1993. "Can Communal Goods Be Human Rights?". In *Liberal Rights: Collected Papers 1981–1991*, 339–69. Cambridge: Cambridge University Press.

Walker, N. 1997. "Hegel's Encounter with the Christian Tradition". In *Hegel and the Tradition: Essays in Honour of H. S. Harris*, M. Baur & J. Russon (eds), 190–211. Toronto: University of Toronto Press.

Walzer, M. 1983. *Spheres of Justice*. Oxford: Martin Robertson.

Walzer, M. 1994. *Thick and Thin: Moral Argument at Home and Abroad*. Southbend, IN: University of Notre Dame Press.

Waszek, N. 1988. *The Scottish Enlightenment and Hegel's Account of "Civil Society"*. Dordrecht: Kluwer.

Westphal, K. R. 1989. *Hegel's Epistemological Realism*. Dordrecht: Kluwer.

Westphal, K. R. 1993. "Hegel, Idealism, and Robert Pippin". *International Philosophical Quarterly* 3(131), 263–72.

Williams, R. R. 1992. *Recognition: Fichte and Hegel on the Other*. Albany, NY: SUNY Press.

Williams, R. R. 1997. *Hegel's Ethics of Recognition*. Berkeley, CA: University of California Press.

Williams, R. R. (ed.) 2001. *Beyond Liberalism and Communitarianism: Studies in Hegel's Philosophy of Right*. Albany, NY: SUNY Press.

Winfield, R. D. 1986. "Conceiving Something Without Any Conceptual Scheme". *The Owl of Minerva* 18(1), 13–28.

Winfield, R. D. 1989. *Overcoming Foundations: Studies in Systematic Philosophy*. New York: Columbia University Press.

Wolff, M. 1992. *Das Körper-Seele-Problem: Kommentar zu Hegel, Enzyklopädie*. Frankfurt: Klostermann.

Wood, A. W. 1990. *Hegel's Ethical Thought*. Cambridge: Cambridge University Press.

Wood, P. 2004. "The Idea of an Abstract Art". In *Art of the Avant-Gardes*, S. Edwards & P. Wood (eds), 229–72. New Haven, CT: Yale University Press.

Wyss, B. 1997. *Trauer der Vollendung: Von der Ästhetik des Deutschen Idealismus zur Kulturkritik an der Moderne*, 2nd edn. Cologne: DuMont.

Wyss, B. 1999. *Hegel's Art History and the Critique of Modernity*, C. Dobson Saltzwedel (trans.). Cambridge: Cambridge University Press.

Žižek, S. 1988. *Le Plus Sublime des Hystériques: Hegel Passe*. Cahors: Point Hors Ligne.

Zoeppritz, R. (ed.) 1869. *Aus F.H. Jacobis Nachlass*, vol. 2. Leipzig: Engelmann.

INDEX